paul
and
empíre

paul and empíre

RELIGION AND POWER IN ROMAN IMPERIAL SOCIETY

EDITED BY

ríchard a. horsley

TRINITY PRESS INTERNATIONAL
Harrisburg, Pennsylvania

Trinity Press International, P.O. Box 1321, Harrisburg, PA 17105
Trinity Press International is a division of the Morehouse Group

Library of Congress Cataloging-in-Publication Data
Paul and empire : religion and power in Roman imperial society /
    edited by Richard A. Horsley.
        p.   cm.
    Includes bibliographical references and index.
    ISBN 1-56338-217-2 (alk. paper)
    1. Church history – Primitive and early church, ca. 30-600.
2. Religion and politics – Rome – History. 3. Paul, the Apostle,
Saint. 4. Emperor worship – Rome.   I. Horsley, Richard A.
BR170.P38 1997
225.9'5 – dc21   97-38319
                                                           CIP

Printed in the United States of America

97   98   99   00   01   02   10 9   8   7   6   5   4   3   2   1

Contents

Acknowledgments

The publisher gratefully thanks the following publishers for permission to reprint the chapters listed below:

Cambridge University Press for *"Laus Imperii"* in *Imperialism in the Ancient World*, edited by P. D. A. Garnsey and C. R. Whittaker. Edited text reprinted with the permission of Cambridge University Press © 1978.

Harvard Theological Review for "Who Is the True Prophet?" by Dieter Georgi in Vol. 79:1–3. Copyright 1986 by the President and Fellows of Harvard College. Edited and abridged version reprinted by permission.

Cambridge University Press for the excerpts from *Rituals and Power: The Roman Imperial Cult in Asia Minor* by S. R. F. Price. Edited text reprinted with the permission of Cambridge University Press © 1984.

The University of Michigan Press for "The Roman Empire of Augustus: Imperial Myth and Cult in East and West" in *The Power of Images in the Age of Augustus* by Paul Zanker. Edited text reprinted with the permission of The University of Michigan Press © 1988, Ann Arbor.

University of California Press for "Social Relations" in *The Roman Empire: Economy, Society, and Culture* by Peter Garnsey and Richard Saller. Edited text reprinted with the permission of University of California Press © 1987.

Sheffield Academic Press for "Patronage in Roman Corinth" in *Patronage and Power* by John K. Chow. Edited text reprinted with the permission of Sheffield Academic Press © 1992.

Gerald Duckworth & Co., Ltd., for "The Veil of Power: Emperors, Sacrificers and Benefactors" in *Pagan Priests: Religion and Power in the Ancient World* edited by Mary Beard and John North. Edited text reprinted with the permission of Gerald Duckworth & Co., Ltd. © 1990.

Verlag Ferdinand Schöningh for "God Turned Upside Down" in *Theocracy in Paul's Praxis and Theology* by Dieter Georgi. Edited text reprinted with the permission of Verlag Ferdinand Schöningh © 1987.

Leuven University Press for "From Paul's Eschatology to the Apocalyptic Schemata of 2 Thessalonians" in *The Thessalonian Correspondence,* edited by Raymond F. Collins. Edited text reprinted with the permission of Leuven University Press © 1990.

Orbis Books for "Chapter 4" of *Liberating Paul: The Justice of God and the Politics of the Apostle* by Neil Elliott. Edited text reprinted with the permission of Orbis Books © 1994.

Cambridge University Press for "The Cults of Thessalonica and the Thessalonian Correspondence" by Karl Donfried in *New Testament Studies,* Vol. 31. Edited text reprinted with the permission of Cambridge University Press © 1985.

The Crossroad Publishing Company for *In Memory of Her* by Elisabeth Schüssler Fiorenza. Edited text reprinted with the permission of The Crossroad Publishing Company © 1983, New York.

Abbreviations

AE	*L'Année Épigraphique*, published in *Revue Archéologique* and separately
AJA	*American Journal of Archaeology*
AJP	*American Journal of Philology*
ANRW	*Aufstieg und Niedergang der römischen Welt*
Ath. Mitt.	*Mitteilungen der deutschen Archäologischen Instituts Athenische Abteilung*
BCH	*Bulletin de Correspondance Hellénique*
BDF	F. Blass, A. Debrunner, and R. W. Funk, *A Greek Grammar of the NT*
BE	*Bulletin Épigraphique*, published in *Revue des Études Grecques*
BETL	Bibliotheca Ephemeridum Theologicarum Lovaniensium
BGU	Griechische Urkunden aus den Koeniglichen Museen zu Berlin
BMC	*British Museum Catalogue*
BTB	*Biblical Theology Bulletin*
CAH	*Cambridge Ancient History*
CBQ	*Catholic Biblical Quarterly*
CIG	*Corpus Inscriptionum Graecarum*
CIL	*Corpus Inscriptionum Latinarum*
EBib	Études Bibliques
EKK	Evangelisch-katholischer Kommentar
FGH	F. Jacoby, *Fragmente der griechischen Historiker*
FRLANT	Forschungen zur Religion und Literatur des Alten und Neuen Testaments
Hesp	*Hesperia: Journal of the American School of Classical Studies at Athens*

HNT	Handbuch zum Neuen Testament
HSCP	*Harvard Studies in Classical Philology*
HSCP Supp.	*Harvard Studies in Classical Philology* — Supplementary Volume
HTKNT	Herders theologischer Kommentar zum Neuen Testament
HTR	*Harvard Theological Review*
IBM	*Ancient Greek Inscriptions in the British Museum*
ICC	International Critical Commentary
IG	*Inscriptiones Graecae*
IGBulg	G. Mihailov, *Inscriptiones Graecae in Bulgaria Repertae*
IGR	R. Cognat et al., *Inscriptiones Graecae ad Res Romanas Pertinentes*
ILS	H. Dessau, *Inscriptiones Latinae Selectae*
Ist. Mitt.	*Istanbuler Mitteilungen*
JAC	Jahrbuch für Antike und Christentum
JBL	*Journal of Biblical Literature*
JETS	*Journal of the Evangelical Theological Society*
JRS	*Journal of Roman Studies*
JSNT	*Journal for the Study of the New Testament*
JTS	*Journal of Theological Studies*
LCC	Library of Christian Classics
LCL	Loeb Classical Library
LSAM	F. Sokolowski, *Lois Sacrées de l'Asie Mineure*
LSCG Supp.	F. Sokolowski, *Lois Sacrées des Cités Grecques* — Supplementary Volume
LSJ	Liddell-Scott-Jones, *Greek-English Lexicon*
MAMA	*Monumenta Asiae Minoris Antiquae*
MEFR	*Mélanges d'Archéologie et d'Histoire de l'École Française de Rome*
MeyerK	H. A. W. Meyer, Kritischexegetischer Kommentar über das Neue Testament

NIC	New International Commentary
NovT	*Novum Testamentum*
NTS	*New Testament Studies*
OCD	*Oxford Classical Dictionary*
OGIS	W. Dittenberger, *Orientis Graeci Inscriptiones Selectae*
OMS	L. Robert, *Opera Minora Selecta*
*ORF*²	H. Malcovati, *Oratorum Romanorum Fragmenta*, 2d ed.
PW	Pauly-Wissowa, *Real-Encyclopädie der classischen Altertumswissenschaft*
RAC	T. Klausner et al. (eds.), *Reallexikon für Antike und Christentum*
Rev. Phil.	*Revue de Philologie*, new series
Rh. M.	*Rheinisches Museum für Philologie*
SBL	Society of Biblical Literature
SBLDS	SBL Dissertation Series
SBLMS	SBL Monograph Series
SBLSBS	SBL Sources for Biblical Study
SBS	Stuttgarter Bibelstudien
SCO	*Studi Classici e Orientali*
SEG	J. J. E. Handins et al., *Supplementum Epigraphicum Graecum*
*Syll.*³	W. Dittenberger, *Sylloge Inscriptionum Graecarum*, 3d ed.
TAM	E. Kalinka and others, *Tituli Asiae Minoris*
TLZ	*Theologische Literaturzeitung*
TWNT	G. Kittel and G. Friedrich (eds.), *Theologisches Wörterbuch zum Neuen Testament*
TZ	*Theologische Zeitschrift*
YCS	*Yale Classical Studies*
ZNW	*Zeitschrift für die neutestamentliche Wissenschaft*
ZPE	*Zeitschrift für Papyrologie und Epigraphik*
ZTK	*Zeitschrift für Theologie und Kirche*

General Introduction

Christianity was a product of empire. In one of the great ironies of history, what became the established religion of empire started as an anti-imperial movement. Although some would still view Jesus as an innocuous religious teacher, it is becoming increasingly evident to many that he catalyzed a movement of the renewal of Israel — a movement over against Roman rule as well as the Jerusalem priestly aristocracy. While some still read Paul through the lens of Lutheran theology, it is becoming increasingly clear that, in anticipation of the termination of "this evil age" at the parousia of Christ, Paul was energetically establishing *ekklēsiai* among the nations that were alternatives to official "assemblies" of cities such as Thessalonica, Philippi, and Corinth. As expressed in the baptismal formula Paul quotes in Gal. 3:28, the principal social divisions of "this world...that is passing away" (1 Cor. 7:29, 31) were overcome in these communities of the nascent alternative society: "There is no longer Jew or Greek, there is no longer slave or free, there is no longer male and female; for all of you are one in Christ Jesus."

By the end of the New Testament era, however, writers of the movement now known as "Christian" had begun to emphasize that they were not a serious threat to the established Roman imperial order. Later Christian apologists and even martyrs about to be thrown to the lions insisted Christians were paradigms of political loyalty to Caesar, despite their exclusive religious loyalty to the one God. Finally, under the patronage of Constantine, Christianity became the established religion of the empire. Thereafter, despite regular tensions and occasional overt conflicts, the "spiritual power" of established Christianity usually collaborated closely with the "temporal power" of kings and emperors.

As a result of the bourgeois revolutions of the late eighteenth century, church and state not only became separate, but agreed not to interfere in each other's designated jurisdictions. Correspondingly, Christian theology and biblical studies, focused primarily on religious affairs, tended to lose sight of the political and economic dimensions of life with which the Bible is concerned.[1] New Testament studies has not been unique among established Western academic fields in confining its focus to matters of the spirit. National literary studies (e.g., "English"), like biblical

---

1. The concept of "religion" as a distinctive entity emerged in eighteenth-century Western European culture. See, e.g., Bernard McGrane, *Beyond Anthropology: Society and the Other* (New York: Columbia University Press, 1989), 55–61.

studies, largely products of the nineteenth century,[2] focused on their chosen jurisdiction of culture to the virtual exclusion of the very national and imperial politics that formed the subject matter of many of the novels they interpreted.[3] As based on its nineteenth-century foundations, New Testament studies, especially study of Paul, focused on the emergence of Christianity as the universal, purely spiritual religion from the parochial and overly political religion of Judaism. Imperial politics were seen as framing the historical context or "background" of the period of Christian origins, in the persecution of Judaism by Antiochus Epiphanes and the Roman destruction of the Temple in Jerusalem. But Jesus and especially Paul were by definition concerned about religious matters, not politics. At most there were only certain social or political "implications" to their ministries. Imperial affairs in particular seemed remote — except for an occasional assist to salvation history, as when Paul managed to escape from imprisonment in Judea by appealing to Caesar.

Other fields of study have recently been discovering the importance of imperial relations for their subject matter, even their own connections with empire, often with prodding by non-Western intellectuals who press for a hearing of different perspectives.[4] Biblical studies more generally is also discovering the importance of imperial relations, particularly its own connection with modern empire, as pointed out by non-European-American scholars.[5] Historians of the Hebrew Bible (Old Testament) have regularly dealt with the importance of ancient Near Eastern empires in the history of Israel, its official histories, and its prophetic oracles. New Testament studies (except on the book of Revelation), however, pays less attention to empire, except as "background."

---

2. Terry Eagleton, *Literary Theory: An Introduction* (Minneapolis: University of Minnesota Press, 1983), chap. 1.

3. This has been explored recently by scholars of literature such as Edward Said, *Culture and Imperialism* (New York: Random House, 1993).

4. See critical reviews of recent discussions such as Arif Dirlik, "The Postcolonial Aura: Third World Criticism in the Age of Global Capitalism," *Critical Inquiry* 20 (1994), 328–56; Rosalind O'Hanlon and David Washbrook, "After Orientalism: Culture, Criticism, and Politics in the Third World," *Comparative Studies in Society and History* 34 (1992), 141–67; with a response by Gyan Prakash, "Can the 'Subaltern' Ride? A Reply to O'Hanlon and Washbrook," 168–84.

5. E.g., essays by Kwok Pui-lan, Itumeleng J. Mosala, and Elsa Tamez in Norman K. Gottwald and Richard A. Horsley, eds., *The Bible and Liberation: Political and Social Hermeneutics*, rev. ed. (Maryknoll, N.Y.: Orbis Books, 1993); Kwok Pui-lan, *Discovering the Bible in the Non-Biblical World* (Maryknoll, N.Y.: Orbis Books, 1995); R. S. Sugirtharajah, *Voices from the Margins: Interpreting the Bible in the Third World*, new edition (Maryknoll, N.Y.: Orbis Books, 1995); Fernando F. Segovia and Mary Ann Tolbert, eds., *Reading from This Place: Social Location and Biblical Interpretation in Global Perspective* (Minneapolis: Fortress, 1995); and Gerald West and Musa W. Dube, *"Reading With": An Exploration of the Interface between Critical and Ordinary Readings of the Bible, Semeia* 73 (Atlanta: Scholars Press, 1996).

A few recent studies of the historical Jesus have made a point of beginning with the Roman imperial context in which Jesus' ministry took place and the Jesus movement(s) and gospel traditions developed. One emphasized the imperial situation in Palestine, another the imperial culture in the Hellenistic-Roman world.[6] And a few recent studies of Paul have finally drawn attention to his opposition to the Roman empire.[7]

Since so little attention has been devoted to the Roman imperial context of Paul's mission and his relations to it, we are only at the point of attempting to formulate appropriate questions and provisional research strategies. The excerpts from various studies and the introductions to them presented here represent only some of the many matters that should be examined, issues that can be explored, and approaches that may prove promising. The closely interrelated issues and selections in Parts I and II (the emperor cult and the imperial patronage system) offer both what appears to have been the principal networks by which Roman imperial power relations were constituted and a significant broadening of our understanding of how power relations are constituted in political-religious and social-economic forms. The topic and selections of Part III represent a significant shift in our understanding of the background and significance of many of the most basic Pauline terms and symbols, that is, over against Roman imperial religio-politics, not over against "Judaism." The topic and selections of Part IV, finally, suggest a serious broadening of how Paul's basic agenda can be understood, that he was not simply catalyzing religious congregations of Gentiles, but was organizing an international anti-imperial alternative society based in local communities.

Each of these sets of selections represents a substantive or procedural shift with regard to previous scholarly understanding in New Testament studies, which should be outlined briefly.

I. *The Gospel of Imperial Salvation:* During the 50s the apostle Paul moved systematically through eastern Mediterranean cities such as Philippi, Thessalonica, and Corinth proclaiming "the gospel of Christ" (1 Cor. 9:12; 2 Cor. 2:12; 9:13; Phil. 1:27; 1 Thess. 3:2). Yet by then "the gospel of Caesar" had already become widespread and well established in those very cities. Paul reassured the Philippians that they could expect a "Savior from heaven." But the imperial savior had long since established "peace and security" throughout the Mediterranean

---

6. Richard A. Horsley, *Jesus and the Spiral of Violence: Popular Jewish Resistance in Roman Palestine* (San Francisco: Harper & Row, 1987); and John Dominic Crossan, *The Historical Jesus: The Life of a Mediterranean Jewish Peasant* (San Francisco: HarperCollins, 1991).

7. Dieter Georgi, *Theocracy in Paul's Praxis and Theology* (Minneapolis: Fortress, 1991); and Neil Elliott, *Liberating Paul: The Justice of God and the Politics of the Apostle* (Maryknoll, N.Y.: Orbis Books, 1994), both of which are excerpted below.

world, and the cities of Greece and Asia Minor had long since established shrines, temples, citywide festivals, and intercity games in which
to honor their savior. Paul taught that God had "highly exalted [Jesus
Christ]...so that every knee should bend...and every tongue confess
that Jesus Christ is Lord" (Phil. 2:9–11). However, the divine lord, to
whom all did obeisance and to whom all declared loyalty ("faith"), was
already enthroned in Rome.

New Testament studies has regularly exhibited an interest in "the emperor cult" as one of the significant "religions" in competition with early
Christianity, although usually more in connection with the book of Revelation than with Paul's mission. Attention usually focuses on the object
of belief, particularly whether the emperor was understood as a god,
and on the individual's personal relationship with (faith in) the (divine)
emperor, on the model of the Christian faith in Christ.[8] According to the
dominant Christian interpretation, the terms and phrases of the emperor
cult quickly became "worn-out formulas" and "hackneyed language."
Thus "the emperor cult never became a new religion as such, or a sub-
stitute for religion during the first two centuries c.e."[9] Recent studies
by classical historians and archaeologists, however, find that honors and
festivals for the emperor were not only widespread but pervaded public
life, particularly in the cities of Greece and Asia Minor, the very area of
Paul's mission.[10] It is even argued, not only that imperial religion and
politics are inseparable, but that the imperial cult, in its multiple manifestations in Greek cities, was the very form by which imperial power
relations were constituted. A reassessment of the emperor cult as a major
factor in the world of Paul's mission is in order.

II. *Patronage, Priesthoods, and Power:* It was suggested some time
ago that "Christianity was a movement sponsored by local patrons to
their social dependents."[11] More recently inscriptions of "benefactors"
have been studied for how they may illuminate New Testament texts.[12]
Moreover, some of those who have been adapting the social sciences for
New Testament interpretation have supplemented historical studies of
Roman patronage with cross-cultural studies of patron-client relations.
They argue that such studies of patron-client relations can help clarify

---

8. As laid out in the most prominent recent scholarly "introduction," Helmut
Koester, *Introduction to the New Testament,* vol. 1: *History, Culture, and Religion of
the Hellenistic Age* (Philadelphia: Fortress, 1982), 366–71.

9. Ibid., 1:370.

10. S. R. F. Price, *Rituals and Power: The Roman Imperial Cult in Asia Minor* (Cambridge: Cambridge University Press, 1984); Paul Zanker, *The Power of Images in the Age
of Augustus* (Ann Arbor: University of Michigan Press, 1988), both of which are excerpted
below.

11. Edwin A. Judge, *The Social Pattern of Christian Groups in the First Century*
(London: Tyndale, 1960), 8.

12. See esp. Frederick W. Danker, *Benefactor: Epigraphic Study of a Greco-Roman
and New Testament Semantic Field* (St. Louis: Clayton, 1982).

"the role that patron-client relations played in the social organization, networking, and expansion of the early Christian movement" and how those relations "provided early Christians the model for conceptualizing and describing their relation to Jesus Christ as mediator and to God as heavenly patron and benefactor."[13]

More important for understanding Christian origins, the Roman imperial patronage system formed one of the most powerful and determinative conditions of the Pauline mission. Recent studies of the early Roman empire and particularly studies of the imperial cult emphasize that concrete patron-client networks with their summits in the local urban elite and even in the imperial family constituted the very hierarchical structure of power through which imperial society operated. "With Roman expansion eastward and the emperor's adoption of patronage as a mode of political administration, the institution assumed ever increasing significance as a model for ordering social relations of dependency."[14] Under the early empire, pyramids of patronal social-economic power relations quickly permeated provincial Greek society in Corinth, Ephesus, Macedonia, and elsewhere, just as they had come to structure political-economic relations in Rome during the previous centuries. Such a hierarchical structure, however, was diametrically opposed to the pattern of horizontal reciprocal social-economic relations with which the Jesus movement(s) began.

III. *Paul's Counter-Imperial Gospel:* Paul has been understood primarily as the paradigmatic individual who underwent a conversion from Judaism to Christianity and, in that connection, as the first great Christian theologian who articulated the tortured transition of *homo religiosus* from justification by works to justification through faith. During the last generation, this view of Paul has undergone severe criticism and deconstruction. Krister Stendahl exposed the "introspective" Augustinian and Lutheran formulation of this understanding of Paul.[15] The "new perspective" on Paul then deconstructed the (mainly German) Lutheran theological construction of Paul as the hero of justification by faith versus works righteousness. The "new perspective," however, was not a major "paradigm shift," for it perpetuated the established theological view that Paul was focused primarily on his new religion of Christianity over against his previous religion of Judaism.[16] In the most

---

13. John H. Elliott, "Patronage and Clientage," in Richard L. Rohrbaugh, ed., *The Social Sciences and New Testament Interpretation* (Peabody, Mass.: Hendrickson, 1996), 152–53.

14. Ibid., 153.

15. Krister Stendahl, "The Apostle Paul and the Introspective Conscience of the West," *HTR* 56 (1963): 199–215; reprinted in *Paul among Jews and Gentiles* (Philadelphia: Fortress, 1976), 78–96.

16. E. P. Sanders, *Paul and Palestinian Judaism: A Comparison of Patterns of Religion* (Philadelphia: Fortress, 1977).

quoted statement of the "new perspective": "In short, *this is what Paul finds wrong in Judaism: it is not Christianity.*"[17] The issues of the law, sin, righteousness, and faith in their "Christian" versus their "Jewish" configuration remain at the center of discussion, with the corresponding focus on the epistles to the Galatians and Romans, where those issues are prominent.

Recent recognition that equally prominent Pauline terms such as "gospel," "the cross/crucified," "salvation," and perhaps even "faith" were borrowed from and stand over against Roman imperial ideology suggests a reexamination of what it is that Paul is against primarily.[18] Sin and death, surely! But does he stand primarily over against "Judaism"? Certainly not in the earliest extant letter, 1 Thessalonians, where the emphasis falls on the coming (or the day) of the Lord Jesus, who will rescue the believers from "the wrath that is coming," while destruction will come upon those who trust in the Roman imperial "peace and security" (1 Thess. 1:10; 2:19; 3:13; 4:13–18; 5:2–3). Not in 1 Corinthians, where Paul opposes Christ crucified on a Roman cross not only to wisdom, but to "the rulers of this age, who are doomed to perish" and to "every ruler and every authority and power" whom Christ is about to destroy (esp. 1 Cor. 2:6–8; 15:24). Not in Philippians, where both Paul and the Philippians struggle against persecution by official and/or local opponents, but will attain martyrlike vindication, and whose real citizenship is in heaven, from which they expect the true "Savior" (Phil. 1:15–30; 2:14–18; 3:20–21). Recently those who have analyzed Romans closely as a letter addressed to a particular community context, like the other letters, insist that it should not be read as Paul's statement over against Jews or "Judaism," but as a letter focused on the welfare and inclusion of Jews as well as Gentiles in the movement awaiting completion of the eschatological events inaugurated in the crucifixion and resurrection of Christ. In the correspondence collected in 2 Corinthians, where Paul is obsessed with the threat posed to his own apostolate by Jewish "super-apostles," he still presses his collection that is to be taken to "the poor among the saints in Jerusalem" (2 Corinthians 8; 9; cf. Rom. 15:25–27). And in Galatians, where "Judaizers" have invaded his turf, he emphasizes the fulfillment of the promises to Abraham in Christ which "set us free from the present evil age" (Gal. 1:4 and chap. 3).

Paul's gospel of Christ announced doom and destruction not on Judaism or the Law, but on "the rulers of this age." Given that the historical context of Paul's mission was the Roman empire, it is not difficult to draw the implications. Precisely in Romans (esp. chaps. 9–11) and Galatians (esp. chap. 3), Paul is asserting that history has been

---

17. Ibid., 552.
18. See esp. Georgi, *Theocracy in Paul's Praxis and Theology* and the excerpts below.

working not primarily through Rome, but through Israel, and that the fulfillment of history has now come about in the fulfillment of the promise to Abraham. Ironic as it may seem, precisely where he is borrowing from or alluding to "imperial" language, we can discern that Paul's gospel stands counter primarily to the Roman imperial order, "this world, which is passing away."

IV. *Building an Alternative Society:* Paul is historically important and intensively studied because he is the principal author represented in the New Testament, the primary scripture of Christianity. Paul is commonly understood as a convert to or founder of a new *religion.* In this respect the "new perspective" on Paul simply perpetuates the standard paradigm of Pauline studies, along with the determinative essentialist anachronism in its fundamental assumptions. It is simply assumed that, as of the mid-first century C.E., both Judaism and Christianity were already religions with normative patterns discernible to a modern theologian.

Many historians, however, have been recognizing three interrelated matters. First, the religious dimension of ancient life and institutions was usually inseparable from others, such as the political, economic, and ethnic. The Temple in Jerusalem along with its high priesthood was the dominant political-economic as well as religious institution in Judean society. Diaspora Jewish congregations were semipolitical and ethnic as well as religious communities. The much later rabbinic circles from which most evidence for first-century "Judaism" had been (anachronistically) taken were concerned with social-economic issues that were inseparable from religious issues.

Second, as suggested by the preceding illustrations, it is difficult to demonstrate that what modern scholars conceive of as Judaism existed yet. Some Jewish historians, in fact, have begun to speak of "formative Judaism" (in pointed opposition to "normative Judaism") as a conceptual compromise between the first-century C.E. historical antecedents of rabbinic Judaism and the rabbinic Judaism that emerged more fully only in later centuries. Similarly, to acknowledge the diversity that existed among and within Judean society and other Jewish communities in late second temple times, some Jewish historians speak in terms of "Judaisms." Resorting to such circumlocutions illustrates how problematic it is to speak of an essentialized "Judaism" in the mid-first century C.E. from which Paul supposedly broke away, as well as to perpetuate the problem of unhistorically separating the religious from other dimensions of ancient Jewish life and institutions. It would obviously be more satisfactory, historically, to recognize both the inseparability of religion from political-economic life and the diversity between and within ancient Jewish communities by indicating more precisely geographical, social, and cultural locations of the groups or persons we have in mind (e.g., Judean scribal circles, Alexandrian Jewish philosophers, Galilean peasants, etc.).

Third, it would also be difficult to claim historically that the religion of Christianity existed already by mid-first century C.E. — particularly as a religion over against Judaism. Not only had the term "Christian" not even been coined, so far as we know, but the movement(s) of those who believed in some way in Jesus (Christ) diversified quickly. Those movements, moreover, including the non-Jewish participants, identified themselves as a continuation, indeed the fulfillment, of the history (and/or cultural heritage) of Israel. Even after the term "Christian" had become current, outsiders continued to identify the movement(s) with Israel/Jews, as evidenced in Luke's desperate attempt in the book of Acts to demonstrate how Paul, his fellow workers, and his communities were different from "the Jews" who (supposedly) regularly stirred up agitation against them.

It is thus simply anachronistic to think that Paul was founding a religion called Christianity that broke away from a religion called Judaism. Paul's mission and communities would not have appeared as distinctively religious to his contemporaries in the Roman empire. The term he uses for the movement as a whole as well as for particular communities, *ekklēsia,* was primarily political, the term for the citizens' "assembly" of the Greek *polis* (city-state). Of the three standard broad categories discussed by Roman intellectuals such as Varro, Paul's assemblies would hardly have fit that of "civil" (i.e., city-state) religion, let alone those of "mythical" or "physical" (i.e., nature of the universe) religion. Where Paul does use typical religious terms, which is rare, he uses them in a metaphorical, social-ethical sense (e.g., "present your bodies as a living 'sacrifice,'" Rom. 12:1). Paul's assemblies were political as well as religious, somewhat as the Greek *polis* was both political and religious.

Paul insisted, however, that his *ekklēsiai* should be exclusive communities, open to recruiting from, but otherwise not participating in, wider imperial society, whether in civil courts or in temple banquets (1 Cor. 5:9–13; 6:1–11; and 10:14–22, respectively). Of course he expected the imminent end of "this evil age," of "this world which is passing away." Meanwhile, evidently anticipating a continuation of some sort of societal form in "the kingdom of God," he was busy forming "assemblies" in the cities of the eastern empire as communities alternative to the existing society. As we can discern particularly in Galatians and in the Corinthian correspondence, it was of utmost importance to his sense of the commission that Christ had given him that those communities be intact at the parousia, when he was to render accounts to his Lord. However vague he was about social forms in "the kingdom of God" which was presumably coming at the "day of the Lord" and (the completion of) the resurrection, in his mission Paul was building an international alternative society (the "assembly") based on local egalitarian communities ("assemblies").

Part I

the gospel of imperial salvation

Introduction

> The whole inhabited world voted him honors usually accorded the
> Olympian gods. These are so well attested by temples, gateways,
> vestibules, and colonnades that every city which contains magnif-
> icent works new and old is surpassed in these by the beauty and
> magnitude of those appropriated to Caesar.
>
> (Philo, *Legatio ad Gaium* 149–50, Loeb adapted)

Roman warlords used crucifixion as an instrument to terrorize subject peoples into submission to imperial rule. Primarily through Paul's
mission, the crucified Christ became the central symbol of the popular
movement that eventually developed into Christianity. Once the crucifix
became surrounded and overlaid by various associations of sacrifice and
atonement for sin, it was easy to lose sight of the terror that the cross
originally evoked as an instrument of torture and punishment for slaves
and peoples resistant to Roman rule.

The Roman patricians established their empire initially by superior
force of arms. While they sometimes bullied their way into control
of an area through negotiations under threat of force, they usually
employed "forceful suasion" — systematic destruction, slaughter, and
enslavement — as their means to the end of *imperium*.[1] As Tacitus has
a Caledonian chieftain comment to his fellow Britons: "[The Romans]
rob, butcher, plunder, and call it empire; and where they make a desola-
tion, they call it 'peace'" (*Agricola* 30). The article by P. A. Brunt below
lays out the political-religious and moral ideology according to which
the Roman elite of the late Republic understood the empire they were
establishing.

Roman military violence established the material, political, and cultural conditions in which the Christian movement originated. Particular
acts of devastation and terrorization framed the period and disfigured
the sites in which the movement took root. During the first century B.C.E. Roman warlords took over the eastern Mediterranean,
including Judea, where Pompey's troops defiled the Jerusalem Temple in
retaliation for the resistance of the priests. Their massive acts of periodic
reconquest of the rebellious Judean and Galilean people included thousands enslaved at Magdala/Tarichaea in Galilee in 52–51 B.C.E., mass

---

1. Edward N. Luttwak, *The Grand Strategy of the Roman Empire* (Baltimore: Johns
Hopkins University Press, 1976).

enslavement in and around Sepphoris (near Nazareth) and thousands crucified at Emmaus in Judea in 4 B.C.E., and the systematic devastation of villages and towns, destruction of Jerusalem and the Temple, and mass enslavement in 67–70 C.E.[2] In the area of Paul's mission, the Romans ruthlessly sacked and torched Corinth, one of the most illustrious Greek cities, slaughtered its men, and enslaved its women and children in 146 B.C.E. Then, a century later, Julius Caesar reestablished the city as a Roman colony peopled with freed slaves and expendables from Rome. The Romans similarly planted colonies of military veterans at Philippi and Thessalonica following the battle of Actium in 31 B.C.E.

For nearly three generations before the time of Paul's mission in Philippi, Thessalonica, Corinth, and Ephesus, however, those areas were completely pacified. In fact, the imperial order in areas such as the provinces of Achaia, Macedonia, and Asia did not even require an administrative bureaucracy, let alone a military presence. One of the truly remarkable changes under Augustus was that the *imperium Romanum* became consolidated into a much more unified entity than a mere collection of provinces.[3] That raises a fundamental question which may seriously undermine previous understanding of the emperor cult and its relation to the nascent Christian movement. In contrast with the more recently conquered areas of the Roman empire such as Judea, which still required occasional intervention by massive military forces, how did the empire hold together and even become somewhat unified in the highly civilized areas such as Greece and Asia Minor?

The emerging answer to this question is somewhat complex. From the beginning of the Principate, apparently, well after the period of conquest in these areas, imperial power no longer functioned in what we ordinarily think of as political interactions. Instead, the imperial power relations developed along two closely interrelated lines. In recent analyses classical historians and archaeologists such as those excerpted below contend that especially in the cities of Greece and Asia Minor imperial power relations became constituted in the images, shrines, temples, and festivals of the emperor cult. Moreover, since the provincial elite, who became imperial clients, were also the principal sponsors of the imperial cult, the political-religious institutions in which power relations were constituted were virtually inseparable from the local social-economic networks of imperial society, as articulated in the selections reprinted in Part II below. After developments under Augustus,

---

2. For the well-known references in Josephus, too numerous to cite, see an edition of *The Jewish War, Jewish Antiquities,* and *Life.* I have dealt with all of these incidents most recently in *Galilee: History, Politics, People* (Valley Forge, Pa.: Trinity Press International, 1995), chaps. 2 and 3.

3. Karl Galinsky, *Augustan Culture: An Interpretive Introduction* (Princeton: Princeton University Press, 1996), 6.

the cohesion and operation of the Roman empire no longer required the exercise of power in military or even a very active administrative form. Instead power was apparently more of a pattern of social relations articulated most visibly in religious, or perhaps we should say, political-religious forms.

These ancient realities have gone unrecognized apparently because of the limiting conceptual apparatus of the interested academic fields, biblical studies and classics (see the excerpt from Price below).[4] The emperor cult, which appeared to be neither political fish nor religious fowl, did not fit comfortably into the agenda of either classical (political) history or Christian-influenced history of religions.[5] Thus in these fields and others, the thesis that imperial power relations became constituted in these institutions and networks requires a serious shift in the ways in which power, politics, and religion in the early Roman empire have been understood. It is necessary, first, for modern Western Christians to reconceptualize religion. If we are thinking of religion primarily in terms of an individual's faith or personal relationship with a god, then we may miss the importance of religious expressions that were far more important in traditional societies, such as sacrificial rituals, community festivals, and the structuring and decor of public urban space. Moreover, although there was a plethora of diverse expression that we might call religious in Hellenistic-Roman society, there was no separation between politics and religion.[6] In fact, as we shall see below, ancient Roman politics was permeated with what we would call religious features. It is requisite, second, for modern intellectuals to reconceptualize politics and the state in at least two interrelated ways in order to understand Roman imperial society. As illustrated in the frequent impossibility of separating the religious from the political dimensions of public life, the modern categories of separate dimensions (even institutions) may

---

4. S. R. F. Price, *Rituals and Power: The Roman Imperial Cult in Asia Minor* (Cambridge: Cambridge University Press, 1984), chap. 1, locates the problem primarily in the narrow Christian understanding of religion as personal faith and the long Christian struggle to define relations between religious faith and political rulers. The problem of limiting conceptual apparatus, however, is far wider and more complex, including debunking of the ancient ruler cult by classics scholars rooted in modern rationalism, one of whose concerns was the claim by kings to divine right. See also Keith Hopkins, *Conquerors and Slaves* (Cambridge: Cambridge University Press, 1978), 241.

5. "If religion is seen as belief in the gods, ruler cults can at best be regarded as a peculiar limiting case of religious belief, at worst as the ultimate degeneration of religion. This view of the degradation of religion of course fits neatly into the picture of the decline of traditional cults in this period. But if ruler cult is really political it has only a marginal importance in that context" (Price, *Rituals and Power*, 23.)

6. The separation between church and state, between religious and political functions and institutions in society that is assumed in much of the modern West, was partly the historical product of the struggle of Christianity to work out its relationship with the Roman imperial state and the imperial cult. Similarly, ibid., 15–16, where he sketches some of the relevant history of ideas.

simply not apply to the workings of the Roman empire. And insofar as politics can work through religion, statecraft through stateliness,
such that mystifying pomp and ceremony make administration (and an
administrative apparatus) unnecessary, what modern Westerners might
consider politics recedes in importance or even seems to disappear. The
concept of power, finally, will be much more useful if reconceived in
relational terms, less as a force possessed by the rulers with which to
threaten (to enforce their will upon) the ruled than a complex and
often subtle set of relations by which the interactions in society are
structured.

The dominant interest in this collection of essays is how Roman imperial power relations were constituted by the combination of emperor
cult and patronage networks in Greece and Asia Minor, and thus formed
the principal conditions of Paul's mission. A parallel and related but distinctive development of a religion-politics focused on the emperor took
place in Rome itself, under Augustus. It is pertinent for comparative purposes to sketch briefly in more relational terms recent reassessment of
the increasing prominence of religious forms, avoiding the old issue of
how the Romans themselves took the unprecedented step of worshiping
the emperor.

The Religion-Politics of Augustan Rome

A major point of the critical new appreciation of Augustan culture is
that "Augustan propaganda" was less a hierarchical "organization of
opinion" than a complex system of multiple autonomous interactions,
more spontaneous than organized. Literature of the Augustan age reveals the close but not authoritarian relationship between poetry and
empire. "There can have been few ages in which poets were so intimately and affectionately connected with the holders of political power,
few regimes with a richer iconography, few poets so profoundly moved
by a political ideal and so equipped to sing its praises with subtlety,
humor, learning, and rapture."[7] The same could be said for sculptors
and architects (see the selection from art historian Paul Zanker printed
below). The spirit of empire ran deep and wide. The remarkable cohesion of Roman society itself at the center of the empire can only
be explained by the way in which the revival of Roman religion and
traditional morality was substituted for what were previously political
processes (albeit religious in their own right) in a reconfiguration of
Roman power relations.

---

7. T. Woodman and D. West, *Poetry and Politics in the Age of Augustus* (Cambridge:
Cambridge University Press, 1984), 195.

An adequate approach to the religious reconfiguration of Roman power relations under Augustus requires that we adopt an understanding of religion appropriate to ancient Greek and Roman social forms and institutions. Roman intellectuals such as Varro understood religion according to three divisions: mythical, referring to traditional stories about the gods; physical, referring to doctrines about the nature of the universe; and civil, referring to the gods, temples, shrines, and rituals that constituted and guarded the city-state. The Roman state was tightly interwoven with the civil religion, and could not have functioned without it. Almost all the various laws Cicero lists that should govern the state are religious laws (*Leg.* 2.18–25). The religious forms in which Roman power relations were reconstituted under Augustus were primarily those of civil religion. Renewal under Augustus, however, went far beyond the previous Roman civil religion, particularly in incorporating Augustus within its complex web of rites, institutions, and eventually even deities. As Cicero had indicated about the close connection of politics and religion: "There is really no human activity in which human *virtus* approaches more closely the divine power [*numen*] of the gods than the founding of new states [*civitatis*] or the preservation [*conservare*] of those already founded" (*Rep.* 1.12). Hence after Augustus restored the state he increasingly approached the *numen* of the gods until, in effect, he joined their company.

In appreciating the remarkable and utterly unprecedented emergence of the mystified and divinized power of the emperor at the center of Roman political religion we must take seriously the importance of *order* in "advanced" ancient civilizations. That there be *cosmos* out of *chaos* is the principal focus and message of ancient Near Eastern myths of origin and New Year festivals (e.g., the Mesopotamian *Enuma Elish*). The divine warrior-king was primarily an orderer, usually by violence. That motif had been central in Hellenistic emperor cults which built on ancient Near Eastern precedents. Not surprisingly *cosmos* out of *chaos* crops up again as a key theme in the Greek cult to Augustus, as in the decree of the provincial assembly of Asia (9 B.C.E.): "It would be right for us to consider him equal to the Beginning (*archē*) of all things ... for when everything was falling [into disorder] and tending toward dissolution, he restored it once more and gave to the whole world a new aspect" (*OGIS* 2, no. 458). It was primarily the wealthy and powerful, of course, who articulated such sentiment. But the Roman civil wars had torn Roman society apart and exhausted Italy in general as well as disrupted the position of the provincial elite. Hence we must appreciate just how deep and widespread the relief and gratitude were in the aftermath of the great victory at Actium by Octavian, who deliberately assumed the posture of Western civilized order over Mark Antony, leader of the Eastern forces of dissolution.

Toward the end of his *Res Gestae*, Augustus focuses on his unprecedented *auctoritas:*

> In my sixth and seventh consulships, after I had extinguished civil wars, and at a time when with universal consent I was in control of all affairs, I transferred the commonwealth from my power to the judgment of the senate and people of Rome. For this service of mine I was named Augustus by decree of the senate, and the doorposts of my house were publicly wreathed with laurel leaves and a civic crown was fixed over my door and a golden shield was set up in the Curia Julia, which, as attested by the inscription thereon, was given me by the senate and people of Rome on account of my courage, clemency, justice, and devotion. After this time I excelled in all *auctoritas*, although I possessed no more official power than others who were my colleagues in the several magistracies. (*Res Gestae* 34.1–3)

The quintessentially Roman and untranslatable term *auctoritas* goes well beyond material and political aspects to the intellectual and ultimately overriding moral authority. A patron's *auctoritas* entailed an active concern for his clients' welfare. It is closely related to other Roman terms such as *fides* (= *pistis* in Greek; "trust," "faith"). Thus a statesman-*auctor* was "a guarantor of the trust that must be operative at all levels of the *res publica*."[8] It was essential, of course, for the patron's or statesman's *auctoritas* that he be wealthy. And Augustus was the wealthiest man and the greatest benefactor in Roman history to that point — much of his wealth gained, of course, from pillage during the civil wars. His wealth enabled him to become the greatest benefactor of Rome, which generated widespread reciprocity and good will. Yet he went far beyond the material and political in a more transformative mode of leadership. He called for moral renewal, as well as the "restoration" of the republic (*res publica* = commonwealth), a dedication to traditional values, virtues, ideas, and ideals.[9] That he followed through on his call for renewal as a paradigm of traditional virtue and public benefaction intensified his power relations with the public. His unprecedented *auctoritas*, moreover, was further enhanced by the divine overtones of the title "Augustus."

> He alone has a name kindred to highest Jupiter. "August" call our fathers what is holy, "august" are called the temples that are duly consecrated by the hand of the priests.... And under the auspices of the gods, and with the same omen as his father, may the heir

---

8. Galinsky, *Augustan Culture*, 15–16.
9. Ibid., 19–20.

of so great a surname take upon himself the burden of (ruling) the world! (Ovid, *Fasti* 1.587–616)[10]

In restoring the Roman commonwealth (*res publica*) Augustus also restored Roman religion and traditional morality. In a deliberate manner he regularly set himself forward as paradigm. Thus his own leadership and *auctoritas* were not simply "charismatic," but were carefully defined in terms of the traditional virtues. As the poet Horace declared in his *Carmen saeculare:* "Now Faith, Peace, Honor, old-fashioned Shame, and Valor, which had been neglected, dare to return" (57–59). In the second selection below, Dieter Georgi explores the religio-politics of Horace's celebrative poetry that resembles certain motifs of Jewish apocalyptic literature. Of the traditional virtues, none was more important than *pietas*. It provided the cooperative counterweight to the drivingly competitive *virtus* (power, force), and included a broad spectrum of obligations to family, country, and gods. *Pietas* also involved a certain sentimental paternalism, caring for people as a father, and evoked reciprocity from others, ideally in unselfish efforts for the common good.[11] In all of this Augustus provided the paradigm. He gave expression to *pietas* toward the gods by building twelve new temples and rebuilding eighty-three temples and shrines that had fallen into disrepair. Aided by the timely discovery of accessible marble, he thus gave the city a whole new aura, rivaling the temples of Greece in expenditure, magnificence, and ornamentation. Not surprisingly, *pietas* came to have connotations of imperial patronage and the corresponding bond of loyalty (*fides*) between ruler and people.[12]

In other ways as well the revival of Roman religion was made to center on the figure of Augustus. Augustus became a member of all priesthoods and sodalities, however inauspicious, thus augmenting his *auctoritas,* climaxing in his appointment as *pontifex maximus.*[13] The previously obscure "Brothers of the Cultivated Fields," for example, suddenly assumed an elevated role in public functions related to the welfare of the emperor. Perhaps the most striking move symbolically was that after Augustus became *pontifex maximus* he did not move to

---

10. See further ibid., 315–16: "*Augos* connotes the power, bestowed divinely, to foster growth; an Augustus therefore is 'the holder of that power, one who awakens life and dispenses blessings.' . . . 'Augustus' was synonymous with being god present, *praesens deus.*" *Praesens* is the equivalent of the Greek *epiphanes,* which meant both alive and powerful (317). Horace speaks of the emperor as a living god. *Sebastos,* the Greek equivalent of *augustus,* meant even more clearly "the worshiped one."

11. Ibid., 86.

12. Ibid., 87, 295.

13. On these matters, see ibid., 292–301; and see the discussion by Richard Gordon in Part II below.

that priest's official residence near the Temple of Vesta in the forum. Rather, compounding the fusion of religion and politics with the blurring of public and private domains, he made part of his house on the Palatine into a *domus publica,* dedicated to the worship of Vesta. The lararium of his household and family thus became in effect also a shrine of the state.

What we may not discern in this process by which Roman religion was not only revived but transformed — partly because we lack adequate concepts to grasp it — is that Roman power relations were being reconfigured into religious (or political-religious) forms. As the role of religion expanded, that of traditional Roman politics receded. The Senate still passed its decrees, for example, that Octavian was now Augustus. In "restoring" the Republic, however, Augustus in effect vitiated the cliquish aristocratic political processes while broadening (not democratizing!) popular participation. The renewed Roman religion became "the conduct of social policy by other means. It afforded participation in the life of the state, and particularly in the new order, to those who were not enfranchised or were second-class citizens while no new political rights needed to be given to them. By way of religion and cult they were granted more of an involvement in Augustus's new order than they had ever had in any other."[14] Communication between ruler and plebs, even slaves, became embodied particularly through the *collegia* that multiplied in the Augustan period. Outside of Rome itself, the new *augustales* provided political-religious expression particularly for wealthy freedmen, an increasingly important segment of the population which otherwise lacked political representation in Rome and the outlying Italian towns.

Much has been made of the Augustan era as the realization of the Golden Age. Virgil's *Fourth Eclogue,* written for Pollio's accession to the consulate, well before the battle of Actium in 31 B.C.E., has been read as prophecy which was then fulfilled by the Augustan dispensation. Yet while Virgil's poem articulates the yearning for relief after decades of civil war, it was hardly a direct anticipation of Augustus's program. The miraculous child about to be born is meant to symbolize or personify the hoped-for time of prosperity, not to evoke faith in a hero-savior.[15] The age of gold or the age of Saturn did indeed become a prominent theme in Augustan literature, but with widely varied meaning. Virgil thinks of the primordial state that must now be surpassed. For Ovid it is virtually the antithesis of the Augustan present.[16] The Golden Age

---

14. Galinsky, *Augustan Culture,* 308–9.

15. Ibid., 91–92.

16. Ibid., 99.

is rarely represented in poetry or art as a paradise of easy bliss.[17] Certainly Augustan writers did not view their time as one of fulfillment, of ease and contentment. Whether as an ideal time in the past or as a possibility for the present, the Golden Age meant a social order and required ongoing effort. The economic realities of the Italian countryside, which underwent a decline during the Augustan era, provided a restraint on writers whose own wealth or that of their patrons depended on income from their lands.[18] Not until decades after Augustus did stability in settlement return to Italy. Many decades later Seneca could declare that the *saeculum* of Nero was "purer" and "happier" than that of Augustus (*Clem.* 2.1.4).

For Augustan writers, achieving the Golden Age required labor. The message of Virgil's *Aeneid* is not that Augustus had already brought Rome to the pinnacle of achievement, but that they were well on their way toward a future that continued to require struggle.[19] The new era for an imperially oriented military society and, moreover, the revival of traditional morality went hand in hand with the perpetuation of war. Just as the farmer's peace and prosperity are based on labor, so the *pax Romana* is based on conquest and war. Augustus was the prince of peace in foreign affairs, but it was *pax* in the Roman sense: making a pact after conquest. Augustus himself wished to be remembered as world conqueror, the most successful of Roman generals, as he signaled in the preamble of the *Res Gestae*: "The deeds of the divine Augustus by which he subdued the earth for the rule of the Roman people." As indicated by the historian Nicolaus of Damascus, client of Herod the Great, Augustus dramatically expanded his empire and conquered people whose names were previously unknown.[20] And such continuing conquest was part and parcel of Rome's moral revival and mission. Stoic philosophers since Posidonius justified Roman conquests as the duty of the better, who had higher moral standards. And Livy, in a prominent theme of the preface to his *History* (9–10), presses Rome's *imperium* as a necessity of her morals.[21]

Augustus's restoration of the commonwealth, reinforced by the supposed revival of traditional virtues and religion, however, involved

---

17. See Andrew Wallace-Hadrill, "The Golden Age and Sin in Augustan Ideology," *Past and Present* 95 (1982): 19–36.

18. Galinsky, *Augustan Culture*, 93, 95, 118–19, 128.

19. Ibid., 125–26.

20. E. S. Gruen, "The Imperial Policy of Augustus," in Kurt A. Raafalub and Mark Tober, eds., *Between Republic and Empire: Interpretations of Augustus and His Principate* (Berkeley: University of California Press, 1990), 395–416; and Galinsky, *Augustan Culture*, 96, 132–33. See also his description on p. 120 of, among other aspects of the Gemma Augustea, a large cameo dating from the last years of Augustus, where Augustus is being crowned by *Oecumene*, the personification of global empire since Alexander.

21. Galinsky, *Augustan Culture*, 133–36. The modern British and French were also proud of their empires.

deep-running contradictions, making his program indeed appear to be an ideology "in the modern sense," contrary to recent assertion.[22] Emphasis on the traditional Roman values was selective. *Simplicitas,* for example, was conveniently left in the past. Neither Augustus nor the senatorial and other wealthy elite retrenched their luxurious lifestyle. Besides transforming Rome into a city of gleaming marble temples, Augustus himself sponsored lavish spectacles: gladiatorial games with up to ten thousand participants, athletic contests, and dozens of other games.[23] As suggested in the term *res publica,* the state as restored by Augustus focused particularly on the protection of private property.[24] In practice that simply reinforced the power of the wealthy landowners at the expense of an Italian peasantry heavily indebted from decades of fighting the battles of their warlord creditors.[25] To tout unremitting struggle as exemplified by the life of the farmer as an essential part of the divinely ordained order was indeed an ideology, that of the nonresident elite who lived from the profits of their latifundia, gained by foreclosing on the peasants' debts and now worked by the labor of slaves made in the imperial conquests. From the perspective of a century later, Roman writers such as Juvenal could appreciate at least part of the problem: "We now suffer the ills of a long peace; luxury presses on us more fiercely than arms and avenges the world we conquered" (6.292–93).

---

22. Ibid., 80, 122.

23. "One could argue that, far from resolving the tension between *publica magnificentia* and *privata luxuria,* Augustus amplified it by denying the aristocracy an outlet for their surplus wealth and a focus for their social competition in the glorification of the City. The luxury of private housing and of consumption at table, the sources assure us, continued to mount. Augustus and his successors neutralized the political threat by demolishing popular elections; and far from setting a model of Roman frugality and restraint, they simply outshone all competitors by abusing public resources on their monstrous villas and palaces" (Andrew Wallace-Hadrill, "Rome's Cultural Revolution," *Journal of Roman Studies* 79 [1989]: 164.)

24. Claude Nicolet, "Augustus, Government, and the Propertied Class," in Fergus Millar and E. Segal, eds., *Caesar Augustus: Seven Aspects* (Oxford: Oxford University Press, 1984), 89–128, emphasizes that while Augustan culture was a conscious return to and rearticulation of basic Roman values, lasting public support of the Augustan restoration rested on its more material function, the protection of private property. Galinsky (*Augustan Culture,* 7) reinforces the point: *Res* has strong connotations of property, and Cicero, who owned eight villas, defined "the protection of private property as one of the chief purposes of the *res publica.*" "The landed gentry that authored the U.S. Constitution recognized this instinctively and hence were attracted to the Roman idea of the state." Galinsky's contention that the material measures of protecting private property were more important than the "power of images" stressed by Zanker (see selection below) may well apply to the Roman patricians. But he appears to miss the more complex dimensions of the imperial order. The "power of images" outside of Rome itself brought the populace, for example, of Greek cities via their elite, into the imperial system, thus enabling the imperial regime to arrange plenty of bread and circuses for the Roman populace, which had been severely displaced from the land and the traditional way of life in the process by which the empire was conquered (Hopkins, *Conquerors and Slaves).*

25. Hopkins, *Conquerors and Slaves,* 1–98.

The Imperial Cult, Primarily in the Area of Paul's Mission

Recent studies have not only placed the emperor cult in a whole new perspective, but made it appear integral to Roman imperial society. In the most civilized areas of the empire, the imperial cult provided the principal means by which disparate cities and provinces were held together and social order produced. This is difficult to grasp because of our previous discounting of the emperor cult as superficial religiously and insignificant politically. However, that the imperial cult pervaded the urban ethos in cities such as Corinth and Ephesus and was the most widespread of religious cults particularly in Greece and Asia Minor has serious implications for our understanding of Paul's mission, which was focused precisely in those areas. Many but not all aspects and implications of the emperor cult are included in the excerpts printed below. It may be useful to highlight several of the key aspects and implications of the imperial cult, especially as evident in Asia Minor (the area of Price's study), with an eye toward the closely interrelated role of "religion" and "politics" in the structuring of power relations in imperial society.

Although the imperial family and officials may have played a role in the proliferation of shrines, temples, and festivals in honor of Augustus and his successors, imperial cult was basically produced by the Greek cities on the basis of traditional Greek religion and in the forms of traditional Greek religion. The initiative to build temples and establish games in the emperor's honor came spontaneously from local urban or provincial elites. The emperor was depicted in mythical guises that were modeled after or easily attached to older Greek myths so that he took on some of the same qualities in the mind of his Greek subjects.[26] The emperor was compared to and made into a god among traditional gods.[27] Imperial images and temples were known by the same names as traditional images and temples (*agalmata* and *naoi*) and were designed and constructed after the same motifs and patterns. Use of standard architectural forms created an association of emperor worship with traditional worship — except that the imperial temple was often larger! A statue or image of the emperor was often inserted into temples to major Greek deities, thus associating the emperor with the traditional gods. Ceremonies honoring the emperor were modeled closely on traditional Greek ceremonies honoring the gods. Sacrifices, one of the principal ways in which people were related to the gods, became one of the key means of relating to the emperor. The emperor was called "god" (*theos*), and the

---

26. Paul Zanker, *The Power of Images in the Age of Augustus* (Ann Arbor: University of Michigan Press, 1988), 301.
27. Price, *Rituals and Power*, 55–56.

main purpose of the cult was to cultivate and express "piety" (*eusebeia,* devotion and socially oriented commitment) towards him.[28]

With the building of new temples to the emperor and the erection of imperial shrines and installation of imperial images in prominent places, particularly in the center of cities, the imperial presence came to permeate public space. New construction to accommodate and appropriately place imperial temples made the emperor the center of attention in cities such as Corinth and Ephesus. Indeed, in Ephesus a new urban center was created around the foundation of the ruler cult, with the Temple of Augustus located at the center of the Upper Square.[29] The imperial presence similarly came to dominate public space in Corinth, with the new (Roman-style) Temple E at the west end of the *agora,* the commanding structure in the extension of the city center, and shrines and images of Augustus and his successors being placed at significant locations around the forum, in front of and in between buildings, and the placement of imperial statues in front of temples to other gods (not to mention inscriptions, etc.).[30] Thus as Greeks went about their lives, they were constantly reminded of the importance of emperor, whose presence pervaded public space.[31] The only comparable way in which "religious" presence invades and permeates the very atmosphere of public (and private) life in modern Western society is at "holiday" time in the United States when the sounds, smells, and sights of "Christmas" permeate ecclesial and office spaces as well as commercial areas, reinforcing the festival of consumption.

Emperor cult, moreover, permeated public life and the culture generally as well as public space. Public festivals focused on imperial events such as birthdays pulled nearly everyone in a given city into participation.[32] The decree of the provincial council of Asia in 9 B.C.E. that Augustus's birthday would be the beginning of the new year serves as an example of how the emperor could become inscribed into the consciousness of the public through the organization of the calendar. "The birthday of the most divine emperor is the fount of every public and private good. Justly would one take this day to be the beginning of the Whole Universe.... Justly would one take this day to be the beginning

---

28. Ibid., 231–32.

29. On Ephesus in particular and the transformation and permeation of public space by the imperial cult, see ibid., 136–46 (excerpted below); and Steven Friesen, "The Cult of the Roman Emperors in Ephesos," in Helmut Koester, ed., *Ephesos: Metropolis of Asia* (Valley Forge, Pa.: Trinity Press International, 1995), 229–50.

30. On Corinth, see James Wiseman, "Corinth and Rome I: 228 B.C.–A.D. 267," in *ANRW* 2.7.1, 438–548.

31. Zanker, *Power of Images,* 298–99; Price, *Rituals and Power,* 136–39.

32. Evidence and analysis of festivals and sacrifices appear in Price, *Rituals and Power,* esp. 102–14 (excerpted on pp. 47–71 below) and 207–20, 229–33.

of Life and Living for everyone."[33] Imperial birthdays and anniversaries, incorporated into the calendar by Greek cities, were celebrated with public sacrifices and ceremonies and often international games, such as the Caesarean Games added to the Isthmian Games at Corinth. The imperial image, which emanated from and represented the center, became omnipresent and was widely venerated in the Greek cities.[34] The appearance of the emperor and his family in images even became the model for clothing and hairstyles.[35]

We need not address the old essentialist question of whether the emperor was divine, or the apparent "distinction without a difference" of whether the Greeks sacrificed to or on behalf of the emperor, to discern that the developing relation between imperial ruler and subject peoples was thoroughly religious as well as political. More appropriately and accurately stated, in the absence of imperial security forces and an extensive imperial administrative apparatus, the relationship between ruler and ruled was taking religious forms. And those religious forms, patterned after traditional Greek religion, whether terminology, architecture, visual representation, or ceremonies, speak for themselves. How the relationship emerged from year to year, emperor to emperor, in Greece and elsewhere can be discerned in the correspondence between Claudius and the Alexandrians in 41 C.E.

> First, I allow you to keep my birthday as a sacred day as you have requested, and I permit you to erect...a statue of me and my family.... But I decline the establishment of a high-priest and temples to myself, not wishing to be offensive to my contemporaries and in the belief that temples and the like have been set apart in all ages for the gods alone. (*P. Lond.* 1912 = *Corp. Iud.* 153 = LCL, *Select Papyri* 212)

The proclamation publicizing this letter, however, went ahead in referring to "the greatness of our god Caesar."[36] The emperor's place among the great gods was steadily secured and elaborated in the many interrelated traditional forms in which gods were honored and worshiped. In statues he was represented in military garb, like the gods, and portrayed naked, like the gods, or overlaid in gold, like the gods, or represented in colossal size, like the gods.[37] The Greeks regularly identified Augustus

---

33. *CIG* 3957b, quoted in Hopkins, *Conquerors and Slaves,* 207. On the degree to which the imperial presence structured the calendar, see Price, *Rituals and Power,* 106.

34. Price, *Rituals and Power,* 206. The critique of idols in Wisdom of Solomon 14:16–21 is highly pertinent in this connection.

35. Zanker, *Power of Images,* 302.

36. Hopkins, *Conquerors and Slaves,* 204.

37. Price, *Rituals and Power,* 180–88.

with Zeus.[38] Sacrifices, rituals, public games, and feasts all celebrated the emperor's supremacy and the benefits of the imperial order.[39]

As excerpted in the selections below, Price and Zanker offer an explanation of what was happening in the rapid development of the imperial cult in Greece, Asia Minor, and elsewhere in the Roman empire. Forced to accept subjection to imperial power external to their traditional political-religious structures, the highly civilized Greek cities created a place for this new power "within the framework of traditional cults of the gods."[40] The power of the emperor was so overwhelming and intrusive that they could not represent him as similar to a local hero. They had instead to represent the new power that constituted the stability of society and the world in the forms traditionally used for the Olympian gods who had previously produced the order of the Greek world.[41] Under Rome "the emperor was set beside the gods, as a power that penetrated into every aspect of the life of the city and its people."[42] That the emperor cult also spread so rapidly in the western areas of the empire, which had no tradition of ruler-cult carrying over from the Hellenistic era, simply confirms this thesis.[43] In the case of the imperial cult in Greek cities and elsewhere in the Roman empire, as in the traditional Greek religion, religion was response to power, the ways in which the society related to the powers that determined its life.[44]

The implications are hardly mysterious or difficult to discern. (Political) power rests not only in armies, taxes, and administrative apparatus.[45] Power can be constructed or constituted in religious forms, of temples, shrines, images, sacrifices, and festivals. Not only does power order, sustain, threaten, and dominate, but people also desire order, sustenance, direction, and protection. Power as constructed in religious

---

38. Galinsky, *Augustan Culture*, 318.

39. Hopkins, *Conquerors and Slaves*, 218, commenting on inscription in the town of Tlos in Asia Minor.

40. Price, *Rituals and Power*, 1. We may also surmise that as the Greek cities declined in power relative to the might and sway, first of the Hellenistic empires and then of Rome, the Olympian gods seemed remote and relatively powerless compared with the imperial power in the person of the emperor among them. As the Athenians had said to Demetrios Poliorcetes in 290 B.C.E.: "The other gods are far away, or cannot hear, or are non-existent, or care nothing for us; but you are here, and visible to us, not carved in wood or stone, but real, so to you we pray" (Athenaeus 6.253e; see further Galinsky, *Augustan Culture*, 314). Cf. Paul's emphasis on "manifestations of the Spirit and power" in Gal. 3:1–5; 1 Cor. 2:1–5; 1 Thess. 1:5.

41. Price, *Rituals and Power*, 1, 225, 233.

42. Zanker, *Power of Images*, 299.

43. It is curious that Zanker (ibid., 302) does not carry his thesis over into explanation of the rapid spread of the emperor cult in the western empire, which he attributes to the operation of "powerful social and political pressures."

44. So also Price, *Rituals and Power*, 29–30. This applies also to the emperor cult in the only slightly Hellenized area of Galatia as discussed in Stephen Mitchell, *Anatolia: Land, Men, and Gods in Asia Minor* (Oxford: Clarendon, 1993), 1, 101–17.

45. Cf. Hopkins, *Conquerors and Slaves*, 198.

forms is thus a relationship, a two-way process. The motive for the association of the emperor with the gods does not come from the ruler alone. Since the subject peoples cannot change the dominant order, they need to justify, perhaps even want to glorify that order and articulate their own place within it. Since the emperor was located at the vortex between the divine and the human, he represented divinity to the society but also needed the divine protection secured by sacrifices to the gods on his behalf. Thus power, or power relations, can be constituted in religious forms as well as political forms — or what are inseparably religious-political. Perhaps the most vivid illustration of this is that diplomacy between the Greek cities and the emperor took what are clearly religious forms (see the Price excerpts below). We cannot continue pretending that political relations are the only or primary mode of power, with religion belonging to some different sphere of reality.[46] But then we cannot pretend either that refusal to go along with or even to create an alternative to that power relationship, which was inseparably religious-political, was politically innocuous, without political implications.

---

46. How deeply ingrained the standard Western separation of religious and political orders is can be illustrated by Price's slip in terminology, e.g., *Rituals and Power,* 248. Surely he does not mean to say only that "The imperial cult stabilized the religious order of the world," but that "The imperial cult stabilized the world."

Laus Imperii

P. A. BRUNT

Roman and Athenian Views of Their Empires

The Romans liked to believe that they had acquired their dominions justly, by fighting for their own security or for the protection of their allies. Victory had conferred on them the right to rule over the conquered, and they were naturally conscious that this right was profitable to them, nor were they ashamed of the booty and tribute they exacted. However, they preferred to dwell on the sheer glory of empire, which made Rome specially worthy of the devotion of her citizens (Cicero, *de orat.* 1.156). Much of this thinking is reminiscent of the interpretation Thucydides put on Athenian imperialism, in the speeches he ascribes to Athens's spokesmen. Like all other peoples, the Athenians had been led to acquire their empire by considerations of security, profit and prestige (*Hist.* 1.76), but it is on the undying fame that Athens had won by reducing the greatest number of Greeks to subjection (2.64) that he seems to lay the greatest weight, and it was the power of the city that should inspire the affection of her citizens and make them glad to sacrifice themselves in her service (2.43). To Romans the glory of their empire was even greater than that which Pericles could claim for Athens, because they had come to think that it properly embraced the whole world. Moreover, this dominion was ordained by the gods, whose favor Rome had deserved by piety and justice, and it was exercised in the interest of the subjects. What was most novel in the Roman attitude to their empire was the belief that it was universal and willed by the gods.

The Glory of Imperial Expansion and the Will of the Gods

In the political program Cicero sketched in his defense of Sestius (96ff.) he maintained that all good men should seek *otium cum dignitate.* *Otium* must have included security from external attack (*de orat.* 1.14), and *dignitas* suggests, among other things, the glory of the whole state (*pro Sest.* 104); *provinciae, socii, imperii laus, res militaris* are expressly named among the *fundamenta otiosae dignitatis*. Much of Cicero's program can have had no appeal to the poor either in Rome or in the country, but the urban plebs at least could apparently be moved by the glamor of imperial glory. No other people had ever had such an appetite for glory (*de rep.* 5.9). He can argue for the propriety or wisdom of any practices which have in the past served to aggrandize the empire (*pro Rosc. Am.* 50; *Phil.* 5.47), or which its long existence in itself justifies. Both Pompey and Caesar are lauded for making its boundaries coterminous with the *orbis terrarum*,[1] a boast that Pompey made for himself on a monument recording his deeds in Asia (Diod. 40.4).

Individual Romans could win no greater renown than victories in war, renown in which the whole people shared.[2] Cicero declared that military talent had brought eternal glory to Rome and compelled the world to obey her commands. The triumph, properly granted only to the general who had slain 5,000 of the enemy in a single battle (Val. Max. 2.8.1), was itself the institutional expression of Rome's military ideal.

The gods were the guardians of city and empire.[3] It was Roman piety that had earned their goodwill. In Propertius's words (3.22.21), *quantum ferro tantum pietare potentes stamus*. Virgil's Aeneas, *pictate insignis et armis*, was the prototype of the people aided and destined by the gods to conquer. In public Cicero gave the most eloquent expression to the notion, which we can trace from a praetor's letter of 193 B.C.E. to the time of Augustine, that "it was by our scrupulous attention to religion and by our wise grasp of a single truth, that all things are ruled and directed by the will of the gods, that we have overcome all peoples and nations."[4]

The Conception of World Empire and Unlimited Expansion

Virgil's Jupiter was to bestow on Rome a dominion without limits in space or time (*Aen.* 1.277ff.). Cicero constantly speaks, and sometimes in quite casual ways with no rhetorical inflation (e.g., *de orat.* 1.14),

---

1. E.g., *in Cat.* 3.26; *pro Sest.* 67; *de prov. cons.* 30, 33; *pro Balb.* 64.

2. *Pro Arch.* 12–32 is the *locus classicus*. Much evidence in U. Knoche's paper, reprinted in H. Oppermann, ed., *Römische Wertbegriffe* (Darmstadt: Wissenschaftliches Buchgesellschaft, 1967), 420–46. On the old Roman *virtus*, manifest in services to the state, see D. C. Earl, *The Political Thought of Sallust* (Cambridge: Cambridge University Press, 1961), chap. 2.

3. E.g., *in Cat.* 2.29; 3.18–22 (a remarkable testimony to popular superstition); *de dom.* 143; *pro Sest.* 53; *in Vat.* 14; *pro Scaur.* 48; *pro Mil.* 83; Sall. *BJ* 14.19.

4. *De har. resp.* 18ff., with particular reference to the skill of the *haruspices* in advising on the placation of the gods. Cicero was bound, if he was to persuade senators who credited this nonsense, not to let his own scepticism appear. Cf. *de nat. deor.* 2.8 ("Stoic"); *Syll.*³ 601; Hor. *Odes* 3.6.1ff.; *Mos. et Rom. Leg. Coll.* 6.4.8 (Diocletian); Aug. *Civ. Dei*, books 4 and 5 passim.

as if Rome already ruled all peoples or the whole *orbis terrarum*.[5] A century earlier, Polybius had held that by 167 B.C.E. the whole, or virtually the whole *oikoumene,* or its known parts, had come under Roman dominion.

Even so, it is obvious that in the time both of Polybius and of Cicero Rome did not herself administer the whole of this political universe. Both must then have conceived that her dominion extended beyond the provinces to the kings, tribes and cities who were bound to Rome by alliances, or who were linked by the looser tie of *amicitia,* which within Rome's own society was often a courteous synonym for clientage. In form the status of such allies and friends of Rome beyond provincial frontiers was no different from that of others like Massilia whose territories constituted enclaves within a province. In reality the degree of their dependence was determined by the advantages or disadvantages that might induce Rome to punish or overlook disobedience to her will.

Augustus was to regard all *reges socios* as *membra partisque imperii* (Suet. *Aug.* 48). Under his more efficient regime "client" states were perhaps more closely controlled than in the republic, but Cicero had already included all kingdoms and *liberae civitates* in the *orbis terrarum,* where every Roman in virtue of his citizenship should be safe from arbitrary punishment (II *Verr.* 5.168). From the second century such rulers had had to look to Rome for recognition, and like free cities and friendly tribes, they were expected to conform their policy to Rome's will, to furnish military aid and money or supplies, when occasion demanded; some were actually tributary. In return they had a moral claim to Rome's protection (e.g., Sallust *BJ* 14, *B. Alex.* 34).

The duty acknowledged by the Romans (but not invariably performed) of protecting their friends and allies could involve them in wars with peoples who had hitherto lain beyond their orbit. Victory made these peoples in turn Rome's subjects. Thus the limits of the *orbis terrarum* within which she claimed dominion were continually advancing. There was no point at which such expansion could halt, so long as any independent people remained. Indeed, as P. Veyne has recently argued, the very existence of a truly independent power was viewed at Rome as a potential threat to her own security.[6]

---

5. J. Vogt, *Orbis* (Freiburg im Breisgau: Herder, 1960), assembles texts and interprets the meaning of the phrase. *Ad Her.* 4.13 is the earliest extant instance in Latin. Alternatively, Cicero speaks of Rome's power over all peoples, II *Verr.* 4.81; *de leg. agr.* 2.22; *de dom.* 90; *pro Planc.* 11; *Phil.* 6.19.

6. P. Veyne, "Y a-t-il eu un imperialisme romain?" *MEFR* 87 (1975): 793–855, is no doubt right that in the third and early second centuries, with which he is concerned, "Rome ne songe pas encore à dominer le monde, mais plûtot à être seule au monde," but "defensive" wars fought for this purpose were bound to appear aggressive to others and to be interpreted in the light of the dominance Rome attained, which in turn created the ideal of world rule.

Even though Romans could see the disaster at Carrhae as divine retribution for an unjust and undeclared war, just as Cicero ascribes the destruction of Piso's army by pestilence to the judgment of heaven on Piso's alleged aggressions (*in Pis.* 85), they continued to assume down to 20 B.C.E. that it was right for them to punish the Parthians and even to conquer them, in order to vindicate Rome's honor and secure her eastern dominions. Whatever the provocation they had received, foreign peoples which attacked Rome could at best be said to wage a *bellum prope iustum* (*de prov. cons.* 4). It would be hard to say how far the conviction that the gods had destined them to rule the world predisposed Romans to treat as legitimate *casus belli* what the uncommitted observer would have thought nugatory. It is then quite mistaken to deny that Roman policy was imperialistic whenever it did not result in outright annexation. Until the first century B.C.E. Rome was notoriously slow to annex territory.

Roman "Clemency"

Wherever necessary, the most brutal methods of repression were in order. Death or enslavement was the common penalty for freedom-fighters. Caesar was alleged to have made a million slaves in Gaul;[7] he himself casually refers to a load of captives he shipped back from Britain in 55 (*BG* 5.23.2), the only kind of booty, Cicero had heard (*ad Att.* 4.16.7), that could be expected from this poor island; he was delighted at Quintus's promise to send him some of them (*ad QF.* 3.7.4). Caesar did all he could to extirpate the Eburones (*BG* 6.34 and 43). On one occasion, like Scipio Aemilianus, that paragon of Roman *humanitas* (App. *Iber.* 94), he had the right hands of all his prisoners cut off (8.44). Yet he speaks, as does Hirtius, of his clemency.[8]

It was characteristic of Romans as early as Cato (Gell. 6.3.52) to boast of what Livy calls their *vetustissimum morem victis parcendi* (33.12.7). Once again Cicero held that Roman practice conformed to Panaetian laws of war; especially when wars were fought for glory, the conquered were to be treated with mercy. Only the destruction of Corinth had perhaps marred Rome's record. Not indeed that Cicero considered that mercy was always proper; it was not due to enemies who were themselves cruel or who were guilty of violating treaties, Rome naturally being the judge, nor when Rome's own survival was at stake. He does not make it clear how he would have justified the destruction of

---

7. Plut. *Caes.* 15; App. *Celt.* 2, misinterpreted by W. L. Westermann, *The Slave Systems of Greek and Roman Antiquity* (Philadelphia: American Philosophical Society, 1955), 63, though naturally unreliable. Note Julius Caesar *BG* 7.89.5.

8. *BG* 2.14.28 and 31ff., 8.3.5, 21.2. In 8.44.1 and 3.16 note apologies for special severity; but cf. Cic. *de offic.* 3.46.

Numantia, which he approves.[9] But Numantia had rebelled; to Romans rebellion was in itself proof of perfidy. Polybius reports Flamininus as saying in 197 that the Romans were "moderate, placable and humane," since they did not utterly destroy a people the first time they fought them (18.37). By implication repeated resistance might call for severity, which was also regarded as a virtue. When Virgil defined Rome's mission as *parcere subiectis et debellare superbos,* he was in effect dividing mankind into two categories, those too insolent to accept her god-given dominion, and those who submitted to it. The latter were to be spared: what of the former? Germanicus was to set up a monument boasting that he had "warred down" the Germans, after exterminating one community with no distinction of age or sex (Tac. *Ann.* 2.21f.).

Naturally this was not the practice Romans preferred. We may readily believe Augustus's claim that it was his policy to preserve foreign peoples who could safely be spared rather than extirpate them (*RG* 3). After all, the dead paid no taxes. Moreover it was usually more expedient to accept the surrender of an enemy, offered in the hope or expectation of mercy, rather than to incur the expense of time, money and blood in further military operations, and then to fulfil that expectation, if only to encourage others not to prolong their own resistance. It was not motivated primarily by humanity, but by rational consideration of self-interest.[10]

Justice for the Subjects

In general Cicero speaks with contempt of provincials. Thus the most eminent of Gauls is not to be compared with the meanest of Romans; they were an arrogant and faithless people, bound by no religious scruples, the true descendants of those who had burned down the Capitol (*pro Font.* 27–36). Conceivably there might be Sardinians whose testimony a Roman court might believe, but most of them were mere barbarian half-breeds, more mendacious than their Punic forebears, and not one community in the island had earned the privileges of friendship with Rome and liberty (*pro Scaur.* 38–45). Even the Greeks, to

---

9. Cic. II *Verr.* 5.115; *de offic.* 1.33–35, 1.82, 2.18, 3.46. Numantia: see A. E. Astin *Scipio Aemilianus* (Oxford: Clarendon Press, 1967), 153–55, on App. *Iber.* 98.

10. Fr. Hampl, "Römische Politik in republikanischer Zeil und das Problem des Sittenverfalls," in R. Klein, ed., *Das Staatsdenken der Römer* (Darmstadt: Wissenschaftliche Buchgesellschaft, 1966), adduces early atrocities to disprove the fable that the Romans became less humane to enemies in the late republic. *Deditio:* W. Dahlheim, *Struktur und Entwicklung des römischen Völkerrechts* (Munich: C. H. Beck, 1968), chap. 1. Especially significant on Roman motives for clemency: Livy 42.8.5ff., 44.7.5 and 31.1; Jos. *BJ* 5.372ff. Cf. generally Livy 30.42.7: *plus paene parcendo victis quam vincendo imperium auxisse.*

whom Rome owed her culture, as Cicero often allowed,[11] were now
for the most part degenerate,[12] yet they stood at a far higher level than
such peoples as Mysians and Phrygians (ad QF. 1.1.19), who constituted
most of the population of the province of Asia. Jews and Syrians were
"nations born for servitude" (de prov. cons. 10). Admittedly in most
of the passages cited Cicero was trying to discredit witnesses hostile
to his clients, and he could speak, when it suited him, honorifically of
provincial magnates and communities, but nonetheless such statements
are eloquent of the prejudice he could easily arouse, and some of his
private remarks even on Greeks are disdainful (e.g., ad QF. 1.2.4).

The "ideal of inclusiveness" which Hugh Last treats as an "outstanding feature of the political technique devised by the Roman Republic"
had not in fact emerged.[13] The third book of Cicero's de republica pre-
serves traces of an argument in which imperial dominion seems to have
been defended in much the same way as the rule of soul over body or
masters over slaves; men who were incapable of governing themselves
were actually better off as the slaves or subjects of others.[14] The theory
naturally did not imply that any actual slaves or subjects belonged to
this category, but a Roman could easily persuade himself that experience
showed the subjects to be unfitted for independence.

Under Roman private law the master was entitled to exploit his slaves
as he pleased, and the iura belli, accepted throughout antiquity, allowed
similar rights to the victor in war. Beyond doubt Romans took it for
granted that Rome was justified in profiting from her empire. Yet in
Panaetius's theory, which Cicero adopted, just as masters were bound
to give slaves just treatment (de offic. 1.41), so an imperial power had a
duty to care for the ruled, which Rome had faithfully discharged in the
"good, old days" before Sulla (2.27). Good government was due even
to Africans, Spaniards and Gauls, "savage and barbarous nations" (ad
QF. 1.1.27).

Many or most of Rome's subjects had come under her sway, not always after defeat, by deditio, which involved the surrender of divina
humanaque omnia (Livy 1.38) and the extinction of the community concerned, but Rome regularly restored to the dediti their cities, lands and
laws, often recognized them as her friends and sometimes concluded
treaties with them; they thus acquired rights that fides or religio bound

---

11. Pro Flacc. 62; ad QF. 1.1.27ff.; de rep. 2.34; Tusc. disp. 1.1–7 (but stressing
Roman moral superiority).

12. Pro Flacc. 9, 16, 57, 61; ad QF. 1.1.16, 1.2.4; pro Sest. 141; pro Lig. 11. He
found it necessary to differentiate the Sicilians (who were almost like old Romans) from
other Greeks, II Verr. 2.7.

13. Hugh Last, "Rome and the Empire," CAH 11, 437.

14. De rep. 3.37–41, whence Aug. Civ. Dei 19.21; cf. W. Capelle, "Griechische Ethnik
und römische Imperialismus," Klio 25 (1932): 93.

Rome to respect. In practice Rome left them all to manage their own internal affairs, at most ensuring that they were administered by persons loyal to the sovereign.[15]

Indemnities or taxes might be demanded from defeated enemies as *quasi victoriae praemium ac poena belli* (II *Verr.* 3.12), and provinces could be described as virtual estates of the Roman people (II *Verr.* 2.7), yet Cicero at least felt it necessary to argue that taxation was in the interest of the provincials themselves: armies were required for their protection, and revenue was indispensable to pay them (*ad QF.* 1.1.34). Thus taxation of the subjects was justified by the benefits conferred on them. Precisely the same argument was to be advanced by Tacitus.[16] There was not even anything new in Tiberius's celebrated dictum that he would have his subjects sheared, not shaved (Suet. *Tib.* 32): Cicero rebutted Verres's claim that he had acted in the public interest by selling the Sicilian tithes at unprecedentedly high amounts, by observing that neither senate nor people had intended him to act in such a way as to ruin the farmers and jeopardize future returns (II *Verr.* 3.48). This, however, is only a question of rational exploitation of the subjects, not of justice towards them.

We may indeed ask how far Cicero spoke for many more than himself in advocating justice to the subjects. Here I attach some significance to his denunciations of the misgovernment prevalent in his time, in the Verrines written for an upper-class audience, in his speech before the people on the Manilian law, and even in a despatch from Cilicia to the senate.[17] He assumes that his own sentiments are generally shared. He actually tells the senate that because of the oppressive and unjust character of Roman government the *socii* are too weak or too disloyal to contribute much to defense against Parthia. About the same time he wrote to Cato that it was his principal object, given the lack of adequate military resources, to provide for the protection of his province by his own mild and upright conduct that would ensure the fidelity of the *socii,* and he later claims that he had reconciled the provincials to Roman rule by the excellence of his own administration.[18] It was indeed a commonplace of ancient political thinking, doubtless based on oft-repeated experience, that in Livy's words *certe id firmissimum longe imperium est quo oboedientes gaudent;*[19] it recurs, for instance, in discussions of absolute monarchy, which teach the king to show justice not

---

15. Dahlheim, *Struktur,* chaps. 1 and 2.

16. *Hist.* 4.74. Dio makes Maecenas add that taxation should be levied on all alike (52.28ff.). That was still not the case when he wrote.

17. See esp. II *Verr.* 3.207 (in 2.2–8, 5.8 he implausibly claims that the Sicilians loved their master, but treats them as exceptional); *de imp. Cn. Pomp.* 65; *ad fam.* 15.1.5.

18. *Ad fam.* 15.3.2 and 4.14; *ad Att.* 5.18.2.

19. Cf. Polyb. 5.11, 10.36; Sall. *BJ* 102.6; Cic. II *Verr.* 3.14; Livy 8.13.16.

only for its own sake but in order to secure the affection of his subjects and make his rule more secure.[20]

However, Cicero's letters from Cilicia and his advice to his brother in Asia (*ad QF.* 1.1) do not suggest that good government was to be practiced purely for this prudential reason. Cicero tells Atticus, for instance, that his integrity as a governor afforded him the greatest intrinsic satisfaction of his life. It mattered to him, he says, more than the fame it brought (*ad Att.* 5.20.6). But the allusion to fame should also be marked. "Fame," he says in the first *Philippic* (29), "is demonstrated by the testimony not only of all the best men but by that of the multitude." It was in this sense that he expected his reputation to be enhanced by his virtues as a governor. So too he surely supposed that denunciations of misrule would evoke indignation — Pompey in 71, he tells us (I *Verr.* 45), had actually roused the people in this way — and equally that there would be a popular response to his laudation of Pompey, not only as a great general but as one whose upright behavior won the hearts of the subjects (*de imp. Cn. Pomp.* 36–42); he does not add in this encomium that his behavior would strengthen Roman rule. In the same way Caesar in his *Civil War* digresses to excoriate the cruelty and rapacity of Metellus Scipio and his officers in the east (*BC* 3.31–3); this was in part a propagandist work, and Caesar evidently hoped that his readers would condemn his enemies for their ill-treatment of provincials. The author of the *Bellum Africum* also contrasts Caesar's care for African provincials (3.1, 7.2) with the depredations, and worse, of his adversaries (26).

Perhaps the constant use of the term *socii* to describe provincials in itself indicates something about Roman attitudes to them; it could hardly have been totally divested of the nuance imparted by its other senses. Much more striking, however, is the history of *repetundae* legislation. At least from the late third century the senate had been ready to hear complaints from the *socii* against Roman officials and to provide for reparation or punishment.[21] The statutes on this subject passed between 149 and 59 B.C.E. were the work of politicians of varying complexion, but according to Cicero (*de offic.* 2.75) each enactment made the law stricter. It is notable that the clause authorizing recovery of money from third parties who had benefited from the governor's extortions, a clause that could affect equites and was apparently often invoked, was introduced by Glaucia, who sought their political backing, and was simply

---

20. E.g., Sen. *Clem.* 1.3, 8.6ff., 11.4, etc., as in Polyb. 5.11.

21. Arnold Toynbee, *A Study of History* (London: Oxford University Press, 1965), 2:608ff. Particularly significant are the activities of the elder Cato in seeking to redress or punish wrongs done to subjects (*ORF*[2] frs. 58ff., 154, 173, 196–99); note also the indignation that Gaius Gracchus tried to arouse at ill-treatment of the Italians (Gell. 10.3). Even if personal or political feuds explain why some or most charges were brought, it would remain true that injustice to subjects was a suitable pretext for assailing personal adversaries.

adopted in later statutes (*Rab. post.* 8–10). Cicero briefly characterizes Sulla's law as *lex socialis* (*div. in Caec.* 18). Caesar's statute, comprising no less than 101 clauses (*ad fam.* 8.8.3), and approved by Cicero (*pro Sest.* 135; *in Pis.* 37), remained in force until Justinian's time and formed the basis of the law throughout the imperial period.[22] Our accounts of the eventful year in which it was passed are fairly full, yet they do not allude to its enactment. It was probably uncontroversial. Like earlier *repetundae* laws, it was concerned only with the wrong-doing of senatorial officials. The governor himself was supposed to protect subjects in his courts against publicans and usurers. On paper even Verres promised heavy damages against the former, if they were guilty of illicit exactions (II *Verr.* 3.26), and some governors gave the provincials real protection.[23]

No proof is needed that provincials found insufficient aid in the *repetundae* laws, *quae vi, ambitu, postremo pecunia turbabantur* (Tac. *Ann.* 1.2), or that many governors, for prudence or profit, connived at or participated in the rapacity of tax-gatherers and moneylenders. Personal or political connections could also distort the conduct of senators who, like Cicero, had no wish for their own part to pillage the subjects.[24] In practice the provincials were usually at the mercy of the proconsul, who was virtually absolute in his province, *ubi nullum auxilium est, nulla conquestio, nullus senatus, nulla contio* (Cic. *ad QF.* 1.1.22). Their best hope lay in his probity and courage. In general he was restrained from indulging in or permitting extortion only by his conscience, or regard for his own reputation. Cicero enjoins upon Quintus and claims for himself, and for Pompey, such virtues as justice, mercy, accessibility and diligence. No quality is more often commended than that elementary honesty for which the most revealing Latin term is *abstinentia.*[25]

---

22. P. A. Brunt, "Charges of Provincial Maladministration under the Early Principate," *Historia* 10 (1961), part I.

23. On the duty of governors and its delicacy, Cic. *ad QF.* 1.1.32–6; *ad Att.* 5.13.1. Posidonius held (with some anachronism) that equestrian control of the courts made governors too fearful to restrain equites in the provinces (Jacoby, *FGH* 87 F 108d and 111b). There were certainly exceptions like Q. Mucius Scaevola and L. Sempronius Asellio (Diod. 37.5 and 8 from Posid.), Lucullus (Plut. *Luc.* 20) and perhaps Gabinius in Syria (Cic. *de pro. cons.* 10; *ad QF.* 3.2.2); Cicero adopted Scaevola's edict on the publicans, while that of Bibulus in Syria was overtly still stricter (*ad Att.* 6.1.15, but see *ad fam.* 3.8.4).

24. From Cilicia Cicero pressed administrators of other provinces to comply with Roman moneylenders' demands (e.g., *ad fam.* 13.56 and 61) in terms perhaps not very different from the pleas on Scaptius's behalf that he resented. Despite his condemnation of Appius, Claudius's conduct as governor (e.g., *ad Att.* 5.15ff. and 6.1.2), he did what he could to hinder his conviction at Rome (*ad fam.* 3.10.1; *ad Att.* 6.2.10), and showed his displeasure with hostile witnesses from Cilicia (*ad fam.* 3.11.3). Similarly in 70 L. Metellus had reversed Verres's *acta* in Sicily (II *Verr.* 2.62ff., 138–40, 3.43–46, 5.55) but obstructed his prosecution (2.64ff., 160–64, 3.122, 152ff., 4.146–49).

25. *Ad QF.* 1.1 (a letter presumably intended for publication) commends *aequitas, clementia, comitas, constantia, continentia, facilitas* (for the meaning of which see *de imp. Cn. Pomp.* 41; *ad Att.* 6.2.5), *gravitas, humanitas, integritas, lenitas, mansuetudo, moderatio, severitas, temperantia.* Several of these virtues (also *fides, innocentia*) recur in Cicero's

The very frequency with which it is ascribed, whether truly or falsely, to individuals shows how little it could be assumed as a common characteristic of officials (cf. n. 28). Still, we must not too lightly treat a Verres or an Appius as typical of republican governors. Others are known to have been men of personal integrity, or, like Scaevola, Lucullus and perhaps Gabinius (n. 23), to have protected the subjects against usurers and publicans. Scaevola remained an exemplar; Cicero took his edict as the model for his own (cf. n. 23). In 50 Cicero tells Atticus that he had heard only good reports of all but one of the eastern governors; they were behaving in conformity with the high principles of Cato, *a quo uno omnium sociorum querelae audiuntur,*[26] and, incidentally, with those which Atticus had himself repeatedly recommended to Cicero.[27] The standards of good government were already recognized and approved in the republic, and the only change that came about in the Principate in this regard was that they were somewhat better observed, an improvement that it is easy to exaggerate.[28]

When Cicero included *provinciae, socii* among the *fundamenta otiosae dignitatis,* I feel sure that he meant among other things care for their welfare (cf. *de leg.* 3.9). But *aerarium* is another of the *fundamenta,* and in his day it was the provinces which supplied most of the revenue. It was probably not until the nineteenth century that any imperial power scrupled to tax subjects for its own benefit; the Romans were not ashamed to do so, and I imagine that most of them would have thought Cicero's justification of the practice, which I cited earlier, as superfluous. In one way or another senators and equites, soldiers and grain recipients at Rome all profited from the empire. In addressing the people Cicero can refer to "your taxes" and "your lands."[29] He did not forget in advocating the Manilian law to argue that it served the interests of the treasury and of Romans with business in the east (*de imp. Cn. Pomp.* 14–19). Pompey boasted of the enormous accretion of revenue his conquests had brought (Plut. *Pomp.* 45). Nor must we overlook what Romans seldom mentioned, that victorious wars stocked Italian estates with cheap slaves.

I will add only one further point. Under the Principate the worst features of republican misrule were obliterated; above all peace and order

---

eulogy of Pompey (*de imp. Cn. Pomp.* 13, 36–42) and in the claims he makes on his own behalf in 51–50 B.C.E. (*ad Att.* 5.9.1, 15.2, 17.2, 18.2, 20.6, etc.; *ad fam.* 15.4.1 and 14), along with *abstinentia* (for whose meaning see also *ad Att.* 5.10.2, 16.3, 21.5; *continentia, innocentia, integritas, temperantia* are more or less synonymous), *iustitia* and *modestia.* See Robert Combes, *Imperator* (Paris: Presses Universitaires de France, 1966), chap. 8.

26. *Ad Att.* 6.1.13; *ad fam.* 15.4.15.

27. *Ad Att.* 5.9.1, 10.2, 13.1, 15.2, 21.5 and 7. Conceivably in pressing Scaptius's case, Atticus did not know all the facts.

28. Brunt, "Provincial Maladministration," part 2.

29. *De imp. Cn. Pomp.* 4ff., 7; *de leg. agr.* 2.80ff.

were better preserved. But exploitation did not end. Italy benefited as much as the provinces from the Roman peace, yet until Diocletian the land there was immune from tax.[30] While contributing less than the provinces to the common needs for expenditure, Italians continued, as late as the third century, to enjoy a share of the higher posts disproportionate to that of provincials, if we simply equate Italy with an area in the provinces of like size and population.[31] Moreover provincial revenues were spent lavishly on feeding and amusing the inhabitants of Rome and beautifying the city, to say nothing of court expenditure. These privileges were not challenged by provincials in the senate or on the throne. Equality as between Italians and provincials was not attained, until all were sunk in equal misery.

---

30. Aurelius Victor, *Caes.* 39.31.

31. G. Barbieri, *L'Albo senatorio da Severo a Carino* (Rome: A. Signorelli, 1952), 441, found that 43 percent of senators whose origins were known or probable were Italian. H.-G. Pflaum, *Les Procurateurs équestres* (Paris: A. Maisonneuve, 1950), 193, assigned an Italian origin to twenty-six out of ninety-one third-century procurators.

Who Is the True Prophet?

DIETER GEORGI

It is rather curious that students of the NT, particularly those making eschatology a battle cry, never mention certain highly eschatological texts
contemporary with Jesus and Paul — namely, Roman texts — despite the
fact that they reflect the origin and consequences of a rather lively propaganda in NT times, a propaganda which extended far beyond Italy.
The only text some will mention here is the Fourth Eclogue of Virgil, and then only to say that the poem is a strange and curious text,
rather foreign in its environment; and since no one really knows how
to interpret this *alienum* the text is dropped again. But Virgil's Fourth
Eclogue is not a strange and singular bird, but the expression of a much
more general and pervasive mood ranging from Cicero's *Somnium Sci-
pionis* to the poems of Statius.[1] The fact that the book of Revelation in
chap. 13 describes the Caesar religion as a prophetic one deserves more
attention.[2]

I would like to single out an "official" Roman text and its context, a
text written by one of the major contributors to the Augustan cultural
renaissance but also, besides Virgil and Augustus himself, the major
theologian/prophet of the budding Caesar religion, the prophetic religion John of Patmos attacks. I am speaking of the *Carmen saeculare*
of Horace. This poem is relatively contemporary with the NT. It originated at a time when the gospel according to Augustus had the world

---

1. Besides the texts of Horace mentioned below and the Fourth Eclogue of Virgil
there are other texts of Virgil which have eschatological overtones, not just the *Nekyia*, the
descent into Hades in the sixth book, or the description of the divine shield in lines 626–
728 of the eighth book of the *Aeneid,* but many more passages of this famous epic. Among
the Eclogues, the First, the Fifth, the Sixth, and the Ninth should be mentioned too, as
well as certain passages of the *Georgics,* e.g., lines 24–42 and 498–514 of the first book,
136–76 and 458–541 of the second, 1–49 of the third, 315–558 of the fourth. The two
fragmentary Eclogues of the Einsiedeln Manuscript, the Caesar Eclogues of Calpurnius
Piso, and the Caesar poems of Statius are further examples of Roman eschatology in NT
times.

2. The Harvard Th.D. dissertation of Steven Scherrer, "Revelation 13 as an Historical
Source for the Imperial Cult under Domitian" (1979), presents excellent material for this
comparison.

spellbound. Because there is not space here to produce a detailed textual analysis of that ode,[3] I will limit myself to certain observations and considerations which are relevant for the understanding of eschatology in NT times.

The *Carmen saeculare* was commissioned for the official celebration of the secular games, the official jubilee for the founding of the republic.[4] This was not an annual affair but was meant only for the end of a *saeculum*.[5] The origin as well as further occurrences of the games are a matter of dispute.[6] The length of a *saeculum* was not firmly established and was open to local variety and political manipulation. The date of the games certainly fell in the province of political expediency, and was therefore easy prey for convenient adjustments. Major occurrences and catastrophes, like the outbreak of the civil war, could also influence the calendar. The games were supposed to propitiate for past sins.[7]

Since Octavian understood himself as the savior of the republic, a celebration of the turn (revolution) of a *saeculum* as centenary of the initial republic fit well into his program. He had the secular games, long overdue, very carefully prepared.[8] Most probably he planned them immediately after the decisive battle of Actium, but then delayed them

---

3. See in particular the commentary on Horace by Adolf Kiessling, *Q. Horatius Flaccus: Werke*, 10th ed., rev. by Richard Heinze (Berlin: Weldmann, 1960), 1. 466–83 (on odes and epodes). See also the epilogue to this volume by Erich Burck with a detailed and annotated bibliography, 569–647. Important also is Eduard Fraenkel, *Horace* (Oxford: Oxford University Press, 1957). On 467–70 Kiessling gives the text of the oracle and of the records for and of the respective games. Relevant texts are also found in Viktor Ehrenberg and Arnold Hugh Martin Jones, *Documents Illustrating the Reigns of Augustus and Tiberius*, 2d ed. (Oxford: Clarendon, 1955), nos. 30–32 (pp. 60–61). See also below n. 11.

4. On the secular games see further Martin Nilsson, "Saeculares ludi," PW 1 A 2, 1696–1720; Lily Ross Taylor, "New Light on the History of the Secular Games," *AJP* 55 (1934): 101–20; Ronald Syme, *The Roman Revolution* (Oxford: Oxford University Press, 1952), 84, 218, 443–44; Franz Altheim, *A History of Roman Religion* (New York: Dutton, 1938), 72, 287–91, 353, 382, 390, 394–407, 442, 458–60; Kurt Latte, *Römische Religionsgeschichte* (Handbuch der Altertumswissenschaften; Munich: Beck, 1960), 248, 298–300; Robert E. A. Palmer, *Roman Religion and Roman Empire: Five Essays* (Philadelphia: University of Pennsylvania Press, 1974), 102–8; J. Gagé, "Beobachtungen zum Carmen Saeculare des Horaz," in Hans Oppermann, ed., *Wege zu Horaz*, Wege der Forschung 99, 2d ed. (Darmstadt: Wissenschaftliche Buchgesellschaft, 1980) 14–36. These authors give more primary data and secondary literature.

5. The idea of a *saeculum* and its use as an instrument for dividing epochs cultically and institutionally seem to have come from the Etruscans. The lengths of these periods were and still are matters of debate. Prodigies played a role. On the concept and the debates see n. 4 and Gerhard Radke, "Saeculum," *Der kleine Pauly* 4. 1492–94. Here also further bibliography and further evidence about the games.

6. Different opinions concerning age and further occurrences of these games in Taylor, "New Light," and Latte, *Römische Religionsgeschichte*, 246, esp. n. 4; new considerations in Palmer, *Roman Religion*.

7. This is the opinion of Latte, *Römische Religionsgeschichte*, 248 n. 3.

8. On these preparations see, e.g., Latte, *Römische Religionsgeschichte*, 298–300.

for political reasons.[9] Like his politics in general his final arrangement showed respect for tradition together with conscious modifications. In fact, his reform of the secular games "changed their character completely insofar as they changed the emphasis from expiation of the past to the inauguration of a new epoch."[10]

The relationship of the *Carmen saeculare* to the games has been a matter of dispute since the discovery of the records of the games and Theodor Mommsen's commentary on them.[11] But it seems certain that Horace's poem played a liturgically important role, that "it presents a uniquely effective rite of propitiating the gods to be gracious."[12] In Ode 4.6, which is contemporary with this "centennial song," Horace describes the situation of origin of the festival hymn. Here he defines his own mission as inspired by Apollo.[13] Horace dedicates this ode as well as the *Carmen saeculare* to the Delphic god who has a temple on the Palatine Mount.[14] The poet of the ode, "Parcus deorum cultor et infrequens,"[15] takes the gods not as a mere foil of poetic hyperbole. Gods for him are a presence laden with power as his ode "Bacchum in remotis carmina rupibus"[16] also demonstrates. The bacchantic inspiration of Horace is also instructive for the student of the NT.[17] A certain phenomenon of composition is important for the *Carmen saeculare:* "Myth

---

9. So, with good arguments, Harold Mattingly, "Virgil's Golden Age: Sixth Aeneid and Fourth Eclogue," *Classical Review* 48 (1934): 161–65.

10. Latte, *Römische Religionsgeschichte*, 248. This official eschatological concept of the new age as political reality is presented in a fascinating way in the famous letter of the proconsul of the province of Asia, and in accompanying decrees on the new calendar. A copy was found in Priene, then also in Apamea, Eumeneia, and Dorylaeum (*OGIS* 458 and *SEG* 4. 490, reprinted in Ehrenberg-Jones, no. 98, pp. 81–83; cf. also the inscription from Halicarnassus, *IBM* 4.1, no. 894; Ehrenberg-Jones, no. 98a, pp. 83–84).

11. For the text of the official records of the Augustan games see *CIL* VI 32323 = *ILS* 5050; and Theodor Mommsen's commentary on them in *Ephemeris epigraphica* 8 (1891): 225–309. Also important is his article, "Die Akten zu dem Säkulargedicht des Horaz," in *Reden und Aufsätze* (Berlin: Weidmann, 1905). See also above n. 3.

12. Gagé, "Beobachtungen," 33. This observation appears correct although some of Gagé's hypotheses concerning models for Horace, i.e., earlier "carmina," may be debatable. In any case the festival song contributed to the efficacy of the rites. Hellenistic religion in general and Roman religion in particular kept the ancient conviction that the word, here the poem, is magically effective. The idea of Horace's poem as a mere melodramatic accompaniment of the festivities, intended only for aesthetic enjoyment, is a typically modern thought, foreign to the ancient mind.

13. " 'Twas Phoebus lent me inspiration, Phoebus the art of song, and gave me the name of poet" (lines 29–30). All quotes of texts and translations are from LCL.

14. Also to the sister of Apollo, Diana/Artemis.

15. "I, a chary and infrequent worshipper of the gods" (1.34).

16. "Bacchus I saw on distant crags" (2.19).

17. Viktor Pöschl, "Dichtung und dionysische Verzauberung in der Horazode III 25," reprinted as "c. 3,25: Quo me Bacche," in *Horazische Lyrik: Interpretationen* (Heidelberg: Winter, 1970), 164–78. The tradition about Dionysiac ecstasy of the poet, which likens him to the Maenads, is already known to Plato. In NT times this idea was still present as Philo shows. See Hans Leisegang, *Der Heilige Geist* (Leipzig: Teubner, 1919), 126–231, 236–37; Hans Lewy, *Sobria Ebrietas*, ZNW 9 (Berlin: de Gruyter, 1929), 3–72; Hans

as the summit and summation of the whole also appears elsewhere in Horace's poetry."[18]

It speaks for this high degree of self-estimation of Horace that he calls himself *vates*[19] as does Virgil. It is most probable that these poets follow the opinion of Varro concerning the meaning of the Latin term. This antiquarian, so important for Augustan reform, had assumed a false etymology and claimed that *vates* originally meant the poet.[20] Virgil and Horace both took this term to mean the inspired singers of ancient times. But then they used the term to refer to themselves, thus putting their own function and importance on the same level as the bards of old.[21]

The poet belongs to the sphere of the extraordinary, the miraculous. According to the ode "Non usitata nec tenui ferar,"[22] the poet is more successful than Icarus because he has turned into a heavenly bird, has turned immortal during his lifetime, and his immortal song has made funeral songs unnecessary. According to Horace's Augustus Epistle,[23] the poet is not merely an educator of youth and comforter of the poor and the sick but also effective in prayer. In these lines from the letter to Augustus the "song" means first of all the *Carmen saeculare,* but it also stands for the poetry of the singer in general. His word is powerful, not only among humans but also among the gods. It has a relationship to prayer, magically invoking the gods, imploring and interceding for the purpose of winning the good and averting the bad. In short, the divine and the human meet on the territory of the song. Bringing this about is the function of the poet as *vates.*[24] His mission thus gains soteriological dimensions. Horace utilizes here the associations of *vates* during his time, namely, that of seer and magician.[25]

The glorification of the *princeps* and of the time of Augustus is not mere courtly poetry. Horace sees it as the immediate fulfillment of a heavenly order and as the execution of divine inspiration. The motif of ecstatic rapture, comparable to the "sweet" danger of the communion of the poet with Dionysus,[26] alludes to the situation at the composition

---

Jonas, *Gnosis und spätantiker Geist* (Göttingen: Vandenhoeck & Ruprecht, 1954), 2. 92–107. Philo proves that Judaism had also become acquainted with this idea.

18. "Dichtung," 169 n. 2.

19. In Ode 4.6.44 and frequently elsewhere.

20. See on this esp. Hellfried Dahlmann, "Vates," *Philologus* 97 (1948): 337–53; further Dietrich Wachsmuth, "Vates," *Der kleine Pauly,* 5. 1146–47.

21. In the *Augustus Epistle* (*Ep.* 2.1.18–49[89]) Horace scolds those who would like to admit and appreciate *only* the old poets and show contempt for the modern ones.

22. "On no common or feeble opinion shall I soar in double form through the liquid air" (2.20).

23. *Ep.* 2.1.126–38.

24. "Vatem ni Musa dedisset" (*Ep.* 2.1.133).

25. See on this association, Altheim, *Roman Religion,* 381–93.

26. Ode 3.25: "Whither, O Bacchus, dost thou hurry me, o'erflowing with thy power?

of his song in honor of Augustus. As the poet wants to put the Caesar among the gods he does not speak as courtly sycophant but as peer, as one who himself belongs to the immortal ones.[27] In fact, it is the power of the poet's word which places Augustus among the gods.

When people discuss the relationship of Horace to Augustus they often overlook this proud self-estimation of the singer. In the fourth Roman Ode (3.4) the divine protection of Horace and of Augustus are put side by side.[28] Horace sees both in the context of the mythical triumph of divine wisdom and moderate rest. The immediate miraculous experiences of the poet are extensively described, those of the Caesar are only hinted at (37–40). The narrative of the wondrous events of Horace's life is steeped in the light of eschatological myth: of paradise in the case of the protection of the boy (9–20), of demonic terror at the ends of the earth, of hope for future preservation (29–35). In between Horace mentions the miracle of rescue during the battle of Philippi but also the wonders of protection from a falling tree and from the waves of the sea (25–28). Caesar and his troops are given rest by the Muses with whom the poet is in intimate conversation throughout his work. They give counsel, too, and through whom but the poet, so divinely saved and thus adorned? Imperial campaign, rest, and poetic counsel to the Caesar then are put into the context of the primordial myth of the rebellion of the Titans and Jupiter's miraculous victory over them (42–80). The recurrence of the mythical past in the end-time is a major tenet of apocalyptic thought.

This ode proves how closely related personal quietude, idyll, and world peace are for Horace. Peace is not merely seen as political status but is put into the light of cosmic processes. Election, inspiration, experience, and linguistic magic all are personal realizations of this cosmic process. The Ode to Maecenas[29] shows in an impressive manner that for Horace the experiences of rest and of composed serenity are divine gifts, miracles indeed, when they happen during hopeless situations. They are comparable, yes superior, to the military and administrative securing of the empire (the business of Maecenas).[30]

Into what groves or grottoes am I swiftly driven in fresh inspiration (*velox mente nova*)? In what caves shall I be heard planning to set amid the stars, and in Jove's council, peerless Caesar's immortal glory? I will sing of a noble exploit, recent, as yet untold by other lips" (25.1–8).

27. In Ode 1.2 Horace speaks of Augustus as a savior who has come down from heaven. See Ernst Doblhofer, *Die Augustuspanegyrik des Horaz in formalhistorischer Sicht* (Heidelberg: Winter, 1966), 113–14. On the deification of Augustus in this song see also Pöschl, "Dichtung," 165–67.

28. *Descende caelo* ("Descend from heaven").

29. Ode 3.29, *Tyrrhena regum progenies* ("Scion of Tuscan kings").

30. See E. Zinn, "Aporos Soteria," in Oppermann, ed., *Wege zu Horaz* (see n. 4 above), 246, about the miraculous aspect of the protection of the poet in the last two stanzas of the poem.

The political and the private for Horace are not two separate spheres; rather they constantly interconnect. The Ode to Maecenas demonstrates this. In this poem, which is so private in one way, Horace also gives political counsel to his patron. Horace wants to be an exemplary Roman in this connection of the political, the religious, and the private. He hopes to restore old civic virtues in contrast to the individualistic tendencies of the previous decades.

In the Augustus Epistle (2.1), one of, if not the last, works of Horace, poetry is described as an essential instrument of political education. Thus the attention that great men of politics pay to great men of the word is very appropriate. Poetry and military-administrative achievements are different expressions of wisdom and, therefore, should appreciate each other. The beginning of this poem sees the *princeps,* the semi-gods, and the singers as colleagues. The poet has the advantage that fame and name, that is, the real divine eternity of the *princeps* and other divine men, depend on the poet's reporting and eternalizing them.

The *Carmen saeculare* celebrates the miracle which occurred: the salvation of the republic. The impossible had happened. The hope expressed in the *Carmen* is miraculous, no doubt, but present, indeed fulfilled. The confidence about the realization of what has been desperately expected before is concrete, and the materialism of the expectation indicates the degree of reality. There are many eschatological themes: the eschatological language of *Urzeit-Endzeit,* the ideal of the miraculous return of the golden age and paradise, and even the ideal of the eschatological savior — in line with the heroes of old. All of this is imbedded in a prophetic framework with reference to the Sibyl at the start of the poem and with the conjuration of the divine prophet and protector of the seers, Apollo, in the beginning and at the end. The reference to the prediction is found at the end as well.[31] There is also the prophetic role of the *vates,* the poet himself.

The recently enacted marital legislation of Augustus[32] at first glance may not appear to be an appropriate subject for a poem of eschatological orientation (lines 13–24). Our readiness to take the ordinary political allusion of Horace seriously is dimmed further by our hindsight: we know of the ultimate lack of success of this legislative measure of Augustus. For the author and the audience of the song, however,

---

31. Christian theologians and scores of other critics throughout the centuries take exception to the "materialistic" interests expressed in Horace's and similar statements. Their religious integrity is doubted. But this criticism only proves that Christians have used eschatology to dematerialize and thus deconcretize the hope for change.

32. Using his tribunal power Augustus had initiated in 18 B.C.E. the *Lex Julia de maritandis ordinibus* — legalizing marriages between freeborn citizens and people freed from slavery (senators, however, were excluded from this liberalized practice), thus rewarding marriage and childrearing, and discouraging abstention from marriage and childbirth — and the *Lex Julia de adulteriis coercendis* — making adultery a public crime.

the marital legislation of Augustus is a new and impressive symbol of Augustus's efforts to reverse the catastrophe of moral and physical decay, the suicide of the republic. It is a sign that far-ranging change is on its way and its duration is secured.[33] The poem prays for stability, prosperity, and peace with impressive language.[34] The hearer receives sufficient indication that these things are not bloodless dreams but present reality,[35] and that the *Carmen* prays for their increase.

The longest single portion of the song (lines 37–52) invokes the tradition which was only alluded to in the Sixteenth Epode, that of Aeneas. At the time of origin of the secular song this tradition was not yet codified in the public consciousness. The epic of Horace's friend, Virgil, was not yet public property.[36] But the tradition was already part of public education, especially since Augustus had started to take active interest in this Trojan hero.[37] Horace mentions only briefly the flight of the great man from Troy and his subsequent adventures, including those in Italy. He uses the divine interference in these experiences as examples for his own prayer, which asks for further divine actions to improve the education of youth and the security of old age.[38]

Then, in lines 49–52 (60), Aeneas suddenly turns into a contemporary figure who brings about worldwide peace through weapons, threat, and persuasion. The miraculous heroic past has become present epiphany in the activity of Augustus. In Aeneas, the Caesar himself has entered the scene. We hear that the age-old virtues of *pietas, pax, honor,* and *virtus* have returned. In the same breath *copia* is mentioned as a quality of similar value; it also experiences a return. It is not just a certain good, but a basic value which guarantees the salvation and duration of the commonwealth.[39] Thus it is not surprising that in the end the song prays not merely for general audition but also for growth of the might and fortune of Rome and Latium (lines 65–68).

The *Carmen saeculare* describes the perfection of the endtime in rural colors. The tones of pastoral idyll as we know them from Virgil's Fourth Eclogue resound in Horace. Although this style fits within the

---

33. Existence and return of the *saeculum,* as such already an eschatological good, depend on this (lines 21–24).

34. Esp. in lines 19–32, 57–60, and 65–68.

35. Cf., besides the references to the marital legislation, the double *iam* ("already") in lines 53 and 57.

36. The *Aeneid* was published after Virgil's death (19 B.C.E.) against the expressed will of the poet but by the request of Augustus.

37. Augustus suggested the topic of the *Aeneid* to Virgil.

38. See lines 45–46, obviously connected with lines 33–36. The third recipient of the beneficial assistance of the gods, proven in history, is the entire progeny of Romulus, all of the Roman people (47–48).

39. One is reminded of the southern panel on the eastern side of the altar of Pax Augusta, erected some four years later, where Italy is depicted as a goddess in the midst of signs of agrarian plenty and peace.

genre of the bucolic poem of Virgil, it is hardly expected in the *Carmen* of Horace. Neither can it be said that eschatological writing requires rural expression. Biblical and Jewish eschatology can work with urban images as the prophecies concerning Zion prove.

Horace does not even offer any harmonization between the rural and the urban image as found in the end of Ezekiel or in Ps.-Aristeas. In these, the harmonization is not a secondary accommodation but an acknowledgment of an important socio-economic problem in antiquity. The antithesis and conflict between urban and rural grew into heavy exploitation of the countryside by the cities during the Hellenistic period. Thus the harmonization in some of the eschatological predictions promised a coming reconciliation of social adversaries and thus the miraculous resolution of a dilemma that history had been unable to solve.

But in the *Carmen saeculare* Horace does not mention the urban world at all. This is striking in a festival song which praises the achievements and blessings of the principate of Augustus, one of the major city builders of the ancient world, and which celebrates the largest city of the age. One of the most important achievements of Augustus was the restoration and improvement of the city of Rome, not merely politically and morally, but also architecturally. In addition, the Augustan reform had brought about a worldwide improvement of urban life, including an increase in the number of cities and of the size of many existing ones. Thus the silence of the *Carmen saeculare* on urban life is very surprising. The traditional interest of Romans in soil and in agriculture is not a sufficient explanation. During the time of Augustus the city of Rome had lost direct contact with the life of farmers and shepherds. In the Hellenistic world in general and especially in Roman society, the city, particularly *the* city, the *urbs* absolute, Rome, had become the central symbol.

There are socio-economic and political reasons for this silence on the city and emphasis on the countryside in the secular song of Horace. These reasons also explain the preference for the idyllic in the preceding works of the two main theologians of Augustus, with Virgil initially being more optimistic than Horace. Although Augustus was the first citizen of the city of Rome and although he very actively improved the image of this city, he still established his own base and his prosperity through Egyptian soil. Under him Egypt grew into a gigantic agricultural domain for the principate. But what developed fully under Augustus had begun before. The trends of Hellenistic society and economy had moved from the direction of worldwide urbanization to that of ruralization.[40] The Romans followed this trend. Augustus built in part on the

---

40. Or, as one might call it, paganization, using the Latin term *pagani*, which denotes

extraordinary position that agriculture held in Roman tradition, which he wanted to restore. But the restoration of the rural world would not have happened if the socio-economic situation had not been ready for it.

Rome's ideology and social structure had remained basically agrarian. Noble and rural, piety and soil, were always related, if not synonymous. Migration to the countryside for the purpose of farming could create a counterweight to the explosive urbanization, reviving old strategies and their potential for social stability and control.

The land issue had been a major element of the Roman civil war. The popular party, that of the Gracchi, of Caesar, and later Augustus, had taken up the banner of the plight of the ever-increasing urban masses. Their impoverishment was supposed to be helped by distribution of public land, and this was to relieve the socio-economic and political pressures of overpopulation on Rome. But during the civil war the Gracchic reforms were only partially realized, and the population of the city continued to grow, with devastating consequences for the labor and housing markets.

Despite the distribution of land since Tiberius Gracchus and the settlement of veterans in rural areas in the subsequent century, there was, nevertheless, an increasing hesitation among the masses to leave the city. The socio-economic development of farming moved away from small farms toward large estates aimed at maximizing profits. Worked and administered by slaves, these estates had turned into centers for the production of profitable goods starting with a limited number of profitable agricultural products, but soon taking advantage of the presence of resources and cheap labor to produce other wares.[41]

Thus, since the end of the first century B.C.E., property in the open country promised to be a better investment of capital with a growing rate of productivity and profit, at least in the case of large agricultural plants. The Ptolemaic system, with its controls and monopolies, had prepared the way for this economic development. Although Augustus provided for the free distribution of wheat to more than 300,000 citizens of Rome, his profit from relatively little expenditure in the Nile

---

persons living in a *pagus* (rural country), the hinterland from an urban, "educated," point of view. The *pagani* happened to be more conservative, holding on to their inherited religion. Thus the term later became synonymous with non-Christian. But the irony of history wills that the move of the church towards power-sharing in the state coincided with the church's increasing missionary success in the countryside. The phenomenon of the massive return first of the Roman elite and then of others to the countryside is also the topic of the book by Werner Raith, *Das verlassene Imperium: Über das Assteigen des römischen Volkes aus der Geschichte* (Berlin: Wagenbach, 1982). But my perception of the character and dimension of the phenomenon and my explanation differ from Raith's.

41. E.g., brick, pottery, glass, and even metal. Agriculturally the big estates would concentrate on whatever proved to give the highest financial yield given local circumstances. In Italy this would mean wine, fruit (particularly figs), and oil. In some suitable areas space was also devoted to the large-scale raising of cattle, sheep, pigs, and poultry.

valley was tremendous. The principle which worked in rural estates and plants also proved to be a better basis for the expensive, long-distance sea trade, which was essential to the economic structure of the empire.[42] This trade needed major capital backing without which it could not survive. It was too expensive and too risky for short-term financing. But, literally, in the long run, it could pay off.

Meanwhile, the social pressure on the city had not yet diminished; on the contrary, the big cities, especially Rome, still attracted many lower-class people. And the slave-operated estates were driving farmers away, and not attracting free laborers. Therefore, a concerted effort was necessary to allay realistic fears among the lower classes regarding their situation on the land. In addition, more landowners needed to be moved to care for their rural estates personally instead of relying on slaves. This would work against the disastrous effects of investment in estates outside of Italy and of absentee ownership of land. Having wealthy Romans invest more in Italian estates and be physically present would create confidence among the smaller farmers because of the shared Roman consensus-structure. An invocation of the old Roman virtues, particularly of thriftiness, could induce restraint in the consumption of luxuries among the rich, thus reducing social envy and improving the catastrophically negative balance of trade.

If more lower-class free people moved to the countryside landlords might also be attracted to invest still more in their estates because they could count on a better labor market. City people might be attracted to work as farm hands which would tempt small farmers to forego economic risks and turn their plots over to the landlords and take up tenancy as a safer way of farming. This would help the landowners since slavery was becoming increasingly expensive.

Augustus was more a symptom than a cause. He stood for the acceleration of an economic and social momentum which later developed into an avalanche: the rise of the owners of the *latifundiae* ("large estates") into the position of essential and decisive producers and promoters and carriers of trade. The flight from the city would eventually end in the dethroning of Rome as the capital city. The centralizing efforts of the Caesars of the first and second centuries were futile attempts to create a

---

42. Land routes were too expensive for long-distance trading because horse power could not yet be economically "harnessed," in the literal sense of the world. Ox power was too slow, clumsy, and costly. On sea routes much space was preempted by grain imported to Italy, especially to Rome, not just from Sicily, but from Africa, Egypt, and as far as the Black Sea. The remaining freight space could be more profitably used to transport luxuries for the well-to-do. This transportation factor is one of the reasons for the absence of interest in mass production in the city. It would have required extensive systems of distribution, particularly for long-distance conveyance. The provision of inexpensive or gratuitous grain to the masses, though expensive to those responsible, was maintained because it proved to be more beneficial politically.

counterweight. They helped neither the empire nor society at large, but aided the deurbanizing decentralization because they tended to make ever larger parts of the empire imperial domains. This turned increasingly larger portions of the populace into an imperial clientele with other investors, proprietors, and producers imitating and competing. Virgil and Horace express the eschatological dimensions of this growing development: the capitalism of the suburbs and of the rural estates as realized eschatology.[43]

---

43. Augustus, the Augustan religion, and all who helped them became pacesetters of an economy and society which turned away from the city and fled to the countryside. The centralizing efforts of the Caesars of the first century were not really of an economic nature in this respect, but a mere passing stage in a contrary development. The Caesars themselves boycotted their centralizing measures by their own private economic activities, arrangements, and establishments.

As it turned out the development which Virgil and Horace promoted and supported did not happen for the sake of the city of Rome. It did not strengthen the situation of small and moderate farmers either, but of the rich, particularly those willing to invest. The political theology as expressed in the poems of Virgil, Horace, and those sharing their opinion in the end gave encouragement and good conscience to the leading class for leaving the cities to the masses, thus turning them into sources of cheap labor for the future heirs of the big country estates, the coming centers of economy and society.

three

Rituals and Power

S. R. F. PRICE

Because mankind address him thus [as Sebastos] in accordance with their estimation of his honor, they revere him with temples and sacrifices over islands and continents, organized in cities and provinces, matching the greatness of his virtue and repaying his benefactions towards them.[1]

The cults of the Roman emperor performed by the Greek cities of Asia Minor during the first three centuries C.E. confound our expectations about the relationship between religion, politics and power. The civilized, complex cities, with their ideals of autonomy and freedom, had to accept subjection to an authority which, while not so alien as to make adjustment impossible, was external to the traditional structures of the city. The answer to the problem lay in finding a place for the ruler within the framework of traditional cults of the gods.

These imperial cults have a particular importance for those interested in the formation of large-scale societies. Much royal ritual — coronations, court ceremonial and funerals — is located in and created by the center. In many kingdoms there is little representation of the monarch outside the center, except in royal progresses, which are occasional and transient. In Asia Minor there were ceremonies to greet emperors who visited provincial cities, but they were rarely called for; no emperor visited the area in the whole of the first century C.E. The rituals with which we are concerned are not irregular and passing events, but cults performed for the emperor in his absence and institutionalized on a regular basis. The Roman empire thus offers an excellent opportunity to explore a ruler cult which was a permanent institution, created and organized

---

Ed. note: The notes to these excerpts from Price do not attempt to reproduce fully the complex references and documentation in *Rituals and Power*. At points the reader is referred to Price's full discussion. References to "Catalogue..." are to *Rituals and Power*, "A Catalogue of Imperial Temples and Shrines in Asia Minor," pp. 249–74.

1. Nicolaus of Damascus, *FGH* 90 F 125. The Latin "Augustus" was a title, implying divine favor, given to the first emperor, whom we call Augustus, and employed by his successors. "Sebastos" is the Greek equivalent, but has a stronger association with the display of religious reverence (*eusebeia*) to the emperor. For other literary references to the cult see Philo, *Legatio* 149–51, and Lucian, *Apologia* 13.

by the subjects of a great empire in order to represent to themselves the ruling power.

Because of the size of the Roman empire, which stretched from Spain to Syria and from Britain to North Africa, I propose to focus on one area, namely Asia Minor, which is roughly equivalent to modern Turkey. Here the basic unit of political organization was the city, and the dominant language Greek, but the cities were always at the mercy of external power. Both Persia and Athens had exercised sway over them, and from the time of Alexander the Great (336–323 B.C.E.) onwards the cities had gradually lost their independence, first to Greek kings and then to Rome. The reign of the first emperor Augustus (31 B.C.E.–14 C.E.) marked a turning point in the consolidation of Roman power. Asia Minor consisted of several provinces, each administered by a governor who came out from Rome. With only a small staff, the governor himself could do little more than handle important legal cases and maintain order. The cities continued to organize themselves, and they, rather than Rome, were the primary centers of attachment for their inhabitants.

We must avoid the difficulties which derive from our own cultural background; Christianizing assumptions and categories have proved a major stumbling block in interpretations of the imperial cult, and of these the most pervasive is our assumption that politics and religion are separate areas; we need also to reject an ethnocentric prejudice for the Romans against the Greeks.

Travelers in the empire would not have been surprised to meet the cult wherever they went: they would have found the cult located both in local communities and in the associations formed of these communities in particular Roman provinces. The actual forms which the cult took varied from place to place. For example, the city of Eresus on the island of Lesbos recorded on an inscription the munificence of a local citizen towards the imperial family in the later years of Augustus's reign and the early years of his successor, Tiberius (Catalogue no. 5).

> In the magistracy of Gaius Caesar, son of Augustus, leader of the youth, he sacrificed again at [the festivals of] the Nedameia and Sebasta and offered sweet-meats to the citizens and Romans and foreigners. In the magistracy of Apollonodotus, when news came of the safety and victory of Augustus he sacrificed at the good news [gospel] to all the gods and goddesses and feasted at the sacrifice the citizens, the Romans and the foreigners and gave to those mentioned a bottle of wine and three pounds of bread. He also dedicated to the sons of Augustus a sanctuary and temple from his own money in the most prominent part of the square, on which his name was also inscribed, wanting to show his gratitude and piety to the whole [imperial] house. . . . He also founded at the harbor

of the market a temple to Augustus god Caesar, so that no notable place should lack his goodwill and piety to the god [namely, Augustus].

This text vividly evokes the range of imperial rituals celebrated in the cities of the empire. The rule of Rome was represented in marble. But the widespread imperial temples and imperial statues did not form the cold grandeur of an alien authority. The visual expression of the emperor was incorporated into the regular life of the communities through public celebrations. Long established festivals, such as the Nedameia, had an imperial element added to them; they were now also called Sebasta. Separate imperial festivals were also founded, where sacrifices were offered and the whole community was involved either in processions or as the recipients of donations from members of the elite, often acting as imperial priests. The honors, temples, priests, festivals, and sacrifices were curiously close to the honors given to the traditional gods. Indeed these honors were designed to display quite explicitly "goodwill and piety to the god."

The sources available for the study of the imperial cult in Asia Minor are rich. Many imperial temples are known. Numerous statues of the emperor survive, some actually discovered in temples, while others are again shown on coins. But their value is limited in comparison with the evidence surviving in thousands of texts inscribed on stone. These texts make it possible to reconstruct what was supposed to happen at particular imperial festivals. They also provide explicit and unforced uses of the conceptual framework of the cults. For example, the various formulae used to describe imperial sacrifices allow us to create a picture of the relationship between the emperor and the gods; the terms in which activities of the local notables are described and praised are important evidence for the overall purpose of the cults; quite explicit reasons are also provided in some documents concerning the establishment of the cults.

Interpretation of Ritual

Royal rituals have long held the attention of historians of other societies, who have written, for example, on the royal touch or on mediaeval European royal insignia.[2] The reason for these studies is that royal rituals and insignia are seen to define the nature of the king and hence of the state itself. I wish to develop the idea that imperial rituals too were a way of conceptualizing the world. I do not see rituals merely as

---

2. See M. Bloch, *Les rois thaumaturges* (Strasbourg: Librairie Istra, 1924) on the royal touch, and on insignia, the useful introductory pieces by P. E. Schramm, *Kaiser, Könige und Päpste* I (Stuttgart: Hiersemann, 1968), 30–58 and IV 2 (1971), 682–701.

a series of "honors" addressed to the emperor but as a system whose structure defines the position of the emperor. Clifford Geertz argues that complexes of symbols, embedded in ritual and lying outside the individual in "the intersubjective world of common understandings," shape the world by inducing in the individual a certain distinctive set of dispositions which result in actions. "The merit of this sort of view of what are usually called 'mental traits' or, if the Cartesianism is unavowed, 'psychological forces' is that it gets them out of any dim and inaccessible realm of private sensation into that same well-lit world of observables" where investigation is possible.[3] The interpretation of ritual as a cognitive system, which has proved fruitful for anthropologists, will, I hope, help to shed new light on the imperial cult.

To treat ritual as a public cognitive system is to shift the perspective of enquiry away from that traditionally adopted. The conventional approach in ancient history attempts to locate meaning at the level of individuals and their mental states. Thus scholars have often searched the imperial cult for evidence of real feelings or emotions towards the emperor. The problem with emotion as the criterion of the significance of rituals is not just that in practice we do not have the relevant evidence but that it is covertly Christianizing. That is to apply the standards of one religion to the ritual of another society without consideration of their relevance to indigenous standards.

The appeal to emotion as a criterion is closely related to another common approach to ritual. One might imagine that although analysis of symbolic knowledge was interesting so far as it went, the important question remained: what did the Greeks really believe about the relationship between the emperor and the gods? That is, the beliefs of individual Greeks are appealed to as a more solid or "real" level than that of symbolism. I would like to suggest that such an appeal is deeply misguided for two related reasons. Firstly, the status of these "real beliefs" can only be private and mental, but fundamental objections have been made to the theory of belief as a private and mental action, from various directions. Indeed the centrality of "religious belief" in our culture has sometimes led to the feeling that belief is a distinct and natural capacity which is shared by all human beings. This, of course, is nonsense. The question about the "real beliefs" of the Greeks is again implicitly Christianizing.

The second reason for objecting to the question is that it lays an improper emphasis on the individual, which is part of the more general issue of the status of the individual in historical explanation. Many ancient historians, relying (often unwittingly) on a realist epistemology,

---

3. Clifford Geertz, "Religion as a Cultural System," in *The Interpretation of Cultures* (New York: Basic Books, 1973), 97.

assume that society is essentially an aggregate of individuals and that explanations of societies have to be couched ultimately in terms of individuals.[4] Methodological individualists can study only the organization of ritual by the elite or by individual members of the elite and the political exploitation of royal ritual for propaganda purposes. That is, they draw a sharp distinction between symbolism and the "real" world of individuals and they cannot treat ritual as an articulation of collective representations.[5] But from Durkheim onwards insistence on the social as the primary area of analysis has been a commonplace in anthropology and now also in modern history.[6] In particular, language is emphasized as the central phenomenon. Language is not a window onto the real world but is, rather, the stuff of thought itself. Individuals are born into a society which already contains sets of institutions, practices and a common language, from which individuals construct the world and themselves. Thus with the imperial cult the processions and the sacrifices, the temples and the images fill our sources. They are the crucially important collective constructs to which the individual reacted. Ritual is what there was.

Religion and Politics

From the theologian Origen in the third century through into the eighth- and ninth-century debates on the role of religious images a distinction was drawn between religious and secular honors.[7] In modern times the preoccupation with this distinction is pervasive. Most scholars agree that the imperial cult was only superficially a religious phenomenon. It was "fundamentally a secular institution,"[8] "more a matter of practical politics than of religion."[9] The conventional formula is that the imperial cult

---

4. S. Lukes, *Individualism* (Oxford: Blackwell, 1973), 110–22, analyzes the problem.

5. Cf. Mary Douglas's distinction between front-stage and back-stage bias (*Implicit Meanings* [London: Routledge, 1975], 120).

6. See, e.g., the survey by P. Burke, "The history of mentalities in Great Britain," *Tijdschrift voor Geschiedenis* 93 (1980): 529. For a philosophical defense inspired by Habermas, see C. Taylor, "Interpretation and the sciences of man," *Review of Metaphysics* 25 (1971): 3.

7. Legitimate secular honors to rulers were termed *proskynesis* in Greek and *adoratio* in Latin, while religious honors were called *latreia* and *cultus*. See K. M. Setton, *Christian Attitude towards the Emperor in the Fourth Century* (New York: Columbia University Press, 1941), 202–11.

8. J. H. W. G. Liebeschuetz, *Continuity and Change in Roman Religion* (Oxford: Clarendon Press, 1979), 78.

9. L. R. Taylor, *The Divinity of the Roman Emperor* (Middletown: American Philological Association, 1931), 35, 237, 238. Cf. D. Fishwick, "The Development of Provincial Ruler Worship in the Western Roman Empire," *ANRW* 2.16.2 (1978): 1253, who concludes: "The real significance of the worship of the Roman emperor, particularly in its provincial application, lies not in the realm of religion at all but in a far different field: that of practical government, wherein lay the historic destiny of the Roman people."

was simply an expression of political loyalty.[10] In Nock's classic dictum, the cult was homage not worship.[11] The distinction must be convicted of perpetuating a Christian debate.

The reasons given for the location of the imperial cult in the domain of politics are two-fold. The first is that the cult was manipulated by the state, an argument that is particularly common in work on the Western provinces. "Like all religious constructions of politicians, [the imperial cult] had a weakness, for it lacked all genuine religious content."[12] But, of course, central promotion does not necessarily imply cynical manipulation.[13] The second reason applies to other parts of the empire, where the initiatives came from below. A study of the imperial cult in the Greek world concludes that the cult discloses "little about the religious life of the Hellenic peoples but much about their ways of diplomacy."[14] The imperial cult is thus essentially a political phenomenon, either because it was exploited by the Roman state, or because the subjects made diplomatic capital out of it. But both arguments assume that an examination of overt initiatives and of the interests served by the cult exhausts the significance of the phenomenon. This is clearly not the case.

To follow the conventional distinction between religion and politics privileges the view of an observer over that of the Greeks and makes it impossible to understand the dynamics of the imperial cult.

Historical Development

Ruler cult shows a decisive change with Augustus.[15] The assembly of the province of Asia decided in about 29 B.C.E. to offer a crown "for the person who devised the greatest honors for the god" (namely, Augustus).[16] When the crown was finally awarded in 9 B.C.E. the assembly explained the reasons for its desire to honor Augustus.

---

10. K. Latte, *Römische Religionsgeschichte* 1 (Munich: Beck, 1960), 312–26, a "Loyalitätsreligion."

11. A. D. Nock, *CAH* 10 (1934): 481–82, though he recognized that there was hardly an equivalent ancient distinction, *Essays on Religion and the Ancient World,* ed. Z. Stewart, 2 vols. (Oxford: Clarendon, 1972), 241.

12. M. P. Nilsson, *Greek Piety* (Oxford: Clarendon, 1948), 178.

13. Keith Hopkins, *Conquerors and Slaves* (Cambridge: Cambridge University Press, 1978), 208–9.

14. Glen W. Bowersock, *Augustus and the Greek World* (Oxford: Clarendon, 1965), 112.

15. S. Weinstock, *Divus Julius* (Oxford: Clarendon, 1971), 401–7, places the significant change earlier with the honors offered Julius Caesar in his lifetime and those promoted by his followers after his death. But there is little evidence from the Greek world datable before the triumph of Augustus, and many cults may have been founded only after it became clear that Augustus was eager to promote the cult of his father.

16. U. Laffi, "Le iscizioni relative all'introduzione nel 9 A.C. del nuovo calendario della provincia d'Asia, *SCO* 16 (1967): 5–98.

Whereas the providence which divinely ordered our lives created with zeal and munificence the most perfect good for our lives by producing Augustus and filling him with virtue for the benefaction of mankind, sending us and those after us a savior who put an end to war and established all things; and whereas Caesar [Augustus] when he appeared exceeded the hopes of all who had anticipated good tidings, not only by surpassing the benefactors born before him, but not even leaving those to come any hope of surpassing him; and whereas the birthday of the god marked for the world the beginning of good tidings through his coming...[17]

The actual proposal, to start the new year on Augustus's birthday, was made by the Roman governor, who expressed similar sentiments about the crucial importance of the birth of Augustus.

(It is hard to tell) whether the birthday of the most divine Caesar is a matter of greater pleasure or benefit. We could justly hold it to be equivalent to the beginning of all things, and he has restored at least to serviceability, if not to its natural state, every form that had become imperfect and fallen into misfortune; and he has given a different aspect to the whole world, which blithely would have embraced its own destruction if Caesar had not been born for the common benefit of all. Therefore people would be right to consider this to have been the beginning of the breath of life for them, which has set a limit to regrets for having been born. And since no one could receive more auspicious beginnings for the common and individual good from any other day than this day which has been fortunate for all...; and since it is difficult to render thanks in due measure for his great benefactions unless in each case we should devise some new method of repayment, but people would celebrate with greater pleasure his birthday as a day common to all if some special pleasure has come to them through his rule; therefore it seems proper to me that the birthday of the most divine Caesar shall serve as the same New Year's Day for all citizens....[18]

The expression of gratitude and enthusiasm found in this document is characteristic of the Augustan period. In its emphasis on the importance of repaying the debts of benefactions the imperial cult was at one with Hellenistic ruler cults, but the language of the Augustan decree has no parallel in the earlier ruler cults of this area. The exaltation of Augustus is carried even further in a lengthy, but poorly preserved, Coan decree

---

17. Translation adapted from *Roman Civilization*, ed. N. Lewis, M. Reinhold, 2 vols. (New York: Harper & Row, 1955), 2:64.

18. Translation adapted from *Ancient Roman Statutes*, ed. A. C. Johnson, P. R. Coleman-Norton, F. C. Bourne (Austin: University of Texas Press, 1961), 119.

which starts "Since Emperor Caesar, son of god, god Sebastos has by
his benefactions to all men outdone even the Olympian gods . . . "[19] Similarly a decree from Mytilene speaks of gratitude for his benefactions
and continues:

> that he should ponder upon his own self-esteem because it is never
> possible to match those honors which are insignificant both in ac-
> cidence and in essence to those who have attained heavenly glory
> and possess the eminence and power of gods. But if anything more
> glorious than these provisions is found hereafter the enthusiasm
> and piety of the city will not fail in anything that can further
> deify him.[20]

In contrast to the decrees of Hellenistic royal cults which simply, as with
Antiochus III and Teos, describe the political benefactions of the king,
the Augustan decrees make explicit and elaborate comparisons between
actions of the emperor and those of the gods. The gods had long been
described as benefactors and Augustus could, in a rhetorical manner,
even be praised to their disadvantage.

These explicit comparisons between gods and emperor are the product of a change in the dynamics of the cult. Whereas the Hellenistic royal
cults were the product of specific royal interventions in the city, Augustan cults were no longer tied to such interventions. The assembly of the
province of Asia was simply reacting to the very existence of Augustus and his general activities rather than requiting him for any specific
benefactions. Consequently the decision that Augustus's birthday should
be the start of the new year was operative not for one city but for the
whole of the province of Asia. Along with this change in dynamics went
the description of Augustus as a benefactor of the whole world. The feeling that imperial rule provided a canopy for all people is also reflected
in the organization of the cults. In contrast again to the Hellenistic period, when, with rare exceptions, royal cults were city cults, the Roman
period saw not only a great flowering of city cults but also prestigious
cults organized by the provincial assemblies. These assemblies, which
were themselves to some extent the product of Roman rule, had the
important task of representing local interests to Rome; they also held
regular imperial festivals presided over by the high priest of the assembly. For example, the province of Asia in 29 B.C.E. established, by leave
of Augustus, a cult of Roma and Augustus with a temple at Pergamum,
where a regular festival was celebrated.

This greater consolidation of cults in the imperial period is part of a
more extensive change in the relationship between the honors and the

---

19. *I. Olympia* 53. For Coan provenance see L. Robert, *Hellenica* II (1946), 146 n. 2,
and *BCH* 102 (1978): 401.

20. *OGIS* 456 = *IGR* IV 39.

ruler. The replacement of piecemeal and isolated cults by a new density and organization of cults helped to strengthen the idea that the cults themselves had real constitutive power. In the third century B.C.E., even though "divine honors" were granted to rulers, no explicit statement was made about their status. But in the course of the second century B.C.E. the latent ideas were elaborated and there developed the idea that the giving of honors deified a person. The culmination of this trend can be seen in the decree from Mytilene which not only awarded Augustus some of the mostly explicit divine honors found anywhere, but also stated that these would deify him, while leaving open the possibility of extra divine honors at a later date. In consequence the system of honors had considerable importance in conceptualizing the political actions of the emperor.

Local Roots

The reasons for the long-term vitality of this fluid and elaborate system of cults lie in its capacity to exploit the competitive values of the urban elite. Within the framework of collective decision-making by the council and people,[21] there was naturally room for initiatives by prominent individuals. Under a regular procedure, a wealthy individual could give the city a sum of money for the purpose of the cult which formed a special fund administered by the city. For example, at Chios an imperial festival, the Caesarea, was celebrated every four years on the income from one such gift.[22] The income was administered by eight officials, elected immediately after the organizer of the imperial games, according to strictly defined rules. The donor himself seems to have been assured of continuing prestige by the inclusion of his descendants in the procession at the festival. Cities also invited individuals to contribute to the cost of building imperial temples.[23] Individual initiatives and resources were thereby incorporated into the service of the city.

Imperial priests played an important role in fostering a dynamic element in the cult. They came from the local elite and were generally among the most prominent figures in the city,[24] a status recognized by

---

21. For additional documents see J. H. Oliver, "Julia Domna as Athena Polias," in *Athenian Studies Ferguson* (*HSCP* Supp. I, 1940), 521 (with *Hesperia* [1941] 84, no. 36 and [1971] 200, no. 53); *TAM* II 549 = *SEG* XXVIII 1227 (Tloan decree referring to Lycian decision); Charitonides no. 14 with *BE* (1970): 422 (Mytilene).

22. *IGR* IV 947 and 948 with Robert, *BCH* 57 (1933): 518–33 = *OMS* I 486–501 (Chios).

23. Cat. nos. 53, 67, 74, 126; *Milet* I 2, 4.

24. F. Geiger, *De sacerdotibus Augustorum manicipalibus* (Diss. Phil. Halle XXIII, 1913), 45–46, on civic priests; A. Stein, "Zur sozialen Stellung der provinzialen Oberpriester," in *Epitymbion H. Swoboda dargebracht* (1927), 300, and J. M. I. West, "Asiarchs" (unpublished B.Litt. Oxford, 1975), on provincial priests as the cream of

their privileged position in the assembly,[25] and as eponymous officials.[26] Like priests of traditional cults they were not specialists and the duration of their period of office varied. While some periods were quite short, there are numerous cases of priesthoods being held for life,[27] or even, occasionally, inherited within one family.[28] An Ephesian family actually succeeded in maintaining an inherited priesthood over five generations.[29] Lengthy tenure of office obviously helped to maintain the existence of individual cults and was thus an element favoring stability in the system, but it is not to be taken as evidence for ossification. Life-long or hereditary priesthoods could actually arise from extreme competition when one person or family succeeded in performing an extraordinary act of generosity, temporarily outstripping other members of the elite. Thus a citizen of Megalopolis in the Peloponnese, during the reign of Augustus, promised to rebuild a temple of "The Mistress" which was in disrepair, and actually built a temple of the emperors and repaired another temple, in addition to other services in the city. In response the city put up images of him in various temples, erected honorific inscriptions at the temples and made him hereditary high priest of the emperors for life.[30] But even in such circumstances this was not the end of the matter; other members of the elite could always respond with further acts of liberality.

While these rivalries within the elite and pressures of the cities on their elites operated within the confines of individual cities, there were also major pressures between cities. The cities were very jealous of their status and titles, and the imperial cult was absorbed into their competitiveness, whose scope it greatly increased.[31] With civic cults the pressures could operate only at the level of very conscious advertisement of their cults, either by the erection of inscriptions in appropriate places or by the invitation of participants to their festivals. With the provincial cults the rivalry between cities was almost unbounded. The decision as to which city should be the site for an imperial temple, and hence for a regular imperial festival, naturally involved the elaborate ranking of the claims of individual cities.

---

society. Also M. Rossner, "Asiarchen und Archiereis Asias," *Studii clasice* 16 (1974): 101–42.

25. *IGR* III 582 = *TAM* II 175 (Sidyma); *SEG* XXVII 938 (Tlos).

26. *IGR* IV 1302 = *I. Kyme* 19; *BGU* III 913 (Myra); *I. Priene* 222; *P. Turner* 22 (Side). Cf. Epictetus I 19, 26–29, and chap. 4, p. 84 on villages, and R. Mellor, *THEA HRŌMĒ* (Göttingen: Vandenhoeck & Ruprecht, 1975), 182–87, on priests of Roma.

27. E.g., Geiger, *De sacerdotibus*, 45–46.

28. Ibid., 58–59.

29. *I. Ephesos* III 710.

30. *IG* V 2, 515. Similarly the founder of the Caesarea at Epidaurus became their first agonothete, *IG* IV I² 652.

31. L. Robert, "La titulature de Nicée et de Nicomédie: la gloire et la haine," *HSCP* 81 (1977). See S. R. F. Price, *Rituals and Power: The Roman Imperial Cult in Asia Minor* (Cambridge: Cambridge University Press, 1984), chap. 5, for the other side of the coin.

Festivals and Cities

Imperial festivals, despite their failure to conform to our expectations of piety, formed the essential framework of the imperial cult. It was at festivals and in their ritual that the vague and elusive ideas concerning the emperor, the "collective representations," were focused in action and made powerful. "It is in some sort of ceremonial form . . . that the moods and motivations which sacred symbols induce in men and the general conceptions of the order of existence which they formulate for men meet and reinforce one another."[32] Here the conceptual systems of temple, image and sacrifice (see Price, *Rituals and Power,* chaps. 6–8) had their living embodiment.

The city as a whole was involved in establishing and running the imperial cult. Cults were generally the product of a joint decision of both the council and the people, whatever the significance of individuals in providing the initial impetus.

Imperial celebrations were organized both irregularly and regularly. The accession of a new emperor or the receipt of good news about the emperor in the course of his reign were met with rejoicings (see Price, *Rituals and Power,* 212–14). Indeed this became so common that a governor of Asia was moved to check the abuses to which the practice led.

> For as often as more cheerful news comes in from Rome, people use this for their own private gain, and, making the outward form of the imperial house a cover, they sell the priesthoods, as if at public auction, and invite men of any type to purchase them.[33]

There was also a regular cycle of celebrations. One way in which the emperor was brought into the life of the community was by adapting a traditional festival in honor of the chief local deity. The emperor was often brought into close relationship with the traditional gods of the city, in joint dedications, in assimilations and in identifications.[34] In particular, traditional festivals often had an imperial title added to them; the Heraea of Samos, for example, became the Sebasta Heraea. The significance of such double titles is at first sight unclear. Some are very transient[35] and do not necessarily entail a close relationship between the

---

32. Geertz, *Interpretation of Cultures,* 112.
33. *I. Ephesos* Ia 18b, 11–17 (translation adapted from Johnson et al., *Ancient Roman Statutes,* no. 171).
34. Nock, *Essays on Religion,* 42–43, on Sebastan gods.
35. Robert, *Hellenica* VI (1948), 43–48, 73–74; *Archaiologike Ephemeris* (1969), 49–58; Mellor, *THEA HRŌMĒ,* 176–80, on Romaea. Cf. Price, *Rituals and Power,* 212. For the transience of imperial civic titles see Robert, *Hellenica* II (1946), 76–79, and *Archaiologike Ephemeris* (1977), 217.

emperor and the traditional cult;[36] others refer to two distinct festivals celebrated at the same time,[37] but double titles usually referred to one festival[38] and represented genuinely joint cults which showed piety to both god and emperor.[39] A foundation at Ephesus gives an idea of the way that the emperor was added to the traditional cult of Artemis.[40] Images of Artemis and busts of the imperial family and various personifications were provided for carrying from the temple of Artemis, where they were kept, to the theater. Here they were put on special bases at various occasions: the new moon sacrifice of the high priestly year, the regular meetings of the assembly, and the festivals of the Sebasta, the Soteria and the quadrennial Great Ephesia.

There were also regular festivals in honor of the emperor alone. The most prominent of these are the major imperial festivals with their associated competitions in athletics or music. The names for these vary, but Sebasteia, Caesarea, Hadrianea, Antoninea and Severeia are particularly common. These civic festivals were generally held once every four years,[41] though a two-year cycle is also found.[42] Provincial festivals and games in Asia were also based on a regular cycle, but the picture is complicated by the number of different cities which celebrated provincial games.[43]

Annual celebrations were regular too in cities, even if there the special celebrations with games were held only every four years. Mytilene, for example, held competitions with prizes every four years, and also annual sacrifices in the temples of Zeus and Augustus; these annual celebrations were often held on the emperor's birthday.[44] There were also in some places more frequent celebrations. Mytilene actually decided also to sacrifice on the birthday of Augustus each month, in accordance with Hellenistic practice.[45] These days, on which distributions and feasts were

---

36. Imperial authorization of expenditure or of a change in rank may explain some, Robert, *Hellenica* XI–XII (1960), 350–68, on Asclepieia Antoninea at Ancyra and *Castabala* 92 on Peraseia Sebasta.

37. Caesarea and Isthmia at Corinth, Robert, *Archaiologike Ephemeris* (1969), 49–58.

38. Robert, *Laodicée du Lycos: Le Nymphée*, ed. J. Des Gagniers et al. (1969), 286, and *Études Anatoliennes* (1937): 35 on Dionysia Caesarea at Teos.

39. *Milet* I 3, 134 = *LSAM* 53; *IGR* IV 98 (Mytilene).

40. J. H. Oliver, *The Sacred Gerusia*, Hesperia Suppl. VI (Baltimore: American School of Classical Studies at Athens, 1941), 3 = *I. Ephesos* Ia 27, lines 48–56, 202–14, 554–60.

41. *IGR* IV 654 = *MAMA* VI 265 (Acmonia); *IGR* IV 579, 584 (Aezani); *IGR* III 778 = *OGIS* 567, *IGR* III 780 = *SEG* XVII 579 (Attalea); Price, *Rituals and Power*, chap. 3, n. 33 (Chios); *IGR* III 382 (Selge). See also *IGR* III pp. 659–60.

42. *IGR* IV 850 with Robert, *Laodicée*, 285.

43. L. Moretti, "Koina Asias," *RFIC* 82 (1954): 276, at Cyzicus, Ephesus, Laodicea, Pergamum, Philadelphia, Sardis, Smyrna and Tralles.

44. *I. Ephesos* IV 1393; Price, *Rituals and Power*, chap. 3 n. 15; *IGR* IV 1666 = *I. Ephesos* VII I, 3245 (near Tire); *I. Ephesos* Ia 26.

45. E. Schürer, "Zu II *Macc.* 6, 7 (monatliche Geburtstagfeier)," *ZNW* 2 (1901): 48;

given by rich benefactors of the city, were known collectively as "the imperial days."[46]

While a special event, such as the arrival of the emperor, could be commemorated by the designation of the day as sacred,[47] it is the regularity of the standard imperial festivals that reflects the Greek perception of the permanence and stability of the Roman empire. The importance of these regular imperial festivals is summed up in a decree of the Asian assembly:

> Since one should each year make clear display of one's piety and of all holy, fitting intentions towards the imperial house, the choir of all Asia, gathering at Pergamum on the most holy birthday of Sebastos Tiberius Caesar god, performs a task that contributes greatly to the glory of Sebastos in hymning the imperial house and performing sacrifices to the Sebastan gods and conducting festivals and feasts. . . .[48]

Festival followed festival in a predictable manner, with but minor adjustments for the play of events and the passage of emperors.

Indeed time itself was changed by the imperial cult. The years were distinguished in some cities no longer by the holders of the old magistracies but by the names of the annual imperial priests (Price, *Rituals and Power,* 63). Within the year time was divided by months, some of which acquired imperial names such as "Kaisarios" or "Tiberios," perhaps to mark the celebration of an imperial festival.[49] A more radical change was the transformation of the calendar of the province of Asia under Augustus (Price, *Rituals and Power,* 54–5). The old luni-solar Macedonian calendar was replaced by a more convenient calendar based on the new Julian system, but the motivation for the change was not so much efficiency as to provide a way of honoring Augustus. Whereas the old year had begun at a point determined by the sun, the autumnal equinox, the new calendar was to commence on Augustus's birthday, September 23, which "we could justly hold to be equivalent to the beginning of all things." There was also a variety of local, civic calendars operating in the province of Asia, sometimes based on a lunar cycle; some

---

Chr. Habicht, *Gottmenchtum und griechische Stadte,* 2d ed. (Munich: Beck, 1970), 156. Also, rarely, daily cult, Price, *Rituals and Power,* 228.

46. *SEG* XIII 258, 39–40 (Gytheum); *IGR* III 739 = *TAM* II 905 ix 951f. (Rhodiapolis); *OGIS* 524 = *IGR* IV 1257 (Thyatira); Robert, *Études Anatoliennes,* 549–50 (Lagina, Panamara). The Pergamene choir had a series of celebrations throughout the year (*IGR* IV 353).

47. Robert, *Hellenica* II (1946), 59. Aristides (*Or.* LI [Keil] 11 and 16) refers to a sacred month of the temple at Cyzicus, which could be the imperial temple there.

48. *IGR* IV 1608c = *I. Ephesos* VII 2, 3801, restored.

49. K. Scott, "Greek and Roman honorific months," *YCS* 2 (1931): 201–78. Cf. R. Merkelbach, "Die ephesischen Monate in der Kaiserzeit," *ZPE* 36 (1979): 157–62.

continued, but many were replaced by a calendar beginning on Augustus's birthday.[50] There is a natural tendency for people to conceive of the calendar not as arbitrary divisions of a continuum, but as actually regulating time itself.

The festivals were not just passing ceremonies but sometimes lasted for several days. The festival at Gytheum lasted for six days with each day designated in honor of a different member of the imperial house, and with two additional days in honor of two distinguished Spartans. The gladiatorial displays, which often formed part of the festivals, ranged in length from two to thirteen days, with an exceptional fifty-one days on one occasion.[51]

At the festivals the towns would be crowded, perhaps with visitors from neighboring villages, perhaps from further afield. Dio of Prusa, in a speech addressed to Apamea Celaenae (XXXV 15) gives some idea of the hustle and bustle in a center used by the Roman governor for his annual assizes, which

> bring together a huge throng of people, litigants, jurors, orators, governors, attendants, slaves, pimps, muleteers, tinkers, prostitutes and craftsmen. Consequently those who have goods to sell get the highest price and there is no lack of work in the city, either for the transport, or houses or women.

Dio is consoling Apamea Celaenae for being only an assize center and not a center for the provincial imperial cult. Even greater numbers gathered at provincial festivals. Provincial delegates mingled with traders who were attracted from Asia and other parts of the Mediterranean by the tax exemptions granted to some of the major imperial festivals.[52] The number of visitors made it an expensive and prestigious task to care for them. It was a mark of special pride for a man to have been responsible at his own expense for all six gymnasia at Pergamum during a provincial festival.[53] The control of the proceedings was the duty of a special official, the panegyriarch, who is found at both local and provincial festivals,[54] and it was sometimes even necessary for there to be attendants with whips or staves to keep order.[55] Imperial festivals were certainly not casual, half-hearted affairs. Some celebrations were attached to festivals of local deities; others were carefully organized on

---

50. A. E. Samuel, *Greek and Roman Chronology* (Munich: Beck, 1972), 174–76, 181–82, 186–87.

51. L. Robert, *Les gladiateurs dans l'Orient grec* (Paris: Champion, 1940), 280–81.

52. *IGR* IV 336 = *AJ* 73, 30; *IGR* IV 1431 (Smyrna).

53. *Alter von Pergamon* VIII (1898ff), 164–65. See in general L. Robert, *Monnaies antiques en Troade* (Geneva: Droz, 1966), 25–30.

54. *IGR* IV 584 (Aezani), 993 (Samos), 1248 (Thyatira). *BCH* 10 (1886): 416, no. 25, and *I. Ephesos* III 724. Cf. Robert, *Gnomon* 35 (1963): 68–69.

55. Robert, *AJP* 100 (1979): 161–62.

a regular basis; they lasted a significant period of time and at the provincial festivals the city would be thronged with visitors. The imperial cult was clearly part of the life of the city.

The Transformation of Civic Space

Space is an important subject, not as a Kantian universal category but because of the significance of the way that it was structured by the Greeks. As anthropologists have long been aware, the ordering of space can be seen both as a representation of social ideas and as a part of the fabric of reality.[56] Political and social changes are likely to consist in part in the reordering of space. For example, the transformation of Athenian political and social organization in the late sixth and first half of the fifth centuries B.C.E. was accompanied by important changes in the organization of civic space of the main square.[57] There were comparable changes in the Greek city in the imperial period.

Imperial temples and sanctuaries were generally located in the most prominent and prestigious positions available within the city.[58] Like Greek sanctuaries in general, imperial sanctuaries could be found scattered throughout the city. In small cities, when there was room, the temples were often placed in the civic center. The imperial temple at Sidyma was in the center (Cat. no. 78), while at Cestrus two imperial temples face each other across the main square (Cat. nos. 146–47). A range of other important locations are also found: facing the city gate (Cat. no. 150, Laertes), at one end of the main civic area (Cat. no. 129, Sagalassus), or on a terrace over the theater (Cat. no. 73, Stratonicea).

The larger cities were able to place their imperial temples in preeminent positions. At Aphrodisias, where the imperial temple was a local landmark, excavations have revealed two facing porticoes of the first century C.E., three stories high, 14 meters apart and 60 meters long (Cat. no. 64). One was adorned with scenes of Republican and Augustan military conquests, the other with panels illustrating mythological figures relating in part to the foundation of Aphrodisias and the imperial family. The porticoes seem to form a monumental processional way, leading to the actual imperial temple. At Miletus there was a temple of Augustus, though its location is not known (Cat. no. 38), and in the

---

56. See generally H. Kuper, "The language of sites in the politics of space,"*American Anthropologist* 74 (1972): 411–15; e.g., on the Berber house: P. Bourdieu, *Algeria 1960* (Cambridge: Cambridge University Press, 1969), 133–53.

57. J. P. Vernant, "Espace et organisation politique en Grèce ancienne," in *Myth and Thought among the Greeks* (London, Boston: Routledge & Kegan Paul, 1983), 212–34.

58. The temple outside Laodicea Combusta (Cat. no. 115) may have been on an imperial estate but the town itself seems not to have been strongly nucleated. There is also an anomalous temple a few minutes outside Hyllarima (Cat. no. 67), as well as other non-imperial sanctuaries.

center of the courtyard of the council house was built in the Augustan period a large and magnificent imperial altar (Cat. no. 39). One could not ask for a more vivid picture of the incorporation of the imperial cult within the institutions of the city.

The impact on the civic space is even more marked at Ephesus, perhaps the richest city of the province. There the whole upper square was redesigned during the reign of Augustus (Fig. 1). Just between the prytaneum (A), the magistrate's building which contained the sacred hearth of the city, and the council house (C) lie the remains of what has been identified as a pair of small imperial temples (B; Cat. no. 27). In front of these key civic buildings there was built in the latter part of Augustus's reign a "royal portico" (*stoa basilikē*) dedicated to Artemis, Augustus and Tiberius (D); at one end of this there was a room containing over life-sized statues of Augustus and his wife Livia (E; Cat. no. 30). In the center of the square there is a free-standing temple which may be a temple of Augustus (F); a head of Augustus found in the area may have come from this temple, and an inscription refers to "the foundation of Augustus and the dedication of the sanctuary," probably in 27 B.C.E. (Cat. no. 29). Towards the end of the first century C.E. a further imperial temple, to Domitian, was built in the center of a huge precinct off one side of the same main square (G). This involved the construction of a platform, which was given a fine façade onto the main street; a contemporary civic decree refers to "the new grandeurs of the imperial works" which were matched by the renovation of old buildings (Cat. no. 31).[59]

The impact of the emperor on the city is marked not only by temples and altars, but also by the provision of special imperial space in the porticoes on the main squares of the cities.[60] There is a tendency to assume that Greek porticoes were purely secular buildings, like shopping centers or bus shelters, but they did in fact sometimes contain shrines and could be used for cult purposes.[61] It was within this tradition that porticoes were built or adapted for the imperial cult. A portico (*stoa*) and Sebasteion are mentioned together in one city, perhaps as a joint building (Cat. no. 74, Choma), and we have already noted the room in the portico at Ephesus. At Priene the Hellenistic sacred portico which ran along one side of the main square included a series of small rooms, in one of which was found a copy of the provincial decree changing the calendar of Asia.

---

59. The well-known "temple of Hadrian" at Ephesus (Cat. no. 32), which is tucked away on one side of the main street, its ground plan ignominiously determined by the baths behind, is not a counter-example; see Price, *Rituals and Power*, 149–50.

60. They were also dedicated to the emperor, e.g., *SEG* XV 454 = *IGBulg* IV 2057 (Pautalia).

61. *SEG* XIV 702 = *LSCG* Supp. 111 (Tymnus) and *OGIS* 511 = *IGR* IV 580 (Aezani). Cf. R. Martin, *Recherches sur l'agora grecque* (Paris: E. de Boccard, 1951), 497–98.

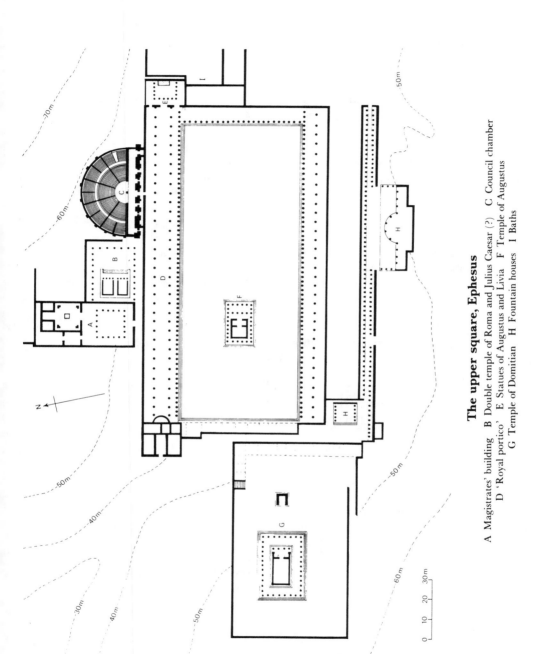

The upper square, Ephesus

A Magistrates' building B Double temple of Roma and Julius Caesar (?) C Council chamber
D 'Royal portico' E Statues of Augustus and Livia F Temple of Augustus
G Temple of Domitian H Fountain houses I Baths

If the imperial cult was an attempt by the city to find a position for the ruler, it is perfectly fitting that the physical expression of this position should be within the civic space rather than in some separate area outside the city. Thus the siting of the imperial temple at Ephesus between the prytaneum and the council house put a permanent expression of the emperor at the heart of the city. The aim of the strategy was to accommodate the rulers within the old framework, and juxtaposition of this sort or the use of a room in a portico on the main square or in the gymnasium was partially successful. But the desire to give the greatest possible prominence to the emperor meant that not all of the architecture of the imperial cult fitted within the limits of the traditional city.

It is preferable to interpret the architectural changes positively as changes parallel to the gradual regularization and restriction of the freedom of action of the Greek city. The formalization of civic space would seem increasingly appropriate in a monarchical world. Within this overall architectural development of the Greek city was embedded the architecture of the imperial cult.

Traditional Sanctuaries, Imperial Temples, and Shrines

I have tried to show positively, and with different material, how the subordination of emperor to god was expressed in architectural terms. There were special imperial buildings in sanctuaries, either freestanding or in porticoes, but these did not approach the temple of the god in grandeur or design. The emperor did sometimes have a part in the temple itself, but in a carefully controlled manner. His name was added in the dedication to the god; he was sometimes actually allocated space at the front or rear of the temple. The pediment might even focus on the emperor in its dedication and decoration. Inside, however, the traditional god was not dethroned or threatened by the emperor. The imperial images that were placed inside the temple of the god seem to have been of different size and in a different position from the traditional cult statue. The limiting case is provided by the building of an entirely new temple to a traditional god and the emperor, which clearly permitted the relationship between god and emperor to be expressed without the constraints of pre-existing architecture.

Temples and shrines devoted solely to the emperor ranged widely. There were special rooms in porticoes and gymnasia; there were freestanding buildings in their own sanctuaries. These buildings varied from simple rectangular buildings filled with imperial statues to buildings with a porch or a colonnade. The most elaborate of them were large and expensive buildings with columns all the way round, which were externally identical to a standard temple of the gods.[62]

The stress upon the dynastic nature of the empire is also found if one passes from the exterior of the temples and the iconography of altars and penetrates within the buildings of the imperial cult.

The stability of imperial rule was perceived to lie in the transmission of power within the imperial family, and, in consequence, considerable importance was attached to the whole imperial house. Modern historians tend to lay too much emphasis on the emperor alone, ignoring the role of the imperial family. Some imperial women played an important part in public diplomatic activity, and not merely in the underhand intrigues of "I, Claudius." Thus the Ephesians tried to aid their claim for a fourth title of "temple warden" by petitioning Julia Domna, the mother of Caracalla, and her reply, tactfully evading any decision, was inscribed by them.[63] At Rome and elsewhere honors were given to women and other members of the imperial family. In addition to the displays of statuary that we have already examined there is the very striking Antonine group from the Artemision at Ephesus. There were statues of Marcus Aurelius, his wife, his son Commodus and five daughters (Cat. no. 28). The empire was in the hands of a family.

The Imperial Cult and Political Power

What is a god? Wielding of power (*to kratoun*).
What is a king? Like a god (*isotheos*).[64]

Consider the implications of this pair of Greek apophthegms. What was the relationship of the imperial cult both to the religious and to the political systems of the Roman empire? Where was power to be found?

We must consider the problem of the relationship between the imperial cult and the political system, between the "dignified" and the "efficient" aspects of the state. The issue is all too often neglected by writers on royal rituals, who tend to stop with a description of the rituals themselves and fail to investigate the relationship between the sacred nature of the king and his political power.[65] In Roman history the conventional approach solves the problem by relegating the imperial

---

62. See now K. Tuchelt, "Zum Problem 'Kaisareion-Sebasteion,' " *Ist. Mitt.* 31 (1981): 167–86.

63. *I. Ephesos* II 212 with L. Robert, "Sur des inscriptions d'Éphèse, 6. Lettres impériales à Éphèse," *Rev. Phil.* 41 (1967): 44–64. Livia had also been important, e.g., Fergus Millar, *The Emperor in the Roman World* (London: Duckworth, 1977), 431–32.

64. *Philologus* 80 (1925): 339, with *Rh. M.* 112 (1969): 48–53.

65. A. I. Richards, "Keeping the King Divine," in *Proceedings of the Royal Anthropological Institute* (1968): 23; R. E. Bradbury, *Benin Studies* (London and New York: Published for the International African Institute by Oxford University Press, 1973), 74–

cult to the sidelines, in favor of diplomacy and administration. Politics, diplomacy and administration form the key to any understanding of the period; the imperial cult does not. Rituals may indeed present a picture of the emperor between human and divine, but they do not really matter. I propose to argue against this view, but it is not easy to pose the question in the appropriate terms. I do not want to suggest that the imperial cult was a part of the ideological superstructure nor that it legitimated political power; these views presuppose too crude a view of the existence and relationship of different aspects of society, economics, politics and religion. Nor should power be seen as a given element of society, located primarily in politics, but as a term for analyzing a wide range of situations. Both diplomacy and the imperial cult were ways of constructing the emperor, and religious language was used in both contexts. Religion is not simply a gloss on politics.

The significance of the imperial cult is dependent on its relationship not only to an autonomous religious system, but also to the political system. There might indeed have been no autonomous political system. As Geertz has shown, the state of nineteenth-century Bali was minimally concerned with administration, which was carried out at the village level, and devoted its energies to elaborate dramaturgical performances. Geertz used this example as the basis for rethinking the relationship between the "dignified" (or ritual) and the "efficient" (or practical) aspects of the state. He argues that it is a misconception to imagine that "the office of the dignified parts is to serve the efficient, that they are artifices, more or less cunning, more or less illusional, designed to facilitate the prosier aims of power."[66] In his view "power served pomp, not pomp power.... The dramas of the theater state, mimetic of themselves, were, in the end, neither illusions nor lies, neither sleight of hand nor make-believe. They were what there was.[67] The problem is quite different in societies, like that of the Roman empire, which had an autonomous political and administrative system. Here it is obviously implausible, if not false, to conclude that rituals are all there was. How then are we to understand the relationship between the dignified and the efficient aspects of the state?

Irrespective of theories about the ultimate springs of religious representations, the significance of ritual has often been seen solely in terms of its practical consequences. Some have felt that the most important function of royal rituals is the preservation of the king's rule.

Ritual has also been examined for its more general consequences or

75, "the key problem of Benin polity — the relationship between political kingship and divine kingship." See more generally Geertz, *Interpretation of Cultures*, 122–27.

66. Clifford Geertz, *Negara: The Theatre State in Nineteenth-Century Bali* (Princeton: Princeton University Press, 1980), 122.

67. Ibid., 13, 136.

functions. The divinization of the Roman emperor has been seen to "function as the legitimation of rule."[68] But functionalist analysis typically fails to examine the conceptual elements of the ritual and leaps to the "obvious" conclusion, as if the actors' perceptions were irrelevant. Rituals are often felt to be "mere" rituals, a "symbolic" aspect of the "real" state, a form of flummery which can safely be left in the care of certain specialists. Such a distinction between the "real" and the "symbolic" wrongly presupposes that the "real," actual imperial rule, is unproblematic. But, as Geertz put it, "the real is as imagined as the imaginary."[69]

This suggests that the terms of the question about the relationship between the dignified and the efficient aspects of the state need rethinking. The terms imply that the efficient aspects are what really count. The political apparatus, the administrative machine, the system of taxation are the fundamental parts of the state. The officials of the state possess political power; if their authority is questioned, they can support their power with force. If one takes this view of the efficient aspects of the state, the imperial cult will necessarily be seen simply as a response to the given phenomenon of political power. One might be tempted to say that it functioned as an accommodation of power and attempted to mystify political reality.

The notion of power as a possession of political leaders is, however, highly questionable. There are objections at two different levels. Firstly, it is surely wrong, as is usually done in historical studies, to treat power in realist terms as a simple datum. Scholars in different fields have shown that this notion of power needs reformulating. As Foucault argues, "Clearly it is necessary to be a nominalist: power is not an institution, a structure, or a certain force with which certain people are endowed; it is the name given to a complex strategic situation in a given society."[70] The argument that power is to be seen as a concept which analyzes relationships is presented more fully by political scientists.[71] Taking for granted that power is relational, they argue that a power relationship between A and B exists when B complies with A's wishes on a matter where there is a conflict of values or plans as a result of calculation of the consequences of non-compliance. That is, a power relationship is rational and compliant. It is easy to see how this view

68. H. Gesche, "Die Divinisierung der römischen Kaiser in ihrer Funktion als Herrschaftslegitimation," *Chiron* 8 (1978): 377.

69. Geertz, *Negara*, 136.

70. M. Foucault, *The History of Sexuality*, vol. 1: *An Introduction* (New York: Pantheon Books, 1978). See further *Power/Knowledge* (New York: Pantheon, 1980).

71. P. Bachrach, M. S. Baratz, *Power and Poverty* (New York: Oxford University Press, 1970), to which S. Lukes, *Power: A Radical View* (London: Macmillan, 1974), does not do justice. See also M. A. Crenson, *The Un-Politics of Air Pollution* (Baltimore: Johns Hopkins University Press, 1971), chap. 1, for a method of studying non-decisions.

could be applied to the political power relationship between the Roman emperor and his Greek subjects. But is it not true that this power
relationship rested ultimately on force? The emperor could execute rebellious subjects by judicial process, or he could send in the army. Force
is, however, a very different concept from power. It applies to a situation
when B is not compliant; it is non-rational and non-relational. What justification can there be for assuming that force is what underpins power?
The cities of the province of Asia, where there was no legion stationed,
were not forced to obey the emperor from fear of his deployment of
violence. That is, power was not a possession of the emperor, wielded
over his subjects and supported ultimately by force; power is a term for
analyzing complex strategic situations.

The second-level objection to the conventional view of power is that
power does not necessarily reside primarily in politics, or the "efficient"
aspects of the state. If power is taken as an analytical term, it makes it
easier to see that there are manifold relations of power which pervade
and constitute society. Religion just as much as politics is concerned with
power. In other words, there is no reason to privilege politics over the
imperial cult.

Furthermore, the constitution of these relations of power requires
analysis. Diplomacy, a major element of politics in the Roman period,
is often seen as essentially practical, or "efficient," a given, empirical
reality requiring no further explanation. But diplomacy is surely not
a simple fact, but a contingent social construct. The endless embassies
from cities to emperors need to be seen as one way of creating and
defining a relationship between subject and ruler. The imperial cult was
another way by which the emperor was constructed.[72] The "efficient"
is no less a construct than the "dignified"; the "dignified" no less an
expression of power than the "efficient."

How, though, do these two means of constructing the emperor relate? The rationalist bias with which we are trained to interpret political
events leads us to suppose that diplomacy was quite separate from the
imperial cult, being based on empirical considerations. But, as has been
argued of modern politics, "political beliefs and perceptions are very
largely not based upon empirical observations or, indeed, upon 'information' at all."[73] It would be mistaken to imagine that diplomacy and
the imperial cult operated in entirely separate spheres. We have already
seen that the linguistic and iconographic classifications of imperial statues were not bounded by ritual contexts (Price, *Rituals and Power,*

---

72. I borrow the term "construction" from (e.g.) P. L. Berger, T. Luckmann, *The Social
Construction of Reality* (New York: Doubleday, 1966).

73. Murray J. Edelman, *Politics as Symbolic Action* (New York: Academic Press,
1971), 31.

179–80). The emperor was not transformed into a totally different being in ritual contexts. I want here to show that the religious language used in diplomatic contexts further weakens the conventional distinction between politics and the imperial cult.

The imperial cult was often associated with diplomatic approaches to the emperor. Offers of cult were sometimes made in association with requests concerning privileges and other matters.[74] Ambassadors to the emperor were frequently also imperial priests. For example, a Samian decree lists the members of an embassy to Augustus as "the priest of Emperor Caesar Sebastos son of god and of his son Gaius Caesar and of Marcus Agrippa, Gaius Julius Amynias... and from the temple builders of Augustus, Menodorus son of Niceratus, and from the other temple builders Saphinios" and others.[75] We do not know in what terms they presented themselves to Augustus, but the city obviously appointed them because of their offices. Little evidence survives of the manner in which ambassadors addressed the emperor, but one Alexandrian embassy addressed Augustus as "unconquered hero,"[76] and ambassadors from Mytilene showed no embarrassment in presenting divine honors to Augustus. The instructions given to them by the city for their speech survive in part; they were to address Augustus as one who had attained the eminence and power of the gods, and were to promise further divine honors which would "deify him even more."[77]

Divine language was used by the Greeks not only in their diplomatic approaches to the emperor but also in response to political actions by the emperor. Gaius made various alterations to the client kingdoms, which modern works describe in purely "factual" terms of administration. ("Rome lost nothing in surrendering the direct government of these districts."[78]) This was not how the action was perceived by the Greeks. A contemporary Greek text reads:[79]

Since the new Sun Gaius Caesar Sebastos Germanicus wanted to cast his own rays also on to the attendant kings of his empire,

---

74. See, for evidence, Millar, *The Emperor in the Roman World*, 492, 537, 542–44 and 375–463 on embassies.

75. *Ath. Mitt.* 75 (1960): 70, no. 1 = P. Herrmann, *Der römische Kaisereid* (Göttingen: Vandenhoeck & Ruprecht, 1968), 125, no. 6. Cf. E. L. Bowie, *YCS* 27 (1982): 35, and Price, *Rituals and Power*, 85–86.

76. *P. Oxy.* 3020 col. ii.

77. *IGR* IV 39 = *OGIS* 456. I infer the nature of this part of the text from the fact that it is in indirect speech. The language of petitions may also have been strongly religious, though the texts of the actual petitions are rarely preserved (and not before the second century). See a decree from Cos (Price, *Rituals and Power,* chap. 3, n. 8) and the use of *theios* (ibid., 246).

78. J. P. V. D. Balsdon, *The Emperor Gaius* (Oxford: Clarendon Press, 1934), 200–203.

79. *IGR* IV 145 = *Syll.*³ 798 (Cyzicus). Cf. also the Neronian freeing of Greece (*Syll.*³ 814).

so that the greatness of his immortality should be in this matter too the more splendid, though the kings, even if they racked their brains, were not able to find appropriate ways of repaying their benefactions to express their gratitude to such a great god (*telikoutos theos*); he re-established the sons of Cotys, Rhoemetalces, Polemon and Cotys, who had been brought up with him and were his friends, to the kingdoms that rightly belonged to them from their fathers and ancestors. Reaping the abundant fruits of his immortal favor they were in this even greater than their predecessors: while they received thrones from their fathers, these men, as a result of the favour of Gaius Caesar, have become kings in the joint government of such great gods (*eis sunarchian telikouton theon*), and the favours of the gods differ from a purely human succession as much as day differs from night and the eternal from human nature.

It is crucially important that the actions of Gaius and Hadrian are presented as the work of "such a great god." The first text also uses language more familiar and more acceptable to us about the restoration of the three men to their kingdom and their friendship with Gaius. But those scholars who screen out the more bizarre aspects of the language used by the participants commit the empiricist fallacy of imagining that social facts can be described in neutral, objective terms. We must not disguise the divergence of the Greek conceptual system from our own.

The importance of this interconnection between religious language and politics can be further demonstrated by an examination of the changes in that relationship and in the terms employed. In the Hellenistic period, when the amount of royal administration over Greek cities was relatively light and variable, the establishment of royal cults does not seem to have affected the terms of politics. The actions of kings towards cities were met by cults; for example, the benefactions of Antiochus III to Teos were followed by the erection of his statue beside that of Dionysus (Price, *Rituals and Power,* 31). But civic decrees do not describe the actions of the king in divine terms and do not elaborate the significance of the cults for the status of the king. By the time of Augustus the relationship of the honors to the political standing of the ruler had changed. The Mytileneans promised Augustus further honors which would deify him even more (see n. 79 above). Cults ceased to be simply responses to particular interventions by the ruler. The more elaborate and systematic nature of the imperial administration in contrast to that of Hellenistic kings was accompanied by a perception that the birthday of Augustus was simply equivalent to the beginning of all things (Price, *Rituals and Power,* 55).

A Christianizing theory of religion which assumes that religion is essentially designed to provide guidance through the personal crises of life and to grant salvation into life everlasting imposes on the imperial cult a distinction between religion and politics. But a broader perspective suggests that religions need not provide answers to these particular questions,[80] and the imposition of the conventional distinction between religion and politics obscures the basic similarity between politics and religion: both are ways of systematically constructing power.

Many societies have the problem of making sense of an otherwise incomprehensible intrusion of authority into their world.[81] The Greeks were faced with the rule first of Hellenistic kings and then of Roman emperors which was not completely alien, but which did not relate to the traditions of the self-governing cities. They attempted to evoke an answer by focusing the problem in ritual. Using their traditional symbolic system they represented the emperor to themselves in the familiar terms of divine power. The imperial cult, like the cults of the traditional gods, created a relationship of power between subject and ruler. It also enhanced the dominance of local elites over the populace, of cities over other cities, and of Greek over indigenous cultures. That is, the cult was a major part of the web of power that formed the fabric of society.

The imperial cult stabilized the religious order of the world. The system of ritual was carefully structured; the symbolism evoked a picture of the relationship between the emperor and the gods. The ritual was also structuring; it imposed a definition of the world.[82] The imperial cult, along with politics and diplomacy, constructed the reality of the Roman empire.

---

80. Cf. Geertz, *Interpretation of Cultures*, and P. L. Berger, *The Social Reality of Religion* (London: Faber, 1969).

81. Kenelm O. L. Burridge, *New Heaven, New Earth* (Oxford: B. Blackwell, 1969), is excellent on millenarian cults and on religion and power in general. Cf. also L. Festinger, *A Theory of Cognitive Dissonance* (Evanston, Ill.: Row, Peterson, 1957).

82. P. Bourdieu, "Sur le pouvoir symbolique," *Annales* (*ESC*) 32 (1977): 405 (translated in *Critique of Anthropology* 13–14 [1979]: 77).

ſ o u ʀ

The Power of Images

PAUL ZANKER

The Empire of Augustus: Greek Reaction

"The whole of humanity turns to the *Sebastos* (i.e., Augustus) filled with reverence. Cities and provincial councils honor him with temples and sacrifices, for this is his due. In this way do they give thanks to him everywhere for his benevolence."

With these words, Augustus's contemporary Nikolaos of Damascus described the spontaneous reaction of the Greek world to the creation of a monarchy after the defeat of Antony. Unlike Rome, the Greek East needed no newly invented symbols or visual imagery of empire. It could apply the old and ingrained "language" of the Hellenistic ruler cult to this new monarch, whose power to bring peace and restore order was everywhere visible, to greet him "with the honors usually accorded the Olympian gods" (Philo, *Legatio* 149–51).

Although the outward forms of the new imperial cult were essentially the same as those with which Greek cities had earlier honored Alexander and the Hellenistic kings, later Roma and individual Roman generals, in its proportions and the extent of its spread it did indeed represent a new phenomenon. Previously, the ruler cult was instituted sporadically in one city or another, usually for a particular occasion. But now it appeared everywhere, almost simultaneously, not only in "free" cities, but in the administrative centers of the provinces, and even in settlements without civic status. The imperial cult rapidly became the most widespread of all cults.[1]

Ed. note: Zanker has "Notes and References for Further Reading" at the end of *The Power of Images,* from which the footnotes here are selected. In the opening paragraph, p. 341, he notes: An overview of historical scholarship of the past several decades is given by D. Kienast, *Augustus* (Darmstadt: Wissenschaftliche Buchgesellschaft, 1982). N. Hannestad, *Roman Art and Imperial Policy* (Aarhus, 1986), now provides a general survey of the subject. His extensive bibliography may be used to complement the sources cited here.

    1. On the imperial cult in the East see now the thorough and stimulating book of S. R. F. Price, *Rituals and Power: The Roman Imperial Cult in Asia Minor* (Cambridge: Cambridge University Press, 1984), where further references will also be found on the phenomena discussed in the following pages. On the archaeological testimonia cf. the

The form and scale of worship naturally varied from city to city, depending on the financial resources of individual patrons and the size and status of the community. The cult of Augustus might be attached to already existing cults and festivals of the gods, but often it was housed in structures built for it alone. "In cities old and new, they build temples, propylaea, sacred precincts, and colonnades for him" (Philo, *Legatio* 149–51). These new sanctuaries for the emperor were often larger and grander than those of the traditional gods, but were otherwise indistinguishable in their outward appearance. There was usually a freestanding, peripteral temple, surrounded by colonnades, or a round temple and monumental altar. But the new style Roman marble temple, with tall podium, heavy pediment, and exuberant decoration, occurs in the East, if at all, only in new Roman foundations. Elsewhere, the use of old and familiar architectural forms reassured the Greeks of the intimate association between traditional religion and the worship of the emperor.

The physical setting of the cult of the emperor was usually in the middle of the city, integrated into the center of religious, political, and economic life. So, for example, a round Temple of Roma and Augustus was built on the Athenian Acropolis, very near the Erechtheum and Parthenon. In Ephesus, the Temple of Augustus lay in the midst of the Upper Square, a new urban center that grew up around the foundation of the ruler cult. King Herod chose a particularly imposing spot for the Temple of Roma and Augustus in the newly founded city of Caesarea (named in honor of the emperor). Set on a high podium, the temple dominated the harbor and shaped the whole outline of the city (Josephus, *Jewish Antiquities* 15.339).

In some places, there was more than one cult site for the imperial house. In Eresos, on the island of Lesbos, for example, a wealthy citizen erected not only a Temple of Augustus at the harbor, like Herod, but also a sacred precinct for C. and L. Caesar in the Agora, then yet a third sanctuary, for Livia. Altars erected for the cult of the emperor were evidently often inordinately lavish, like the one in the Hellenistic bouleuterion of Miletus which has only recently been reconstructed. All of this was a constant visual reminder to every city-dweller of the importance attached to the worship of the emperor. It also expressed a new consciousness within cities of the Greek East, which could identify much better with the monarchy than they had with the large and continually changing administration of the Republic. Direct communication with the emperor, through the medium of cult, gave rise to a new and positive sense of belonging to the Roman Empire.

Greek ruler cults had, since the fourth century B.C.E., linked the ruler,

---

lists of monuments in C. C. Vermeule, *Roman Imperial Art in Greece and Asia Minor* (Cambridge, Mass.: Harvard University Press, 1968).

as the incarnation of earthly power, with the traditional cults of the gods. Usually sacrifices were made to the old gods *for* the ruler, but occasionally people might entreat him directly. Even Augustus and his successors were not treated as fully equal to the gods, despite the extravagant temples and ritual. But the emperor was set beside the gods, as a power that penetrated into every aspect of the life of the city and its people. Historians of religion have often questioned the depth of emotional and religious experience in the ruler cult and dismissed it as a routine expression of allegiance to the state, a view which stems from the Christian conception of religion as faith. But, whatever Greeks in the time of Augustus may have thought or experienced in a sacrificial procession in honor of the emperor, such rituals were linked with parades, public meals, and lavish games. Imperial feast days became the high points of the entire year, when the citizenry could experience a sense of community. As part of the excitement, people streamed in from neighboring towns, markets were held, and self-important embassies came from distant parts. An imperial feast day was also a bright spot in the lives of the poor. Rituals performed for the emperor in faraway Rome blended with high spirits and pride in one's own city. For prominent citizens, it was an opportunity to show off their own status and how much they could afford to lavish on honors for the emperor and enjoyment for their fellow citizens.

But every day of the year, a permanent architectural stage set, against which people played out their lives, was a constant reminder of the emperor. One encountered pictures and statues of him everywhere, and there were also, of course, the coins with his likeness, minted in almost every city. This in itself represented a unique means of honoring the world ruler on a scale never seen before. At first, however, the coin portraits were not by any means uniform. A thorough study of these could ascertain interesting gradations and emphases in the praises thereby accorded the emperor.

While the architecture, as well as forms of ritual and ceremony, were largely traditional, honorific statues for the emperor and his family were apparently most often imitative of models originating in Rome. The widespread togate statue with veiled head presented the emperor as pious Roman, an appropriate counterpoise to the many cult statues. In his images, Augustus was thus manifest as both god and man, corresponding precisely to his special status in the imperial cult. But other types of statues seem also to have been taken over more or less directly from Rome: the figure with garment about the hips, the cuirassed statue, and the heroic nude in Classical style. The same is true of female divinity types, used to celebrate women of the imperial family as a new Aphrodite, Hera, or Hestia, sometimes also as personifications, as was done in the West. In short, the visual language used to express the myth of the emperor shared many common elements in East and West.

Nevertheless, it is probably still true that in the East the emperor was linked more directly with the ancient myths of gods and heroes than in the West. This is, at least, the implication of various later monuments, such as one erected ca. 170 to Lucius Verus in Ephesus, commemorating his victory in Parthia, and a building belonging to the imperial cult recently excavated at Aphrodisias, dating to the Early Empire.

The latter was decorated with two series of large-scale relief sculpture. One series presents familiar mythological subjects — Meleager's hunt, Leda with the Swan, et al. — while in the other, the emperor himself appears in various mythological guises. For example, he subdues Britannia like a new Achilles, the composition borrowed from the familiar group of Achilles and Penthesilia. Several of the reliefs depict him as victor, surrounded by divinities and personifications. In these scenes, the ruler is shown either nude or wearing a cuirass, both reflecting statue types then popular in the West. The various personifications, such as the Genius Senatus and the Genius Populi Romani, are also represented in the standard Roman way. The female deity who crowns Nero accords perfectly with the new type of "political" divinity in Rome, both in her classicizing pose and in the fact that she bears the portrait features and hairstyle of an empress, in this case Agrippina Minor, the wife of Claudius and mother of Nero.

These examples illustrate how East and West early on were able to make use of the same formulaic expressions of praise for the emperor, and how Roman personifications and symbolic depictions of the emperor in mythical guise were easily attached to much older Greek myths, so that the former, in the eyes of the Greek viewer, took on at least some of the same qualities.

Portraits of the emperor and of his family are also usually faithful to models originating in Rome, sometimes extremely so. There are, to be sure, instances where the Roman model has been adapted to the emotional style of Hellenistic portraiture or even assimilated to earlier ruler portraits, but these are quite rare. The question is, why did the Greeks imitate so slavishly their Roman models? Were there no artists whose imaginations were sparked by the new ruler? Or was their intention simply to reproduce his "authentic" features, which were by now so well known from numerous statues in both East and West and from so many coin portraits?

In any event, the result of the copying process was that, thanks to the abundance of honorific statues, a uniform conception of the emperor's appearance and that of his family prevailed, and these images in turn, owing to the new political order, became models for clothing and hair styles — in life no less than in art — throughout the Empire. From the time of Augustus, private portraits, even in the East, consistently display the hairstyles favored by the emperor and other women and men of his house. This in itself was a significant step toward the creation of a uniform imperial culture.

The Imperial Cult: Competition among Cities

Cults and honors for the emperor spread rapidly and had a momentum of their own.[2] Only rarely did Augustus himself or members of his circle take the initiative. The erection of altars of Roma and Augustus for the new provincial assemblies of Gaul and Germany, in Lyon and Cologne, constitute an exception, whose purpose was primarily to convey the permanent bond between the imperial house and the leading men among the recently subjugated peoples. Mostly, however, Augustus made a modest impression and never tired of reassuring his fellow Romans that he was a mere mortal and that they should reserve divine honors for the gods. As *princeps,* he could not do otherwise.

Yet once Augustus had granted permission, in the winter of 30/29 B.C.E., to the provincial assemblies of the Greeks in Bithynia and Asia for cult worship of his person — with, however, the conditions that the goddess Roma must be associated with him in the cult and that he not be named explicitly as a god — there was no turning back. Here too, the various roles were clearly defined. For the emperor's subjects, it was an opportunity to express their allegiance, while he himself had constantly to impose restrictions, occasionally refuse to allow excesses, or even forbid certain forms of worship altogether. Cult worship created a direct link to the emperor. On those occasions when he granted petitions for support or special privileges, when he proclaimed a victory, when a death or birth in the imperial family was announced, when the anniversary of his rule came around, or anything else of the sort, he might expect even more elaborate honors than usual. We are reminded in a way of the practice of reciprocal gift-giving in archaic religion.

Unlike the provincial assemblies, the big cities were largely independent of Rome in managing their own affairs. They could decide for themselves whom they wished to honor, and how, and as a rule did not need to seek Rome's approval. They were just as free as any private individual to accord the emperor religious honors, and Augustus had no reason to stand in their way. This was as true in the West as it was in the East. The only place where he made sure that no temples were built to him while still alive was in Rome itself. For here decisions were taken by the Senate, and Augustus was the Senate's most prominent member. But we may still ask how much difference it made for the worshiper —

---

2. On the imperial cult under Augustus see C. Habicht, in *Le culte des souverains dans l'empire romain,* vol. 19. of *Entretiens Fondation Hardt* (Geneva: Fondation Hardt, 1973), 39ff.; Kienast, *Augustus,* 202ff.

aside from the question of labels — that the *genius* of Augustus, and not Augustus himself, was worshiped together with the Lares in the local district sanctuaries of Rome.

In any case, the imperial cult did spread throughout the West, only not quite as early on as in the East. Yet by the end of Augustus's reign, there was probably not a single Roman city in Italy or the western provinces that did not enjoy several cults linked directly or indirectly to the imperial house. There was, however, no tradition of a ruler cult in the West: on the contrary, Italic religion made a much sharper distinction than Greek between mortal and immortal. There must, therefore, have been powerful social and political pressures operating here. Naturally, we should also take account of the substantial Hellenization of the West. But in any case, the imperial cult became a pillar of the new order in every Roman city in the West.

At first, cities in the West drew inspiration from models in the East, sometimes quite directly. In 27 B.C.E., when the city of Mytilene on Lesbos voted a whole series of honors for Augustus — temple, priests, games, statues in the temples of the ancient gods, monthly sacrifices of a white bull on the day of Augustus's birth, and more — the local magistrates proudly sent an embassy to Rome to announce all this and, in addition, set up copies of the honorary decree not only in the house of Augustus on the Capitoline, but in a variety of cities all around the Mediterranean.

One copy of the decree which chances to survive, though not complete (*IGR* IV 39), names the following cities: Pergamum, Actium, Brundisium, Tarraco, Massilia, and Antioch in Syria. All these cities were important administrative or commercial centers or harbors, where the inscription would surely be read by many. We happen to know that in one of these cities, Tarraco (Tarragona), an altar to Augustus with appropriate ritual was set up at about this very time. Of course we cannot be sure that the display of the Mytilenian inscription was the immediate stimulus that galvanized the people of Tarraco into action. There were literally hundreds of cities all around the Mediterranean that set up altars and temples to Augustus at this time. But in general it seems clear that mutual competition among cities played a decisive role in the swiftness with which the imperial cult spread.

But this is not all we know about the altar at Tarraco. Among all such altars it had a special distinction in that a miracle was associated with it: in the course of time a palm tree grew up on it, all by itself! The city council of Tarraco excitedly sent messengers to inform the emperor of the miracle, but he replied dryly, "One can see how often you have lit the sacrificial fires" (Quintilian 6.3.77). Beside attesting to Augustus's remarkable wit, the response indicates clearly how he took such sacrifices for granted. The miracle of the palm nevertheless enjoyed a certain recognition, for the city of Tarraco later minted coins with the altar and palm tree, in order to boast of the miracle to other cities.

There is epigraphical evidence to suggest that the practice of sending such embassies to Rome and to allied cities was quite common. For the leading men of provincial cities, this presented a unique opportunity to establish personal contact with Augustus. The real reason behind these embassies was not simply the hope of receiving certain privileges, financial support for building projects, or help in times of need, but also the chance for the city to present itself as an important, well-run, and loyal member of the Empire. Copies of honorary decrees in Rome could be read by envoys from throughout the Empire, when Augustus granted them an audience, or when they conducted sacrifices in the Temple of Jupiter on the Capitol. In other provincial allies as well, these inscriptions were displayed in prominent places.

Competition among cities in the worship of the emperor leaves little doubt how fully accepted the monarchy was everywhere. Through the imperial cult, ties with and orientation toward Rome took on a new dimension. In the early years, we can still observe efforts at originality in the various initiatives of some cities, but the trend very quickly became one of standardization and uniformity. The story of the contest sponsored by the provincial assembly of Asia provides a good example. In 29 B.C.E., a golden wreath was offered to whoever could invent the greatest honor for the new god. When the prize was finally awarded twenty years later, it went to the Roman proconsul Paullus Fabius Maximus (consul in 11 B.C.E.), for, of all things, his suggestion that the solar calendar be introduced in the province of Asia and that in the future the new year begin on Augustus's birthday.

In earlier times, cities in the East and in the West had competed among themselves, in central Italy, for example, where they built the great terraced sanctuaries to proclaim their self-assurance. The intention was to impress the visitor on his arrival and so to enhance the prestige of the sanctuary. This type of competitive spirit was now a thing of the past. Every city directed itself primarily to the emperor, and only as an afterthought considered its own needs or its immediate rivals.

It was then not long before the most important stimuli came not from within the cities themselves, but from Rome. In the first instance, the Senate determined which deeds or events in the imperial house should be celebrated or mourned, then individual cities followed suit, more or less voluntarily and each according to its means. Just recently, substantial parts of an inscription were found near Seville, preserving a decree of the Roman Senate and people (*tabula Siarensis*), part of which was already known from other inscriptions. All the fragments now constitute one of the longest known Latin inscriptions. It concerns the enumeration of honors that the Roman Senate and people voted after the death of Germanicus in 19 C.E. These include monumental arches, whose sculptural decoration is described in detail, statues of Germanicus in triumphal garb, which were to be added to several already existing portrait galleries of the imperial family in Rome, annual sacrifices, and much else. The most interesting passage in the present context is the provision that copies of this decree be set up in all the *municipia* and *coloniae* of Italy, as well as in all *coloniae* in imperial provinces. The recent discovery in the remote province of Baetica proves that this provision was indeed carried out. Thus, by this time, the Senate was proceeding as earlier the city of Mytilene had, only much more systematically. Accordingly, what emanated from Rome as "inspiration" was perceived in the provinces more as requirement and obligation. And in fact, arches and statues in honor of Germanicus were erected, just as cults and altars had been instituted everywhere some twenty years before, after the early deaths of Augustus's grandsons Gaius and Lucius, the Senate in Rome leading the way.

The Local Elite and the Augustan Program

The various examples of cults and honors voted by city councils should not obscure the fact that most public building activity, whether religious or secular, was sponsored by private individuals. This quickly led to competition and pressures within every social class, which contributed significantly to the rapid and natural spread of the imperial cult and to the "spontaneous" takeover of the Augustan cultural program in the West.[3] Many people felt they had to put up a building or make a dedication, simply because someone else had done it.

Leading the way were of course the local aristocracy in each city, but they competed not only against members of their own class. As in Rome, wealthy freedmen in the provinces used the imperial cult to win for themselves public recognition and honors, even though they were excluded from holding office. For such "social climbers," the need for recognition in society was of course especially great, and they were among the first to seize upon the new opportunities. It is conceivable that these freedmen, many of whom will have come from the East originally, were in some cities the first to set up, on their own initiative, a cult of the emperor, thus forcing the local aristocracy to come up with a similar undertaking.

A particularly revealing example is known to us from the excavations at Tibur (modern Tivoli). There, a freedman named M. Varenus, who served as *magister Herculeus,* set up a small shrine in the Forum "with

---

3. On the rituals of the imperial cult in the West see now D. Fishwick, *The Imperial Cult in the Latin West* (Leiden: E. J. Brill, 1987).

his own money," on the occasion of the safe return of the emperor, as the dedicatory inscription informs us: *pro reditu Caesaris Augusti.* The reference must be to Augustus's travels either in 19 or 13 B.C.E. On those two occasions the Senate and people in Rome had erected the famous altars of Fortuna Redux and Pax Augusta, both of which, along with the later honors for the deceased princes, were especially influential in the provinces.

The freedman thus celebrated his emperor in the guise of world ruler, as was commonplace by now in Rome, and probably with a private cult as well, just as Herod was doing, albeit on a grander scale, at the same time in Caesarea. Indeed, the *princeps* himself, as well as his successors, evidently had no objection to this rather grandiose image, as long as it was not displayed directly under his nose, in Rome. This much, at any rate, can be inferred from the numerous statues of the emperor in the guise of Jupiter, many of which bear the portrait features of Tiberius or Claudius and were certainly put up while the subject was still alive.

It is surely no accident that a man like Varenus threw himself into the worship of Augustus so early on and with such abandon. To a freedman, the old traditions of the Republic meant little or nothing, whereas the power of Augustus meant everything. Besides, none of the *decuriones* on the city council was about to say no to his request for a site in the Forum for this particular purpose.

Our wealthy freedman, for whom all public offices and honors were inaccessible, was evidently at great pains despite this to call attention to himself. This is clear from the marble tables (*mensae ponderariae*) which he set up just next to the shrine of Augustus, practical and hence surely much-used objects on which the donor's name appeared twice, rather conspicuously. But in addition, on either side of these *mensae*, Varenus put up statues of his *patrona* and *patronus*. The honorific inscription for his former owners gave him another opportunity to include his own name, along with the fact that the site had been granted him by decision of the *decuriones*. The one thing he could not put up was a statue of himself, but he did everything possible to turn this double monument into a monument to himself.

Perhaps it was such cults sponsored by individual freedmen that gave Augustus the idea of encouraging district cults of the Lares in Rome. The next step was the creation of the *augustales* as cult associations patterned after the model of the Roman *compital* cults. This gave wealthy freedmen the opportunity to make public appearances, usually in a *collegium* of six. The imperial cult thus allowed them to sponsor games and public meals, and, in this capacity, to enjoy, if only temporarily, certain prerogatives of public officials, such as the *toga praetexta,* an honorary seat, and official attendants. Later, on their tomb monuments, they boast of the games they paid for and recall those cherished moments when they were allowed to sit on a tribunal in official garb. In this manner the freedmen could try to establish themselves as a kind of recognized class, second to the *decuriones,* at least in outward appearance. Membership in the college of *augustales* was the greatest goal a freedman could attain.[4]

The little temples and local cults associated with this remarkable social and political institution were usually located in the Forum, and thanks to the frequent and highly visible festivals and cult activities they became way stations in the transmission of the imperial mythology. In Rome, the shrines of the Lares served a similar purpose. The extraordinary prestige that the *augustales* attached to their own office is illustrated by the enormous oak wreaths that they had carved not only on altars for the emperor and for the divinities associated with him, but also on their own funerary altars and above the doors of their houses.

As important as the activities of the freedmen may have been, the cults they established did much less to shape the overall appearance of a city than those of the *domi nobiles,* or local aristocracy. Statistical studies have attempted to compare the extent of private donations made by the two principal social classes. These suggest that the leading families, which held political office, spent on average at least twice as much money for public construction and other dedications as the middle class, comprising primarily successful freedmen. The archaeological evidence, though of course subject to accidents of preservation, presents a roughly analogous picture. As a rule, the *decuriones* had a say in the size and setting of each dedication, and they will have seen to it that the proportions of a building accurately reflected the social status of the benefactor.

In Pompeii, we can reconstruct to a great extent the competing activities of the leading families and their important role in the life of the city. The four major, identifiable donors, two men and two women, all belong to the top level of the local aristocracy, and all four held priestly office. The men were both priests in the imperial cult and were also leading political figures in the city.[5]

Such local worthies, always striving to outdo one another, were not only the focus of city politics, but as priests invariably played the leading roles at imperial festivals, performed rituals, and inaugurated the games. They were the *principes* of their local communities, as Augustus and his family were in Rome. In this role they were also responsible for translating the new values into action and seeing to it that the program of cultural renewal was carried out as effectively in the western provinces as it was in Rome.

---

4. On the Augustales and other cult associations: K. Latte, *Römische Religion* (Munich: Beck, 1960), 307, with references.

5. On Pompeiian society: P. Castren, *Ordo populusque Pompeianus* (Rome: Bardi, 1975).

In return for their services they were accorded appropriate honors. Statues of them were put up in public places, especially, of course, in the buildings they had dedicated. In the Temple of Fortuna Augusta and in the market-aedicula in Pompeii, statues of the patron stood in the cella and were thus neighbors of the emperor and the imperial divinities, just as in Rome statues of Augustus stood in temples of the traditional gods. Eumachia's building makes clear how important such honors in the form of statuary were. In the niche behind the cult image, the fullers' guild "spontaneously" dedicated, after the completion of the building, a statue of their patroness Eumachia, which in reality had been planned from the start.

The statues of these local benefactors betray in their very form how they conceived of their role, for the types are the same employed to honor the emperor and his family. Instead of the nude, dramatic figure so popular in the previous generation, they chose a togate statue with veiled head. And of course priestesses had themselves represented just like the pious and chaste women of the imperial house, wearing a veil and the virtuous *stola,* performing a sacrifice.

Cities of Marble:
The New Self-Assurance in the West

It is primarily due to these local aristocracies and their new self-image that the face of many Roman cities in the West was fully transformed in the Early Empire. The leading families could boast of having done for their cities what Augustus did for Rome: turning them to marble, at least their temples, public buildings, piazzas, and monumental gateways. In some instances they had help from the emperor or a member of his family, or another of the Roman nobility. Such occasional subsidies were most likely to go to the *coloniae* founded by Augustus himself. But for the most part, local *domi nobiles* had to rely on their own resources to bring about an architectural revival patterned on that in Augustan Rome. If we discount for the moment those cities of Campania and Central Italy that had been Hellenized as early as the second to first century B.C.E., then indeed most cities in Italy and the western provinces received their first public buildings in marble, streets, squares, and gateways at all comparable with those of the average Greek city only at the time of the Augustan revival.

The building activity for the imperial cult that we have just considered will have made clear how closely the architectural revival was linked to the new political situation and the sense of excitement that went with it. Even purely aesthetic refinements or, at the other extreme, mundane engineering projects involving road- and bridge-building or the water supply system cannot be fully divorced from the ideological foundations of the Augustan cultural program.

A particularly important component in the architectural renewal in every city, not only in Rome, was the theater, whose significance went far beyond its practical purposes.[6] As in Pompeii, so too in almost every city in the West a theater was either newly built or enlarged or renovated during the Early Empire. Unlike in colonies founded during the Republic, the theater was now usually a conspicuous part of any new city founded under Augustus. The theater was regularly situated at a central or easily accessible site, its soaring facade, clad in marble and richly ornamented, towering over the surroundings. As in Rome, seating was by social status, so that the *cavea,* when full with spectators, presented a vivid reflection of the carefully structured social hierarchy within each city. At the front were seats for city magistrates, priests, and *decuriones,* as well as others which by law had to be kept free in the event of senators from Rome passing through the city. Stalls separated the seats in the middle area, reserved for the *plebs,* from those of the nobility, which in Pompeii occupied twenty rows. In some cities, the forward section will probably have had further subdivisions, though good evidence for this is lacking. Those at the bottom of the social ladder — women, foreigners, and slaves — sat at the very back.

At the rear of the theater in Pompeii, at the uppermost section of the *cavea,* the brothers Holconii built a vaulted passage (*crypta*), which contained additional, tightly packed rows of seats. This is surely more than a routine expansion to meet local needs and is not typical. Augustus's policies were based on a clear separation of social classes, but they nevertheless strove to include all those on the fringes of society in greater numbers than ever before. This is evident not only in the imperial cult, but at games and festivals as well.

The *princeps* was of course unable to appear in person in all these local theaters, as he did in Rome. This may help explain how the custom arose, as early as the time of Augustus, of placing statues of him and his family in the *scaenae frons,* the colonnaded facade behind the stage, where previously figures of gods, muses, and Greek masterpieces were displayed.

In the building inscription at the theater in Pompeii, the Holconii brothers make reference to another of the improvements they made, the *tribunalia.* These are seats reserved for the magistrates in charge of the games, located over the barrel-vaulted side entrances to the orchestra,

---

6. On the theater buildings see G. Béjor, "L'edificio teatrale nell'urbanizzazione augustea," *Athenaeum* 57 (1979): 126–38; M. Fuchs, *Untersuchungen zur Ausstattung römischer Theater* (Mainz am Rhein: P. von Zabern, 1987). On the differences between the Roman and Greek theater see M. Bieber, *The History of the Greek and Roman Theater,* 4th ed. (Princeton, N.J.: Princeton University Press, 1971).

and with their addition, the essentially Hellenistic theater of Pompeii was turned into a Roman one. The particular importance of this feature for the Augustan Age is evident in Leptis Magna, where the dedicatory inscriptions are displayed just here, on the *tribunalia*. Leading magistrates appeared on these elevated seats before the populace like statues on a triumphal arch come to life. Thus the local powers were also incorporated into the stage set, though in a clearly subsidiary position to the statues of the emperor in the *scaenae frons*.

The Augustan theater was surely no place to go to forget politics and lose oneself in a spontaneous, Dionysiac entertainment. We do not know whether even outside Rome one was required to wear a toga to the theater, but certainly the ennobled spirit of the new age was ever-present in the form of statues and other images. Everywhere were carved altars, little temples, Victories, arms and armor, and vines. In Rome, later on, the theater curtain was even decorated with pictures of bound barbarians. Symbols of the imperial cult were on hand on various forms, some more blatant than others. So, for example, above the auditorium of the theater in Leptis Magna stood a small temple with a statue of Ceres Augusta with the coiffure and portrait features of Livia. Similarly, the famous altar with the swans of Apollo stood in the theater at Aries.

In the construction of any theater or other public building, the decorative scheme was of course an integral part of the planning, by both patron and architect, from the start. But in public squares, especially in fora, on the other hand, honorary statues and other monuments accumulated gradually. Even allowing for the fact that most of these were put up on an ad hoc basis, there emerged a distinctive and expressive whole, which was fundamentally different from a public square of the Republic.

We must again turn to Pompeii to gain an impression of such a square in its full effect. The Republican Forum had apparently been characterized by monuments of roughly equal size, to judge from the socles of equestrian statues along the west side. On the south side, in front of the administrative buildings, more monuments were originally lined up in this same egalitarian arrangement, until they had to make way, first for a monumental arch, probably to Augustus, then for two colossal bases for other imperial monuments, perhaps triumphal chariots. Not long after, an oversize equestrian monument was set up before the arch of Augustus. All these new monuments naturally relegated the equestrian statues of local nobility to secondary importance. That the hierarchy of status according to size of monument was everywhere an important principle during the Early Empire is confirmed by a charge against the proconsul Marcellus, reported by Tacitus (1.74), that he set up his own statues higher than those of the *caesares*. It is also striking that bases for equestrian statues were more prominently displayed than those for simple standing figures (*statuae pedestres*). In Pompeii, *statuae pedestres* now no longer stood in the square, but in the porches of the new buildings. Socles of the same type were probably erected simultaneously in front of the Macellum and in the Chalcidium of Eumachia's building, to carry older images of local worthies, following the model of the *summi viri* displayed in the Forum of Augustus. Although these *statuae pedestres* imitate the body types, hairstyles, and even expressions of statues of the imperial family, their scale and location, relative to those of the overwhelming imperial monuments, indicate clearly their true rank in society.

This picture of the Forum in Pompeii would be incomplete without the two honorific arches on either side of the Temple of Jupiter. They may have been among the honors voted after the early deaths of the princes Gaius and Lucius, or Germanicus. Augustan models for the linking of temple facade and honorary arches can be found in the Forum Romanum and later in the Forum of Augustus as well. Similarly situated arches of early imperial date have also been found in other cities, as in Spoleto. It need hardly be emphasized how such a setting enhanced the effect of such arches, with their statues, tropaea, or quadrigas. The sacred aura of the temple facade was thus pressed into the service of whichever member of the imperial house was honored by the arch.

Theater and public square were the places where the ordinary citizen lingered the longest, apart from the baths. In both places he was confronted with an impressive collocation of imagery, which vividly illustrated for him not only the power structure and social organization of the state, but also his own place within society.

But it was not only the cities themselves that were transformed, but their surroundings as well. The traveler along the roads of Italy in the first century C.E. — roads largely built by the *princeps,* with a pillar set up every mile to proclaim in big letters to whom it was owed — would have continually encountered new city walls and towers. Augustus and Tiberius personally gave many Italian cities the money to build such walls, even in peacetime. Why, we may ask, just when the Empire was enjoying the much-touted Pax Augusta?

In the Late Republic, the city wall had become in many parts of Italy an important element of self-promotion. Now, in changed circumstances, it became a symbol of defense, particularly defense of the *virtus* recently restored by the *princeps.* In places like Hispellum (Spello) in Umbria, the prospect of a city protected by great walls, carefully staged by the layout of the road network, turned Virgil's poetic vision into a reality. *Mores* and *moenia* went together (*Aeneid* 1.264; 6.403), and the new walls gave proof of the new spirit.

In reality, the young men of Italy were being called upon less and less for active military service. But the militarization of visual imagery, for which a whole series of other examples could be cited, was intended at least to instill in them, through the appropriate symbolism, the correct mentality. The military towers in the city gates of Spello or Turin are the outward expression of military preparedness. As in Saepinum, which received money from Tiberius to build walls and towers, in many other towns statues of captured barbarians recalled not only the victories of the imperial house, but more generally, the self-appointed mandate of the Romans as world rulers.

This necessarily abbreviated glimpse over the Empire shows how, from the foundation of the monarchy, a uniform visual language began to develop, one based almost entirely on forms of paying homage to the imperial house. As in Rome, this followed a course of natural progression, without the need for explicit directives from above. After Actium, both East and West must have felt an overwhelming need to establish direct contact with Augustus, with the one individual who, for the first time in the history of the Mediterranean world, had created a stable and recognizable universal rule. Only the East, however, had an instrument already in place for establishing lines of communication, in the form of the ruler cult. There, people had long felt the lack of a genuine ruler and of an empire with which they could identify.

It was inevitable that the West would take over the ruler cult, since it gave local aristocracies a new vehicle for expressing and maintaining their positions of power. The integration of the ruler cult into traditional religious ritual allowed each individual, and the community as a whole, to share the feeling of participation in the restoration of the state.

The new monarchy also inherited, along with the Hellenistic ruler cult, a fully developed system of visual communication, into which the specifically new imagery and symbolism were easily integrated. Viewed somewhat differently, the entire sequence of events is a further stage in a gradual process of acculturation in Rome. The adoption of the ruler cult represents a new watershed in the Hellenization of the Roman cities in the West.

The leading families in each city, in both East and West, were those who contributed most to the ruler cult and also profited most from it. Those in the West had the added advantage that they could, as Romans, identify personally with Augustus's program of cultural renewal. In these areas, the imperial cult went hand in hand with the visual expression of new moral values, especially in the complete architectural remodeling of the cities themselves. The impact of the new imagery in the West thus presupposed the acceptance of a complete ideological package. Temples, theaters, water systems, and city gates, all of specifically Roman type, gave every city in the West a uniform look, one which remained essentially unchanged.

Part II

patronage, priesthoods, and power

Introduction

The ruling nobility, priests, magistrates, judges, legal counsel, and generals rolled into one, stood astride all the major lines of communication with the centre of state power and the resources it had to distribute. Their success in control lay as much in their power to refuse as in their readiness to deliver the goods. In this light, the inability of a few hundred to satisfy the needs of hundreds of thousands, their manifest failure to alleviate poverty, hunger, and debt, indeed their exploitation of these circumstances to secure themselves advantage need not be seen as arguments for the inadequacy of patronage, so much as the conditions of its flourishing.

(Andrew Wallace-Hadrill[1])

The problem addressed in Part II is the same as that addressed in Part I: what held the far-flung empire of Rome together, given that the Romans did not develop an imperial administration commensurate with the complexity of their empire? How were power relations constituted in the civilized areas of the empire such that no force was required to maintain social control? Prior to the recent theory that the imperial cult was instrumental in this regard, some held that a vast web of patronage relations held the empire together.[2] According to Pliny (*Panegyric* 2, 21) and modern studies that follow his lead, the emperor was not so much an efficient administrator as a paternal protector and benefactor, granting to communities or individuals status, privilege, resources, or a favorable hearing.[3] Comparative studies suggest that patron-client relations tend to arise where "authority is dispersed and state activity limited in scope, and in which considerable separation exists between the levels of village, city, and state."[4] Patron-client relations supply part of the answer to how such a large empire was governed by so small an administration

---

1. Andrew Wallace-Hadrill, "Patronage in Roman Society: From Republic to Empire," *Patronage in Ancient Society* (London: Routledge, 1989), 73.
2. G. E. M. de Ste. Croix, *The Class Struggle in the Ancient World* (London: Duckworth, 1981), 364.
3. Peter Garnsey and Richard Saller, *The Roman Empire: Economy, Society, and Culture* (Berkeley: University of California Press, 1987), 20–26, 149; Fergus Millar, *The Emperor in the Roman World, 31 B.C.–A.D. 337* (Ithaca, N.Y.: Cornell University Press, 1977).
4. Alex Weingrod, "Patrons, Patronage, and Political Parties," in Steffen W. Schmidt et al., eds., *Friends, Followers, Factions: A Reader in Political Clientelism* (Berkeley: University of California Press, 1977), 325.

not simply "within the sphere of politics and administration,"[5] but in a far wider social-economic sense as well. Seneca's comment about patron-client relations became true of the imperial order as well as Roman society itself: the exchange of favors and services "binds together human society" by easing conflicts provoked by divisions and inequalities.[6]

The cross-cultural studies of patron-client relations in modern Mediterranean societies will likely be of little help in this connection, except for comparison and contrast. "It is inadequate simply to look for the presence of patron-client relations...; what we need to look at is the strategic function of such relations within a particular social system as a whole."[7] In this case we are attempting to understand a particular strategic function of networks of patronage at specific social locations in the Roman imperial order. In the ancient Mediterranean the patron-client patterns that came to structure Roman society prior to the empire were distinctively Roman. We cannot simply assume that other peoples around the Mediterranean had similar patterns of patron-client relations.[8] There is clear evidence that the development of patronage patterns was resisted in the evolution of Athenian democracy.[9] The emergence of patron-client relations in Greece in Roman times may thus

---

5. Richard P. Saller, *Personal Patronage under the Early Empire* (Cambridge: Cambridge University Press, 1982), 205.

6. Garnsey and Saller, *The Roman Empire,* 148.

7. Wallace-Hadrill, introduction to *Patronage in Ancient Society,* 8.

8. This is simply assumed by some New Testament scholars who borrow data as well as "models" from functionalist anthropological studies of modern Mediterranean societies done largely in the 1960s. See the literature cited by John H. Elliott, "Patronage and Clientage," in Richard Rohrbaugh, ed., *The Social Sciences and New Testament Interpretation* (Peabody, Mass.: Hendrickson, 1996), 144–56. Application of any generalizations from modern Mediterranean societies to the ancient Mediterranean world by social scientists who tend to exclude historical explanation involves a certain historical question-begging. For example, David Gilmore makes an illuminating and unobjectionable observation (in "Anthropology of the Mediterranean Area," *Annual Review of Anthropology* 11 [1982]: 192–93) that John Dominic Crossan then applies to ancient Roman imperial society (in *The Historical Jesus: The Life of a Mediterranean Jewish Peasant* [San Francisco: HarperCollins, 1991], 67): "Mediterranean societies are all undercapitalized agrarian civilizations...[with] sharp social stratification...[and] little social mobility. Power is highly concentrated in a few hands, and the bureaucratic functions of the state are poorly developed....Patronal relations provide a consistent ideological support for social inequality and dependency...." But when he adds, "These conditions are of course ideal for the development of patron-client ties and a dependency ideology," he simply ignores the reality of historical change and development. The patronage system that provided the forms for Roman imperial relations with subject societies was the historical product of earlier Roman history, and the spread of the patronage system from Rome itself into the empire, where it came to structure social relations for several centuries, was surely a powerful historical factor in the later history of Mediterranean societies which did not develop state bureaucracies and more democratic social-political forms.

9. See esp. Moses I. Finley, *Politics in the Ancient World* (Cambridge: Cambridge University Press, 1983), 70–96; and Paul Millett, "Patronage and Its Avoidance in Classical Athens," in Wallace-Hadrill, *Patronage in Ancient Society,* 15–47, who outlines deliberate steps taken in Athens to underwrite the economic independence of the poor, such

be the result of Roman influence and domination. We cannot simply assume, moreover, that patronage patterns pervaded Roman society so completely that it included most of the peasantry. Like the relevant inscriptions, the literature in which patronage was discussed was written by the elite and focuses on the elite, leaving us with virtually no evidence for client status of the rural poor. Political-economic dependency such as sharecropping and debt slavery is not the same as patron-client relations.[10]

Many discussions of patron-client relations exclude consideration of its effect on the ordinary people (rural or urban) and how they may have felt about their dependency. The personal but asymmetrical (vertical) reciprocal exchange of goods and services in patron-client relations stands diametrically opposed to the horizontal associations and reciprocity embodied in kinship and villages. The vertical bondings of some peasants undermine the solidarity of local peasant communities.[11] Precisely this subversion of solidarity among the peasantry and the urban poor is one of the key facets that makes it important in the circumstances of Paul's mission to build a movement of solidarity among the peoples of the eastern Mediterranean. Among the Roman urban poor, for whom we have at least minimal evidence of dependency on patronage, we should not imagine either that the poor were happy about their dependency or that patronage really alleviated poverty and hunger. Patrons promised help, but kept their clients in suspense about whether they would receive any. The attempts at antipatronal legislation (e.g., secret ballot) indicate that patronage was not all that popular among the clients (cf. Cicero, De leg. 3.33–34). The Roman elite used patronage as an instrument of social control. As noted by Wallace-Hadrill in the epigraph above, the ruling nobility's "success in control lay as much in their power to refuse as in their readiness to deliver the goods," and they failed "to alleviate poverty, hunger, and debt." In fact their exploitation of these circumstances to secure advantage for themselves was the precondition for the

---

as redistribution of income as an antidote to patronage — which explains why wealthy conservatives such as Plato and Isocrates objected so vehemently to state pay.

10. Peter Garnsey and Greg Woolf, "Patronage and the Rural Poor in the Roman World," in Wallace-Hadrill, *Patronage in Ancient Society,* 153–70, esp. 152, 154, 158, acknowledge the risk that study of patronage will overrate the significance of this one way among many by which the rural poor may have survived the many threats to their subsistence, but distinguish inadequately between different forms of dependency relations. To the extent that they were pulled into patron-client relations, of course, they did not survive as independent peasant families.

11. S. N. Eisenstadt and L. Roniger, "Patron-Client Relations as a Model of Structuring Social Exchange," *Comparative Studies in Society and History* 22 (1980): 50; Garnsey and Woolf, "Patronage and the Rural Poor," 157: "Patronage works by distributing resources and services preferentially to some of the poor but not to others, and the ideal rural client (from the patron's perspective) is concerned with his own interests to the exclusion of those of his fellows."

patronage system.[12] Thus the vertical patron-client relations that came to structure much of Roman society must have been located primarily in Rome itself and the Italian towns. There, as Tacitus put it, the "good" people of the city were included in established social order, while the "bad" either wished to avoid the humiliation of dependence or were thought to have nothing to offer in return for the favors of aspiring would-be patrons. Even the members of the *collegia* which imitated the hierarchical features of the upper eschalons of the patronage pyramids, while humble men, were not from among the very poor or destitute.

In any case, our interest focuses on patronage not only as an instrument of social control, but as the means of social cohesion — the networks of personal relations by which first the different interests within Roman society and then the disparate peoples of the Roman empire were held together. That depends on how the pyramids of patronage relations fit together at the highest levels of the hierarchical Roman society and, later, at the highest levels of the imperial order. Earlier in the Roman Republic the webs of patron-client relations cut across the conflicting class interests of plebs and patricians as well as the lesser tensions between families and factions within the upper orders of Roman society. Democratic reforms were thus effectively blocked, since large numbers of the plebs were tied, against their own interests, to the wealthy and powerful senatorial families. Until the later Republic the competition between the powerful men, each supported by his network of clients and clients of clients, proved effective for the domestic cohesion necessary for continual foreign wars and conquests. Internal cohesion turned into civil war, however, when the great warlords such as Julius Caesar and Pompey, Octavian and Mark Antony, each supported by a social-economic-political power base of extensive pyramids of patronage, could not control their own ambition, greed, and drive for greater glory.

Augustus and the Principate brought about a profound transformation in the system of patronage in Rome itself, which included and was partly caused by running the empire as a vast new network of patronage. Despite the abolition of elections, in which the patronage pyramids had played a key role during the Republic, patronage patterns continued. The mass of people in Rome itself became more and more dependent on the emperor's patronage (Tacitus, *Hist.* 1.4). But although he became the universal patron, he did not displace other patrons at the top of the system. Instead, he manipulated the pluralist system, both in Rome

---

12. Andrew Wallace-Hadrill, "Patronage in Roman Society: From Republic to Empire," in *Patronage in Ancient Society,* 73. "Dionysius of Halicarnassus saw in the patronage instituted by Romulus an instrument of social control, that kept the population in subjection to the ruling class.... Juvenal, *Satire 5,* has the clients as the dupes, for the patrons have no intention of rewarding their services" (72–73).

itself, and particularly in the administration of the empire, so that all strands in the competing pyramids of patronage converged on the emperor at the center. This has been argued and documented by important historical studies[13] and is summarized in the excerpt by Garnsey and Saller printed below. In effect, the emperor became patron of the great senatorial and equestrian figures, and exercised his power through them.

This consolidation of power through the transformation of the system of personal patronage is dramatically evident in the emergent administration of the empire from the imperial city itself. The patronage system was rooted in the basic Roman value that honor and prestige, for which all were clamoring, derived from the power to give what others needed or wanted. Augustus and his successors governed by distributing *beneficia* as personal favors to senators and knights. "All senatorial magistracies, offices, and honors were at the disposal of the emperor.... All were used — either directly by the emperor or indirectly by those close to him — as *beneficia* in patronal exchange relationships.... Patronage was also assumed to be the usual method by which new men in particular secured advancement in a senatorial career."[14] Within the transformed system of imperial patronage, brokering of offices by well-placed senators became increasingly important for secondary offices. By means of such brokerage, the emperor encouraged development of vertical bonds of patronage between the highest-ranking senators and administrators of lower rank. Successful emperors thus skillfully utilized "the offices, honors, statuses and administrative decisions at their disposal to produce cohesion in a web of personal exchange relationships extending from themselves."[15]

Besides becoming the form taken by the structure of Roman society itself, particularly among the elite, and the imperial administration in Rome, the transformed patronage system was widened into the network by which the empire as a whole was integrated, from the imperial family at the top through the provincial elite in each major city. Already under the Republic, the empire was structured through patronal relations. The patron-client relationship provided the pattern on which the relationship with a subject people was modeled as a client city or a client kingdom. Even more important, perhaps, the subject city and prominent figures within it became clients or "friends" of the great Roman generals and prominent governors, who were even proclaimed explicitly as "patrons" in public inscriptions and statues. To a considerable extent, city councils, provincial officials, or client kings dealt with the Roman

---

13. See especially the survey in ibid., esp. 78–84.

14. As argued and documented by Saller, *Personal Patronage*, 41–58; quotation from p. 45.

15. Ibid., 77–78; on how the imperial aristocracy functioned through the patronage system, see further chap. 4.

state through personal patrons.[16] Students of Jewish history and New Testament will be familiar with how the young Hyrcanus's chief minister Antipater and his son, the young Herod, ingratiated themselves with prominent Romans such as Julius Caesar, Mark Antony, and Octavian. As the system of imperial patronage extended and became more pervasive, public and private dimensions were scarcely distinguishable. It was simply taken for granted that personal patronage should take precedence over proper administrative procedures if a conflict should arise.[17] By the end of the Republic, the system of patronage had already extended into, indeed become the relationship between, Rome and her subject cities and kingdoms, which were in turn bound up with personal patron-client relationships at the center of power.[18] In the complex web of patronage, the more formal patron-client relationship between Rome and the subject city or kingdom was "supplemented by numerous informal patronal links between members of the local elites and members of the Roman elite."[19] In language that for many will be more familiar from Paul's letters than from Latin and Greek writers and inscriptions, a central feature of the ideology of Roman imperialism, derived from patron-client relations, was that the Romans show their *fides* = *pistis,* protection, by helping their "friends," while the friends of Rome are praised for their *fides* = *pistis,* that is, loyalty to Rome.[20]

While the extension of patronage networks into subject cities and kingdoms under the Republic became a key factor in the expansion into the empire at large of the Roman "civil war" between the great Roman patrons and warlords, such conflicts were resolved under the emperors. The interests of the state and those of the ultimate patron were now the same, since the emperor was the state. The desperate need and desire of the provincial elite for access to the center of decision making and favorable judgments in Rome, moreover, became a powerful motive force in the consolidation of power precisely through patronage relations. Plutarch's advice to a young man about to pursue local political office indicates how the system worked:

> Not only is it necessary for a statesman to keep himself and his home city blameless toward the rulers, but also always to have some friend in the circles of the most powerful (in Rome) as a firm support for the city. For the Romans themselves are best disposed

---

16. David Braund, "Function and Dysfunction: Personal Patronage in Roman Imperialism," in Wallace-Hadrill, *Patronage in Ancient Society,* 139.

17. Ibid., 142–46. Braund lays out how an imperial administrator of the Republic who prided himself on his own integrity articulates the point explicitly.

18. Ibid., 148–49.

19. Wallace-Hadrill, "Patronage in Roman Society," 75.

20. John Rich, "Patronage and Interstate Relations in the Roman Republic," in Wallace-Hadrill, *Patronage in Ancient Society,* 128–31.

toward the civic exertions of friends. And it is good that those who enjoy benefits from friendship with the powerful use it for the prosperity of the people. (*Moralia* 814C)

In effect, the local notable needed two sorts of connections in the patronage system near the top. He must cultivate the actual office holders, whether the Roman governor or the emperor (or imperial family) who had favors to dispense. And particularly failing the first, he needed close relations with influential provincials close to the governor or senators or others close to the emperor who could function as friends of friends on his behalf.[21] Plutarch (*Moralia* 814D) writes of ambitious provincial figures in Rome seeking appointment as governor or procurator "growing old haunting the doors of other men's houses" (presumably attending the morning *salutationes* at their patrons' houses). Prominent provincials proudly publicized their gratitude to their Roman patrons in public inscriptions in every major city of the empire. It was precisely through this system of personal patronage that Rome as a "predatory state" functioned in the provinces. "The traditional idea that Rome supported municipal aristocracies across the empire and in return benefitted from their allegiance had its parallel here at the personal level. Just as the emperor distributed his stock of *beneficia* to buy the loyalty of the Roman aristocracy, so the governor built up a loyal and useful clientele among the provincial aristocracy, both by favoring clients in local disputes and by supplying the patronage needed to enter the imperial aristocracy."[22]

The selection from Garnsey and Saller below sets out the general picture of the patronage system centered in the emperor, while the excerpts from Chow's study display the particular pattern and prominent individual members of the elite in Corinth as an illustration of how the system extended into provincial power relations. Some of the material included, especially in Chow's discussion, indicate further how the patronage system served to integrate the empire in its extension even into the basic social relations within subject cities. It seems likely, given the documented gradual consolidation of economic resources into the control of a few wealthy families,[23] that patron-client relations gradually extended downwards into the social structure of cities such as Corinth and Ephesus, although we have little direct evidence. More evident is that *collegia* such as those in Rome and Italian towns were replicated in provincial cities. And such *collegia* not only sought and attracted wealthy and powerful patrons, whose birthdays they then cele-

---

21. For a study of how the patronage system worked in the provinces based mainly on inscriptions from North Africa, see Saller, *Personal Patronage,* chap. 5.

22. Ibid., 166.

23. See especially Susan E. Alcock, *Graecia Capta: The Landscapes of Roman Greece* (Cambridge: Cambridge University Press, 1993).

brated, but further replicated the hierarchical social patterns modeled in standard patron-client relations, with differential rank and even graded portions and quality of food at banquets. Also documentable from studies of slavery and emancipation in the Roman empire, freedpersons remained under the domination of and, in effect, clients of their former masters,[24] constituting an ever renewing extension of patron-client relations at the lower levels of society. In a more general form, of course, the provincial/urban elite posed as the patrons of their cities in sponsoring festivals and public buildings, in return for which they received the honor and prestige of election to the most important public offices.

The article by Richard Gordon below, finally, along with certain points in the selections from Zanker and Price in Part I (above), indicates how the (political-economic-social) system of patronage was articulated parallel to and eventually in fusion with the political-religious system of sacrifices and emperor cult. As Price and Zanker explain, both among the more prominent families within particular cities and among the cities of a province, intense competition emerged to honor the emperor with festivals, temples, and monuments. And, as Gordon lays out, with the emperor as the model for the outlying cities as well as Rome, the provincial as well as Roman elite clamored for prestige in appointment to priesthoods, particularly as officiants at public sacrifices, the rituals that manifested the solidarity of the bodies politic in cities, provinces, and empire. The religious elite was the same as the political-economic elite. The political-economic elite dominated urban and provincial society precisely by their sponsorship and control of public sacrifices and the emperor cult! In Pauline and deutero-Pauline language, the "principalities and powers" may well have seemed like superhuman cosmic forces. But they were also very concrete, human products of political-religious institutions and patronage relations that had come to constitute the power relations of the Roman imperial order.

To paraphrase Gordon's conclusion, the fusion of the religious system of sacrifices and emperor cult with the social-economic system of patronage served to veil as it constituted the imperial network of domination and power relations. Euergetism, established throughout the empire as the socially responsible use of wealth, proclaimed the necessity of social inequality, grounded in the divine world of the gods. Local euergetism in the combination of the sacrificial system and the emperor cult transformed community into a hierarchical system controlled by a tiny elite, effectively blocking the emergence of any social forms through which the aspirations of the ordinary people might have been articulated.

---

24. Orlando Patterson, *Slavery and Social Death: A Comparative Study* (Cambridge: Harvard University Press, 1982), chaps. 8, 9, 10; Susan Treggiari, *Roman Freedmen during the Late Republic* (Oxford: Clarendon Press, 1969).

Patronal Power Relations

PETER GARNSEY AND RICHARD SALLER

The place of a Roman in society was a function of his position in the social hierarchy, membership of a family, and involvement in a web of personal relationships extending out from the household. Romans were obligated to and could expect support from their families, kinsmen and dependants both inside and outside the household, and friends, patrons, protégés and clients. In the eyes of Seneca, whose longest moral essay was devoted to the subject, the exchange of favors and services (*beneficia*) which underlay these relationships "most especially binds together human society" (*Ben.* 1.4.2).[1] Seneca's emphasis on reciprocal exchange is justifiable on several grounds: it eased tensions and conflicts provoked by divisions and inequalities; and it provided many of the services for which today we turn to impersonal governmental or private institutions.[2]

Honor, Status, and the Reciprocity Ethic

Despite the general comment about human society quoted above, Seneca's *On Benefits* is not a work of sociology or anthropology, but an ethical treatise about how men ought to conduct themselves in the giving and receiving of favors and services. His central premise is that a man in receipt of a favor owes his benefactor gratitude and a return in kind. Of the man who neglects this ethical precept, Seneca wrote: "Homicides, tyrants, traitors there always will be; but worse than all these is the crime of ingratitude" (*Ben.* 1.10.4). A century earlier Cicero expressed the same view: "To fail to repay [a favor] is not permitted to a good man" (*Off.* 1.48). The ideal benefactor was supposed to act without thought of what was due to him, but this was unrealistic. It was understood by both the author of the *Handbook on Canvassing*

---

1. R. Kaufman, "The Patron-Client Concept and Macro-Politics: Prospects and Problems," *Comparative Studies in Society and History* 16 (1974): 286–87, on the cohesive effects of patronage.

2. A. R. Hands, *Charities and Social Aid in Greece and Rome* (London: Thames & Hudson, 1968), 32ff.; J. Michel, *Gratuité en droit romain* (Brussels: Université Libre de Bruxelles, 1962), 562; P. Veyne, *Bread and Circus* (London: Penguin, 1976), 17.

attributed to Q. Cicero and by Tacitus in his *Dialogue on the Orators* that the orator and politician would succeed by distributing benefits that would subsequently be reciprocated. Consequently, Seneca could use the metaphor of treasure for benefits that could be recalled in time of the benefactor's need (*Ben.* 6.43.3), and the language of debt and repayment regularly appeared in discussions of exchange between friends or patrons and clients.[3]

Just as a loan created a relationship between creditor and debtor, so a favor or service gave rise to a social relationship between Romans. Because benefaction and requital were matters of honor, the dynamics of the exchange partially determined the relative social standing of the men involved. Very little pretense was made about egalitarianism in friendships. A man might have "superior friends," "equal friends," "lesser friends" and humble "clients," and the categorization of others into one or another of these depended on their resources (Pliny, *Ep.* 7.3.2, 2.6.2; Seneca, *Ep.* 94.14). Those who could exchange comparable benefits were friends of equal social standing, whilst most stood higher or lower in the hierarchy by virtue of their capacity to provide superior or inferior services in return. Some Romans tried to conceal the favors done for them precisely to avoid the implication of social inferiority arising from the fact that they had to turn to someone else for help. The proper conduct of a recipient was to acknowledge and advertise his benefactor's generosity and power.

The Emperor as Patron

Augustus sought to establish his legitimacy not only by restoring the social order, but also by demonstrating his own supremacy in it through the traditional modes of patronage and beneficence. Much of the *Res Gestae,* his own account of his reign, was an elaboration of the staggering scale of his benefits and services to the Roman people (15–18). In Pliny's *Panegyric* (e.g., 2, 21), the ideology of the good emperor was one not so much of an efficient administrator as of a paternal protector and benefactor.[4] Since subjects could not repay imperial benefactions in kind, the reciprocity ethic dictated that they make a return in the form of deference, respect and loyalty. Consequently, as Seneca pointed out, the emperor who played the role of great patron well had no need of guards because he was protected by his "benefits" (*Clem.* 1.13.5).

---

3. Richard P. Saller, *Personal Patronage under the Early Empire* (Cambridge: Cambridge University Press, 1982), 21 and, more generally, chap. 1 for the language of exchange.

4. J. Béranger, *Recherches sur l'aspect idéologique de Principat* (Basel: F. Reinhardt, 1953), 259.

The emperor distributed his benefits individually to those who had access to him and, more broadly, to favored groups, notably the Roman plebs and the army. Proximity to the emperor opened up to a privileged circle, including friends of high rank, relatives, and servile members of his household, a wide range of benefits from offices and honors to financial assistance to citizenship and the right of tapping the water supply. The norms guiding the distribution of these goods and services were openly particularistic, in contrast to the universalistic rules associated with modern bureaucracies. They were treated as personal favors granted to the loyal, not as governmental services and positions to be distributed on the basis of impersonal competition and universally available to all qualified citizens or subjects. In return, devoted service and gratitude were expected, one manifestation of which was the naming of the emperor in the will. T. Marius Urbinas caused a scandal by failing to acknowledge Augustus's generosity to himself in this way (Valerius Maximus 7.8.6). From more conscientious friends and clients Augustus received 1.4 billion sesterces in bequests over the last twenty years of his reign (Suetonius, *Aug.* 101).[5]

The emperor also took on the role of benefactor of the plebs, in the cause of order and the security of his regime. Augustus's interest in the tribunate, the prerogatives of which he gradually assumed between 36 and 23 B.C.E., is to be explained in these terms. The appeal of the tribune lay in its historic role as the champion of the common people. More important, Augustus saw to the material needs of the masses by tending to their supply of food, water and housing, by providing public shows and by occasional distributions of considerable sums of money to all male citizens of the city. The sums cited in *Res Gestae* were the equivalent of at least several months' rent for the poor (15). Whatever their feelings about these handouts, later emperors felt compelled to continue in this role. Though the plebs lost all semblance of constitutional power with the transfer of elections to the senate in 14 C.E., they still possessed means of making their discontent known and the emperor's position awkward, whether through protests at public spectacles or riots in the streets.[6]

Emperors did not and could not monopolize patronage. They did not attempt to be universal patrons to all their subjects, since universality would have undermined the incentive for personal gratitude on the part of the subjects.[7] Far from contemplating the suppression of the

5. Fergus Millar, *The Emperor in the Roman World* (London: Duckworth, 1977), 153ff. and chaps. 6, 8; Saller, *Personal Patronage,* chaps. 1–3.

6. Zvi Yavetz, *Plebs and Princeps* (London: Oxford University Press, 1969), chaps. 2, 5–6; H. Kloft, *Liberalitas Principis* (Cologne: Boehlau, 1970).

7. Pliny, *Pan.* 23.1, with Saller, *Personal Patronage,* 68, 73–74, and P. A. Brunt, *Times Literary Supplement,* 19 November 1982, p. 1276.

patronal networks of the aristocratic houses in Rome, emperors positively encouraged them by providing some of the resources that helped aristocratic patrons like Pliny to reward their clients. The letters of Pliny show Trajan granting offices and citizenship at Pliny's request, thus bolstering Pliny's status as an effective mediator. The successful emperors were the ones who kept the imperial aristocrats content by allowing them to maintain their exalted social status, and that implied a willingness to permit the great houses to display their patronal influence in the traditional way.

Patrons and Clients

Tacitus in writing of the "part of the populace...attached to the great houses" (*Hist.* 1.4.) attests the patronal ties linking aristocrats and members of the lower classes in the city of Rome. The *salutatio* and other Republican customs characteristic of patronage continued throughout the Principate, though with a different complexion. After 14 C.E. the relationship could no longer revolve around the electoral process. In the *Handbook on Canvassing* (11) it was stressed that a Republican candidate for high office had to make every effort to win followers of all ranks, even to the extent of lowering himself by mixing with and flattering members of the lower classes who would ordinarily be beneath his dignity. In the imperial era the impotence of the popular assemblies deprived the ordinary people of their political leverage and, with it, the incentive for aristocrats to treat their humble clients with a modicum of respect.[8] The patron's arrogance toward his clients was a common motif in imperial literature (e.g., Martial, *Epig.* 2.68).

Nevertheless, some *quid pro quo* was still possible and provided the basis for patronal exchange. Clients could contribute to their patron's social status by forming crowds at his door for the morning *salutatio* (Tacitus, *Ann.* 3.55) or by accompanying him on his rounds of public business during the day and applauding his speeches in court. In return, they could expect handouts of food or *sportulae* (small sums of money, customarily about six sesterces in Martial's day) and sometimes an invitation to dinner. Martial lists attendance on a patron as one way that an immigrant to the city of Rome might hope to support himself, though he warns that the *sportulae* were not enough to live on. They must have been just one of the possible supplements to the grain dole (*Epig.* 3.7 and 8.42). These epigrams were written after the inauguration of Vespasian, whose more austere habits were supposed to have set an example for a retreat from the lavish clientèles of the Julio-Claudian

---

8. G. E. M. de Ste. Croix, "Suffragium: From Vote to Patronage," *British Journal of Sociology* 5 (1954): 33, 40.

era (Tacitus, *Ann.* 3.55). Martial's verses and other evidence, however, leave no doubt that the *salutatio* and other patronal customs continued to characterize life in Rome throughout the Principate.[9]

Patron-client bonds extended out from Rome to the provinces. Like the emperor, governors and other officials representing his power had a patronal role. In a speech before a governor of Africa Proconsularis, Apuleius claimed that provincials esteemed governors for the benefits they conferred (*Flor.* 9). This is corroborated by a number of north African inscriptions dedicated by provincials to governors as their "patrons." In their official capacities governors could help provincials secure citizenship, offices and honors from Rome, and they could also make administrative and legal decisions in their favor. The public dedications to governor "patrons" from lawyers (*advocati*) may strike the modern reader as an ominous sign of corruption, but in fact highlight the differences between ancient and modern ideologies of administration (e.g., *CIL* VIII.2734,2743,2393).[10] Governors also received from grateful provincials gifts (or, differently interpreted, bribes) and support in case of a prosecution for maladministration after the governor's term of office. For his part in discouraging a prosecution against a senatorial ex-governor of Gaul, T. Sennius Sollemnis received from the former governor a tribunate on his staff in Britain (salary paid in gold), several luxury garments, a sealskin and jewelry (*CIL* XIII.3162).[11] The advertisement of all these details on a public monument demonstrates that the exercise of patronage in government was not considered dishonorable or corrupt.

The Plebs: Patronage, Self-Help, and Coercion

Patrons did not enter into relationships with their social inferiors indiscriminately. In his division of the ordinary people of the city of Rome into the good and the bad (*Hist.* 1.4), Tacitus characterizes the former by their attachment to the great houses — an implicit commitment to the social order as it was.[12] The latter were not caught up in patronal relationships with the rich, because they were thought to have nothing to contribute to a reciprocal exchange relationship or because they wished to avoid the humiliation of dependence.

Upper-class writers show little interest in vertical links between the high and the low, but have even less to say about horizontal bonds

---

9. L. Friedlaender, *Roman Life and Manners under the Early Empire*, 7th ed. (London: Routledge, 1908–13), I, 195ff.; Saller, *Personal Patronage*, 1270–79.

10. De Ste. Croix, "Suffragium," 43–44; Saller, *Personal Patronage*, 151–52 and Table III.

11. H.-G. Pflaum, *Le Marbre de Thorigny* (Paris: Champion, 1948).

12. A parallel in Livy 9.46.13.

between the latter. A plethora of informal relationships between individual neighbors and work associates have gone largely unrecorded. However, one institutional manifestation of these relationships, the *collegium,* is well known from numerous inscriptions and some largely hostile references in the literary sources.[13]

Collegia, made up of a few score or few hundred urban residents, were essentially mutual aid societies formed to meet basic needs of their members. Organized around cults to patron deities or by occupation, these associations provided for decent burial of the dead as well as periodic festive dinners for the living. Unable to rely on family, many Romans took the precaution of arranging burial before their death by joining a *collegium* and paying small monthly dues. In a long inscription detailing the rules of a *collegium* in the small Italian town of Lanuvium, the membership fee was specified as 100 sesterces, with dues of slightly more than one sesterce per month, which guaranteed a funeral attended by club members.[14] These fees were meant for modestly prosperous men, as were the club dinners with a menu of good wine, two *asses* worth of bread and four sardines per member. Lower down in the social hierarchy was another stratum, the impoverished who could not afford club membership and whose bodies, consequently, were dumped unceremoniously into mass graves.

Though these *collegia* were associations of humble men, they still exhibit some of the hierarchical features so characteristic of Roman society. Like the larger community, *collegia* were often patronized by the wealthy.[15] In the case of the association in Lanuvium, Caesennius Rufus provided an endowment of 15,000 sesterces to finance club dinners honoring the birthdays of himself and his family. Further, the club rules show a typically Roman appreciation for rank and the authority of office: the chief magistrate of the club, the *quinquennalis* (the title taken from municipal office), received double portions at the banquets and was protected from "insolent language" by a special fine of twenty sesterces.

Despite the conservative attitudes implied by such rules, the authorities were always suspicious of these associations and fearful lest they become sources of unrest. In the late Republic, demagogic tribunes like P. Clodius had made use of the *collegia* in their campaigns to undermine

---

13. J. P. Waltzing, *Etude historique sur le corporations professionelles chez les Romains* (Louvain: C. Peeters, 1895–1900); F. M. de Robertis, *Il fenomeno associativo nel mondo romano* (Naples: Liberia scientifica editrice, 1955); F. Ausbuettel, *Untersuchungen zu Vereinen in Westen des römisches Reiches* (Kallmunz: M. Lassleben, 1982); Keith Hopkins, *Death and Renewal* (Cambridge: Cambridge University Press, 1983), 211–17.

14. *CIL* XIV.2112 = *ILS* 7212, translated in N. Lewis and M. Reinhold, *Roman Civilization* (New York: Harper & Row, 1955), 273–75.

15. G. Clemente,"Il patronato nei collegia dell'Impero Romano," *SCO* 21 (1972): 22.

the authority of the Roman magistrates by violence. Under the Principate, those *collegia* that had achieved respectability because of their long
histories and the special public services they were held to perform (apparently in the area of fire fighting, building construction and religious
ceremonial) were allowed a continuous and even a privileged existence.[16]
Religious and burial clubs were also authorized. But the emperors remained suspicious of plebeian organizations as seedbeds of undercover
political activity. Hence, an imperial rule prohibited meetings of these
associations more often than once a month. Pliny, Trajan's special en-
voy in Bithynia/Pontus, a province with a bad reputation for disorder,
was instructed to issue a decree prohibiting associations. Christian gatherings were assumed to fall under the general prohibition (Pliny, *Ep.*
10.96.7), and also groups with an apparently utilitarian function. Trajan
rejected a request from the people of Nicomedia for a fire brigade. Pliny,
who had viewed the proposal sympathetically, was reminded by the emperor that "this province and especially these cities have been troubled
by cliques of this type. Whatever name we may give for whatever reason to those who come together for a common purpose, political clubs
emerge quickly from them" (Pliny, *Ep.* 10.34).

Imperial regulation of urban gatherings and distribution of benefits
were not enough to prevent violence in the cities. Republican magistrates had had no police forces to suppress urban unrest, and military
units were by tradition forbidden from crossing the "sacred boundary"
(*pomerium*) around the city. In the midst of recurring urban violence the
senate in 52 B.C.E. dispensed with tradition and summoned Pompey to
reestablish order in the city with troops.[17] Augustus then organized the
first standing forces in Rome: the praetorian guard, the urban cohorts
and the night watch (*vigiles*). The initial impetus for these organizations
was partially political in the beginning — to support Augustus against
challenges — but they did come to perform various policing functions
in the city. Despite their presence, pervasive street crime aroused constant fear among urban residents (Pliny, *HN* 19.59). The military units
were more effective in controlling the crowds at public spectacles. When
a theater crowd in 32 C.E. abused Tiberius for allowing grain prices
to rise, the emperor resorted to the traditional Republican response of
asking the senate and the magistrates to use their authority to suppress
the verbal insolence (Tacitus, *Ann.* 6.15). To prevent vocal protest from
developing into a riot, the presence of a praetorian cohort became a
regular feature of public spectacles. In 55 C.E., Nero experimented by
removing the guard at the games, "in order that there might be a greater
show of freedom, that the soldiery too might be less demoralized when

---

16. *AE* 1966, 277.
17. W. Nippel, "Policing Rome," *JRS* 74 (1984): 20–29.

no longer in contact with the licence of the theater, and that it might be proved whether the populace, in the absence of a guard, would maintain their self-control" (Tacitus, *Ann.* 13.24–5). The soldiers were brought back the following year, but it is noteworthy that a consideration in Nero's initial decision was freedom of expression.

Away from Rome, the authorities had both less to offer urban populations in the manner of subsistence and entertainment, and less institutional apparatus for repressing disorder or other activities classified as undesirable. Army detachments were sometimes available for policing purposes, especially in provincial or regional centers. Thus soldiers are much in evidence in accounts of actions taken by authorities against Christians. To a large extent, however, communities were left to police themselves. Many Greek cities of the East had magistrates, irenarchs, charged with the maintenance of order, but they had only small forces at their disposal and no power to punish. In addition, sources as diverse as the New Testament (Acts 18:12–17) and Apuleius's *Golden Ass* (*Met.* 10.28) testify to initiatives taken by ordinary local men to capture criminals and troublemakers and bring them before Roman officials for imprisonment and punishment. The local or imperial authorities (away from military zones) established full control only in and around the cities. In the countryside, especially in rough terrains, banditry was a constant problem.[18]

---

18. Ramsay MacMullen, *Enemies of the Roman Order* (Cambridge: Harvard University Press, 1966), app. B; B. D. Shaw, "Bandits in the Roman Empire," *Past and Present* 105 (1984): 3–52.

Patronage in Roman Corinth

JOHN K. CHOW

On a monument made in the middle of the first century c.e. in Corinth, the following words were inscribed to honor Julius Spartiaticus, a man of influence, an important patron to the tribe of Calpurnia and a contemporary of Paul:

> Gaius Julius, Son of Laco,
> Grandson of Eurycles, [of the tribe] Fabia, Spartiaticus,
> Procurator of Caesar and Augusta
> Agrippina, Tribune of the Soldiers, Awarded a Public Horse
> By the Deified Claudius, Flamen
> Of the Deified Julius, Pontifex, Duovir Quinquennalis twice,
> Agonothete of the Isthmian and Caesar-
> Augustan Games, High-Priest of the House of Augustus
> In Perpetuity, First of the Achaeans.
> Because of his Virtue and Eager
> And all-encompassing Munificence toward the Divine House
> And toward our Colony, the Tribesmen
> Of the Tribe Calpurnia
> [Dedicated this] to their Patron.[1]

From the relationships recorded in the above inscription, a rough picture of how social relationships were organized in Roman Corinth is displayed before our eyes. While Spartiaticus was a patron to one of the tribes in Corinth, he himself was under the Roman emperor, an even more powerful man. We see here a chain of patron-client ties.

According to one political scientist, patron-client ties tend "to arise within a state structure in which authority is dispersed and state activity limited in scope, and in which considerable separation exists between

---

1. A. B. West, *Latin Inscriptions 1896–1926. Corinth: Results,* VIII.2 (Cambridge, Mass.: Harvard University Press, 1931), no. 68. The translation is adapted from D. C. Braund, *Augustus to Nero: A Sourcebook on Roman History, 31 B.C.–A.D. 68* (London: Croom & Helm, 1985), no. 469, and R. K. Sherk, *The Roman Empire: Augustus to Hadrian* (Cambridge: Cambridge University Press, 1988), no. 164B.

the levels of village, city and state."[2] One ancient historian actually suggests that patronage was the secret to the integration of the Roman Empire.[3] The institution of patronage has also helped to explain how the Roman rulers were able to rule such an enormous empire with the minimal number of officials.[4] The networks of relationships in Corinth can roughly be seen as a hierarchy made up of the emperor, Roman officials, local notables and the populace. A kind of patronal hierarchy may be seen in the structure of relationships in different institutions, such as the association and the household.

Patronage and Society

As defined before, a patron-client tie is basically an asymmetrical exchange relationship. The parties on both ends of such a tie are unequal in the control of resources, and so differ in terms of power and status. They are bound together mainly because their tie can serve their mutual interests through the exchange of resources.

The Emperor

If the Roman emperor was comparable to the patron of the entire Empire, in some ways, he was the patron of Corinth too. That he was able to bring peace and order to a vast Empire naturally would inspire reverence and awe. Not surprisingly, in some parts of the Empire, especially in the Greek east, such reverence for the Roman rulers was expressed by showering them and members of the imperial family with honorific titles like "patron," "benefactor," "saviour" and "son of a god," which suggest a greatly superior status.[5] In Corinth, some of these titles, even the

---

2. Alex Weingrod, "Patrons, Patronage, and Political Parties," in S. W. Schmidt et al., eds., *Friends, Followers, Factions: A Reader in Political Clientelism* (Berkeley: University of California Press, 1977), 325.

3. G. E. M. de Ste. Croix writes, "Patronage, indeed, must be seen as an institution the Roman world simply could not do without" (*The Class Struggle in the Ancient Greek World* [London: Duckworth, 1981], 364).

4. Richard Saller, *Personal Patronage under the Early Empire* (Cambridge: Cambridge University Press, 1982), 205–6.

5. Just to give some examples:

(a) "Patron": Marcus Agrippa (Ilium [Braund, *Augustus to Nero*, no. 67]); Lucius Caesar, son of Augustus (Pisa [V. Ehrenberg and A. H. M. Jones, *Documents Illustrating the Reigns of Augustus and Tiberius,* 2d ed. (Oxford: Clarendon Press, 1955), no. 68 = Braund, *Augustus to Nero*, no. 62]);

(b) "Benefactor": Marcus Agrippa (Myra [Ehrenberg and Jones, *Documents,* no. 72 = Braund, *Augustus to Nero*, no. 66]); Augustus (Myra [Ehrenberg and Jones, *Documents,* no. 72 = Braund, *Augustus to Nero*, no. 66]); Tiberius (Myra [Ehrenberg and Jones, *Documents,* no. 88 = Braund, *Augustus to Nero*, no. 107]);

(c) "Saviour": Marcus Agrippa (Myra [Ehrenberg and Jones, *Documents,* no. 72 = Braund, *Augustus to Nero*, no. 66]); Augustus (Asia [Ehrenberg and Jones, *Documents,*

title "patron,"[6] were also found in some of the inscriptions dedicated to the emperors or members of the imperial house.[7]

To get a better picture of the Roman emperor as a supreme patron, the ultimate center of power granting favors and expecting loyalty and honor in return, I suggest the need to look further into the life situation in the colony and the relationships between the emperors and the local leaders rather than to study the occurrences of the word "patron" in the inscriptions. The image of the Roman emperor as one who dominated the life of the colony could hardly be overlooked by the people in Corinth. The name of the colony, *Colonia Laus Julia Corinthiensis*, stood as a constant reminder of the grace of Julius Caesar who helped to refound the colony. The names of the voting tribes or local political divisions would also remind people of the imperial presence in Corinth. Some of these names are Agrippia, Atia, Aurelia, Calpurnia, Claudia, Domitia, Hostilia, Livia, Maneia, Vatinia and Vinicia.[8] It is clear that these tribes were named after members of the imperial families or close friends and associates of Augustus.[9] When Paul walked down the streets of Corinth, other symbols which conveyed the presence and power of the Roman emperor could also be seen. Coins which circulated in the market

no. 98 = Braund, *Augustus to Nero*, no. 122]; Gytheum [Ehrenberg and Jones, *Documents*, no. 102a = Braund, *Augustus to Nero*, no. 127]); Tiberius (Myra [Ehrenberg and Jones, *Documents*, no. 88 = Braund, *Augustus to Nero*, no. 107]);

(d) "Son of a god" or "god": Augustus (Gytheum [Ehrenberg and Jones, *Documents*, no. 102 = Braund, *Augustus to Nero*, no. 127]); Tiberius (Cyprus [Ehrenberg and Jones, *Documents*, no. 134 = Braund, *Augustus to Nero*, no. 164]); Caligula (Didyma [Braund, *Augustus to Nero*, no. 181]); Claudius (Volubilis [Braund, *Augustus to Nero*, no. 680a]).

6. Between 18 and 12 B.C.E., Marcus Agrippa was honored as a patron of the tribe Vinicia (West, *Latin Inscriptions*, no. 16 = Ehrenberg and Jones, *Documents*, no. 73 = Braund, *Augustus to Nero*, no. 69). But it is actually possible that Agrippa was a patron of the colony (West, *Latin Inscriptions*, 15).

7. The title *theou huios* was used to designate Augustus (B. D. Meritt, *Greek Inscriptions, 1896–1927. Corinth: Results*, VIII.1 [Cambridge, Mass.: Harvard University Press, 1931], no. 19). The title *divus* was also given in Julius Caesar (J. H. Kent, *The Inscriptions, 1926–1950. Corinth: Results*, VIII. 3 [Princeton: American School of Classical Studies at Athens, 1966], no. 50) and Augustus (Kent, *Inscriptions*, no. 52).

8. Agrippia (West, *Latin Inscriptions*, no. 110); Atia (West, *Latin Inscriptions*, no. 86); Aurelia (West, *Latin Inscriptions*, no. 97); Calpurnia (West, *Latin Inscriptions*, no. 68); Hostilia (West, *Latin Inscriptions*, no. 109); Maneia (West, *Latin Inscriptions*, no. 56); Vinicia (West, *Latin Inscriptions*, no. 16); Domitia (Kent, *Inscriptions*, no. 249); Livia (Kent, *Inscriptions*, no. 259); Vatinia (Kent, *Inscriptions*, no. 222). On the identification of the tribe of Claudia, see J. Wiseman, "The Gymnasium Area at Corinth," *Hesp* 41 (1972): 37.

9. Aurelia and Calpurnia were names of the mother and the wife of Julius Caesar. Atia and Livia were names of the mother and the wife of Augustus. The tribe Vatinia could be named after P. Vatinius, legate and friend of Caesar. The tribe of Agrippia was named in honor of Marcus Agrippa. M. Vinicius, consul in 19 B.C.E., a personal friend of Augustus, was probably remembered by the tribe of Vinicia. It is to be expected that the other three tribes were also named for close friends and associates of Augustus. Later, in either the reign of Tiberius and Claudius, the tribe of Claudia was added. See West, *Latin Inscriptions*, no. 110 and commentary; Kent, *Inscriptions*, nos. 23 and 249 and commentary; J. Wiseman, "Corinth and Rome I," *ANRW* 2.7.1 (1979): 497–98.

bore the images of the emperors.[10] Imperial images of Augustus and his sons were erected.[11] A Roman temple, or Temple E, which was built probably in the reign of Claudius[12] for the cult of the imperial family, stood at the west end of the forum, witnessing to the transcending status of the Roman rulers.[13] In addition, there were, of course, many other monuments and inscriptions which were made to honor the emperors.[14]

For different reasons, whether to honor the benevolent rule of the imperial house or otherwise, many celebrations organized in Corinth were related to the Roman emperors. Some of them were occasional while others were recurrent. One of the occasional events which probably called for celebrations, as it did elsewhere,[15] was the coronation of the new emperor.[16] Other occasional events which concerned the Roman emperors were celebrated as well. A cult was founded to celebrate the safety of the emperor, possibly at the time when Sejanus's plot against Tiberius was discovered.[17] Another was established to celebrate Claudius's victories in Britain.[18]

---

10. For a discussion on coins found in Corinth, see K. N. Edwards, *The Coins, 1896–1929. Corinth: Results,* VI (Cambridge, Mass.: Harvard University Press, 1933). Coins which bear the images of the Roman emperors and some members of the imperial family are as follows: Augustus, nos. 28, 30, 32, 34, 35; Agrippa, no. 36; Tiberius, nos. 40, 43; Livia, nos. 41, 42; Caligula, nos. 45, 46, 47; Claudius, nos. 50, 51; Nero, nos. 54, 55, 56, 57, 59, 61, 62, 63, 64.

11. F. P. Johnson, "The Imperial Portraits at Corinth," *AJA* 30 (1926): 158–76; idem, *Sculpture, 1896–1923. Corinth: Results,* IX.1 (Cambridge, Mass.: Harvard University Press, 1931), 70–78; E. H. Swift, "A Group of Roman Imperial Portraits at Corinth," *AJA* 25 (1921): 142–59, 248–65, 337–63; B. S. Ridgway, "Sculpture from Corinth," *Hesp* 50 (1981): 429–35.

12. Wiseman, "Corinth and Rome I," 519. Cf. S. E. Freeman, *Architecture. Corinth: Results,* I.2, ed. R. Stillwell, R. L. Scranton and S. E. Freeman (Cambridge, Mass.: Harvard University Press, 1941), 168–79. D. W. J. Gill has suggested that the temple might have been built prior to 38/39 C.E. ("Roman Corinth: A Pluralistic Society?" [1989 Tyndale New Testament/Biblical Archaeology Study Groups Paper], 10).

13. Most scholars regard Temple E as the Temple of Octavia, the sister of Augustus (Wiseman, "Corinth and Rome I," 522; C. K. Williams's view quoted in V. P. Furnish, *II Corinthians* [Garden City, N.Y.: Doubleday, 1984], 19; Gill, "Roman Corinth," 10–11). But Freeman prefers to see the temple as the Temple of Jupiter Capitolinus ("Temple E," *Architecture,* I.2, 179–236).

14. From Julius Caesar to Nero, all had inscriptions dedicated to them in Corinth: Julius Caesar (Kent, *Inscriptions,* no. 50); Augustus (Kent, *Inscriptions,* nos. 51, 52, 53, 69); Tiberius (Kent, *Inscriptions,* no. 72); Claudius (Kent, *Inscriptions,* nos. 74, 75, 77, 79); Nero (Kent, *Inscriptions,* nos. 80, 81).

15. When Claudius became emperor in 41 C.E., the Alexandrians sent envoys to express their desire to honor him (Braund, *Augustus to Nero,* no. 571).

16. In the reign of Caligula, envoys were sent from Achaea in 37 C.E. to express the loyalty of the League of Achaeans to the new emperor with a proposal to honor him in different parts of Achaea. The program included the offering of sacrifices for the safety of the emperor, the holding of festivals and the setting up of his statues in various places, including Isthmia (Braund, *Augustus to Nero,* no. 564).

17. West, *Latin Inscriptions,* no. 110 = Ehrenberg and Jones, *Documents,* no. 113 = Braund, *Augustus to Nero,* no. 140.

18. See West, *Latin Inscriptions,* nos. 86–90. Cf. also no. 11.

Apart from these occasional events, there were the recurrent festivals. As in other parts of the Roman world, the birthdays of the Roman rulers were often celebrated,[19] and it is highly likely that such dates were also celebrated in Corinth. Above all, the most important celebration which emphasized the power and glory of the Roman rulers was probably the holding of the imperial games at the same time as the famous biennial Isthmian games.[20] By the time Paul visited Corinth, two new programs were already added alongside the Isthmian games to sing praises to the imperial house. They were the Caesarea and the "imperial contests." The Caesarea was the first program added in honor of Augustus[21] c. 30 B.C.E. after the battle of Actium.[22] Its first three contests included an encomium of Augustus, an encomium of Tiberius, and a poem in honor of Livia.[23] A second series of contests or the "imperial contests" was added later, possibly in the reign of Tiberius,[24] to honor the reigning emperor.[25]

The story of the family of C. Julius Eurycles in Spartan Greece may be cited as an exemplary case to highlight the power of the emperor as the supreme patron in the Greek east and the instrumental nature of the relationship between the emperor and the local rulers and notables. C. Julius Eurycles,[26] the famous Spartan dynast, probably did not come from a respected family. His father was alleged to be a pirate.[27] But be-

---

19. In Forum Clodii, Etruria, sacrifices were offered on the birthday of the emperor (Ehrenberg and Jones, *Documents*, no. 101 = Braund, *Augustus to Nero*, no. 126). In 9 B.C.E., as an attempt to honor Augustus, it was proposed that the calendar in Asia should be changed so that time began with his birthday, that is, 23 September (Ehrenberg and Jones, *Documents*, no. 98 = Braund, *Augustus to Nero*, no. 112). See also W. F. Snyder, "Public Anniversaries in the Roman Empire," *YCS* 7 (1940): 226–35.

20. For a general discussion of the imperial cult in the early empire, see especially S. R. F. Price, *Rituals and Power: The Roman Imperial Cult in Asia Minor* (Cambridge: Cambridge University Press, 1984). For references to the imperial cult in Corinth, see West, *Latin Inscriptions*, nos. 14–16, 81; Kent, *Inscriptions*, nos. 152, 153, 156, 209, 210, 213, 218, 224, 272. Cf. also Kent, *Inscriptions*, pp. 28–30.

21. See West, *Latin Inscriptions*, no. 81 and commentary.

22. The date of the introduction of the Caesarea was not recorded. But it is possible that the Caesarea was first established c. 30 B.C.E., shortly after the battle of Actium (West, *Latin Inscriptions*, 65; Kent, *Inscriptions*, 28).

23. Meritt, *Greek Inscriptions*, no. 19; Kent, *Inscriptions*, 29, no. 153 and commentary.

24. Kent, *Inscriptions*, 28.

25. In honor of Tiberius, the contests were called the *Tiberea Caesarea Sebastea* (Kent, *Inscriptions*, nos. 153, 156). In the time of Claudius, the name of the contests was changed to *Isthmia et Caesarea et Tiberea Claudiea Sebastea* (West, *Latin Inscriptions*, no. 82). By the time of Nero, the title became *Neronea Caesarea et Isthmia et Caesarea* (West, *Latin Inscriptions*, nos. 86–90). See Kent's discussion, *Inscriptions*, 28–29.

26. For detailed discussions of the Euryclids, see G. Bowersock, "Eurycles of Sparta," *JRS* 51 (1961): 112–18; idem, *Augustus and the Greek World* (Oxford: Clarendon, 1965), 59–60; P. Cartledge and A. Spawforth, *Hellenistic and Roman Sparta: A Tale of Two Cities* (London: Routledge, 1989), 97–104.

27. Plutarch, *Antony* 67. The island of Cythera, which was given to Sparta, was perhaps the base which his father once used. See Polybius, 4.6.

cause he helped to bring victory to Octavian at Actium, he was able to win the *philia* of Augustus. Consequently he was granted Roman citizenship and the control of Sparta c. 30 B.C.E.[28] In return for such benefactions he founded the imperial cult in Sparta as an expression of his loyalty to the imperial house.[29]

After the death of Eurycles, his descendants continued to enjoy power and prestige in Greece in the early Empire. In an inscription from Gytheum (or Gytheion),[30] dated c. 15 C.E., the proposal to honor the imperial house was followed by another proposal to stage thymelic performances in honor of the deceased Eurycles, the benefactor, and his son Laco, the guardian, for their benefactions. This suggests that, by the end of the Principate of Augustus and the early reign of Tiberius, Laco, the son, was in a position comparable to that of his father, a good friend of Augustus.

By the time of Claudius, the third generation of the Euryclids was able to befriend the Roman ruler. The most representative example was a grandson of Eurycles, namely Spartiaticus.[31] As a procurator of Caesar and Augusta Agrippina, Spartiaticus was by now part of the imperial system.[32] He was also awarded the equestrian rank. The reason why Spartiaticus was able to enjoy power and prestige is not clear. It is quite likely that the past ties between his family and the imperial house formed an important basis for his rise to power. Perhaps not by mere accident, like other members of his family, he also held many priestly posts besides his political offices. He was *flamen* of the deified Julius, *pontifex,* and high priest of the House of Augustus in perpetuity. Such explicit and unequivocal expressions of loyalty to the imperial house might also have helped him a great deal. Of course, his enormous wealth might have been another reason for his winning the favor of the ruler in Rome.[33]

In the rise and the fall of the Euryclids, one of the decisive factors, if not the most decisive factor, in determining their fate seems to be their relationships with the Roman emperors. It serves to highlight the Roman

---

28. Bowersock, "Eurycles," 112; Cartledge and Spawforth, *Sparta,* 98.

29. Cartledge and Spawforth, *Sparta,* 99.

30. Ehrenberg and Jones, *Documents,* no. 102a = Braund, *Augustus to Nero,* no. 127.

31. An inscription which was made to honor him in Corinth is listed at the beginning of this chapter. Cf. also Meritt, *Greek Inscriptions,* no. 70.

32. The recruitment of people like Spartiaticus into the imperial system has been interpreted by Syme as a subtle move by Claudius to establish trustworthy clients without arousing unnecessary opposition (*The Roman Revolution* [Oxford: Oxford University Press, 1939], 506).

33. According to Dio Cassius, 59.9, in the reign of Caligula people from good family and with wealth were chosen to fill the equestrian rank. This may be another factor, among others, contributing to the rise of Spartiaticus (cf. West, *Latin Inscriptions,* 52). That Spartiaticus was a man of great wealth is suggested by his being able to serve as the *agonothete* of the Isthmian and Caesarean games which required great outlay of capital (Kent, *Inscriptions,* 30; Wiseman, "Corinth and Rome I," 500).

emperor as the supreme, though somewhat capricious, patron in those days. Hence it might be essential to maintain a good relationship with him if one wanted to climb high on the power ladder and to stay there. Against such a background one can perhaps better understand why the imperial cult was strongly promoted in first-century Corinth.

Roman Officials

The role of a Roman official within the hierarchical structure of the Roman Empire has to be defined in context.[34] We can again take Spartiaticus as an example. In relation to Claudius he would look not unlike a friend or a client. As a procurator of Caesar in his province, however, he would assume the role of a broker or mediator, representing the interests of his superior in a locality. But at a local level, because he had access to the emperor, was apportioned a certain amount of power, and possessed enormous wealth, he probably would have become an authority to be honored and respected. No wonder he was named as the patron of a tribe in Corinth. To illustrate further the different roles of a Roman official in a province, that is, as a middleman between the emperor and the local people, I will look at P. Memmius Regulus, an important governor in Achaea in the late thirties and the early forties.[35]

Since Achaea was part of an imperial province from 15 to 44 c.e., its governor was appointed by the emperor to represent him in the province.[36] His power and term of office were naturally defined by the emperor. In that case, it is reasonable to expect that the emperor most probably would appoint only those who were loyal to him. It is also likely that the appointee would also work to please the emperor as well as to secure his present position and a better prospect in the future.[37]

---

34. In a simplified way, one may suggest that the hierarchical structure of the early Empire was made up of the emperor (the supreme patron), officials of the government or local leaders (mediators), and the community (clients). Such a structure can be seen in some of the inscriptions which recorded events in the reign of Claudius. Two examples may be given. (a) In 44 c.e., M. Valerius Severus, a local magistrate who once helped Claudius to suppress a rebellion, successfully secured Roman citizenship, exemption from imperial taxes for 10 years and other rights for the city of Volubilis in Mauretania from the emperor (Braund, *Augustus to Nero,* no. 680b). (b) In 48–49 c.e., through the work of Marcus Valerius Iunianus, member of Claudius's household, the Dionysiac performers were able to get their rights confirmed by Claudius (Braund, *Augustus to Nero,* no. 580b).

35. West, *Latin Inscriptions,* no. 53.

36. The governor of an imperial province was called a legate and was usually chosen from the rank of ex-praetor and ex-consul (F. Millar, *The Roman Empire and Its Neighbours,* 2d ed. [London: Duckworth, 1981], 54–55; Peter Garnsey and Richard Saller, *The Roman Empire: Economy, Society, and Culture* (Berkeley: University of California Press, 1987), 22). For a discussion of the provincial officials in Corinth, see A. Bagdikian, "Civic Officials of Roman Corinth," M.A. thesis, University of Vermont, 1953, 4–6.

37. Garnsey and Saller, *Roman Empire,* 34–36. Note F. Millar's warning against drawing too clear a line between the imperial provinces and the senatorial provinces ("The Emperor, the Senate and the Provinces," *JRS* 56 [1966]: 156–66).

P. Memmius Regulus was not of particularly distinguished ancestry.[38] He began his career in the reign of Tiberius as *quaestor*. He then became praetor. In the autumn of 31 C.E. he was made consul.[39] Later he was appointed as the governor of Achaea, Moesia and Macedonia. He held the post from 35 to 44 C.E., that is, for eight years and under three emperors, Tiberius, Gaius and Claudius.[40] In 47 C.E., he was proconsul of Asia.[41] He died in the reign of Nero in 61 C.E. Memmius was able to earn favor and trust[42] from most of his superiors, that is, the emperors. In this respect, Memmius Regulus was not unlike Eurycles, the Spartan dynast. But he differed from the latter at one crucial point, that is, Memmius Regulus was able to rise steadily to power and to remain in power until he died. How did he manage to do it despite his undistinguished background?

Under Tiberius[43] he showed himself to be a loyal friend of the emperor by helping him to strike down the mighty opponent Sejanus. When Caligula came to power, he proposed to marry Regulus's rich and perhaps beautiful wife, Lollia Paulina. Regulus complied with the demand of the emperor, and even personally escorted her to Rome.[44] Equally noteworthy was the development of the imperial cult in Achaea under his governorship. Probably with his encouragement, a larger *koinon* was formed to promote the cult. Games were held in honor of the imperial house and envoys were sent to see Caligula with a proposal to express the loyalty of Achaea to Rome.[45] It is thus not surprising that he held priestly titles like *sodalis Augustalis*,[46] Arval brother[47] and one of the

---

38. Tacitus, *Ann.* 14.47.

39. Ehrenberg and Jones, *Documents*, no. 217 = Braund, *Augustus to Nero*, no. 388.

40. Dio Cassius 58.25. See also West, *Latin Inscriptions*, 29–31.

41. Ehrenberg and Jones, *Documents*, no. 218 = Braund, *Augustus to Nero*, no. 389; L.R. Dean, "Latin Inscriptions from Corinth, III," *AJA* 26 (1922): 456.

42. Tacitus, *Ann.* 14.47.

43. Tacitus, *Ann.* 5.11; 6.4. See also M. P. Charlesworth, "Tiberius," in *Cambridge Ancient History*, X, 637–38; B. Levick, *Tiberius the Politician* (London: Thames & Hudson, 1976), 177–78.

44. Dio Cassius 59.12. Cf. Suetonius, *Gaius* 25. See also J. H. Oliver, "Lollia Paulina, Memmius Regulus and Caligula," *Hesp* 35 (1966): 150–53.

45. Braund, *Augustus to Nero*, no. 564. See also West, *Latin Inscriptions*, 30–31.

46. A *sodalis Augustalis* or a "Fellow of the priesthood of (the deified) Augustus" was a member of a chosen group of eminent Romans whose function was to superintend and promote the imperial cult. The *sodales Augustales* were first founded by Tiberius after the death of Augustus. Claudius instituted the *sodales augustales Claudiales* and later emperors organized similar *sodales*. For further discussion, see L. R. Taylor, *Divinity of the Roman Emperor* (Middletown: American Philological Association, 1931), 230; Kent, *Inscriptions*, 84; Sherk, *Roman Empire*, 266.

47. The *fratres Arvales* was a priestly college in Rome, responsible for offering worship for the well-being of the imperial house. The college was made up of 12 members. The reigning emperor was always a member. The others were chosen from the most distinguished senatorial families by cooption (*OCD*, 447). Memmius Regulus held this title

seven for feast.[48] Interestingly enough, his later years in Rome were also spent actively offering sacrifices for the emperor with other Arvales brothers.[49] Such preparedness to demonstrate his loyalty to the imperial house and to serve the emperors at whatever cost may to a large extent account for his steady rise to power without being deposed later on.

The position of P. Memmius Regulus as a node in the patronage structure of the early Empire would not be fully understood if we looked only at his relationship with the Roman emperors without at the same time considering his relationship with the people he governed, especially those in Achaea. From the very many inscriptions made in honor of P. Memmius Regulus in Corinth[50] and other places in the Greek east,[51] it looks probable that Regulus was well-supported and well-connected in the region.[52] Though he was named as a patron in Ruscino, Narbonensis,[53] such a title is not found on the inscription which honored him in Corinth. Nonetheless, his image as a patron in the region is still visible in some of the benefactions he bestowed. In the reign of Caligula [he] made the risky attempt to delay the delivery of the statue of Zeus at Olympia to Rome.[54] Whether he might have dispatched other kinds of benefactions, such as helping to promote provincials[55] or making legal decisions in favor of his clients,[56] is not clear. Apparently he had helped quite a number of people in Corinth to secure Roman citizenship. P. Memmius

---

since at least 38 C.E. (West, *Latin Inscriptions*, 29; R. Syme, *Some Arval Brethren* [Oxford: Clarendon Press, 1980], 67).

48. The *septemviri epulones* were priests who organized the banquet of Jupiter and other banquets at various festivals. Many of them were formerly the partisans of the emperors (Sherk, *Roman Empire*, 266).

49. A. H. Smallwood, *Documents Illustrating the Principates of Gaius, Claudius, and Nero* (Cambridge: Cambridge University Press, 1967), nos. 16–22. Cf. N. Lewis and M. Reinhold, *Roman Civilization*, 2 vols. (New York: Harper & Row, 1951, 1966), II, 554–55.

50. West, *Latin Inscriptions*, no. 53.

51. E.g., Delphi (Smallwood, *Documents*, no. 225 = Braund, *Augustus to Nero*, no. 389); Athens (P. Graindor, "Inscriptions attiques d'époque romaine," *BCH* 51 [1927]: 269, no. 36).

52. West, *Latin Inscriptions*, 30.

53. Ehrenberg and Jones, *Documents*, no. 217 = Braund, *Augustus to Nero*, no. 388. It may be added that Roman officials could be requested to serve as patrons of certain towns to represent their interests in Rome (e.g., *ILS*, no. 6106 = Sherk, *Roman Empire*, no. 193). Actually, a kind of patron-client agreement was sometimes made between a Roman official and his client communities. For samples of these agreements, see Ehrenberg and Jones, *Documents*, no. 354 = Braund, *Augustus to Nero*, no. 668 (Brixia, 28 C.E.); Smallwood, *Documents*, no. 413 = Braund, *Augustus to Nero*, no. 686 (Hippo Regius, North Africa, 55 C.E.).

54. Josephus, *Ant.* 19.8–10. See also M. P. Charlesworth, "Gaius and Claudius," in *Cambridge Ancient History*, X, 664.

55. Saller, *Personal Patronage*, 169–75.

56. Ibid., 152–54; Millar, *Roman Empire*, 63–64; Garnsey and Saller, *Roman Empire*, 151–52.

Cleander,[57] a prominent leader in Corinth in the sixties, was probably one of them.

Just as the emperor was courted by some of his officials because he had the power to promote or depose them, there are also indications that some Roman officials at a local level were also befriended by cities and local notables. In an inscription which was made possibly in 52/53 C.E. the governor Aquillius Florus Turcianus Gallus was honored by two *duoviri*, namely Ti. Claudius Anaxilas and Ti. Claudius Dinippus.[58] Such a good relationship between a government official and local elites is intriguing. Presumably it was one which would benefit both parties. For the officials, the support of the local notables would be needed, among other things, to protect them from any future troubles, such as complaints about their maladministration.[59] For the local elites, they would be in a more advantageous position than other people in the pursuit of ambitions, be it power, honor or material benefit, for themselves or their hometowns,[60] if they could have a good relationship with the Roman officials or, even better, with the emperor himself. In order to secure the favor of local Roman officials, gifts were sometimes exchanged, despite the fact that it was illegal for Roman officials to receive gifts from the provincials.[61] If the local notables were eager to establish "friendly" relationships, patronal relations in a local community could only be reinforced.

Local Notables

In the politics of a local community the *decuriones* were often the local aristocrats, men of great wealth and often men who had once served as local magistrates.[62] The authority of such people might even be higher

---

57. Smallwood, *Documents*, no. 62 = Braund, *Augustus to Nero*, no. 262. P. Memmius Cleander was the *duovir quinquennalis* at the time of Nero's visit in 67 C.E. He probably received his Roman citizenship during Regulus's time in Greece (West, *Latin Inscriptions*, 31; Kent, *Inscriptions*, 26). On the Memmi in Sparta, see Cartledge and Spawforth, *Sparta*, 163.

58. West, *Latin Inscriptions*, no. 54 and commentary.

59. Eulogies from some local people could help to cover up a governor's offenses against the law in court (P. A. Brunt, "Charges of Provincial Administration under the Early Principate," *Historia* 10 [1961]: 212–17).

60. Here some comparable cases can be given. (a) To bring glory to their town and perhaps to themselves too, some of the people in Prusa cultivated their relationship with the proconsuls, but Dio negotiated directly with the emperor (Dio Chrysostom, *Or.* 45.2–3). (b) Through the recommendation of Pliny, the governor of Bithynia, one of his friends was able to secure from Trajan the privileges granted to parents with three children (*Ep.* 10.94). Pliny also made recommendations for the promotion of his friend and his friend's son (*Ep.* 10.26, 87).

61. The prohibition in the law did not deter Julius Bassus, praetorian proconsul of Bithynia and *amicus* of Domitian, from receiving such gifts on occasions like his birthday. The whole scandal was later revealed in a court case handled by Pliny (*Ep.* 4.9).

62. W. T. Arnold, *The Roman System of Provincial Administration to the Accession of Constantine the Great*, 3d ed., rev. E. S. Bouchier (Oxford: Basil Blackwell, 1914),

than that of the administering officials, including the *duoviri,* who were elected by the assembly of citizens. They could request that matters relating to public accounts and public lands and buildings be referred to them for investigation or decision. The right to give honorary titles to benefactors of the city was under their control. Appeal against the *duovir*'s verdict could be directed to them. Furthermore, they might even be able to exercise influence over the recruitment of new council members, if not the actual election of magistrates.[63] Under such circumstances, it would be natural for the magistrates to try to please the *decuriones.*[64]

As mentioned above, well-connected and unusually rich families like the Euryclids were already very active in the politics of Corinth in the first century C.E. That such were the famous people in Corinth already indicates that good family background and wealth were important in the making of a local notable.[65] But in Corinth wealth appears to have been an especially important precondition. For if a person was especially rich, even though that person was not of distinguished family, there might still be a chance that he could make a name for himself.[66] So rich freedmen in Corinth were not barred from holding such offices as *aedilis* and *duovir,* even though, in other places, they were excluded from the magistracies and the local council.[67] One such freedman was Erastus, a figure who interests students of the New Testament greatly. He was made an *aedilis* of the colony,[68] probably after his promise to lay the pavement outside the theater.[69]

Another rich freedman in Corinth who succeeded in making himself

---

245, 251–52; Garnsey and Saller, *Roman Empire,* 114–15. For a sample of a colonial charter, see F. F. Abbott and A. C. Johnson, *Municipal Administration in the Roman Empire* (Princeton: Princeton University Press, 1926), no. 26 = Lewis and Reinhold, *Roman Civilization,* I, 420–28.

63. *Decuriones* were usually recruited from ex-magistrates. The ones responsible for such recruitment were the *quinquennales* who served as local censors (Arnold, *Provincial Administration,* 254). Cf. Abbott and Johnson, *Municipal Administration,* 78–79; C. P. Jones, *The Roman World of Dio Chrysostom* (Cambridge, Mass.: Harvard University Press, 1978), 97–98.

64. G. H. Stevenson, *Roman Provincial Administration* (Oxford: Basil Blackwell, 1939), 171.

65. According to Pliny, such were the people the Roman government wanted to help govern the common crowd (Pliny, *Ep.* 10.79.3).

66. It should be noted that there was a basic property requirement to be met before one could hold civic office (Millar, *Roman Empire,* 82). As Corinth was a well-known and rich city, it is likely that the amount required would not be inconsiderable. Moreover, to compete for local honors in first-century Corinth, one probably would have to do more than simply meeting the basic requirement.

67. A. M. Duff, *Freedmen in the Early Roman Empire* (Oxford: Clarendon, 1928), 137.

68. Kent, *Inscriptions,* no. 232. Kent identifies this Erastus, a freedman, with the Erastus of Rom. 16:23 (*Inscriptions,* 99–100).

69. Bagdikian, "Civic Officials," 17.

prominent in the first half of the first century C.E. was Babbius Philinus.[70] If the imperial temple in the west end of the forum was a witness to the majesty and power of the Roman ruler, the buildings donated by Babbius Philinus around the city could be seen as indications of his power and wealth. The most notable piece of architecture was the Babbius monument, a circular structure set on the northwest corner of the *agora*, just outside the site where Temple E would later be built.[71] Possibly the fountain next to it, a dedication to Poseidon, was also donated by Babbius. In addition, the reconstruction of the southeast building too might be due to the generosity of Babbius and his son.[72] Presumably because of these gifts he was voted not only to the office of *aedilis*, but also of *duovir*. It should also be noted that Babbius held two other priestly offices, *pontifex* and a priest of Neptune.[73] So his wealth was able to win him some honors and power. But not insignificantly, for some reason, he had not been able to get the highest honor, that is, the agonotheteship of the Isthmian games.[74] The fact that he was a freedman may help partly to explain his failure to obtain further advancement, despite his tremendous wealth.

L. Castricius Regulus was awarded the highest honor.[75] In fact, not only was he one of the *agonothetai* of the Isthmian games, but also the one who brought the management of the games back to Corinth, sometime between 7 B.C.E. and 3 C.E.[76] Needless to say, he was an extremely rich man. He not only paid for the expenses of the games,[77] but also put in money to repair the sanctuary at Isthmia and to give a banquet of celebration for all the inhabitants of the colony upon the completion of the repair work. With such magnificent benefactions it would be unthinkable if he was not rewarded with appropriate honors in Corinth. Unsurprisingly, during his politically active period from c. 10 B.C.E. to 23 C.E., he was able to hold most of the important mu-

---

70. West, *Latin Inscriptions*, nos. 2, 3, 98–101, 130, 131, 132; Kent, *Inscriptions*, nos. 155, 241. For evidence that Babbius Philinus probably was a freedman, see West, *Latin Inscriptions*, 108.

71. R. L. Scranton, *Monuments in the Lower Agora and North of the Archaic Temple. Corinth: Results*, I.3 (Princeton: American School of Classical Studies, 1951), 17–32; Wiseman, "Corinth and Rome I," 518. See also West, *Latin Inscriptions*, no. 132; Kent, *Inscriptions*, no. 155.

72. West, *Latin Inscriptions*, no. 122; Kent, *Inscriptions*, no. 323. See also Wiseman, "Corinth and Rome I," 514.

73. West, *Latin Inscriptions*, nos. 2 and 3. Such combination of political and priestly roles has already been seen in the career of people like Spartiaticus and Memmius Regulus and will also be seen in the career of many of the local notables in Corinth.

74. The *agonothetes* of the Isthmian games was the highest honor the colony could bestow (Kent, *Inscriptions*, 30; Wiseman, "Corinth and Rome I," 500).

75. Kent, *Inscriptions*, no. 153 and commentary; Edwards, *Coins*, 7.

76. After 146 B.C.E. the Isthmian games were under the control of the Sicyon (Pausanias 2.2.2; cf. Wiseman, "Corinth and Rome I," 496).

77. Kent, *Inscriptions*, 30; Wiseman, "Corinth and Rome I," 500.

nicipal offices which included *aedilis, praefectus iure dicundo, duovir, duovir quinquennalis, agonothetes* of the Isthmian and the Caesarean games and *agonothetes* of the *Tiberea Caesarea Sebastea*. The climax of his career as the *agonothetes* of *Tiberea Caesarea Sebastea* in 23 C.E. is most interesting. In the games of that year, not only was the reigning emperor honored, but more significantly, Livia was honored as divine Julia Augusta with the introduction of a poetry contest in her honor. In other words, she was deified in Corinth before her death in 29 C.E., even before her formal deification in 42 C.E.[78]

Whatever the significance of such an action was, this concern to honor the imperial house and to demonstrate one's loyalty to it appears to be quite common among local notables in the first half of the first century. For a similar but slightly different action was devised by T. Manlius Juvencus, another *agonothetes* and a young contemporary of L. Castricius Regulus.[79] Like Castricius Regulus, Juvencus started as an *aedilis* and ended up being the *agonothetes* of the Isthmian and Caesarean games. The most distinctive mark of his career was his close relationship with the imperial family. Having served as an *aedilis,* he was chosen to be a *praefectus iure dicundo,* possibly representing Tiberius.[80] As *agonothetes* of the Isthmian and Caesarean games, he was the first man to schedule the Caesarean games, the games which honored the imperial house, ahead of the Isthmian games, the traditional games.

Such apparent affection for the imperial rule was seen again in the actions of another important figure in the colony, namely Tiberius Claudius Dinippus.[81] Dinippus served as *cura annonae* or curator of the grain supply three times. That suggests strongly that he was a very rich patron of the colony.[82] We know that there were several famines in the reign of Claudius, and that the one in 51 C.E. was especially serious.[83] Dinippus probably became an important benefactor to the city in this period. This would make him a contemporary of Paul. With such

---

78. Kent, *Inscriptions,* 73.

79. West, *Latin Inscriptions,* nos. 81, 86; Kent, *Inscriptions,* no. 154.

80. See discussion in West, *Latin Inscriptions,* 65–66.

81. West, *Latin Inscriptions,* nos. 86–90; Kent, *Inscriptions,* nos. 158–63. Cf. also L. R. Dean, "Latin Inscriptions from Corinth," *AJA* 22 (1918): 189–90. So far, at least, ten inscriptions with the same cursus and the same order have been recovered. They possibly were made by different tribes in Corinth. The sheer number of inscriptions made in his honor suggests that this man was no ordinary leader. It is also noteworthy that one inscription was authorized by a decree of the local senate (West, *Latin Inscriptions,* no. 89).

82. These curators were appointed in times of threatened or actual famine with a responsibility to relieve the needs of the city, either by purchasing grain or by handing out money, often out of their own resources (West, *Latin Inscriptions,* 73; Bagdikian, "Civic Officials," 18–19; P. Garnsey, *Famine and Food Supply in the Greco-Roman World: Responses to Risk and Crisis* [Cambridge: Cambridge University Press, 1988], 230–31).

83. Tacitus, *Ann.* 12.43; Suetonius, *Claudius* 18.

pivotal benefactions it was inevitable that Dinippus was made *duovir,* then *duovir quinquennalis* (c. 52/53 C.E.) and *agonothetes* of *Neronea Caesarea* and of the Isthmian and Caesarean games (c. 55 C.E.).[84] Like Babbius Philinus, Dinippus also held some priestly roles. He was an *augur,* that is, a member of an honorable priesthood in the Roman empire.

If one wanted to get ahead of other competitors, something more than wealth perhaps was needed. Good family background was help-ful. But since most of the distinguished notables were eager to honor the imperial house in one way or another a connection with the Roman authorities might have given an ambitious person the edge. By the same token, the support of influential men in the city council might also be sought by men who wanted to climb the ladder of power in Corinth, especially if they did not have a particularly good background.[85] Proper public relations were an important factor contributing to one's success in the pursuit of fame and power.

In short, patronage was *one* of the ways through which society in Corinth was organized. Because of such relations, people at different lev-els, from the emperor down to a citizen in a town, were linked together, even though their interests might not be the same.

Patronage and Institutions

If patronage was such a pervasive phenomenon in Corinth one naturally would wonder how far such relationships might have been established within the society as a whole.

Patronage and the Associations

Rome was suspicious of clubs or associations,[86] but associations, legal[87] or illegal,[88] were still organized.[89] Many of the associations were formed by people who worked in the same trade.[90] That there were associations

---

84. West, *Latin Inscriptions,* 72–73.

85. Cf. Dio Chrysostom, *Or.* 45.7–8; 50.3.

86. See Trajan's reply to Pliny's request for organizing an association of firefighters (*Ep.* 10.34).

87. The poor were allowed to form associations, provided that they met once a month (*Digest,* 47.22.1 = Sherk, *Roman Empire,* no. 177A).

88. Tacitus, *Ann.* 14.17.

89. My purpose here is to show that the structure of many of these associations was similar to a patronal hierarchy. For further studies on associations, see, e.g., S. Dill, *Roman Society from Nero to Marcus Aurelius* (London: Macmillan, 1905), 251–86; M. N. Tod, *Sidelights on Greek History* (Oxford: Basil Blackwell, 1932), 71–96; K. Hopkins, *Death and Renewal: Sociological Studies in Roman History,* II (Cambridge: Cambridge University Press, 1983), 211–17.

90. For example, the association of band-players (*ILS,* no. 4966 = Sherk, *Roman Empire,* no. 177B); the association of mule-and-ass-drivers (*ILS,* no. 7293 = Sherk, *Roman*

in Corinth at the turn of the first century C.E., if not earlier, is suggested by a monument erected by the association of the Lares of the imperial house in the early second century.[91]

Members of this Corinthian association, under the leadership of two of its outstanding members,[92] met to offer worship to the Lares of the imperial house. Presumably sacrifices and meals formed an important part of their activities.[93] The two outstanding members were Titus Flavius Antiochus, a freedman of the emperor, and Tiberius Claudius Primigenius, probably a freedman's son. The structure of the association was hierarchical. There were the deities, the patrons or leaders, and the members.

Not accidentally the underlying structure of many other associations resembles that of a patronal hierarchy. Perhaps because the law allowed people to form associations for the sake of religion, many associations were formed in honor of one or more deities.[94] These deities can be compared to a sort of divine patron. Under them were their human counterparts, the patrons. In the early Empire, it was not uncommon for associations to invite rich men or men of influence to serve as patrons.[95] Rich and powerful men were honored or praised by the members for their benefactions.[96] An association was actually founded to perpetuate the name of a rich man.[97] On the other hand, the ordinary members

---

Empire, no. 177C); the association of hay merchants (*ILS*, no. 1577 = Sherk, *Roman Empire*, no. 177E).

91. Kent, *Inscriptions*, no. 62. The presence of such an association gives further support to my suggestion above that the imperial house was highly honored in Corinth. According to Kent, the members of the association were likely to be freedmen in the colony (*Inscriptions*, 35). If so, it would mean that the imperial rulers were honored not only by the local ruling classes, but also by the freedmen.

92. Ibid., 35.

93. While incense, wine and flowers were used in the worship of the *genius* of an individual *paterfamilias*, a victim was sacrificed to the *genius* Augusti (I. S. Ryberg, *Rites of the State Religion in Roman Arts* (Rome: American Academy in Rome, 1955), 55, 62). On the development of the cult of Lares Augusti, see Taylor, *Divinity*, 184–85.

94. For example, Silvanus was honored by the carpenters (*CIL*, 13.1640) and the woodcutters (*ILS*, no. 3547), Annona and Ceres were adopted by the grain-measurers (*ILS*, nos. 3816, 6146). Sometimes the *genius* of its patron was honored (*CIL*, 5.7469). See Duff, *Freedmen*, 116–17; R. MacMullen, *Roman Social Relations, 50 B.C. to A.D. 284* (New Haven: Yale University Press, 1974), 82–83.

95. In Ostia, Gnaeus Sentius Felix was such a rich and powerful patron (*ILS*, no. 6146 = Sherk, *Roman Empire*, no. 182). He was not only elected to hold important municipal offices, like *aedilis, quaestor* of the Ostian treasury, and *duovir*, but also honorable posts, like patron of different groups and clubs.

96. One association proposed that a bronze tablet with the resolution of the association to elect a certain man as patron inscribed should be placed in the patron's house if he accepted the post and, presumably, supported the association (*ILS*, no. 7216 = Lewis and Reinhold, *Roman Civilization*, II, 276).

97. A college of Aesculapius and Hygia was founded by a rich lady called Salvia Marcellina to commemorate her deceased husband (*ILS*, no. 7213; Dill, *Roman Society*, 262).

would also like to have influential and rich men as their patrons, giving them protection and benefaction.[98]

The structure of a patronal hierarchy with the patron deities at the top, rich and powerful men as patrons and leaders in the middle, and ordinary members at the bottom is most clearly revealed in an often quoted inscription from Lanuvium which recorded the by-laws of a burial society.[99] With the approval of the Roman Senate, the society was founded in the name of its deities Diana and Antinous.[100] They met in the temple of Antinous where the inscription containing the by-laws of the society was found. In honor of the patron deities their birthdays were celebrated with worship followed by a banquet. Like many other associations, it also had a prominent man as its patron. He was Lucius Caesennius Rufus, who happened to be the patron of the municipality. He promised to make an endowment to the society. Under the protection of such a patron, the association could probably be sure that they could meet without interruption. With his endowment the members could have some more money to spend on their feasts. To repay and perhaps also to exploit further the generosity and kindness of the patron, it was proposed that the birthdays of the patron and his family members, including the patron's father, mother and brother, should also be celebrated by banquets. Thus the way the patron was honored strikes an interesting parallel with the way the patron deities were honored. Likewise, the honoring of the patron along with his family members also calls to mind the honoring of the emperor and members of the imperial family.

The society had its own administrative officials. They were elected by the members. The chief official was called *quinquennalis*. The *quinquennalis* was eligible to receive a double portion of the food, and even his helper had a share and a half. It is possible, though not certain, that the difference in rank might also be reflected in the seating arrangement. For in contrast to the patron and the leading official who put in large sums of money to the association, a person who wanted to join the associa-

---

98. It was not unheard of that an association could get so poor that it had to dissolve (*ILS*, no. 7215a = Lewis and Reinhold, *Roman Civilization*, II, 276–77). On the use of patrons to secure interests of the association in the Republic, see M. Gelzer, *The Roman Nobility* (Oxford: Blackwell, 1969), 92.

99. *CIL*, 14.2112 = *ILS*, no. 7212 = Lewis and Reinhold, *Roman Civilization*, II, 273–75 (136 C.E.). For further discussion, see Dill, *Roman Society*, 259–61; MacMullen, *Roman Social Relations*, 78–79; R. L. Wilken, *The Christians as the Romans Saw Them* (New Haven: Yale University Press, 1984), 36–39; Garnsey and Saller, *Roman Empire*, 156–57.

100. It is worth pointing out that Antinous was not exactly a god, but a deified man. He was a favorite of Hadrian and was given divine honors after his death in 130 C.E. Perhaps as a custom, good wishes for the well-being of the imperial house were also expressed in the inscription.

tion and to enjoy himself only had to pay a relatively small sum for the entrance fee and an amphora of good wine, plus a monthly fee.

From the above picture of the organization of the association in Lanuvium it is perhaps not difficult to see that the structure resembles a kind of patronal hierarchy. In this respect the association was not unlike a mirror of the larger political structure of the day. The special treatment the patron and leading members received was also in line with the reciprocal principle which undergirded the patronage system. But the parallels between the two seem to go beyond the way relationships were structured in the association. For the title given to the chief official, *quinquennalis,* was actually an honorable office in a municipal government.[101] Whether such a borrowing of terms was intentional or not, the similarity in structure between the association and the political system is simply too striking to be overlooked. Perhaps they just reinforced one another.

Patronage and the Household

Trimalchio was a freedman,[102] he had a patron over him.[103] He became rich through trade. So it was appropriate for him to adopt Mercury, the god of trade, as his patron deity.[104] As a rich man he had his own clients. Such is seen clearly in his relationships with three groups of people. They were his freedmen, his literary friends and those who sought his help, financial or otherwise.

When slaves in a household were manumitted by their masters, in name they were freed persons. But in reality, they were neither totally free from the domination of nor equal in status to their patron. So even though the relationship between a freedman and his former master was compared to that between a son and a father,[105] it was one way of saying that the freedman was still under the power of the patron, just as the son was under the power of the father. Against this background, the taking of the *praenomenon* and *nomen* of the patron by the freedman may be understood as a symbol of the patron's power, however shadowy, over

---

101. Sherk, *Roman Empire,* 265; cf. also Stevenson, *Roman Provincial Administration,* 149, 172. Other titles of offices in local government which were given to officials in associations are *magistri, praefecti* and *quaestores* (Dill, *Roman Society,* 269–71).

102. Petronius, *Satyricon* 57.

103. Petronius, *Satyricon* 52.

104. Petronius, *Satyricon* 29, 77. Mercury was believed to be the one who helped to push him into the office of *sevir,* that is, a municipal office responsible for the imperial cult (J. P. Sullivan, *Petronius: The Satyricon; Seneca: The Apocolocyntosis,* rev. ed. [Harmondsworth: Penguin Books, 1986], 188). It is also worth noting that Lares of the household were also worshiped by Trimalchio (*Satyricon* 29).

105. *Digest* 37.15.9: "By freedman or son the person of patron or father should always be honored and held sacred" (Duff, *Freedmen,* 36). See also T. C. Sandars, *The Institutes of Justinian* (London: Longmans, 1952), 21.

the rest of the freedman's life. It would, in a very subtle way, remind the freedman that he owed his freedom (or new life?) to his patron. So he should be grateful to him and honor him. That such a response was sanctioned by law is most striking.[106]

But there was other legislation made to protect the interests of the patron. On the one hand, a freedman was not allowed to act in such a way as to harm his patron.[107] Under this condition, unless the freedman had special permission from the praetor, he was not allowed to bring certain cases against his patron.[108] So, in actual effect, it meant that a freedman would hardly be able to bring his patron to court, even if he had suffered injustice. On the other hand, a freedman had a duty to continue serving his former master.[109] It is noteworthy that the right of the patron was extended even to the property of the freedman for, according to law, the patron was entitled to have a share in the freedman's legacy.[110] Of course, as one party in an exchange relationship, a patron, in theory, also had some obligations to fulfil.[111] But the unequal relationship between a patron and his freedman should be quite obvious.

A second group of people who clustered around a rich patron were the literary friends or men with special skills, such as philosophers or religious persons. The fact that it was common for some satirists to denounce their colleagues for associating themselves with the rich and the powerful and for flattering them suggests how common it was for literary men to attach themselves to rich houses.[112] Ironically, many of the famous satirists themselves actually were clients of rich patrons.[113]

---

106. It has been suggested that ungrateful freedmen could be punished in the early Empire (Suetonius, *Claudius* 25; Dio Cassius 60.13; Sandars, *Institutes,* 60–61).

107. J. A. Crook, *Law and Life of Rome* (London: Thames & Hudson, 1967), 51–55.

108. *Digest* 2.4.4; Sandars, *Institutes,* 500; Duff, *Freedmen,* 37–40; P. Garnsey, *Social Status and Legal Privilege in the Roman Empire* (Oxford: Clarendon, 1970), 182.

109. A patron could demand a freedman to provide different kinds of services, such as taking care of his children, attending to his friends, even to help the patron if he was in poverty. For further details, see Duff, *Freedmen,* 40–46.

110. Sandars, *Institutes,* 21, 63–64. In the time of the Republic, a patron could claim half of the estate from the legacy of his freedman. In the time of Paul, the freedman had to have three actual descendants to bar the patron from sharing equally with the one or two descendants if the estate was worth 100,000 sesterces. If the descendants were not actual descendants, the patron could claim half of the estate. See W. W. Buckland, *A Textbook of Roman Law,* 3d ed. (Cambridge: Cambridge University Press, 1968), 597; Duff, *Freedmen,* 43–44; Crook, *Law and Life,* 53–54.

111. For example, a patron had the right to act as a *tutela* to protect the interests of a freedwoman, no matter how old she was, or a freedman under 20 years of age, giving them legal advice and guiding them in the handling of their property. Likewise, if a freedman was really in need, a patron was obliged to feed him. And if a freedman was murdered, a patron was required to help to bring the murderer to justice. For further discussion, see Duff, *Freedmen,* 43, 48–49.

112. Horace, *Ep.* 1.19.35; Persius, *Prologue, Satires* 1; Pliny, *Ep.* 5.19.

113. Horace, *Satires* 2.6.40–41; *Ep.* 1.7; Persius, *Satires* 1.108–9; Martial, *Epigrams* 1.20; 3.60; Pliny, *Ep.* 3.21; Juvenal, *Satires* 5.

On the matter of courting rich houses, philosophers seemingly were not far behind.[114] Like the satirists, some of them also debated over the problem of receiving gifts from the rich patrons.[115] Besides poets and philosophers, religious figures such as soothsayers might also be among the followers of a rich and powerful patron.[116]

Unlike the patron-client relation between the former master and his freedman which was formal and sanctioned by law, the patronal nature of the relation between a rich patron and his literary friends was much more informal and subtle. Apart from tangible things,[117] literary clients might also be able to get intangible benefits such as opportunities to display their talents which ultimately might win them fame.[118] In a different way, the patron too needed the companionship of his literary friends. For with a group of literary men around him, the dignity of the patron, as a cultured man, would be enhanced.[119] They could be sure that there would always be people to applaud their actions,[120] not to mention literary works which praised their benevolence and virtues.[121]

Having said this, it should be noted that differences and inequalities between the patron and the literary clients would always exist. These features of their relationship were usually unfolded on two occasions, namely, the dinner party and the morning salutation. While the dinner table was a place for the patron to show off his wealth, to congratulate himself and to reward the services of his clients,[122] it was also the place where the clients had to fulfil their duty, even if it meant inconvenience for themselves.[123] Food first bore witness to their unequal positions. It was not uncommon for the satirists to protest against the serving of inferior food and wine to the clients when good food and

---

114. Tacitus, *Ann.* 16.32; *Hist.* 4.10. Cf. Dio Chrysostom, *Or.* 77/78.34–35.

115. So in the Socratic letters, those philosophers who found shelter under the roofs of the rich houses became a type to be attacked by the ascetic Cynics (*Ps.-Socratic Ep.* 8, 9).

116. A *duovir* and an *aedilis* of a town were allowed to keep a soothsayer as their assistant (Abbott and Johnson, *Municipal Administration,* no. 26, LXII = Lewis and Reinhold, *Roman Civilization,* I, 421).

117. A literary friend could be invited to dinners (Horace, *Satires* 2.7.32–42; Martial, *Satires* 3.60; Juvenal, *Satires* 1.52.5; *Ps.-Socratic Ep.* 9). Or he could be given gifts in the form of money (Persius, *Prologue;* Martial, *Epigrams* 10.75; Juvenal, *Satires* 1.128; *Ps.-Socratic Ep.* 9; Pliny, *Ep.* 3.21.3), clothing (Persius, *Satires* 1.54; *Ps.-Socratic Ep.* 9), even land (Horace, *Satires* 2.6; Juvenal, *Satires* 9.59). He could also be taken on journey with the patron (Horace, *Satires* 2.6.40–41).

118. Pliny, *Ep.* 8.12.

119. Petronius, *Satyricon* 48, 55.

120. Such actions might be a speech in the forum (Martial, *Epigrams* 6.48; Juvenal, *Satires* 1.128), a recitation (Martial, *Epigrams* 4.49; 10.4, 10; Juvenal, *Satires* 1.52), even wit at the dinner table (Petronius, *Satyricon* 34–35, 41, 48).

121. Horace, *Satires* 2.6; Persius, *Satires* 1.50–56; Pliny, *Ep.* 3.12.

122. Juvenal, *Satires* 5.12–15.

123. Horace, *Satires* 2.7.32–34; cf. Juvenal, *Satires* 5.15–23.

good wine were reserved for the host and his honorable friends.[124] Seating arrangements told the same story.[125] The place of honor or the third position in the middle couch, sometimes next to the host, was reserved for the chief guest.[126] Ordinary clients understandably would have to occupy less honorable positions,[127] and so would the freedmen.[128] Slaves and the poor simply had to dine on pallets or sitting upright.[129] But the difference between the patron and his clients went further than these arrangements. For in order to be a successful client, one had to follow the golden rule, that is, to please the patron and try to accommodate oneself to his opinion.[130]

Before the rich patron and some of his client-guests could recover from the tiresome party the night before, they had to get up early to fulfil their duties at the morning salutation.[131] Receiving the salutation of his clients, the patron could once more satisfy his desire to be superior and different both before his peers and his inferiors. Paying their visits to the patron, some poor clients could get limited financial help to support their wretched lives.[132] But it should be stressed that probably not all the clients were treated in the same way. In a reference to the custom of morning salutation Seneca suggested that friends or clients were classified and treated accordingly by patrons in the great houses.[133] The closest friends were seen in private, the less close friends in company with others, and the rest were seen *en masse*. That may be why some clients complained that they did not get to see the patron while others did.[134] Although some might complain, the same people perhaps would come again the next morning. Some might do it out of a sense of duty as

---

124. Martial, *Epigrams* 3.49, 60; 6.11; Juvenal, *Satires* 5.24–25. Note also Pliny's apparent distaste for such a practice (*Ep.* 2.6).

125. For more discussions of the Roman seating arrangement, see "Triclinium," in *A Dictionary of Classical Antiquities: Mythology, Religion, Literature and Art,* rev. H. Nettleship and J. E. Sandys (London: Swan Sonnenschein, 1894), 653; J. E. Sandys, ed., *A Companion to Latin Studies,* 3d ed. (Cambridge: Cambridge University Press, 1921), 206–7; *OCD,* 1093–94.

126. N. Rudd, *Horace: Satires and Epistles; Persius: Satires* (Harmondsworth: Penguin Books, 1979), 122.

127. Juvenal, *Satires* 5.15–18.

128. Sullivan, *Petronius,* 189 n. 9.

129. *OCD,* 1094.

130. Horace, *Ep.* 1.18; Seneca, *De Ira* 3.8.6; 3.35.

131. Martial, *Epigrams* 10.82; Juvenal, *Satires* 1.95–138; Seneca, *De Brev. Vit.* 14.4; Pliny, *Ep.* 3.12.2. See also J. P. V. D. Balsdon, *Life and Leisure in Ancient Rome* (London: Bodley Head, 1969), 21–24.

132. By attending the door of the rich a poor client might get a *sportula* which is either a basket of food or some money to buy food for the day (Juvenal, *Satires* 1.128).

133. Seneca, *De Ben.* 6.34.2.

134. Seneca, *De Const.* 10.2; Juvenal, *Satires* 1.100–101. To solve this problem, the advice of experienced clients was to bribe the servants or to wait for the patrons on the street (Horace, *Satires* 1.9.56–58; Juvenal, *Satires* 3.189).

faithful clients.[135] But others had to do it because of necessity. The latter group of people made up the third group of clients under an influential patron. They were those who sought the help of a patron in different matters. Some wanted the support of an important patron in the pursuit of a public career.[136] Others needed the help of a patron in legal matters.[137]

Conclusion

> Look at those whose prosperity men flock to behold; they are smothered by their blessings. To how many are riches a burden! From how many do eloquence and the daily straining to display their powers draw forth blood.... To how many does the throng of clients that crowd about them leave no freedom! In short, run through the list of all these men from the lowest to the highest — this man desires an advocate, this one answers the call, that one is on trial, that one defends him, that one gives sentence; no one asserts his claim to himself, everyone is wasted for the sake of another. Ask about the men whose names are known by heart, and you will see that these are the marks that distinguish them: A cultivates B and B cultivates C; no one is his own master.[138]

We can say with some confidence that patronage provided *one* of the ways through which relationships in Corinth would have been organized. The relationship complexes in the community, which involved the common people, the local notables, the Roman officials, and in a way the emperor, may also be seen as interlocking nets of patrons and clients.

The patron was expected to provide protection and favors which might not have been accessible through other channels. In return, he could expect to get power, honor, support and perhaps more benefits. So the emperor established his loyal officials in his provinces who would support him and served his interests. The local notables used their wealth to take care of the common crowd who voted them to honorable offices and special privileges. Likewise, the patrons of the associations and the heads of individual households were also able to enjoy special privileges and powers because of their positions in the respective groups. While in first-century Corinth honor and power, whether political or religious, were sought by the ambitious men, the way to fame was probably marked by strong competition. In order to climb the ladder of

---

135. Martial, *Epigrams* 10.28.
136. Martial, *Epigrams* 12.26; Seneca, *De Brev. Vit.* 14.3; 20.1; Plutarch, *Moralia* 814D.
137. Seneca, *De Brev. Vit.* 11.4.
138. Seneca, *De Brev. Vit.* 2.4 (LCL).

power and honor, one would have to do more than fulfil the basic property requirements. Hence it was essential for those who did not come from a good family background, like freedmen, to have proper personal connections. One of the necessary and honorable things to do was to cultivate relationships with men of influence and, if possible, the Roman authorities. Perhaps that is why many of the local notables were at the same time priests of the imperial cult.

The values and structure of the patronal society were also reflected in institutions, such as associations and households. In such contexts it is of particular interest to note that patronal relations can be seen as projected beyond the realm of human relations into that of human-divine relations. So even though a rich householder could be the patron of many, he himself would need the protection of a patron god.

If patronage formed such an important part of life in Roman Corinth, it would be most unrealistic to expect the Christians there to be wholly untouched by its influence and to behave in a completely new way immediately after their conversion. On the contrary, it is most likely that patronage would become the background for understanding the relational ties in the church and some of the problems Paul discussed in 1 Corinthians.

The Veil of Power

RICHARD GORDON

To construct a history of religion in the Roman Empire is a well-nigh impossible task: there are topics but no subject, quantities of information but little sense to be made of it. The difficulties that beset the historian of the religion of archaic and classical Greece reappear, still more intractable. One of the reasons for this is the assumption that the proper study of the history of religions is divinity and beliefs about divinity: and no one has ever succeeded in counting the number of divinities worshiped in the Roman Empire. A book dedicated to the study of priesthood in the ancient world provides an excellent opportunity to move away from divinities towards fundamental institutions of the religious system, above all the practice of sacrifice, and the group which controlled public sacrifice, the emperor and the elites, both in the center and in each locality. Sacrifice was a "natural" institution in the ancient world, but that does not mean that it has no history or that its relation to the political order did not change.

The system as a whole can be understood only by tracing the relationship between the *princeps,* the crucial figure in the center, and those in Rome and in the provinces who found in him support for their own social and political status. Of course the Roman Empire was not in the ordinary sense a society, rather a congeries of settlements only loosely integrated with one another. In such circumstances, most of the links they had with each other and with the center were symbolic, above all religious. But these religious links were at the same time an essential part of the domination enjoyed by the elites of the empire.

This paper considers first the sacrificial or "priestly" role of the *princeps,* starting from the visual representations of sacrifice on major monuments of "official" Roman art. It argues that the emperor's sacrificial role cannot be divorced from his role as benefactor or euergete on a massive scale; but rather that these roles *together* (and I stress *together*) provided a model for the elite more generally, both in Rome and in the provinces. The second part of the paper focuses particularly on the elite itself. It explores the nature of the "civic compromise" — that is the failure within traditional Graeco-Roman cult to differentiate sharply between magistracy and priesthood; and it suggests that this refusal is not just a curious "fact" about the Roman system but a central mode of domination.

The Emperor as Priest and Sacrificer

Taken as a whole, one of the peculiarities of Roman sacrificial iconography is the massive domination of the emperor. The ideal monopoly by emperors of sacrificial iconography is confirmed by the coin-series, beginning with Trajan.

The visual representation of public sacrifice at Rome summarily reproduces key aspects of the social and political system: one could hardly wish for a more direct, if unconscious, testimony to the relationship between religion and the social order. But it is the control by the *princeps* over the visual representation of sacrifice which demands our attention. One of the important new uses of sacrificial imagery by the emperors was in response to a difficult and indeed intractable problem, the character of the relationship between the "religion of Rome" and the "religion of the Roman Empire."

It is clear that one of the roles of the *princeps* as *pontifex maximus* was to safeguard the integrity and continuity of the traditional public rituals of Rome.[1] But at the same time it is obvious that by far the greater number of innovations in the ritual calendar of Rome was in connection with the imperial house. The artificiality of Augustus's revival made this consumption of Roman religion by imperial festivals entirely plausible. For during the last two centuries of the Republic Roman religion had increasingly depended upon the conflicts of the elite for its ability to continue to generate meanings. The removal of those conflicts by Octavian/Augustus removed the argument from religion, turning it into a naked instrument of ideological domination. And one of its ideological functions in the early Principate was to insulate Rome from the cultural consequence of her own imperialism: the religion of Rome became a guarantee not merely of her supremacy but also of her freedom from contamination by her subjects. Rome was different from her Empire and her religion was an emblem of that difference. The so-called tolerance of the indigenous religions of the provinces is rather to be understood as a consequence of this colonial attitude.

But the historical choices made by successive emperors eroded this difference continually. Without constant repression, with all its impossible costs, the provinces had to be induced to love their servitude. If

---

1. W. Speyer, "Das Verhältnis des Augustus zur Religion," *ANRW* 2.16.3, 1777–1805, esp. 1779–82; D. Little, "Politics in Augustan Poetry," *ANRW* 2.30.1, 254–370, esp. 260–71 and 277–86.

that meant above all the recruitment of local aristocracies into the central elite, it also meant the widening of the citizen base (culminating in the universal extension of citizenship to all free inhabitants of the Empire in 213–14), the army as an agent of acculturation, the mobility of shippers, craftsmen, tourists and slaves, the manipulation of their imperial masters by provincial elites, the spread of the cult of Jupiter and above all that of the emperors. All these developments meant that the desire to maintain a symbolic distance between center and periphery was doomed to ineffectiveness. And it seems to me that the institution of sacrifice was one of the key means whereby some kind of synthesis was effected between the religion of Rome, in the narrow sense, and the religion of the Empire taken very broadly. It became a sort of code for membership in this unwieldy congeries of disparate cultures.

To a very considerable degree we are dealing with processes that were scarcely conscious, as so often with religious developments. But during the course of the Principate sacrifices by emperors seem to have lost their implication in particular rituals of the traditional religion of Rome (above all triumphs and public *vota*) and to have become symbols of a very generalized conception of "piety" sustained by the emperors in the name not of the *Senate and People of Rome* but of the Empire as a whole. I would go further and claim that sacrifices by emperors also became paradigms or exemplars of public sacrifice throughout the empire, ideal and grandiloquent versions of the proper means of communication with the other world. There was an elective affinity between this symbolic paradigm and the real-world changes also encouraged by the imperial system, the absorption of more and more wealth by small numbers of the elite in each locality. Just as the emperor's symbolic capital was bound up with his acquisition of offices as well as his vast euergetism, so the same system, allying office to prestation, was encouraged in imitation all over the Empire: one of the interesting developments of the Principate is the restriction in fact but not in theory of office, including priesthood, to a smaller and smaller circle of gilded families in each locality. The Principate also encouraged further changes: the massive extension of cities on a Graeco-Roman model through the Empire and the corresponding religious changes; the extension of the Roman model of office-holding and priesthood to areas not controlled by cities, for example in Egypt and in the great temple-states of Asia Minor, and more generally into "villages"; the transformation of existing native priesthoods into Graeco-Roman priests. Moreover, since these processes depended entirely upon the maintenance, and further development, of an already enormously unequal and steeply stratified society, symbolic means of integration were invaluable. The paradigmatic quality of the emperor's sacrificial activity encouraged the spontaneous demand for access to public sacrificial positions such as those of the *vicomagistri* and *VIviri Augustales*, and beyond that for access to quasi-public positions, such as priesthoods of *collegia* (local or trade associations), and in the cults of the Magna Mater and of Isis. If small numbers of the very rich in each town monopolized official sacrificial positions, the Empire was sufficiently differentiated to provide alternatives.

Diverse as it was, the Roman Empire had particular need of symbols of unity. One of the images already present in the political language of the Republic, that of the body, could be easily adapted.[2] In these terms, the emperor would represent the head, the directing intelligence of the whole body; his power and authority would be the sinews of coherence. Without him, the body is useless.[3] Connected with this imagery of unity is the idea of the emperor as affording an example to the rest of the empire, just as he was "regulator of the world and father of the earth."[4] It has been well observed that the title *optimus* (best) implies that the emperor had a paradigmatic role, and the clearest expression of the idea duly turns up in Pliny's *Panegyric of Trajan:* "We do not need strict rule so much as an example."[5] But the idea was already "a regular topos in panegyric or in other writings about the *princeps.*"[6] Augustus already implies his own function as a model in *Res Gestae:* "By introducing new laws I have reintroduced numerous traditional *exempla* which had already begun to disappear from our age, and have myself left *exempla* in many things to be handed down to our descendants"; and he is said by Suetonius to have been fully conscious of his own imitation of great men of the past and of the exemplary role of the *princeps.*[7] Velleius Paterculus, for whom the *religio* of Tiberius was an important part of his moral claim to authority, asserts: "for the best of emperors (*princeps optimus*) teaches his fellow citizens to do right by doing so himself, and though he is the greatest in authority, he is still greater in the examples which

---

2. See J. Béranger, *Recherches sur l'aspect idéologique du Principat* (Basel: F. Reinhardt, 1953), 218–52.

3. Ibid., 231–36; note esp. Seneca, *Clem.* 1.5.1 (addressing Nero): "animus reipublicae tuae es, illa corpus tuum" ("you are the soul of the state and the state your body").

4. Martial, 7.7.5 (92 C.E.); cf. 9.6.1. On this theme in general, see J. Vogt, *Orbis Romanus: zur Terminologie des römischen Imperialismus,* Philosophie und Geschichte 22 (Tübingen, 1929), 18–22.

5. *Pan.* 45.6, with the entire section; also Ovid, *Met.* 15, 833–34 and *Fast.* 6.647–48. Seneca, *Clem.* 2.2.1, offers the idea of the diffusion of the quality of *mansuetudo* throughout the Empire thanks to the display of it. For *optimus* implying example, Ch. Wirszubski, *Libertas as a Political Idea at Rome during the Late Republic and Early Principate* (Cambridge: Cambridge University Press, 1950), 153–54.

6. A. Woodman, ed., *Velleius Paterculus: The Tiberian Narrative* (2.94–131) (Cambridge: Cambridge University Press, 1977), 245.

7. *Res Gestae* 2, 12–13. See also Suetonius, *Aug.* 31, 5 and 89 (one of his most boring habits, no doubt).

he sets"; while Quintilian observes that it is characteristic of Romans to work by example.[8]

Augustus's revival of religion was intended to exemplify the *pietas* of his rule. Coinage also provides important images of imperial, sacrificial activity. Sacrificial implements occur commonly on coins from imperial mints. It is generally agreed that they register a non-specific message of the piety of the emperors rather than particular priesthoods or events.[9] Indeed when PIETAS AVG ("piety of the emperor") is the legend of the coin, it is commonly illustrated by an act of sacrifice, either by Pietas herself or by the emperor. It is as if the exemplary piety of the emperor was best imaged by displaying him (as on commemorative arches) in a sacrificial context. The "religion of Rome" is now seen to be conducted wherever the *princeps* happens to be, and in relation to the central political and military needs of each successive regime. What we witness is the universal quality of imperial sacrifice, its disengagements from the narrow world of the City of Rome, and its paradigmatic, exemplary intention.

Priesthood and Euergetism at Rome

The sacrificial role of the *princeps* is not, of course, to be understood in isolation: it is inextricably linked with his *philanthropia* (benevolence), his *liberalitas* (generosity), and so with his accumulation of symbolic capital. In that respect, his sacrificial activity serves as an example to all the elites in the Empire. Overtly, sacrificial activity fulfils a specific duty, to maintain satisfactory relations with the gods; but it is never clear whether this duty is allocated to the elite or appropriated by it. What is clear is the way in which the visual record of sacrificial activity of a public kind in the Principate is virtually monopolized, in several modes, by the imperial system; and also how local religious life in the Empire became suffused with references to the emperor and in a sense dependent upon his presence.[10] It is as though the nexus, evident to the modern historian, between (a) the political structure of the Empire (summarized in the emperor's relations with both center and periphery), (b) the use of inequality of wealth to perpetuate structures of dependence more effective than those based on mere violence, and (c) the sacrificial system, could not be fully veiled, but found expression in the dynamic extension of a particular kind of civic priesthood. It is to this matter that we must now turn.

---

8. Velleius Paterculus 2, 126, 5; Quintilian 12, 2, 30.

9. H. Mattingly, *BMC* III, xl–xliii, is the best brief discussion.

10. For the East, see especially S. R. F. Price, *Rituals and Power: The Roman Imperial Cult in Asia Minor* (Cambridge: Cambridge University Press, 1984).

By far the most active agent of change, social, economic and symbolic, in the Roman Empire was the institution of the Principate itself. As often, of course, the intended changes were either illusory or ineffective; of far greater importance were unintended changes that resulted from long-term or invisible forces.

Along with the perception of continuity with the remote past went recognition of the instrumental value of sacerdotal offices. So evident is it that successive emperors used the appointments as instruments of patronage that the study of the priesthoods of the Principate has usually been seen as an aspect not of Roman religion but of the history of the senatorial elite.[11] Calculations have been made of the proportions of men who entered priesthoods at different points in their careers; of the proportions of consuls, praetors, quaestors, and even more junior magistrates, who might expect, if they were not already appointed, to enter a college. Almost endless inferences can be drawn about the status of individuals in relation to the emperor, the standing of families and the workings of the patronage system. Moreover the symbolic advantages of priesthood to members of the senatorial elite were considerable, and assisted them in their own extension of their patronage-networks (the equivalent of politics in the imperial system). Because they had this double quality — collectively symbols of continuity and changelessness, as well as day-to-day instruments of imperial patronage — it was inevitable that the "reality" of the latter role was much more significant to ordinary ambitious senators that the symbolic function.

But even the emperors could not resist the changes which they themselves had brought about. The legitimating role of the sacerdotal colleges gradually faded, as the emperor's own religious role vastly increased. The emperors' innovations in the religious system could hardly be sensibly, let alone critically, discussed.[12] It is a truism that at Rome religion and politics were inextricably intertwined; but the converse is also true: the abolition of politics involved also the break-down of the Republican religious synthesis predicated upon the appropriation of religious authority by the political elite. The emperors took over the religion of Rome.

But in one area tradition could be built upon. In the Republic, it seems, it had been customary for a priest on election to provide some expensive public entertainment and to underwrite the cost of the sump-

11. Martha W. Hoffmann Lewis, *The Official Priests of Rome under the Julio-Claudians: A Study of the Nobility from 44 B.C. to 68 A.D.* (Rome: American Academy in Rome, 1955), 2.

12. Note Dio's remark on Octavian's consultation (in 38 B.C.E.) of the *pontifices* over his proposed marriage to Livia (while pregnant): "Perhaps they really found (their answer) among the *patria,* but certainly they would have said (what they said), even had they not found it" (48, 44, 2).

tuous feast he had to give to his new colleagues.[13] The Roman senatorial elite treated the acquisition of priesthoods in the Roman sacerdotal colleges as symbolic but highly desirable goods. The emperors used these posts just as they used their other means of patronage, as means of creating an enduring relation of dependence, gratitude and respect towards themselves, in short to create symbolic capital. But priesthood had another facet, as the *summa honoraria* show, as a vehicle for the institutionalization of euergetism towards the people of Rome, as a means of compelling the senatorial elite to imitate the emperor's generosity. Their generosity is no longer overtly political, as in the Republic, but it serves a social purpose nonetheless in displaying as spectacularly as possible the social inequality which enabled them to give so generously and forced the recipients gratefully to receive. If the emperor alone gives, he makes impossibly wide the gulf which separates him from all others — he becomes as it were an evident *god;*[14] if the leading members of the senatorial order also give, euergetism becomes a sign of the social responsibility of an entire order. And that they give in consideration of a non-political good, a priesthood, a purely symbolic good, makes it clear that the euergetic system is for the good of the people, who receive real benefits in return for giving honor. Mask and veil here coincide: for the true purpose of giving is not to receive honor, but to maintain the power and wealth of the elite. It cannot be sufficiently emphasized that the relative "success" of the Roman Empire, by comparison with other much more violently extractive, and unstable, pre-industrial empires, lay largely in the extension of the euergetic system of unequal exchange very widely through the Empire.[15]

Priesthood and Euergetism among the Provincial Elite

The same pattern can be perceived throughout the Roman Empire. The Roman forms of local government also brought with them the institution of the *summum honorarium,* civil as well as religious: it was not merely the forms and names of central priesthoods that were imposed. The key associations between wealth, public office, beneficence

---

13. "Yet the *cena aditialis* has often cost a most careful man a cool million HS" (Seneca, *Ep.* 95.41). See also the augural dinner given before 67 B.C.E. by Q. Hortensius Hortalus, mentioned by Varro, *Rust.* 3.6.6; Pliny, *HN* 10.23.45; Macrobius, *Sat.* 3.13.1; and Cicero's excuses for being absent from M. Apulleius's feast, *Att.* 12.13.2; 14.1; 15.1.

14. Note S. Martin's comment, "The senate (better "senators") seems to have provided an important link between the emperor and his subjects. As emperors became more elevated and more remote figures — they had to rely more, not less, on the mediation of their own dependants" (*JRS* 75 [1985]: 225).

15. The concealed "bottom line" means that: giving + gratitude/honor = power for the elite.

and the religious system could thus be disseminated throughout the Roman world. This complex relationship is unselfconsciously evidenced by thousands of honorific inscriptions and statues set up as marks of these transactions. But it is the East, and particularly Asia Minor, that provides the most striking examples of priestly generosity, as of generosity on appointment to an ordinary magistracy. I propose to consider in some detail two examples of this — so as to explore different facets of the connection between euergetism and local civic priesthood.

The first is that of Cleanax, son of Sarapion, of Cyme in the Aeolid. He is known only from a fragmentary stele, now in the J. Paul Getty Museum in Malibu, erected on the occasion of his quitting the office of *prytanis* (a local magistracy in Cyme).[16] It probably dates from the period 2 B.C.E.–2 C.E., and documents in exhaustive detail the fact that Cleanax has never lost any opportunity to bestow his beneficence upon the council, the Roman community, and the people of Cyme (ll. 7–8). Only those which concern his priesthood are of relevance here. As priest of Dionysus Pandamos, "he celebrated the mysteries founded by the city, and paid all the expenses necessary for the five-yearly celebration of the mysteries, at which time the magnitude of the sums involved... displayed his *philodoxia* (love of honor, i.e., reputation for munificence) and *eusebeia* (respect for the worship of the gods), sums he alone paid and which he was the first to engage to pay... " (ll. 12–16). He also invited by public proclamation the citizens, the Roman (Italian) community, the *paroikoi* (the dependent population that worked the land) and the foreigners to a feast in the sanctuary of Dionysus and "entertained them magnificently; and he did this every year" (ll. 16–19). In other words, Cleanax has invented a new kind of charge upon himself (and doubtless his successors) by putting on a public festival entirely at his own expense (l. 16); by putting up posters, he attempts to ensure the largest possible attendance, but he also objectifies his munificence in the litter of the placards making the announcement, which are a physical sign of the generation of that hidden gratitude which is to become his symbolic capital. More important, however, is Cleanax's transformation of the cult of the gods into an opportunity to accumulate symbolic capital for himself: a delicate boundary, between use of the religious system by the elite and its usurpation, has been crossed; and such gestures become increasingly common in the Principate.[17]

---

16. P. Hodot, "Décret de Kymè en l'honneur du prytane Kleanax," *The J. Paul Getty Museum Journal* 10 (1982): 165–80. J. and L. Robert, *Bulletin Épigraphique* 1983, no. 323 is an essential addendum, whose interpretation I have generally followed.

17. Pauline Schmitt-Pantel, "La Festin dans la Fête de la cité grecque (hellenistique)," *La Fête: Pratique et discourse* (Paris: Université Besançon, 1981), 85–99," points out that this process begins already in the second century B.C.E. See also Pauline Schmitt-Pantel, "Euergétisme et mémoires du mort," in G. Gnoli and J.-P. Vernant, eds., *Le mort,*

The list of Cleanax's benefits during his subsequent magistracy illustrates the closeness of the relation between civic office and religious
function in the Graeco-Roman city. For as *prytanis* Cleanax, on entry
into office on the first day of the year (probably Augustus's birthday,
23 September), "performed the sacrifices to the gods according to custom, distributed sweet wine to all the inhabitants of the city (without
restriction of category), offered splendid entertainments for the goddesses and performed the (annual) vows for a prosperous new year and
sacrifices according to custom, and entertained many citizens and Romans for several days in the *prytaneum* (civic hall)" (ll. 30–34). On the
usual day for celebrating the festival of the dead, "he performed the
customary sacrifices, and had the *chondrogala*[18] distributed to all the
inhabitants of the city, slave and free"; there followed another festival,
in the month of Corydon: "On his own initiative, he invited by verbal
proclamation the citizens, the Romans, the *paroikoi* and the foreigners
to banquet in the *prytaneum*, and gave out portions to the people in the
same way as the other *prytaneis;* he provided laurel for the processions
(the *daphnephoria* in honor of Apollo) and gave a feast for the priests,
for the victors in the sacred games, to the magistrates and many citizens" (ll. 36–40). Finally, during an imperial festival celebrated by the
province of Asia, "he offered the sacrifices and the banquets at which
the meat is consumed, as he had promised, first of all sacrificing a bull
to Caesar Augustus, his sons (Gaius and Lucius Caesar) and to the other
gods, sacrifices with which he entertained in (?) the market-place the
Greeks, the Romans, the *paroikoi* and the foreigners, by proclamation
on posters..." (ll. 40–45).

The inseparability of civic and religious functions is abundantly plain:
the generosity of Cleanax expresses itself in the manner most directly
and concretely advantageous to his fellow-citizens, in feasts, meat-eating
and the distribution of wine. We hardly need to note the way in which
such social occasions, both the rituals themselves and the organized
feasting in and out of *prytaneum*, recapitulate an ideal version of the
local social hierarchy.[19] Religious celebrations provide a privileged context within which a certain notion of community can be evoked: all are
united in gratitude to the generosity of Cleanax. The actual, and fundamental, divisions of the local society are repeatedly rehearsed, in an
almost incantatory manner, reminding us that the wealth of Cleanax almost certainly derived from his dominant roles in reproducing the very
social relations that his activity as *euergete* serves to veil. And finally

---

les morts dans les sociétés anciennes (Cambridge and Paris: Cambridge University Press,
1982), 177–88.

18. The *chondrogala* seems to have been a sort of milk soup made from coarse ground
flour.

19. Schmitt-Pantel, "Festin," 93.

the insertion into the text of the shadowy figures of the emperor Augustus and his two adoptive sons (Gaius and Lucius) neatly demonstrates the Chinese-box structure of the Roman Empire: as one penetrates further down the social hierarchy and out towards the periphery, one finds systems of relationship which recapitulate on a smaller, local, scale the pattern of domination which enabled the personal rule of Octavian to be transformed into the institution of the Principate.[20]

The second illustration concerns the gifts of an exceptionally wealthy woman, Menodora daughter of Megacles from Sillyon in Pamphylia. The first point to make about Menodora's gifts, apart from their sheer size and the minute attention to detail, is that the hierarchy of the city is given monetary expression. It is evident that the major purpose of this philanthropy is not to relieve poverty. Part of the function of philanthropic gestures is to register and naturalize the inequalities of the social system in each community, just as the emperors' patronage and generosity marshals and orchestrates the overall hierarchy of the system as a whole. The gifts objectify the relations of respect, dependence, authority and power upon which the entire euergetic system rests. Moreover, the fusion of the euergetic system with the sacrificial system in civic priesthood evokes both the divine necessity and the social responsibility of the existing social order. The relationship proposed by the sacrificial system between god and man (inferiority; reciprocity between unequals; providential beneficence; changelessness) is implicitly offered as a model of the relationship between the elite and the rest of the community. On the one hand, the Roman Empire institutionalized the figure of the *princeps* who, if he were not a god, was certainly not a man; on the other, by imitating the *princeps*'s genial fusions of sacrificial activity with euergetism on a grand scale, the elite at every level, even in the miserable town of Pamphylian Sillyon, by the subtle alchemy of symbolic capital, forged its own subordinate legitimacy.

Secondly, the nature of what is given, the distribution of food, wine, oil and money; the buildings, the art products, the silver goods for rituals; the foundations and orphanages, construct an image of what is needful to the community, an idea constructed by the elite in terms of its own judgments of value.[21] Lavish goods for the gods are set side by side with necessaries for orphans. Just as the elite takes responsibility for the community it takes responsibility for the gods. It thus sets itself up as the major carrier of central values in the community. At the same

---

20. Price, *Rituals and Power*, chap. 9, denies "that the imperial cult was part of the ideological superstructure (or) that it legitimated political power." This seems plain daft: to deny the relationship is in fact to undo the good done by his earlier analyses.

21. P. Debord, *Aspects sociaux et économiques de la vie religieuse dans l'Anatolia gréco-romaine* (Leiden: EPRO, 1982), 74–75; cf. J. Andreau, "Fondations privées et rapports sociaux en Italic romaine, Ier–IIIe s. ap. J.C.," *Ktema* 2 (1977): 157–209.

time, the community becomes dependent upon the elite for the means of worshiping "piously," that is, equipped with suitably lavish items of religious paraphernalia: the elite inserts itself surreptitiously into the communication between here and the other world, not by claiming some special mediatory status but by means of the provision of the agencies of worship.[22]

Finally, women appear here, as frequently in the Principate (and earlier, to some extent), not merely as occupants of priesthoods, which had always been possible, but in the role of *euergetês,* that is, as honorary men. The dynamic of the euergetic system gradually erodes one of the principles of the traditional political systems of the Greek cities: these euergetic women are symptoms of changes in local inheritance systems and of the pressure of Roman law upon them; and also of the pressure which the obligation to give puts upon all wealthy families in a locality. They do not mark any particular shift in the social power of women in general, as Menodora's gifts to the wives of the local elite — and the complete absence of the women lower down the social scale — testify.[23]

Patriotism and piety are fused in these inscriptions. To what end? What is the ideological value of this odd fusion? A hint at the answer is provided by one of the inscriptions from the sanctuary of Leto in the city of Xanthos in Lycia, in honor of Q. Veranius Tlepolemus, high priest of the emperor in 149 C.E.[24] The inscription describes him as "gentlemanly, honorable, patriotic, noble, notable for his moral character, his conversation and his lack of excessive display." The most interesting feature of this description is its praise of restraint in self-display, in a context in which quite evidently enormous amounts of money and energy were expended in display. The fusion between patriotism and piety ensures that the social functions of "philanthropy" can be veiled: the object of erecting inscriptions and statues can be suppressed in consideration of the true disinterestedness of generosity. In giving one seeks literally for nothing, as true piety does not look for a reward. Duty is the most delicious disguise of self-interest. And the very fact of the continuity of many of these elite families was sufficient proof of the pleasure the gods took in their piety.[25]

•

22. Schmitt-Pantel, "Festin," 89: the banquets of benefactors create new religious feasts in the city, constructed entirely around their own social and political concerns.

23. For a full discussion of these women commanding wealth, see R. van Bremen, "Women and Wealth," in A. Cameron and A. Kuhrt, eds., *Images of Women in Antiquity* (London: Croom & Helm, 1983), 223–42. P. Veyne, *Bread and Circus* (London: Penguin, 1976), classes magistracies held by women with those held by children, dead persons, and gods (though this list is not, as it stands, without difficulties).

24. *TAM* II. 1, no. 288 = *IGR* III, 6286–98.

25. A clear example of a family dominant (and holding priesthoods) in generation after generation is provided by the Claudii of Panamara in Caria. These generations can be

Insofar as there is an overall development discernible in the complex history of civic priesthood in the Principate, its rationale surely lies in this fusion of the religious system with the socio-political system, a fusion which served to veil from the central and local elites the true character of their domination. There is a consistent set of attitudes throughout the Empire, despite numerous institutional and detailed differences. The sacrificial system is one of the key links between the imperial system organized at the center and the local control exercised by the local elites at the periphery. Euergetism is the socially responsible use of wealth, and so, as a system, proclaims the necessity of social inequality; the existence of social inequality is a natural phenomenon, because it is based on the distinction, entirely natural, between this world and the other world. Moreover, sacrificial euergetism contributes powerfully to a remodeling of the notion of community in the absence of political structures through which the aspirations of the mass of the population might have been articulated. This process is dynamic: the potentially disruptive consequence of new forms of social power achieved through the wealth (whose accumulation was encouraged by the fiscal system of the Empire) could be absorbed into the status quo through the sacrificial system.[26] The profusion of priestly roles among the non-elite and upwardly mobile — the *vicomagistri,* the *VIviri Augustales* and the innumerable collegiate organizations — may be seen as so many testimonies to the ideological effectiveness of the sacrificial system. In its turn, the part played by the elites, central and local, in the maintenance of the sacrificial system was not disinterested but rather a crucial element in their domination.

---

traced in A. Laumonier, "Recherches sur la chronologie des prêtres de Panamara," *BCH* 61 (1937): 236–98 and *I. Stratonikeia* I, 67; 76; 90.

26. For the important economic role of the fiscal system, see K. Hopkins, "Taxes and Trade in the Roman Empire," *JRS* 70 (1980): 101–25. I broadly support this account, without necessarily believing in the details.

Part III

Paul's counter-imperial gospel

Introduction

> But *our government* is in heaven, and it is from there that we await
> a *Savior,* the Lord Jesus Christ. He will transform the body of our
> humiliation that it may be conformed to his body of glory, by the
> power that also enables him to make all things subject to himself.
>
> (Phil. 3:20–21)

The starting point in recognizing that Paul was preaching an anti-
imperial gospel is that much of his key language would have evoked
echoes of the imperial cult and ideology. The selection by Dieter Georgi
below explores this point with reference to Paul's epistle to the Romans,
the text previously read as a theological treatise about *homo religiosus*
and the supersession of justification by works of the law to justification
through faith — of Judaism by Christianity. By featuring such "loaded
terms as *euangelion* [the "gospel" of the imperial Savior], *pistis* [the
"loyalty" or faithfulness of Caesar/Rome, to be reciprocated by the
"loyalty" of her subjects], *dikaiosynē* [the "justice" imposed by Cae-
sar], and *eirene* [the "peace" or good order secured by Roman conquest]
as central concepts...he evokes their associations to Roman political
theology."[1] Insofar as Paul deliberately used language closely associated with the imperial religion, he was presenting his gospel as a direct
competitor of the gospel of Caesar. Once this is discerned, then other
features of Romans suddenly take on their true political significance,
for example, the introductory creed in 1:3–4 in which Jesus Christ (not
Caesar) is the true king, "designated Son of God in power." "For Paul,
Jesus is what the *princeps* claimed to be: representative of humanity,
reconciler and ruler of the world."[2]

The "imperial" language found in Romans is paralleled and extended
in Paul's other letters. Perhaps the most vivid examples come from Philippians and 1 Thessalonians. Whatever the other connotations (and

---

1. Dieter Georgi, *Theocracy in Paul's Praxis and Theology* (Minneapolis: Fortress,
1991), 83. In a more elaborate and focused study, Stanley Stowers argues that Paul pur-
posely posed his argument in Romans over against the ancient ethic of self-mastery which
Octavian had co-opted in constructing an imperial ideology, with himself as paradigm
(*A Rereading of Romans: Justice, Jews, and Gentiles* [New Haven: Yale University Press,
1994], esp. chap. 2).

2. Georgi, *Theocracy,* 99. Classics scholars such as Keith Hopkins (*Conquerors and
Slaves* [Cambridge: Cambridge University Press, 1978], 199 n. 3) had also noted that "the
parallels between the cults of the emperor and Christ are striking." And Adolf Deissmann
had discussed the parallels some time ago (*Light from the Ancient East* [London: Hodder
& Stoughton, 1910], 346–84 [ET of 4th ed., 1927, 338–78]).

biblical roots) of "salvation" in Paul, his use of *sōtēria* (see 1 Thess. 5:8–9; Phil. 1:28; 2:12; Rom. 1:16; 10:1; 11:11; 13:11) would have been understood as an alternative to that supposedly already effected by Augustus and his successors. The selection by Helmut Koester below explores the skill and nuances by which Paul alludes to and bluntly opposes the "peace and security" that imperial propaganda boasted of having been established for the whole world.

Precisely because he does not elsewhere use the corresponding term *sōtēr* = savior, the pointed employment of the term in an unmistakably political context at the climax of the argument in Philippians 3 (vv. 20–21, cited as the epigraph just above) sharply opposes Jesus Christ as Lord to the imperial savior. Translations and interpretations of the passage have attempted to tone down the implications through devices of individualization ("citizenship") and spiritualization ("heavenly"), but the meaning is abundantly clear once considered in the imperial context. The Philippians would hardly have been unaware that since the battle of Actium they already had a savior who was their lord and that the government of Philippi had long since been established as a Roman colony of army veterans (to which they were subordinate, politically and socially). Philippians also indicates that Paul was not alone in his opposition to the imperial gospel. The portrayal of "Jesus' exaltation and entrance into heaven in the 'pre-Pauline' hymn that he cites in Phil. 2:6–11 must have suggested the events surrounding the [death] of a *princeps* and his heavenly assumption and apotheosis."[3] Paul's borrowing from and allusions to language central to the imperial cult and ideology reveal and dramatize just how anti-Roman imperial his own gospel was.

Surely the most blatantly anti-Roman imperial aspect of his gospel was its focus on the crucified Christ. The selection by Neil Elliott below lays out just how blatant this would have been in the Roman imperial context. Crucifixion, of course, was the distinctively horrendous means by which the Romans tortured to death subject people who resisted the Roman order for its "demonstration effect" on others. Paul refers to this Roman means of terrorizing subject peoples in describing his preaching to the Galatians: "It was *before your eyes* that Christ was *publicly exhibited* as crucified!" (Gal. 3:1). In the long-pacified Greek cities dominated culturally and politically by the philo-Roman elite and their aristocratic values, it would indeed have been "folly" (1 Cor. 1:23) as well as an anti-Roman political statement to proclaim and organize communities around a crucified political criminal as a central symbol. The rest of Paul's fundamental gospel, of course, was that the political insurrectionary crucified by the Romans had then been enthroned as the

---

3. Georgi, *Theocracy,* 72–74.

true Lord of the world and was imminently to return in *the* (eschatological) *parousia* (a reference to an imperial entrance to a subject city). The one crucified by the Roman rulers was now the Lord who would soon subject "all things," presumably including the Roman rulers (see esp. 1 Cor. 15:24–28; Phil. 3:20–21).

Georgi, Koester, and Elliott all indicate that Paul's anti-imperial use of imperial language and symbols is part of his own Jewish apocalyptic background and view of the world. Established scholarly interpretations, however, with their Christian theological perspective and agenda, have obscured the political anti-imperial thrust of Paul's statements, partly because they have tended to follow the deutero-Pauline spiritualization of Pauline language. The first selection by Elliott below takes some crucial steps toward peeling away the deutero-Pauline and subsequent Christian readings that mystify Paul's original anti-imperial gospel. The key passages are 1 Cor. 2:6–8 where, in God's apocalyptic "mystery" (plan), "the rulers (*archontes*) of this age, who are doomed to perish," made the mistake of crucifying "the Lord of glory," and 15:24 where Christ "hands over the kingdom of God to the Father, after he has destroyed every rule (*archē*) and every authority (*exousia*) and power (*dynamis*)."

Apparently out of modern apologetic motives, even advocates of an "apocalyptic" Paul have interpreted the "powers" here in terms of the "anthropological" or "ontological" powers that determine "the human situation" (death, sin, the law, the flesh) prominent in Romans 6–7.[4] In the deutero-Pauline Colossians and Ephesians, "Paul" is made to "pull his political punches" by portraying the now cosmic "rulers" and "powers" as created by a (non-Pauline) preexistent Christ (Col. 1:16; cf. 2:10), over whom he then triumphs in his crucifixion (Col. 2:15; vs. 1 Cor. 2:8; 15:24). The author of Ephesians, apparently grasping the political thrust of Paul's gospel only too well, has "Paul" protest that "our struggle is *not against enemies of blood and flesh,* but against the rulers, against the authorities, *against the cosmic powers* of this present darkness, [i.e.,] *against the spiritual forces of evil in heavenly places*" (Eph. 6:12).

However, as can be seen from Rom. 13:1–3 (on this passage so overlaid by Christian interpretations, see the second selection by Elliott below), by *archontes* (1 Cor. 2:6–8) and *exousiai* (1 Cor. 15:24), Paul has in mind the concrete political rulers and authorities, although the latter passage appears to mix them with the more vague and ab-

---

4. Neil Elliott, *Liberating Paul: The Justice of God and the Politics of the Apostle* (Maryknoll, N.Y.: Orbis Books, 1994), 114–15 (see pp. 176–77 below), in response to J. Christiaan Beker, *Paul the Apostle: The Triumph of God in Life and Thought* (Philadelphia: Fortress, 1980), 189–90, who is heavily influenced by Bultmann's *Theology of the New Testament.*

stract "rule" and "power." As Elliott and others have recently argued, Paul is here rooted in Jewish apocalyptic thinking, which understands current historical struggles as caught up in God's struggle against super-human forces.[5] But that is a religious-theological interpretation of the historical political struggles, not a denial or avoidance of them. And that religious-theological interpretation makes all the difference for Paul. The crucifixion, resurrection, and *parousia* are all significant, historical, *political* events, the first two already having taken place and the third imminent, with obvious implications for the Roman imperial order.

Recent studies of the "social world" of Paul and the "social function" of his apocalypticism perpetuate a depoliticization of his anti-imperial apocalyptic gospel similar to previous, theologically grounded interpretations. Such studies have relied on the "functionalism" that dominated North American social science in the 1950s and 1960s. Taking the dominant political-economic system as a given, this approach focuses primarily on the ways in which sects or cults are "functional" for the system. The most influential construction of the social world of Paul takes "Pauline Christianity" as the "society" or system to be studied, and then finds his apocalypticism functional insofar as it reinforces group solidarity.[6] Paul's "master eschatological picture... both explains present experience and recommends a specific outlook and set of dispositions." Lacking any attempt to ascertain what that "present experience" and "specific outlook" were for Paul and his communities, we are left with only vague generalizations. "The primary function of such doomsday language... is less specific. It reinforces the sense of uniqueness and cohesion of the community."[7] Paul's own apparent reference to being "set free from the present evil age" is reformulated as "evil and its reversal" and discussed in terms taken largely from Colossians and Ephesians, language that "Paul himself rarely uses."[8] Judgment at the imminent "end of the present age" involves the defeat or reconciliation of the "cosmic powers," but apparently not the imperial "rulers and authorities."[9] Correspondingly, although joining the *ekklēsia* meant "replacing other relationships and sources of identity... [and] hostility from the outside society," this "strong social change" was basically "cultic," with no apparent political implications.

Ironically, the "social world" approach, like earlier theological interpretations of Paul's apocalyptic gospel, leaves largely out of account

---

5. Elliott, *Liberating Paul,* 111 = pp. 173–74 below.

6. Wayne A. Meeks, *The First Urban Christians: The Social World of the Apostle Paul* (New Haven: Yale University Press, 1983), 171–90; and "Social Functions of Apocalyptic Language in Pauline Christianity," in David Hellholm, ed., *Apocalypticism in the Mediterranean World and the Near East* (Tübingen: Mohr [Siebeck], 1983), 687–705.

7. Meeks, *First Urban Christians,* 174–75.

8. Ibid., 183–89.

9. Ibid., 184–90.

the wider "social world" in which ancient Jewish apocalypticism was born and "functioned." Like contemporary Judean apocalyptic literature, Paul's letters arose in and addressed an imperial situation. Because of its heavy determination by Christian theology, New Testament studies has usually treated Jewish "apocalyptic" as a system of religious thought. The concept of Jewish "apocalyptic(ism)" that dominates many discussions of Paul is a synthetic construct of features abstracted from a variety of Jewish literature ranging over several centuries. Ironically attention often focuses on what are merely instrumental features in one or two apocalypses (heavenly architecture) or subordinate general features ("cosmic" disturbances when God intervenes in historical affairs). If we instead examine each Judean apocalyptic document as the product of a particular historical situation, then it is evident that Judean apocalyptic literature addresses particular crises in the imperial relations between the dominant empire and Judeans as a subject people.[10]

More precisely, Judean apocalyptic literature such as the book of Daniel, the various sections of 1 Enoch, (layers of) the Testament of Moses, and some of the Dead Sea Scrolls was produced by dissident (or former) scribal retainers of the Judean priestly aristocracy at points of acute crisis in their relationship with the imperial rulers. The Persian imperial regime of the sixth to fourth centuries had apparently sponsored the return of the Judean ruling class to Jerusalem to rebuild the Temple and to consolidate Judea's legal and cultural traditions. The succeeding Hellenistic and Roman empires, however, imposed a policy of cultural as well as political-economic imperialism, encouraging the ruling classes of subject Near Eastern peoples to assimilate into the dominant Greek culture as well as to adopt Greek political forms. This policy placed Judean scribal retainers, the professional guardians and interpreters of the ancestral Judean laws and traditions who assisted the high priestly aristocracy in governing the Judean temple community, in a most difficult situation. When the Jerusalem high priestly rulers moved into close collaboration with the Hellenistic or Roman imperial rulers, even adopting some of the dominant political-cultural forms, some scribal circles felt their own position threatened, along with the traditional way of life.

The best-known case is the crisis that escalated into the Maccabean Revolt in the 170s–160s B.C.E. Leading high priestly families and their allies appeared to "sell out" completely to the dominant imperial ethos, even attempting to transform Jerusalem into a Hellenistic *polis* with its

---

10. The following builds on the analyses of Daniel 7–12, the sections of 1 Enoch, and the layers of the Testament of Moses in John J. Collins, *The Apocalyptic Imagination: The Jewish Matrix of Christianity* (New York: Crossroad, 1984); George W. E. Nickelsburg, *Jewish Literature between the Bible and the Mishnah* (Philadelphia: Fortress, 1981); and Richard A. Horsley, *Jesus and the Spiral of Violence: Popular Jewish Resistance in Roman Palestine* (San Francisco: Harper & Row, 1987), 1–9, 129–46, 157–60.

attendant culture. The scribal-sapiential circle known as the *maskilim,* among others, staunchly resisted the Hellenizing "reform." In the course of their persecution and repression, they received revelations in the form of dreams and interpretations that both explained how history had come to such an acute crisis and reassured the faithful that God would eventually take action to deliver them from this situation that threatened the very survival of the Judean people and its way of life. The resulting literary products of the *maskilim,* chapters 7–12 of the book of Daniel, became the prototypical Judean apocalyptic literature.

The revelatory visions of the book of Daniel and subsequent apocalyptic literature in late second-temple Judea thus address specific crises in the continuing imperial relations between subject people and imperial (and local) rulers, although we cannot always determine the precise circumstances from allusions in the texts. The message or agenda of this literature is remarkably consistent from Daniel to the Testament of Moses and Dead Sea Scrolls. Whatever the visionary elaborations, the basic message focuses on a twofold resolution to the historical crisis: God will intervene to judge the oppressive imperial (and/or Judean) rulers and to restore the people.[11] Closely connected with the restoration of the people is the third main theme in the apocalyptic agenda, the vindication of those (leaders) martyred in the struggle to maintain the traditional way of life. All three principal concerns of such Judean apocalyptic literature appear in sequence at the climax of the revelation in Daniel 10–12: the emperor Antiochus Epiphanes will be defeated, the people will be restored after intervention by the protective angel Michael, including the resurrection of the dead, and the *maskilim* martyred in the struggle against imperial violence will "shine . . . like the stars forever" (Dan. 11:45–12:3). In the close connection between the vindication of martyred leaders and the deliverance of the people, the motifs of resurrection and exaltation vary in their application to the one or the other from text to text.[12] When examined in their concrete historical sit-

---

11. As in traditional biblical portrayals of the divine warrior's action against Israel's oppressors and prophetic portrayals of "the day of the Lord" (e.g., Judg. 5:4–5; Isa. 13:10), God's intervention to defeat the oppressive imperial rulers in apocalyptic literature is often accompanied by disturbances in the cosmic order. Ironically, the latter, which are secondary to the main agenda of God's intervention to judge and restore in Judean apocalyptic literature, have become the focus of the modern scholarly misunderstanding of a "cosmic catastrophe."

12. All three of these principal concerns of Judean apocalyptic literature — defeat of the oppressive empire, restoration of the people, and the vindication of the martyrs — can be seen again at the conclusion of the Testament of Moses. It takes the form of an elaborate assurance to potential martyrs that God will avenge them. "Then God's kingdom will appear throughout his whole creation" as God acts against his people's enemies. "Then you will be happy, O Israel! And you will arise upon the neck and wings of the eagle [Rome?] and they will be brought to an end. . . . And God will raise you to the heights . . . in the heaven of the stars . . . and you will see your enemies on the earth" (Test. Mos. 10).

uations, it is clear that Daniel, Testament of Moses, and other Judean apocalyptic writings were expressions of political as well as cultural resistance to Western empires and the social and political forms that they imposed on subject peoples.

Paul's gospel belongs in this same tradition. The renewal of the people, judgment of imperial rulers, and vindication of martyr(s) that Judean apocalypses placed in the future, however, Paul believed had already been inaugurated and would soon be completed. He gave all three more specific form than in Judean apocalyptic literature, and he gave the renewal of the people a radically new twist that indicates all the more clearly how directly his gospel opposed the Roman empire. In the crucifixion and resurrection of Jesus Christ the promise to Abraham, including that all peoples would receive blessing through him, had been fulfilled. Paul understood this to mean that in Christ all peoples, and not simply the children of Israel, could now become "heirs according to the promise,...adoption as children" (Gal. 3:6–4:7). The implication for Roman rule should be clear in the imperial context. Paul's younger contemporary, client of the Flavian emperors, Josephus, who also claimed to have been a Pharisee, argued in the hindsight of the devastating Roman suppression of the Judean revolt of 66–70 that in God's guidance of history he had granted sovereignty currently to Rome. Whatever his view of history had been prior to this commissioning by Christ in his apocalyptic vision (Gal. 1:15–16), Paul became convinced that God, having focused world history in Israel, had brought it to fulfillment in the crucifixion and resurrection of Christ. Indeed the further international implementation of that fulfillment was underway in his own gospel and mission (Gal. 1:17–2:10; cf. Romans 9–10; 15). History was running not through but against Rome and its empire. "Sudden destruction" was about to come upon the "peace and security" of the Roman imperial order (1 Thess. 5:3). But those who had responded to Paul's gospel, whose *politeuma* was in heaven, had a genuinely secure political future, for God had destined them "not for wrath but for obtaining salvation through our Lord Jesus" (Phil. 3:20–21; 1 Thess. 5:9).

If Paul's gospel was opposed to the Roman empire, however, then how do we account for his apparent endorsement in Rom. 13:1–7? — "Let every person be subject to the governing authorities; for there is no authority except from God, and those authorities that exist have been instituted by God...." Rom. 13:1–7 has been used as a justification for tyrants and a basis for acquiescence in the face of rulers' gross injustice and abuse of their subjects. Such abuse of scripture is rooted in two closely interrelated facets of how the Bible has been understood: as separate individual statements or lessons (or "pericopes") taken out of the context of a narrative or a longer argument, and as the "word of God" abstracted from historical context and directly applicable to any context. An adequate alternative requires the combination of both the recently rediscovered rhetorical criticism by which, in this case, Paul's full argument in Romans can be grasped, and a rigorous quest for the historical context in which that argument can be appropriately understood. In the fourth selection below, Neil Elliott not only provides a review of recent interpretations of Romans 13, but combines rhetorical and historical criticism in a convincing argument for how Romans 13:1–7 can be understood: both in the particular volatile historical context in which Jews were under fire and in the general Roman imperial context in which diaspora Jews such as Philo had developed a certain strategy of coping with hostile imperial authorities in such circumstances. In Judean apocalyptic theology, if God was ultimately in control of history, then God must be at least allowing the current imperial regime to rule. But God was also holding that imperial regime accountable for oppression and injustice. Advocating judicious restraint in certain volatile circumstances did not in any way lessen the general opposition to the Roman imperial regime.

Perhaps the most striking opposition between the imperial gospel and Paul's gospel is their "theology" in relation to politics. The imperial ideology emphasized that Jupiter and the gods had handed power over to Augustus. Paul, by contrast, insisted that Christ was now reigning in heaven and, "after every rule and every authority and power," would "hand the kingdom over to God the Father . . . so that God may be all in all" (1 Cor. 15:24, 28). In the end, no human, including the now exalted Jesus Christ, would have a monopoly on power.

---
eíght

God Turned Upside Down

DIETER GEORGI

Romans: Missionary Theology and Roman Political Theology

Romans, Paul's last extant letter, summarizes his varied experiments, both practical and theoretical, in a single grand outline. It is this outline that he sends to the congregation of Jesus' followers in Rome, both as introduction and as groundwork for his prospective conversation with them. In the first chapter Paul suggests (and states explicitly in 15:20) that visiting Rome would actually run counter to his own principles because a congregation of Jesus' followers already existed there. By insisting on this visit, a "temporary sojourn," Paul violated these principles. In doing so he indicates that this city has a special significance, which makes him not want to bypass it. What could this significance be other than its position as world capital?

Furthermore, every page of the letter contains indications that Paul has very concrete and critical objections to the dominant political theology of the Roman Empire under the principate. By using such loaded terms as *euangelion, pistis, dikaiosynē,* and *eirēnē* as central concepts in Romans, he evokes their associations to Roman political theology. Monuments of this theology were familiar to his contemporaries throughout the Empire, both east and west. And everyone carried the flyers of this ideology about in the form of Roman coins.

All attempts to derive the Pauline use of *euangelion* (gospel) from the Septuagint have failed. The noun does not appear there with the Pauline double meaning, which denotes both the act and the content of proclamation. Nevertheless, in extrabiblical Greek usage the term possesses a dynamic meaning that also embraces content and action. The dynamic tendency finds expression above all in the predominance of the plural. The closest parallel (albeit in the plural) to the Pauline usage of *euangelion* occurs in an inscription from Priene.[1] At the suggestion of the Roman proconsul, this city decided to shift the beginning of the new

---

1. Wilhelm Dittenberger, *Syll.*[3], 458.

year, and thus the installation of all city officials, to September 23, the birthday of Augustus. The shift was made on the grounds that this day had given a new aspect, as it were, to the universe and marked a new beginning for all things.

This savior (*sōtēr*) had above all brought the world peace. But among his other benefactions he also had created an order of fairness in all matters. The variety in this salutary experience is reflected in the spreading of the message of universal salvation like a grass-fire (whence the plural). The Caesar-religion is based primarily on these tidings.

The word *pistis* has been encountered already in Galatians 2 and 3. One can see there that the translation "faith" does not exhaust its meaning. "Faithfulness" or "loyalty," which includes the notion of "trust," comes nearer to the Pauline usage of the term. This more objective sense of the Greek word from Gal. 3:23–25 is maintained in Romans. Rom. 3:3 uses it to speak expressly of God's "faithfulness" or "reliability." I want also to point to the Greek translation of the *Acts of Augustus*. This fundamental gospel of the Caesar-religion speaks of *pistis*. There, in the context of chapters 31–33, which describe universal friendship with foreign powers and rulers, one finds the summary statement that under the principate of Augustus many previously unbefriended peoples "discovered the *pistis* of the Roman people." Beginning in the time of Augustus, *fides*, the Latin synonym of *pistis*, was reassessed and assumed weightier dimensions.

The Caesar represented the *fides* of Rome in the sense of loyalty, faithfulness to treaty obligations, uprightness, truthfulness, honesty, confidence, and conviction — all, as it were, a Roman monopoly. The ancient cult of the goddess Fides was revived under Augustus. It is significant too, in the period of the principate, that the word appears frequently on coins.[2]

The *Acts of Augustus* also speak of *dikaiosynē* (chap. 34) as one of the four attributes demonstrated by Augustus and recognized by law. By decree of the senate and the popular assembly, the attributes were inscribed upon golden plates and presented to the *princeps*.[3] It is also noteworthy that Ovid, describing the dedication of a temple to Justitia,[4] identifies the *princeps* with Justitia.[5] On the whole, however, the Pauline term *dikaiosynē* is derived more from the Jewish Bible. As I have argued

---

2. See also Werner Eisenhut, "Fides," in *Der kleine Pauly* (Stuttgart: Druckenmüller, 1964), 2:545–46; and H. Le Bonniec, "Fides," in *Lexikon der Alten Welt* (Zurich: Artemis, 1965), 969.

3. *CIL,* 9:5811.

4. Ovid *Ex Ponto* 3.6.23–29.

5. "Iampridem posuit mentis in aede suae" ("long ago already he has enshrined her — justice — in the temple of his mind").

elsewhere in discussing Galatians 2, it denotes first and foremost the solidarity of God with mortals.

The peace ideology of the Roman Empire had long been a force in Roman praxis and propaganda. It achieved worldwide recognition in consequence of the miraculous peace established by Augustus. The statistics of *eirēnē* in Paul suggest that he is looking for critical engagement with this ideology. In Romans, the theme of peace plays a more extensive role than anywhere else in Paul (or the remainder of the New Testament): the word *eirēnē* appears ten times, the expression "to have peace" once. There are also many words of related meaning: *dikaiosynē, charis, chara, oikodomē, zoē, elpis* ("solidarity, grace, joy, constructive activity, life, hope").

Almost all the Pauline letters proceed by interpreting in the body of the epistle the traditional formulas or phrases appearing either at the beginning or in the introduction. This is also true in Romans, where the formula is found in 1:3–4:[6]

> ...the gospel concerning [God's] Son, who was descended from David according to the flesh and designated Son of God in power according to the Spirit of holiness by his resurrection from the dead, Jesus Christ our Lord.

The exegete must explain why a text like this should be cited in a letter addressed to the seat of Roman power. The formula, which speaks of the origins and significance of the royal messiah Jesus, reflects the two-phase structure of the biblical law of kingship.[7] More is at stake here than spiritualized religious questions.

In Romans, Paul introduces the figure he considers to be the true king into the kingship debate. The antagonist is not so much the royal messiah of Jewish missionary theology; this figure enters into the picture, but not in any pivotal role. The adversary is rather a different figure, a power that in fact considers itself politically and religiously central, a force that claims universal dominion in the political and social realm but bases this claim on a religion and a theology: the Roman Caesar. Here, in Romans, there is a critical counterpart to the central institution of the Roman Empire. This institution, after all, purported to hold the world together, and even for Jews represented a worldwide society. It

---

6. See the detailed discussion of these verses in Ernst Käsemann, *Commentary on Romans* (Grand Rapids, Mich.: Eerdmans, 1980), 8–11; Ulrich Wilckens, *Der Brief an die Römer* (Cologne: Benzinger; Neukirchen: Neukirchener Verlag, 1978–82), 1:56–61, 64–66.

7. The future king was first declared God's elect by prophetic designation and then, in a second step, adopted as God's son, i.e., enthroned as king. In the case of the kings of Judah, the oracle of the prophet Nathan assumed once and for all the function of prophetic designation. It was interpreted as applying to the entire dynasty — the phrase "from the seed of David" in Rom. 1:3–4.

was a power that in the first century was still looked upon as a savior throughout the world — not only by the upper-class elite but also by a broad cross-section of the lower classes.

Speaking out of the Jesus tradition of Hellenistic Judaism, Paul introduces the Nazarene as the true king in Rom. 1:3–4. But are not his qualifications and the circumstances of his accession rather dubious? By "normal" standards, there is something highly irregular here. Is an element of satire intended? A year before Paul wrote Romans,[8] a change of regime had taken place in Rome under most unusual circumstances. Following the violent death of Claudius, the senate decreed his *consecratio* — i.e., not only his life after death but also his assumption and apotheosis. Among other things, this event evoked the ridicule of Seneca in his satirical *Apocolocyntosis,* "The Pumpkinification of Claudius." Claudius's violent death brought Nero to the throne. But Jesus, too, came to power through a violent death — in this case his own — which was brought about by the Romans.

Paul's use of terminology drawn from the law of royal succession in Rom. 1:3–4 shows that he is making more than a religious claim. The following verse shows that something more is involved than nationalistic Jewish propaganda. Is Paul using the traditional formula in order to support an alternative theory concerning true rulership and the legitimate *princeps?* Is he offering an alternative to the social utopia of Caesarism, with its promise of universal reconciliation and peace as the prerequisite for undreamed-of achievements resulting in unimagined prosperity? Roughly contemporary with Romans are the two fragmentary eclogues of the Einsiedeln Papyrus that celebrate the accession of the young Nero as the beginning of the golden age. Is it Paul's intention to measure King Jesus and his program by this yardstick?

The first step in Paul's exposition of the Christ formula is Rom. 1:5. Here he interprets apostolic preaching as a mission to the peoples.[9] In 1:14, Paul speaks of his obligation to both Greeks and barbarians, a typical formula in Hellenistic propaganda, especially political propaganda, for the unity of the human race. This mission is led by the brush-fire of the good news of Jesus.

---

8. See Dieter Georgi, *Remembering the Poor* (Decatur, Ga.: Abingdon, 1992).

9. By *ethnē,* Paul means all the nations, not simply the Gentiles. I have elsewhere pointed out that even the biblical prophets thought of themselves as prophets to the peoples of the world. Furthermore, when compared with the remaining letter, Rom. 1:5 does not suggest that Paul is using "we" simply to refer to himself. In 1:8–15 and 15:14–32, where he discusses his personal intentions with respect to Rome, he uses the first person singular. Paul stands to gain strong support for his trip to Rome if he can show that his sense of having a worldwide mission is not his own invention but that a mission to the nations is fundamental to the apostolate. Rome, the capital of the world, belongs to everyone; it is certainly justifiable and appropriate that the apostles, who are sent to the peoples of the world, should visit it.

If the terms chosen by Paul for his Roman readers have associations with the slogans of Caesar religion, then Paul's gospel must be understood as competing with the gospel of the Caesars. Paul's gospel enters into critical dialogue with the good news that universal peace has been achieved by the miracle of Actium. This was a prodigious miracle that brought respite and new life to a world tortured by a century of civil war. Even a devout Jew like Philo could celebrate this marvel, secured by the law and might of Rome.[10] The *sōtēria* represented by Caesar and his empire is challenged by the *sōtēria* brought about by Jesus. Like that of Caesar, the *sōtēria* of the God Jesus is worldwide (1:16).

But here I have already come to Paul's next step in his interpretation of Jesus' kingship — his concentration on God's loyalty (*pistis*) as affirmed and expressed in God's solidarity (*dikaiosynē*) with the human race. The good news of Jesus refuses to employ threats and the exercise of power and violence — even the law — as instruments of rulership. According to Paul, the *sōtēria* of the God Jesus has made loyalty a two-way street (*ek pisteōs eis pistin* 1:16): it demonstrates and creates loyalty, but demands loyalty as well (1:16–17).

Sovereignty and Solidarity

In Rom. 5:6–8, Paul gives his interpretation of Jesus' death without reference to any traditional formulas:

> While we were still weak, at the right time Christ died for the ungodly. [7]Why, one will hardly die for a righteous person — though perhaps for a good person one will dare even to die. [8]But God shows his love for us in that while we were yet sinners Christ died for us.

Here he brings the Christ event more distinctly into the realm of sinners. He describes Jesus' association with all humanity as an association with a company of weak and godless sinners. In the language of sin used by scripture and Rom. 1:18–3:20, Christ associates himself with a company of chaotic anarchists and rebels. He becomes a strange first among equals, a very singular sort of *princeps*. The ruler of the world joins company with those in rebellion against him. This claim defies both Jewish and Roman moral principles, not only as phenomena of individual or religious morality, but as phenomena of social and political ethics and administrative efficiency. Romans 5:6–8 turns martyrdom into a death that establishes solidarity with the rebel and the enemy. This view of martyrdom protests the one-sided understanding of loyalty which prevailed in contemporary social and political life. There, loyalty means

---

10. Philo, *Legatio ad Gaium* 143–53.

first and foremost the loyalty of subjects to their rulers. Paul declares
an end to the deadly cycle of power, privilege, law, justice, and violence.

The unilateral preemptive act of Christ brings about the deliverance
of all human beings — not only from sin, but also from the law and the
alienation and corruption[11] brought about by the law.[12] The death of
Jesus establishes solidarity between humanity and God. Yet in 3:27 Paul
can speak of the law in positive terms, as the bar to any kind of privilege.[13] Paul asks: what law really reflects the demand that law should bar
all kinds of privilege? He answers: not a law concerned with works,[14]
which promotes achievement; but the law that is concerned with *pistis,* the loyalty of Christ (described above), the confidence displayed by
Christ in his active engagement with the human condition. Hellenistic
civilization aspired to an ideal of justice that it failed to realize and instead perverted. The confidence of Christ makes this ideal reality. Christ
does not demand renunciation of privilege but bestows and realizes privilege by giving himself freely.[15] Romans 3:31 makes it absolutely clear
that in 3:27–31 Paul identifies God's law and God's fidelity: God's loyalty is God's law; establishment of solidarity with humanity is God's
sovereignty.

Romans 5:12–21 explicates Phil. 2:6–11, Galatians 3, and 1 Corinthians 12. It presents Jesus as the one who through his obedience
became the embodiment of a new and authentic humanity. In this new
humanity justice means participatory solidarity and therein signifies the
sovereignty of all (5:17). This sovereignty is not in obedience to the will
expressed in law but in obedience to the creaturely limitations of human
existence, vulnerability, and weakness.[16]

---

11. Compare Rom. 3:21 with 1:18–3:20, and 5:6–8 with 5:20–21.

12. Including Jewish and Roman law, which supposedly represent law in its "liberal"
and "humane" form.

13. Hellenistic thought, notably since Aristotle, emphasized even more than biblical
thought that the law treats all people the same and renders them equal. Roman law in
particular addressed all without distinction, both subjects and rulers. Roman jurisprudence
required *aequitas,* that is, identical verdicts in identical cases.

14. The genitive in *nomos ergōn* ("law of works"), as well as in the following phrase
nomos pisteōs ("law of loyalty"), is explicative.

15. Romans 3:28 does not speak about human faith but about the loyalty of God and
of Jesus, which irresistibly and irreversibly establishes solidarity with humanity. Romans
3:29 radicalizes the Jewish affirmation that God is one: the God who is one is the God of
all. That is why in the future, too, God will declare God's solidarity with all, including the
Gentiles. This is also the argument of Romans 4.

16. Romans 1:5 and Romans 5 undertake a revision of the concept of obedience, an
attitude in which the Romans were well versed. Romans 6 develops this revision further:
obedience is not an appropriate subordination to the superior authority of rulers and
judges but a responsible reaction to demonstrated solidarity in the surrender of privileges,
rights, and power (see esp. vv. 13, 22). Obedience is thus not a one-way road to subjection
but a confident response to demonstrated loyalty and solidarity.

In Rom. 5:6–11 and 15–21, Paul competes with Augustus and his successors. They were, allegedly, the first among equals, and according to their propaganda, representatives of a new kind of human being. Paul, however, makes Jesus of Nazareth, who accepts death, represent the new humanity. Moreover, Jesus signifies the new world of reconciliation and peace — not as a model of hegemony or authority, but as an exemplar of partnership. He is not a paradigm of the force bound to death, but rather the prototype of a community pledged to life.[17]

Romans 5, to be sure, also uses Jewish ideas (Adam/Christ, etc.). But they have been permeated by Jewish Gnosticism[18] and are intended to compete in a critical fashion with the notions of a new age (*saeculum*) which have been embodied in a single individual, the Caesar. This idea flourished once again during the period of the principate. Romans was written at the very beginning of Nero's rule, when propaganda based on such prophetic and theological speculations, with intense eschatological expectations, enjoyed great popularity.[19] For Paul, Jesus is what the *princeps* claimed to be: representative of humanity, reconciler and ruler of the world. Jesus is all this because he demonstrates the association and identification of God with those in rebellion against God. He represents the weakness of God and thus the dominion of grace, the sole form of dominion befitting both humanity and God. The return of the golden age expected under Nero comes face to face with a humanity whose solidarity is established by Jesus.

It has become commonplace to look upon personal affirmation of faith and affiliation with ecclesial institutions as conditions for receiving the righteousness and reconciliation of Jesus. Romans 5 flatly contradicts any such mindset. Solidarity (righteousness, justice), reconciliation, and peace are *givens,* and they are for *everyone.* They are the reality of Jesus, which applies to the whole world. Here Paul leaves Roman ideas about peace far behind. Despite all the talk about one world united in peace, these ideas are still based on social and geographical boundaries,

---

17. The *Pax Romana* is based on the theory of an eternal Rome, whose foremost representatives are divine and immortal, as well as on the power of the Roman army and Roman money. The result — not only in the view of the rulers — was deliverance from foreign domination and internecine warfare, self-determination, and the freedom to form coalitions with others in a world civilization and world economy that people thought they could enjoy freely but that in fact enslaved them to the principle of achievement and the constraint of possessions. The *Pax Christi* is based on acceptance of human existence with all its limitations and mutual interdependence. *Pax Christi* means the freedom and the surrender of all privileges by everyone. This renunciation of privilege, according to Romans 5, is the true authority which moves and shapes the world.

18. See Egon Brandenburger, *Adam und Christus: Exegetisch-religionsgeschichtliche Untersuchungen zu Römer 5, 12–21 (1. Kor. 15),* Wissenschaftliche Monographien zum Alten und Neuen Testament 7 (Neukirchen: Neukirchener Verlag, 1968), passim.

19. See the Neronian Eclogues of the Einsiedeln Papyrus as well as the first, fourth, and seventh eclogues of Titus Calpurnius Piso.

on superiority and inferiority. They have, in other words, conditions and prerequisites for admission.

In Rom. 8:2, as in 3:27 and 3:31, Paul speaks of the law in positive terms. In the latter he speaks of the law of *pistis*. Here he speaks about the law of the spirit. The hortatory section of Romans (chapters 12–15), like the exhortations of the other Pauline letters, arises from this spiritual law, the law of Christ of Gal. 6:2. This law is not a demand, a norm, or an authority. It is, rather, an environment of loyalty and solidarity, of fidelity and confidence, of spirit and community. Thus the law becomes a prophetic entity, an expression of creative power and imagination. It establishes neither the past nor the present, binding and limiting the future. It opens the future and is a message of freedom.

Chapter 8 speaks of creative freedom in spiritual community, a community that transcends all hard and fast boundaries. This community includes the natural world. For Paul, nature and humanity share a common fate (8:12–30, esp. vv. 18–25). This idea distinguishes Pauline theology sharply from the political theology of Rome. There, nature plays an important role, but it is discussed in idyllic terms.[20] Paul speaks instead of how all creation, including the physical world, groans under the corruption brought about by the collaboration between humanity and the law.[21] For Paul, the difference between humanity and nature is the fact that the latter will come to share in the freedom of creation only in the future, when it is delivered from all the consequences of human depravity. The eschatological freedom envisioned in 8:12–30 is freedom from all dominion, freedom to be children.[22]

The end of the law in the reality of Jesus (10:4) means not only the end of norms but also the end of normative and authoritarian (allegedly protective) power. It also signals the end of the prestige that accompanies this power including the prestige of God.[23] Salvation is opposed to power and authority. The Roman theology of peace, on the other hand, is intimately associated with the restoration of legal authority and power. It promises the revival of institutional and cultic prestige, along with the revival of *auctoritas* (sovereignty). These are the principles that establish and uphold society. In Romans 12, however (recalling and elaborating the image of the body which he applied in 1 Corinthians 12), Paul enlists the idea of peace he has been developing throughout Ro-

---

20. Typical are the eclogues from Virgil to Piso, but see also the *Carmen saeculare* and the odes and epodes of Horace; see Dieter Georgi, "Who Is the True Prophet?" in *Christians among Jews and Gentiles,* ed. George W. E. Nickelsburg with George W. MacRae (Philadelphia: Fortress, 1986), 102–21, excerpted above, chap. 2.

21. Romans 8:18–22, retrospectively summarizing Rom. 1:18–3:20 and 7:7–24.

22. Verses 14–17 and 26–30 provide the essential context for vv. 18–25 and describe proleptically the nature of this eschatological freedom: the freedom to be vulnerable.

23. This is the theme of Romans 9, which speaks of God in terms of despotic capriciousness.

mans to call for a democratized worship closely tied to everyday life.[24] Such worship is not exalted above the ordinary workaday realm like the cream of society. Rather it goes much further: Romans 12 maintains that worship is ethics and that recognition of ethical responsibility is worship. But ethics is not the dictation and regulation of life. It is not a body of commandments and prohibitions, either individual or collective. True ethics means charismatic responsibility in communal interchange and dialogue based on love, that is, in participation inspired by the Spirit.

Paul's treatment of the relationship of Christians to the political and legal authorities is an example of his critical imagination. The period was one of increasing political centralization, and there was a great emphasis on the ideology of Caesar's authority and power. Yet Paul, in this letter to the citizens of the capital, never mentions the *princeps* or the special status of Rome. And in Rom. 13:1–7, he borrows a fragment of Jewish tradition from the republican period. By citing this anachronistic tradition (particularly during this time of increasing centralization), Paul gives the passage a critical slant: he urges decentralization and undermines the ideology that supports the majesty of the state. The summation and interpretation of Rom. 13:1–7 in 13:8–14 makes it clear that political ethics cannot be separated from the ethics of love. The later (largely post-Constantinian) distinction between secular and spiritual, visible and invisible, private and civic, shatters Paul's goal of solidarity and unification. For Paul, eschatology belongs to the present world and the separation of ethics is abrogated. Not just Romans 12–13 (a distinct unit) but the entire letter demands the inclusion of politics in the spiritual realm — never its exclusion.[25]

Romans 14, moreover, gives practical examples for the realization of the solidarity of God in the workaday world. This solidarity appears as a continuous reconciliation between ideological divisions as they manifest themselves in praxis. Paul sees the congregation as pluralistic model-society.

The universality of Paul's vision stands in the foreground once again in Rom. 15:7ff., an undisguised echo of the popular picture of Alexander. Romans 15:3, 5, 7–8 depicts Jesus once more as the archetype of solidarity, overcoming all distinctions of class and system. From Jesus' solidarity with the Jews, Paul deduces the solidarity of Jews and Gentiles. Paul's own mission is a sign of this universal solidarity (15:14–33). His journey to Jerusalem and delivery of the collection are also instru-

---

24. See Ernst Käsemann, "Gottesdienst im Alltag der Welt," *Exegetische Versuche und Besinnungen,* 6th ed. (Göttingen: Vandenhoeck & Ruprecht, 1975), 2:189–203.

25. I have discussed Rom. 13:1–7 in n. 40 of the exegetical notes on the "Theologische Auseinandersetzung reit den Einwänden gegen die Thesen der Bruderschaften" of the Badische Theologische Sozietät in Ernst Wolf, ed., *Christusbekenntnis im Atomzeitalter?* Theologische Existenz Heute 70 (Munich: Chr. Kaiser, 1959), 130–31.

ments of this solidarity. Paul's mission continues and fulfills the mission of Jesus (prematurely interrupted, like that of Alexander). Paul's activity signifies the mission of all the witnesses to Jesus (see also 15:4–6). By completing the unfinished work of Alexander with the help of Jesus' followers in the capital of the world, the Pauline engagement serves the entire human race, including the peoples of the western regions of the Mediterranean, which Alexander never reached.

No exegesis of Romans can ignore the fact that its author was almost certainly a prisoner when he came to Rome, the city where he was to be tried and executed. On the indirect evidence of Acts 28:30–31 and 1 Clement 5, both Paul and Peter were charged and convicted independently of (and probably before) the persecution ordered by Nero. There is no reason to believe that the Jewish charges of desecrating the temple in Jerusalem could have endangered Paul before an imperial court in Rome. A normal criminal charge is out of the question, as is a charge of *superstitio*.[26] The eloquent apologetic silence of Luke, friend to both Paul and the Romans, suggests a different explanation: the *crimen* (*laesae*) *maiestatis,* or treason. The argument employed by Paul in Romans, especially if its protective code is cracked, could easily lead to such a trial and justify a negative verdict. The difference between Paul's arraignment and the later persecutions (and convictions) of the Christians would be that Paul's crime was not passive resistance (refusal to sacrifice to the emperor). Rather, it was an active one, an act of political aggression. This explanation would account well for the apologetic smoke-screen laid down by Luke and the Pastorals (and by the later ecclesiastical tradition). 1 Clement already exhibits this tendency, albeit not so clearly as Luke or the Pastorals. Still, it is noteworthy that 1 Clem. 5:7 uses the phrase *dikaiosynēn didaxas* ("having taught righteousness") to describe Paul's preaching which led to his martyrdom, thereby echoing the theme of Romans. When Luke turned Paul into a religious hero, the fool for Christ was given a belated state funeral. When the victorious wing of the church allied itself with the Caesar, Paul, the rebel for Christ whom Caesar had slain, was consigned to a golden hell. Since that day, has up been up and down been down? Can the gods once again dwell in peace in heaven and rulers stand secure once more upon the backs of their subjects?

---

26. See, e.g., the charges in the Bacchanalia trial of 186 B.C.E. (Livy *Ab urbe condita* 9.2–19.2); see Dieter Georgi, "Analyse des Liviusberichts über den Bacchanalienskandal," in *Unterwegs für die Volkskirche, FS Dieter Stoodt,* ed. Wilhelm-Ludwig Federlin and Edmund Weber (Frankfurt/Main: Lang, 1987), 191–207. Under such circumstances, the judiciary and the police would certainly have investigated the entire Christian community, at least in Rome. There is no trace of such an investigation even during the persecution of 64 C.E.

Imperial Ideology and Paul's Eschatology in I Thessalonians

HELMUT KOESTER

The term *parousia* is used with reference to the coming of the Lord four times in 1 Thessalonians (2:19; 3:13; 4:15; 5:23) and twice in 2 Thessalonians (2:1, 8) — elsewhere in Paul only once (1 Cor. 15:23).

It has been a general assumption that the *parousia* is used as a technical term for the eschatological coming of Jesus or the Son of Man. However, there is no evidence in pre-Christian apocalyptic literature for such technical usage.[1] If there is any "technical" use of *parousia* it appears in the terminology for the arrival of a king or an emperor.[2] In the traditional formula quoted by Paul in 1 Thess. 1:9–10 the term does not occur, although this formula ends with an eschatological reference to the coming of Jesus (*anamenein ton huion autou . . . Iēsoun*).[3] Also elsewhere in 1 Thessalonians, *parousia* is never part of traditional materials used by Paul.

I would therefore conclude (1) that the term *parousia* has been introduced by Paul in this letter, and (2) that it is a political term which is closely related to the status of the community. The traditional formula quoted in 1:9–10 contains elements typical for Hellenistic-Jewish propaganda in which individuals are asked to convert to the true worship of the "Living and True God." But Paul, in his own language, describes the coming of the Lord like the coming of a king or Caesar for whose

---

1. See the frustrated attempt to establish such a technical usage by A. Oepke, *Parousia pareimi*, in *TWNT* 5 (1954), 859–63. The problem is clearly stated by T. Holtz, *Der erste Brief an die Thessalonicher*, EKK 13 (Neukirchen: Neukirchener Verlag, 1986), 119.

2. Oepke, *Parousia*, 857–58; see also LSJ s.v.; especially the references of B. Rigaux, *Saint Paul: Les Épître aux Thessaloniciens*, EBib (Paris: Gabalda, 1956), 198, to the use of *parousia* with respect to the arrival of Demetrius Poliorcetes, Ptolemy Philometor and Cleopatra, and Germanicus.

3. G. Friedrich ("Ein Tauflied hellenistischer Judenchristen," in *TZ* 21 [1965]: 502–16) has attempted to show that Paul is quoting a Jewish-Christian baptismal hymn. Holtz (*Erster Thessalonicher*, 54–62) rejects this hypothesis, but recognizes that the terminology is not Pauline and has parallels in Hellenistic-Jewish conversion language.

arrival the community must be prepared. *Parousia* always occurs in contexts in which the preparedness of the entire community is in view: The community in Thessalonica is the "hope, joy, and crown" in Paul in the *parousia* of the Lord Jesus (2:19). The reference to the *parousia* in 3:13 is preceded by an admonition to mutual love (3:12). In 1 Thess. 4:15, *parousia* appears in a context in which the question of the joint presence of those who are still alive and those who have died is discussed, and 5:23 concludes an admonition to the entire community which speaks of their joint and mutual obligations. Paul's personal role is closely related to this event, because his task is fulfilled and his reward certain, if the community is indeed found prepared when the Lord arrives.

The discussion of the fate of those who have died in 1 Thess. 4:13–18 belongs to this context of community concern. Its topic has often been described as "the delay of the parousia": since Paul was expecting the parousia to occur very soon, he did not say anything about the resurrection of the dead.[4] This is misleading. Neither here nor elsewhere is Paul concerned with this problem. The "recollection of the creed" in 1 Thess. 4:14[5] presupposes that the Thessalonians believed that Christ's dying and rising was the basis for the Christians' hope for the resurrection of the dead. But instead of quoting the expectation of the resurrection in the second part of the formula, Paul alters the sentence: "God will lead through Jesus those who have died with him,"[6] that is, Paul replaces the traditional reference to the resurrection by a statement about God leading the dead with him (namely, Jesus). His concerns here are the concerns of the community in Thessalonica: will those who have died be united with us at the parousia? That this question was raised by the Christians in Thessalonica demonstrates that they had very well understood Paul's message and the aim of his missionary work, namely the founding of communities who are united in their expectation of the arrival of the Lord.

The question discussed here is not a religious question ("Will there be a resurrection of the dead?"), but a communal question: "Will the dead be united with us in order to meet the Lord when he arrives?"

---

4. More recently again W. Marxsen, *Der erste Brief an die Thessalonicher,* Zürcher Bibelkommentare, NT 11,1 (Zurich: Theologischer Verlag, 1979), 63–65; also Holtz, *Erster Thessalonicher,* 205–6.

5. Raymond F. Collins, *Studies on the First Letter to the Thessalonians,* BETL 66 (Louvain: Louvain University Press, 1984), 158. On the complexity of the interpretation of this formula, including its linguistic awkwardness, see Wolfgang Harnisch, *Eschatologische Existenz: Ein exegetischer Beitrag zum Sachanliegen von 1. Thessalonicher 4,13–5,11,* FRLANT 110 (Göttingen: Vandenhoeck & Ruprecht, 1973), 29–36; however, there is no reason for Harnisch's assumption that such interpretation of the traditional formula was directed against Gnostic opponents (37–38).

6. "*Dia tou Iēsou* corresponds to the *dia tou Christou* formula" and "must be taken as a modifier of the verb *axei* rather than as a qualification of the participle *koimēthentas*" (Collins, *Studies,* 159).

The precise definition of the "saying of the Lord" in 4:16–17 can be left aside here.[7] It is important that, in the context of this discussion, another term from the political realm is employed: *apantēsis*. That this term was introduced by Paul and does not belong to the apocalyptic "saying of the Lord" quoted in 4:15–16 has long been recognized. *Apantēsis* is a technical term describing the festive and formal meeting of a king or other dignitary who arrives for a visit of a city.[8] It is the crucial term for Paul's description of the festive reception of the Lord at his coming. The united community, those who are alive and those who have died and have been raised, will meet the Lord like a delegation of a city that goes out to meet and greet an emperor when he comes to visit.[9]

One might argue that "being caught up into the air on clouds" reflects mythical apocalyptic language and is not taken from the realm of political terminology. To be sure the language is mythological. But at this point of his argument Paul does not quote any particular apocalyptic tradition. Rather, the mythological language serves to transcend the horizon of the earthly realm and to describe the eschatological meeting of the Lord in cosmic dimensions.

The apocalyptic tradition, quoted in the preceding verses as a saying of the Lord, implies a specific sequence of eschatological happenings — or has at least been pressed into this service by Paul. However, this sequence of events is not designed to determine the present standing of the community with respect to the apocalyptic timetable. Its only purpose is to argue that, at the parousia of the Lord, the dead will be raised before the *apantēsis*. As the Lord draws near in his *parousia*, the archangel who goes before him like a herald, accompanied by a trumpeter, will effect the resurrection of the dead. If one wants to have a visual image of this event, it may be allowed to draw on archaeology: everywhere in ancient Greek cities, the cemeteries line the main roads leading into the city, often for miles.

Paul had no interest in an apocalyptic timetable per se. All emphasis is put on "being *with* the Lord (*syn kyriō*) at all times" (cf. also *axei sun autō* in 4:14).[10] Paul customarily uses the formula *syn kyriō* to describe the future relationship of the believers to their Lord — al-

---

7. It is clear that apocalyptic traditions are used here; see the discussion in Collins (ibid., 159–62), who points to the freedom with which Paul uses a number of apocalyptic motifs.

8. The decisive arguments for the political use of this term were presented by E. Peterson, "Die Einholung des Kyrios," in *Zeitschrift für systematische Theologie* 7 (1929/30): 682–702; cf. also idem, *apantēsis*, in *TWNT* 1 (1933), 14–15.

9. It is not possible to understand this passage as a statement about the "rapture" of the believers into heaven.

10. The question where the believers will be after this festive meeting of the Lord is unnecessarily speculative. Paul's only interest lies in the statement that they will be "with the Lord."

though *syn* with *christō* or *kyriō* is relatively rare — while the present relationship is called being *en christō*. Thus, the "being *with* the Lord" in 1 Thess. 4:18 seems to point to the future. 1 Thess. 4:13–18 does not obliterate the line between present and future existence.

1 Thess. 5:1 turns to a new topic (*peri de*): the question of the "seasons and times" (*chronoi kai kairoi*). The formulation which says that there is no need to discuss the topic makes it very unlikely that Paul is answering a question addressed to him by his readers.[11] The following, therefore, must be read as a deliberate exposition by Paul that does not have any specific reference to concerns of the readers.

The question is, whether Paul's own arguments begin in 5:2 or in 5:4. If the former, Paul wants to juxtapose the early Christian view of a sudden coming of the Lord that cannot be calculated to a Jewish apocalyptic understanding that tries to reckon the dates and sequences of the eschatological events. However, this explanation is not possible.[12] Both the discussion of the times and seasons and the emphasis upon the suddenness and inevitability are topics of the prophetic and apocalyptic traditions of Israel, and both occur also in early Christian statements. Also the citation of the metaphor of the thief and the reference to the onset of labor that suddenly comes upon a woman with child remain in the realm of traditional apocalyptic language.[13]

But it is difficult to place the slogan "peace and security" (*eirēnē kai asphaleia*) into the context of apocalyptic language. Because parallels in apocalyptic writings are lacking, one usually points to Jer. 6:14: *legontes Eirēnē: kai pou estin eirēnē*; and assumes that Paul has replaced the second *eirēnē* with the synonym *asphaleia*.[14] But nothing else in this context points to a use of Jer. 6:14 or similar prophetic passages. Moreover, the LXX never uses *asphaleia* as an equivalent for Hebrew *šlm*. The reference to traditional apocalyptic materials is thus interrupted by Paul with the phrase *hotan legōsin...tote...*,[15] in order to introduce the slogan *eirēnē kai asphaleia*. What is the origin of this slogan?

It is unlikely that Paul has coined the slogan. The first of the two terms, *eirēnē*, is never used by Paul for the description of a false illusion of peace. The second term, *asphaleia*, never occurs again in the entire Pauline corpus.[16] The term *asphaleia* is missing in the LXX in all of the

---

11. Cf. Harnisch, *Eschatologische Existenz*, 51–54.

12. Ibid., 54–77.

13. On the traditional apocalyptic character of these verses, see also Collins, *Studies*, 163–66.

14. Rigaux, *Thessaloniciens*, 558; Holtz, *Erster Thessalonicher*, 215–16.

15. The construction *hotan...tote* is not unusual in Paul, cf. 1 Cor. 15:28, 54; 2 Cor. 12:10 (Harnisch, *Eschatologische Existenz*, 76 n. 9); for *legōsin* see 1 Cor. 15:12. I agree with Harnisch, "daß Paulus in 5:3 (*hotan...tote*) selbständig formuliert...."

16. In the entire New Testament, *asphaleia* occurs only here and in Luke 1:4 and Acts 5:24.

prophetic characterizations of false security. But it is widely used for the security that is guaranteed by treaties or promises or by strong defenses, like "security of the cities" or "safe conduct."[17] With this meaning, it also occurs in the LXX, especially in 1 and 2 Maccabees.[18] It is a political term.[19] As a political slogan, *eirēnē kai asphaleia = pax et securitas* is best ascribed to the realm of imperial Roman propaganda.[20] If this interpretation of the phrase is correct, it would imply that Paul points to the coming of the day of the Lord as an event that will shatter the false peace and security of the Roman establishment. Of course, such a view is entirely in keeping with older Jewish and later Christian apocalyptic protest against imperial establishments.

On this basis the following discussion of the position of the Christian community becomes much clearer. The Christian community is not one that has to fear the sudden coming of that day.[21] In verse 4, and not earlier, Paul begins with his own arguments concerning the community. The play on the metaphors "night and day" (thief in the night, children of the day, etc.) is rhetorically fascinating. It serves to introduce a new terminology for the description of the community: they are "children of the light."

"Children of light" is certainly not typically baptismal, but can hardly be understood without reference to the Qumran literature.[22] The children of light are the elect people of God who are prepared and ready for the eschatological battle, fighting on the side of God against the kingdom of Belial. That this notion of eschatological battle lies much closer

---

17. See LSJ s.v. §2.

18. E.g., *katoikēsete meta asphaleias epi tēs gēs humōn* (Lev. 26:5; cf. Deut. 12:10); *asphaleia estai en tē emē polei* (Isa. 18:4); about Simon, 1 Macc. 14:37 reports that he forced the gentiles to vacate the acra in Jerusalem and that he placed Jewish soldiers there: *kai ōchyrōsen autēn pros asphaleian tēs chōras kai tēs poleōs*. In his letter to the Jews, Antiochus writes that he found it necessary to provide for the security of all people (*tēs koinēs pantōn asphaleias*, 2 Macc. 9:21).

19. That it can also be used as a legal terminus technicus for "pledge" or "bond" can be left aside here.

20. This suggestion was made by E. Bammel ("Ein Beitrag zur paulinischen Staatsanschauung," in *TLZ* 85 [1960]: 837) but has been largely ignored. Holtz (*Erster Thessalonicher*, 215) takes notice of Bammel's article but states: "Eine kritische Anspielung auf 'das Programm der frühprinzipalen Zeit,' das in der Formel pax et securitas enthalten ist,... liegt jedenfalls kaum vor."

21. There is no indication that it is a polemical discussion which is directed against an attitude of the community in Thessalonica which Paul criticizes; pace Holtz (*Erster Thessalonicher*, 216): "eine allgemeine Stimmung der Sicherheit in diesem Leben, die' Gemeinde bedroht"; and Harnisch (*Eschatologische Existenz*, 80): "die Einstellung gnostisch orientierter Enthusiasten, welche das Telos mit dem Aufstieg des Pneuma-Selbst in die himmlische Heimat bereits erreicht zu haben meinen."

22. For a discussion of the Qumran parallels to "children of the light" and of the relevant older literature on this terminology, see H. Braun, *Qumran und das Neue Testament* (Tübingen: Mohr/Siebeck, 1966), 1: 219–22 and 234 ("Die 'Lichtkinder'... sind eindeutig qumranisch," 221); further E. Lohse, *huios,* etc., in *TWNT* 8 (1969), 359.

to Paul's thought here than some kind of baptismal piety is evident in his subsequent use of the images of the weapons of God.

But before moving to the interpretation of the weapons for the battle of the "children of light," Paul interjects an admonition that is modeled upon traditional apocalyptic calls for watchfulness and sobriety.[23] If the statements about sleeping and drunkenness at night (5:6–8) are not trivialities, they do not speak about the watchfulness required of those who are expecting the "day," but of those who are already now "children of the day." Thus, they underline the position of the community in a realm of realized eschatology. To this extent, the distinction between present and future has been obliterated.

The admonition to sobriety is connected closely with the call for putting on the weapons fitting for the children of light (5:8). There are parallels in the Qumran texts for the use of these metaphors.[24] But Paul's terminology is more directly related to the classical text for this language, Isa. 59:17. Paul was familiar with that passage and drew directly upon it, that is, there are no intermediary stages like a "tradition" or a baptismal liturgy.[25] Like Isa. 59:17, Paul uses only defensive weapons: breastplate and helmet. The latter he connects, like Isa. 59, with "salvation," and adds the word "hope" (*elpis sōtērias*), but in the former he replaces "righteousness" (*dikaiosynē*) with "faith and love" (*pistis kai agapē*). Thus, the triad of Christian virtues, already alluded to in 1 Thess. 1:3, is established as the communities' weaponry for the eschatological battle.

At this point, however, Paul has moved beyond the implications of the traditional apocalyptic language with which he had started the passage. If 5:1–3 seemed to suggest that the "peace and security" of the empire will be shattered by the sudden coming of the "day of the Lord," it is now made clear that, for the believers, "the day" is realized in the presence of faith, hope, and love in the community; these are the weapons in the battle of God. In faith, love, and hope, the "day" becomes a reality in the life of the community. "The children of the day" or "the children of light," in their "work of faith, labor of love, and patience of hope" (1 Thess. 1:3), are the architects of the new eschatological community in which the future is becoming a present reality.[26]

---

23. Parallels are cited comprehensively in Rigaux, *Thessaloniciens*, 563–66, and in most other commentaries.

24. Braun, *Qumran und das Neue Testament*, 222–24; K. G. Kuhn, *hoplon*, etc., in *TWNT* 5 (1954), 297–300.

25. Most exegetes prefer to resort to the hypothesis of intermediary stages; cf. Holtz, *Erster Thessalonicher*, 226; see also the extensive discussion and comparison of all relevant materials in Rigaux, *Thessaloniciens*, 567–70. There is, of course, good cause for the assumption that Paul knew both, the passage from Isaiah as well as traditional interpretations.

26. It should not be overlooked that the occurrence of the triad of faith, love and hope, in 1:3 and 5:8 forms an *inclusio* within the rhetorical structure of the letter.

This elimination of the distinction between present and future is summarized in the enigmatic statement of 5:10. It is useful to state the problems of the sentence before suggesting a solution: (1) While 5:9 recalls the non-Pauline formula of 1:10 (salvation from the *orgē*), 5:10 connects this very closely with the typical Pauline formula of Christ's death and resurrection which had already been used in 4:14. (2) This latter formula is not quoted in full; only the part that speaks about Christ's death (*tou apothanontos hyper hēmōn*) appears. (3) Before quoting the conclusion referring to the life of believers, Paul inserts the phrase *eite grēgorōmen eite katheudōmen*. (4) Paul uses *katheudein* here, as in the preceding verses (5:6–7) where the word refers to physical sleep, albeit metaphorically; but in 4:13–14 he had used the verb *koimasthai* in order to refer to those who have died. (5) The aorist subjunctive *zēsōmen* is ambiguous, because it does not necessarily refer to the future;[27] if Paul wanted to refer unambiguously to the future, he could have used the future indicative.[28]

Solutions to each of these peculiar features have been suggested by various commentators. A comprehensive interpretation which accounts for all the peculiar features quoted above is difficult. I can do no more here than to make a few suggestions for a solution of the enigma. The intimate connection between the emphasis upon the dying of Jesus Christ for us and the preceding statement (v. 9) makes clear that the destination for the possession[29] of salvation has already been accomplished through the death of Christ for us. Salvation from the *orgē* is not, as the traditional formula of 1:10 might suggest, an event to be expected in the future, nor is it an event connected with the believers' future resurrection — thus, there is no mention of Christ's resurrection in 1:10.[30] Paul speaks about the life of all believers in such a way that the salvation is not simply tied to a future eschatological event.

The recipients of this life are characterized by the *eite...eite...* ["whether...or...," NRSV] phrase. One can argue that those who watch are the ones who are still alive and those who sleep are the Christians who have died at the time of the parousia, as most exegetes do.[31] But if this is the meaning of the phrase, why does Paul not use terms

---

27. I assume with most exegetes that the variant readings which bring the verb in the future indicative *zēsomen* and present subjunctive *zōmen* are secondary.

28. For future indicative after *hina* in Paul, cf. 1 Cor. 9:15 (*hina tis kenōsei*); 1 Cor. 13:3 (*hina kauthēsomai*). See BDF §369.2.

29. *Peripoiēsis* must be understood as "possession" (not "acquisition"), see Rigaux, *Thessaloniciens*, 571; Holtz, *Erster Thessalonicher*, 228–29.

30. In 4:14 mention of the resurrection of Jesus is important, because Paul wants to argue for the future resurrection of those who have died.

31. Cf., e.g., Holtz, *Erster Thessalonicher*, 230–31; Marxsen, *Erster Thessalonicher*, 70.

which clearly describe "to be alive" and "to die"[32] as he does in Rom. 14:8? On the other hand, *grēgorein* and *katheudein* cannot simply refer to the physical state of being awake and being asleep.[33] In the preceding verses, both terms had already been used metaphorically; *grēgorein* was equated with *nēphein,* and *katheudein* with *methuein* (vv. 6–8). No reader of v. 10 could have forgotten the metaphorical use of *grēgorein* and *katheudein* in vv. 6–8 where Paul emphasized a crucial distinction of attitudes with respect to the future. Deliberately using the very same words, v. 10 makes this distinction irrelevant with respect to "living with him." Without the intervening verse 8, this would be nonsensical. But verse 8 states why the existence of the believers is no longer dependent upon watching for the "day" that comes like a thief in the night: Those who belong to the "day" have put on the weapons of the eschatological battle — faith, love, and hope. They are no longer subject to the dangers arising from the lack of watchfulness or, vice versa, the catastrophe of "being asleep" or "dying" when the Lord comes. "To live *with* him" (*syn autō zēsōmen*) describes the status of a community that is independent of the eschatological timetable. The terms *grēgorein* and *katheudein* are chosen in verse 10 because Paul does not only intend to say that to be alive or to have died at the time of the coming of the Lord is irrelevant — all will go out to meet the Lord — he also wants to emphasize that the believers' existence is not determined by the watchfulness that is focused on the "day of the Lord."

The concept of a community which realizes the presence of the eschatological future in its *oikodomē* (5:11) and which obliterates the distinctions between being watchful and being asleep, and between life and death, is certainly utopian, especially in its political implications. But that, it seems to me, was exactly what Paul was talking about.

It may be permitted to add a note regarding the notorious question of the "delay of the parousia." It has been argued above that 1 Thess. 4:13–18 is not concerned with the problem of the resurrection of the dead in general — as if Paul had failed to talk about the resurrection because he expected the coming of the Lord before any deaths would occur. It seems to me that it is altogether wrong to assume that Paul began to talk about the resurrection of the dead only later when he realized that the parousia might be delayed and that people were dying. 1 Thess. 5:1–11 makes the existence of the believers independent of the

---

32. For the latter, at least *koimasthai* would have been more in keeping with the terminology used in 1 Thess. 4:13–18.

33. R. Jewett (*The Thessalonian Correspondence: Pauline Rhetoric and Millenarian Piety* [Philadelphia: Fortress, 1986], 190), taking up a suggestion of T. R. Edgar (*The Meaning of "Sleep" in 1 Thessalonians 5:10,* in *JETS* 22 [1979]: 344–49), argues that *katheudein* here must be understood as physical sleep: "Paul did not really intend to support Christian insomnia, so he sought to allay [the] fear . . . that if Christ returns while you are asleep you are irrevocably lost."

eschatological timetable. They are already now the children of light who have put on the armor of God, faith, love, and hope. That the day of the Lord will come suddenly and unexpectedly is not their concern, but will be a disastrous surprise for those who proclaim "peace and security." That the existence of the community had thus been freed from such concerns does not imply that Paul no longer expected the day of the Lord, the raising of the dead, and the coming of the Lord. On the contrary, one could argue that the expectation of the nearness of these events was even intensified in the later writings of Paul. Rom. 13:11–14, using the same terms which were employed in 1 Thess. 5:1–11 (*kairos, ex hupnou egerthēnai, sōtēria, nux, hēmera, skotos, endusasthai ta hopla tou phōtos*) even radicalizes the expectation of the nearness: *nun gar egguteron hēmōn hē sōtēria ē hote episteusamen* (Rom. 13:11). Neither 1 Thessalonians nor Romans was written by someone who was worried about the "delay of the parousia." But both letters base the existence of the community of believers on the statement that they already belong to the "day" in their present existence.

Traditional apocalyptic sequences of events are known to Paul and are presupposed in 1 Thessalonians. Some of these elements are used in order to answer specific questions of the community in Thessalonica. This, however, is done in such a way that the distance between presence and future is made almost irrelevant. Paul envisions a role for the eschatological community that presents a utopian alternative to the prevailing eschatological ideology of Rome. In doing so, he radicalizes traditional apocalyptic topics, ascribing a dignity to the building-up of the community that is equal to the presence of the future in faith, love, and hope. He thus makes traditional apocalyptic postures irrelevant and interprets the situation of the community in a way that even transcends the distinction between life and death.

The Anti-Imperial Message of the Cross

NEIL ELLIOTT

"When I first came to you, brothers and sisters," Paul wrote to the Christians in the Roman colony of Corinth, "I resolved to know nothing among you except Jesus Christ, and him crucified."

It is impossible to exaggerate the importance of the cross of Jesus Christ to Paul. Not only did his encounter with Jesus *as the crucified* generate the revolution in his conviction and action that we customarily call his "conversion," it energized his entire apostolic endeavor. His proclamation in the cities of the Roman Empire consisted in the "public portrayal of Jesus Christ crucified" (Gal. 3:1). The entrance rite of baptism was in his eyes nothing less than co-crucifixion with Christ (Rom. 6:1–5); the common sacred meal, the "Lord's supper," a solemn and public proclamation of the Lord's death (1 Cor. 11:26). The atmosphere of the congregation was to be charged with constant regard for the brother or sister "for whom Christ died" (Rom. 14:15; 1 Cor. 8:11).

As soon as we recognize the centrality of the cross of Christ for Paul, the common view that Paul was uninterested in political realities should leave us perplexed. The crucifixion of Jesus is, after all, one of the most unequivocally political events recorded in the New Testament. Behind the early theological interpretations of Jesus' crucifixion as a death "for us," and behind centuries of piety that have encrusted the crucifixion with often grotesque sentimentality, stands the "most nonreligious and horrendous feature of the gospel,"[1] the brutal fact of the cross as an instrument of imperial terror. If in his theologizing Paul muted or suppressed the politically engineered horror of the cross, then we would have to conclude that Paul himself mystified the death of Jesus, accommodating his "word of the cross" to the interests of the very regime that had brought about that death.

Martin Hengel's study of crucifixion in the Roman world highlights

---

1. J. Christiaan Beker, *Paul the Apostle: The Triumph of God in Life and Thought* (Philadelphia: Fortress, 1980), 207.

its political significance.[2] As a means of capital punishment for heinous crimes, crucifixion was the "supreme Roman penalty," yet "almost always inflicted only on the lower class (*humiliores*); the upper class (*honestiores*) could reckon with more 'humane' punishment" (such as decapitation). Crucifixion was "the typical punishment for slaves," practiced "above all as a deterrent against trouble," the most spectacular example being the crucifixion of six thousand followers of the slave rebel Spartacus in 71 B.C.E. A special location was reserved on the Campus Esquilinus in Rome for the public crucifixion of slaves: Hengel compares it to Golgotha, outside Jerusalem.[3] The Roman lawyer Gaius Cassius explained this use of crucifixion as he pressed in court, in the face of mass protest by people from the lower classes, for the execution of four hundred slaves after their master, the prefect of Rome, was murdered by one of them: "You will never restrain that scum but by terror" (Tacitus, *Annals* 14.42–45).[4]

Only those Roman citizens who by acts of treason "had forfeited the protection of citizenship" might be crucified, but this happened only very rarely. Much more commonly, crucifixion served as "a means of waging war and securing peace, of wearing down rebellious cities under siege, of breaking the will of conquered peoples and of bringing mutinous troops or unruly provinces under control." First among these "unruly provinces," of course, was Judea, where the Romans crucified tens of thousands of Jews. The Roman general Varus put down a rebellion there in 4 B.C.E., crucifying two thousand suspected rebels at once (Josephus, *War* 2.5.1–3). The Roman procurator Felix, confronted by widespread resistance and sporadic guerrilla action in the 50s of the common era, won the hatred of his subjects by indiscriminate mass crucifixions, putting to death "a number of robbers [*lēstai*] impossible to calculate" (*War* 2.13.2: Josephus uses the pejorative term preferred by Rome for its most ungrateful subjects). His successor, Florus, provoked full-scale rebellion first by plundering the Temple treasury, then by suppressing the ensuing (nonviolent) protest with mass crucifixions even of Jews who held equestrian rank as citizens of Rome (*War* 2.14.6–7). During the subsequent siege of Jerusalem, the Roman general Titus crucified as many as five hundred refugees from the city per day, until "there was not enough room for the crosses" outside the city walls (*War* 5.11.1–2).[5]

In the Roman practice, "whipping, torture, the burning out of the

2. Martin Hengel, *Crucifixion*, trans. John Bowden (London: SCM Press, 1977); reprinted with *The Son of God* and *The Atonement* in *The Cross of the Son of God* (London: SCM Press, 1986). Citations are from the reprint edition.

3. Hengel, *Crucifixion*, 125–37.

4. Cited by G. E. M. de Ste. Croix, *The Class Struggle in the Ancient Greek World, from the Archaic Age to the Arab Conquests* (Ithaca: Cornell University Press, 1981), 409.

5. Ibid., 138–42.

eyes, and maiming often preceded the actual hanging."[6] Josephus reported that Titus's troops captured poorer Jews escaping from Jerusalem to seek food outside the walls, and tortured, scourged, and crucified them in the sight of the city's defenders. In one instance they hacked off the hands of torture victims and drove them back, mutilated, into the city to coerce its inhabitants into surrender (*War* 5.11.5).

As Hengel summarizes the point with regard to crucifixion, the chief reason for its use was "its allegedly supreme efficacy as a deterrent." The Romans practiced crucifixion above all on "groups whose development had to be suppressed by all possible means to safeguard law and order in the state."

The brutality of crucifixion was not exceptional in the order established by Rome. The so-called Pax Romana, the cessation of "hot" wars of expansion and competition among military rivals, was celebrated in rhetoric and ritual as a new golden age, the gift of the gods; but it was a "peace" won through military conquest, as Roman iconography clearly shows. The "altar of the peace of Augustus" was placed on the Hill of Mars, god of war. Coins struck under Augustus link the armed and armored First Citizen with Pax, goddess of peace, trampling on the weapons of subdued enemies, and Victoria, goddess of conquest, treading upon the globe itself.[7]

Most of our literary sources for this period, coming from the hands of the upper classes, who benefited from the "sheer rapacity" of an empire that "plundered the provinces on a vast scale,"[8] speak of the arrangement in the most admiring terms. "Not surprisingly, the imperial regime was hardly legitimate in the eyes of the conquered."[9] The last point bears emphasis. In a speech put on the lips of a Briton by the Roman historian Tacitus:[10]

> Harriers of the world, now that earth fails their all devastating hands they probe even the sea; if their enemy has wealth, they have greed; if he is poor, they are ambitious; East and West have glutted them; alone of mankind they behold with the same passion of concupiscence waste alike and want. To plunder, butcher, steal, these things they misname empire; they make a desolation and call it

---

6. Beker, *Paul the Apostle,* 206 (citing Josephus, *War* 5.44.9).

7. A less enchanted view of the Pax Romana comes from the Marxist historian de Ste. Croix. The cessation of war was "made inevitable by the exhaustion of Italian manpower...too many Italians had been fighting for too long" (*Class Struggle in the Ancient Greek World,* 358).

8. Ibid., 355.

9. Richard A. Horsley, *Jesus and the Spiral of Violence: Popular Jewish Resistance in Roman Palestine* (San Francisco: Harper & Row, 1987), 20–29; he cites Dom Helder Camara, *Spiral of Violence* (London: Sheed & Ward, 1971), 29–31.

10. Klaus Wengst, *Pax Romana and the Peace of Jesus Christ,* trans. John Bowden (Philadelphia: Fortress, 1987), 52–53.

peace. Children and kin are by the law of nature each man's dearest possessions: they are swept away from us by conscription to be slaves in other lands; our wives and sisters, even when they escape a soldier's lust, are debauched by self-styled friends and guests: our goods and chattels go for tribute; our lands and harvests in requisitions of grain; life and limb themselves are used up in levelling marsh and forest to the accompaniment of gibes and blows. Slaves born to slavery are sold once for all and are fed by their masters free of cost; but Britain pays a daily price for her own enslavement, and feeds the slavers.

And again, a Judean voice, the seer of 4 Ezra describing a vision in which a lion (the messiah) addresses the Roman eagle:

Are you not the one that remains of the four beasts which I had made to reign in my world, so that the end of my times might come through them? You, the fourth that has come, have conquered all the beasts that have gone before: and you have held sway over the world with much terror, and over all the earth with grievous oppression; and for so long you have dwelt on the earth with deceit. And you have judged the earth, but not with truth; for you have afflicted the meek and injured the peaceable: you have hated those who tell the truth, and have loved liars; you have destroyed the dwellings of those who brought forth fruit, and have laid low the walls of those who did you no harm. And your insolence has come up before the Most High, and your pride to the Mighty One. And the Most High has looked upon his times, and behold, they are ended, and his ages are completed! Therefore you will surely disappear, you eagle...so that the whole earth, freed from your violence, may be refreshed and relieved, and may hope for the judgment and mercy of him who made it.

The "peace" that Rome secured through terror was maintained through terror,[11] through slavery, fed by conquest and scrupulously maintained through constant intimidation, abuse, and violence;[12] through the ritualized terror of gladiatorial games, where the human refuse of empire — captives of war, condemned criminals, slaves bought for the arena — were killed in stylized rehearsals of conquest, their fate decided by the whim of the empire's representatives;[13] through the pomp

---

11. Horsley, *Jesus and the Spiral of Violence*, 29.

12. See K. R. Bradley, *Slaves and Masters in the Roman Empire: A Study in Social Control* (New York: Oxford University Press, 1987); Orlando Patterson, *Slavery and Social Death: A Comparative Study* (Cambridge: Harvard University Press, 1982).

13. The standard reference is L. Robert, *Les gladiateurs dans l'Orient grec* (Paris: Champion, 1940).

of military processions, which often culminated in the execution of vanquished captives;[14] and on the ideological plane, through imperial cult
and ceremonial, the rhetoric of the courts (where the torture of slaves
was a routine procedure for gathering evidence), and an educational
system that rehearsed the "naturalness" of Rome's global hegemony.[15] It
was within this civilization of terror that crucifixion played its indispensable role. Among the massive applications of force were the enslavement
of 150,000 Epirots in 167 B.C.E. and the destruction of Corinth in
146 B.C.E., to which we should add the best documented case, the suppression of Judea in 66–73 C.E.[16] Acts of exemplary violence such as
crucifixion make large-scale social control possible.

The Political Character of Jesus' Death

Paul's letters show little interest in recounting the words or deeds of
Jesus. Of course, since these letters are written to already established
congregations, we should not assume that they reproduce either the content of Paul's initial proclamation, the "teaching" or "traditions" he has
handed on, or the extent of his knowledge of the Jesus tradition (with
which he may be more familiar than his few explicit citations would suggest).[17] We should nevertheless take seriously Paul's declaration that he
sought to know "only Jesus and him crucified" among the Corinthians
(1 Cor. 2:2).

In his letters Paul does not rehearse the historical course that led Jesus
to the cross. But that does not mean that he was unaware of, or uninterested in, the historical causes of Jesus' death. Comparing Paul and
the Gospels on this point can be misleading. Paul may be less interested
than the Evangelists in recounting the words and deeds of Jesus because
he does not share their need, in the wake of the Judean war, to provide Jesus with a dramatically messianic past.[18] He is, rather, concerned
constantly to stir up among his congregations a fervent expectancy of

---

14. See Paul Duff, "Processions," *Anchor Bible Dictionary,* vol. 5, ed. David Noel
Freedman (New York: Doubleday, 1992), 469–93.

15. See de Ste. Croix's discussion of "Class Struggle on the Ideological Plane," in *Class
Struggle in the Ancient Greek World,* chap. 7; on the emperor cult, Duncan Fishwick, "The
Development of Provincial Ruler Worship in the Western Roman Empire," *ANRW* II:16:2,
ed. H. Temporini and W. Haase (Berlin and New York: de Gruyter, 1972ff.), 1201–53.

16. De Ste. Croix, *Class Struggle in the Ancient Greek World,* 344.

17. Paul refers rather frequently to the "teaching" he expects Christians to remember
and hold fast to (*tēn didachēn,* Rom. 16:17; *typon didachēs,* Rom. 6:17; *tas paradoseis,*
1 Cor. 11:2; *ton logon akoēs tou theou,* 1 Thess. 2:13). For a concise discussion of Paul's
contact with the Jesus tradition, see Joseph A. Fitzmyer, *Paul and His Theology: A Brief
Sketch* (Englewood Cliffs, N.J.: Prentice-Hall, 1989), 32–34, and the bibliography there.

18. Paula Fredriksen, *From Jesus to Christ* (New Haven: Yale University Press, 1988),
chaps. 3, 9.

the Messiah's future (see Rom. 8:18–25; 1 Cor. 15:59–58; 1 Thess. 5:1–11).

In contrast to the Gospels, Paul is content to say no more about Jesus than that he was "obedient," and that this obedience was the cause of his death, which Paul specifies was by crucifixion (Phil. 2:6–8). The obedience of the one equal to God (2:6) consists not simply in becoming human, but in taking a particular place within humanity, as a slave (2:7); not simply in taking on mortality, but in being so humbled as to accept the most humiliating of deaths, the form of execution reserved for slaves under Roman rule, crucifixion (2:8).[19] That very emphasis on the manner of Jesus' death, shameful and horrific, yes, but also unavoidably political in its connotations, stands in sharp tension with the view that Paul sought to obscure or mystify Jesus' death. The cross was for Paul the signature in history of the forces that killed Jesus.

Nevertheless, "Paul appears totally uninterested in tracking down and identifying the villains responsible for Jesus' crucifixion, nor does he offer any historical reasons why they did it."[20] There are only two possible exceptions to this statement: 1 Thess. 2:15–16, where "the Jews" are blamed for killing "the Lord Jesus," a passage rightly regarded as an interpolation made by a Christian scribe in the wake of the Judean war, and 1 Cor. 2:8, where Paul writes that "the rulers [*archontes*] of this age" crucified "the Lord of glory." Since this latter passage might be the only place in Paul's letters where he alludes to the human actors in Jesus' death, it clearly merits our attention.

Just what does Paul mean by the phrase "the rulers of this age"? Unfortunately, this is one of many places where the apostle's style is abrupt and elliptical. To make matters more complicated, he uses a term, *archōn,* that can have a range of meanings in classical and koine Greek. Although elsewhere in the New Testament *archontes* refers straightforwardly to human rulers,[21] the word could also refer to superhuman beings (e.g., the angelic "princes" behind the Persian and Greek empires in Dan. 10:13, 20).

It is evident from the immediate context, however, that Paul is not interested in examining political tensions in Judea or the vicissitudes of Pilate's career some two decades earlier. *The context of his interpretation of Jesus' crucifixion is the mythic symbolism of the Jewish*

---

19. Ernst Käsemann, "The Saving Significance of Jesus' Death in Paul," *Perspectives on Paul* (Philadelphia: Fortress, 1971), 36; see now the discussion in N. T. Wright, *The Climax of the Covenant* (Minneapolis: Fortress, 1992), chap. 4.

20. Charles B. Cousar, *A Theology of the Cross: The Death of Jesus in the Pauline Letters* (Minneapolis: Fortress, 1990), 26.

21. Luke 23:13, 35; 24:20; Acts 4:8–10, 26; 13:27–28; John 7:26. See Walter Wink, *Naming the Powers* (Philadelphia: Fortress, 1984), 40.

apocalypses. In the cross of Jesus, the Wisdom of God decreed "before the ages" (2:7) has confounded the rulers of this age who are being destroyed (*katargoumenōn*, 2:6). The terms used here are echoed in the prophecy at the end of 1 Corinthians: At the end, Christ will "deliver the kingdom to God the Father after destroying every rule and authority and power" (15:24). The parallelism, including both the verb "destroy" (*katargoumenōn*, 2:6; *katargēsē*, 15:24) and the related nouns "rulers" (*archontes*, 2:8), "rule" (*archē*), "authority" (*exousia*), "power" (*dynamis*, 15:24), suggests that "the rulers of this age" in 2:8 should be taken to include potentially "every rule and authority and power" that remains hostile to God (as Death is "the last enemy," 15:26). Further, the language echoes the apocalyptic vocabulary of the book of Daniel, where we are told that God disposes "rule" (*archē*), "sovereignty" (*basileia*), "power" (*ischys*), "honor" (*timē*), and "glory" (*doxa*) to the rulers of earth (2:37, Septuagint), until at the end God establishes a kingdom (*basileia*) that will "shatter and bring to an end" all the other kingdoms of the earth (2:44).

Earlier scholarship, heavily influenced by the "religio-historical school," tended to find 1 Corinthians saturated with gnostic motifs; the "rulers of this age" were set within a gnostic scheme of supernatural powers through which a "redeemer" would descend to bring salvation.[22] More recent scholarship has decisively criticized this interpretation, however, pointing out that the construct of a pre-Christian gnostic redeemer myth is a retrojection into the time of Paul of a pattern that first appears in gnostic literature a century or more later, a pattern often dependent on Paul's letters.[23] Recent studies of 1 Corinthians 2 tend to set Paul's language within the conceptual world of Jewish end-time speculations, seeing "the wisdom of God as an apocalyptic

---

22. Bultmann sees in the passage an allusion to the gnostic redeemer myth (*Theology of the New Testament* [New York: Scribner's, 1951], 1:175, 181). See also H. Conzelmann, *First Corinthians*, Hermeneia (Philadelphia: Fortress, 1975), 61; Gerhard Delling, "*archōn*," *Theological Dictionary of the New Testament*, ed. Gerhard Kittel, trans. G. W. Bromiley (Grand Rapids: Eerdmans, 1964), 1:488–89; Martin Dibelius, *Die Geisterwelt im Glauben des Paulus* (Göttingen: Vandenhoeck & Ruprecht, 1909), 89 (cited by Wink, *Naming the Powers*, 40).

23. C. Colpe, *Die religionsgeschichtliche Schule: Darstellung und Kritik ihres Bildes vom gnostischen Erlösermythus* (Göttingen: Vandenhoeck & Ruprecht, 1961); a similar presentation in English, depending in part on Colpe's work, is Edwin Yamauchi, *Pre-Christian Gnosticism: A Survey of the Proposed Evidences* (Grand Rapids: Eerdmans, 1973); and now see Simone Pétrement, *A Separate God: The Christian Origins of Gnosticism,* trans. Carol Harrison (San Francisco: Harper San Francisco, 1990). Birger Pearson's demonstration that Paul used terms like *pneumatikoi* and *psychikoi* differently from later Gnostics was also decisive in undermining the "Gnostic" interpretation of 1 Corinthians: see *The Pneumatikos-Psychikos Terminology in I Corinthians: A Study in the Theology of the Corinthian Opponents of Paul in Its Relation to Gnosticism* (Missoula: Scholars, 1973).

power."[24] Indeed, this passage is one of the most important evidences of Paul's apocalypticism in his letters.[25]

"Apocalypticism" is, of course, another scholarly construct, and its precise definition in relation to the ancient sources continues to attract debate.[26] It is sufficient for our purposes to observe the symmetrical language in 1 Corinthians 2 and 15, the characteristic apocalyptic tendency to "view reality on two levels: behind the events of human history lies the cosmic struggle of God with the forces of evil." The references to "the rulers of this age" or to "rules, authorities, powers" reveal that *Paul experiences the present time as under the dominion of evil rulers.* That Paul describes the rulers as "being destroyed" (*katargoumenōn,* 2:6) shows that Paul sees in the cross the beginning of the destruction of the evil powers — but only its beginning. When Paul refers at "the climax of the whole letter" to every rule and authority and power being destroyed and all things being subjected to the Messiah, it is clear that Paul looks forward to the completion of God's victory in the imminent future.[27]

Recognizing that Paul conceives Jesus' death as the decisive event in a cosmic struggle may disappoint our sense of history. After all, other writers in Paul's age could describe Pilate's savagery in Judea in journalistic detail. For Paul, however, Pilate's individuality seems to have dissolved within the apocalyptic category of "the rulers of this age."

But this hardly means that Paul has softened the political force of the crucifixion.[28] Two illuminating comparisons are at hand in the writings of Paul's near contemporaries, Philo of Alexandria and Flavius Josephus, both Jews. When in his *Embassy to Gaius* Philo described Pontius Pilate as "naturally inflexible, a blend of self-will and relentlessness," guilty of "briberies, insults, robberies, outrages and wanton injuries, executions

---

24. See E. Elizabeth Johnson, "The Wisdom of God as Apocalyptic Power," in *Faith and History: Essays in Honor of Paul W. Meyer,* ed. John T. Carroll, Charles H. Cosgrove, and E. Elizabeth Johnson (Atlanta: Scholars, 1990), 137–48.

25. Judith Kovacs, "The Archons, the Spirit, and the Death of Christ: Do We Really Need the Hypothesis of Gnostic Opponents to Explain 1 Cor. 21:6–16?" in *Apocalyptic in the New Testament: Essays in Honor of J. Louis Martyn,* JSNT Supplement 24, ed. Joel Marcus and Marion L. Soards (Sheffield: JSOT Press, 1989).

26. See Paul D. Hanson, A. Kirk Grayson, John J. Collins, and Adela Yarbro Collins, "Apocalypses and Apocalypticism," *Anchor Bible Dictionary,* 1:279–82. For issues in recent scholarship see the essays in John J. Collins, ed., *Apocalypse: The Morphology of a Genre, Semeia* 14 (1979); David Hellholm, ed., *Apocalypticism in the Mediterranean World and the Near East: Proceedings of the International Colloquium on Apocalypticism, Uppsala, August 12–17, 1979* (Tübingen: Mohr-Siebeck, 1983); Adela Yarbro Collins, *Early Christian Apocalypticism: Genre and Social Setting, Semeia* 36 (1986); and a judicious synthesis, John J. Collins, *The Apocalyptic Imagination: An Introduction to the Jewish Matrix of Christianity* (New York: Crossroad, 1987).

27. Kovacs, "Archons, the Spirit, and the Death of Christ," 224–25.

28. Jon Sobrino discusses the tension between the "eschatologization" of Jesus' death and its historical significance as a death taking place among the poor: *Jesus in Latin America* (Maryknoll, N.Y.: Orbis, 1987), 39–40.

without trial constantly repeated, ceaseless and supremely grievous cruelty" (301–2), he took care to point out that Pilate's brutality violated the intentions of Tiberius, who had instructed his procurators to "speak comfortably to the members of our nation in the different cities" and to regard Jews and their customs with respect (161). Philo reserved the greatest praise for Tiberius's predecessor, "who first received the title of Augustus for his virtue and good fortune, who disseminated peace everywhere over sea and land to the ends of the world" (310). The point of Philo's argument is that even the barbarities of a renegade officer like Pilate did not come near the horror Gaius proposed to inflict on the Jews when he ordered that his statue be erected within the Temple itself. Thus Philo can contrast the depradations of Pilate, which he attributes to grave personal defects, to the benevolent policies of the preceding Caesars. His rhetoric suggests that Philo is prepared, of necessity, to make peace with the Roman order, so long as the excesses of a Pilate or a Gaius are curtailed.

In recounting Pilate's massacre of Jews protesting his expropriation of Temple funds for a building project, Flavius Josephus restricts his moral judgments to noting that Pilate's soldiers "inflicted much harder blows than Pilate had ordered" (*Antiquities* 18:60–62). When he relates the crucifixion of Jesus, apparently because he is aware that "the tribe of the Christians" persists in his own day, he is satisfied to note that Pilate condemned Jesus "on the accusation of men of the highest standing among us" (18:63–64); no questions of justice disturb the account. Pilate's massacre of Samaritan villagers in Tirathana was answered by an embassy from the council of the Samaritans to Vitellius, governor of Syria, accusing Pilate of slaughtering refugees, not suppressing rebels. Vitellius sent Pilate to Rome to answer the charges, but Tiberius died before he could hear the case; Josephus shows no interest in pursuing the matter further (18:85–89). Josephus's concern in this section of the *Antiquities* is to emphasize the unscrupulous violence of Jewish agitators, motivated by personal greed, who infected Judea with perversely revolutionary sentiments and thus invited disaster throughout the decades leading up to the war (*Antiquities* 18:6–10); he is not prepared to question Roman policy in Judea.[29]

Neither writer impugns the legitimacy of Roman order as such. Paul

---

29. Between his accounts of these incidents in Judea and Samaria, Josephus narrates two "scandals" in Rome that reveal a similar disposition toward Roman order. First, a senator's wife was seduced with the connivance of the staff at a temple of Isis; Tiberius crucified the temple staff and the maidservant of the seduced woman but banished the seducer (who was after all a Roman citizen). "Such," Josephus concludes, "were the insolent acts of the priests in the temple of Isis" (18:65–80). Again, when another senator's wife was bilked by Jewish conmen, Tiberius exiled the whole Jewish population of Rome, impressing four thousand able-bodied Jewish men into a military campaign on Sardinia — to suppress popular "brigandage," Suetonius tells us (*Tiberius* 36) — and "punishing"

shows no such reserve, however. The crucifixion of Jesus is not for him an instance of official misconduct, a miscarriage of Roman justice. It is an apocalyptic event. It reveals "the rulers of this age," indeed "every rule and authority and power" — procurators, kings, emperors, as well as the supernatural "powers" who stand behind them — as intractably hostile to God and as doomed to be destroyed by the Messiah at "the end." Jesus' crucifixion "is the crux of God's plan for unmasking and overthrowing the powers of this world."[30]

Paul's view of the cross of Jesus is certainly informed by the symbolism of Jewish apocalyptic mythology. But it would miss the point to set this symbolic background over against the "naked facts of history," as if these were available to the impartial observer. If there were a position of neutral objectivity from which the violence of the cross might have been regarded, neither Paul nor Philo nor Josephus was apparently able to find it. Rather, we should compare Paul's apocalyptic interpretation of the cross with other interpretations of violence in Judea that acknowledge, however subtly, the legitimacy of Roman rule implicit in the mythology of empire. We should marvel, not that Paul can speak of his "word of the cross" without specifically identifying Pilate, but that his indictment goes beyond Pilate to include all the powers of heaven and earth together that stand hostile to God. Nevertheless, the reference to crucifixion prevents this symbolic interpretation of Jesus' death from losing its moorings in history and becoming a strictly otherworldly drama.

Far from "denationalizing" the cross, Paul has, so to speak, internationalized it. He insists that the Roman colonists of Corinth, thousands of miles from the troubles in Judea, must mold their lives into a constant remembrance of one particular crucifixion in Judea, because through that crucifixion God has revealed the imminent end of the Powers and has begun to bring "the scheme of this world" to an end (1 Cor. 7:31).

Paul and "the Powers"

The political force of the "word of the cross" could hardly be announced more powerfully. If we are unaccustomed to perceiving this force, part of the reason may be that it has occasionally been blunted by scholarship. Interpreters have often slighted these passages from 1 Corinthians as "less central" to Paul's thought than the more "anthropological" or "existential" understanding of what Bultmann called "the

---

any who refused; this, Josephus concludes, resulted from "the wickedness of four men" (18:81–84).

30. Robert Hamerton-Kelly, *Sacred Violence: Paul's Hermeneutics of the Cross* (Minneapolis: Fortress, 1992), 82.

powers of this age: Law, Sin, and Death," as these appear in Romans 5–8.[31]

Even when Paul's thought is construed as genuinely apocalyptic, however, interpretation may slight the global horizon of God's struggle against the Powers as we find it in 1 Corinthians 2 and 15. J. Christiaan Beker, an advocate of an "apocalyptic Paul," has distanced Paul from the mythology of the apocalypses and emphasized his "transformation" of Jewish apocalyptic. Beker observes, first, that Paul "does not engage in apocalyptic timetables, descriptions of the architecture of heaven, or accounts of demons and angels; nor does he take delight in the rewards of the blessed and the torture of the wicked." Second, he asserts that even when "traditional apocalyptic terminology" does appear (in Rom. 8:38–39, 1 Cor. 2:6–8, and 15:24–28), Paul uses these motifs only "sparingly" and interprets them "anthropologically." Thus "the major apocalyptic forces are, for him, those ontological powers that determine the human situation," that is, "the 'field' of death, sin, the law, and the flesh" that figure in Romans 6–7. Beker finds Paul's own apocalyptic interpretation of the cross more in the latter texts than the former, and consequently writes that "the death of Christ now marks the defeat of the apocalyptic power alliance."[32]

But Paul never declares that the existential powers of sin, death, or the Law have been defeated. He says rather that those who are "in Christ" are no longer to let sin rule as lord over them, not because sin has ceased to exist as a power, but because Christians have "died to sin" (Rom. 6:2, 6). Similarly, Christians are "free from the Law," not because the Law has ceased to be valid (to the contrary, as Paul insists in Rom. 3:31; 7:12, 22, 25!), but because Christians have "died with regard to the law" (Rom. 7:1, 4).[33] Further, Paul clearly affirms that the cosmic power of death remains unconquered (1 Cor. 15:26). If for Paul the field of cosmic powers opposed to God "operates as an interrelated whole . . . no power can be viewed in isolation from the others," the powers continue as active and insubordinate to God, although (with the exception of death) they no longer have any dominion over the Christian.

Moreover, even when Paul does use more "traditionally apocalyptic" language, he clearly insists that the Powers remain unconquered (1 Cor. 15:24). This insistence plays an important role in Paul's argument in

---

31. Bultmann, *Theology of the New Testament*, 1:298. Bultmann and his followers also insisted that Paul's theology of the Powers in 1 Corinthians 2:6–8 was both uncharacteristic of the apostle's own thought and completely separate from the "word of the cross," which represented the genius of Paul's theology in demythologizing apocalyptic and gnostic mythologies into "believing self-understanding" (ibid., 1:293).

32. Beker, *Paul the Apostle*, 189–90.

33. On the translation of the dative (*tō nomō*) see Neil Elliott, *Rhetoric of Romans: Argumentative Constraint and Strategy and Paul's Debate with Judaism* (Sheffield: Sheffield Academic Press, 1990), 243–45.

1 Corinthians.[34] It is not clear, therefore, why the apocalyptic conception so important in one letter (1 Corinthians) should be subordinated to the so-called anthropological categories of another (Romans). Indeed, it appears arbitrary to declare that the Powers as understood in 1 Corinthians have in fact been "reinterpreted" as the Powers of Romans, and on this basis to conclude — contrary to the intention of 1 Corinthians 15 — that Paul understands the Powers to have been decisively defeated; how much more arbitrary to support this judgment with texts from the pseudo-Pauline Colossians and Ephesians![35]

It may be to the point here to observe that what Beker describes as "traditional apocalyptic elements" do in fact appear in Paul's letters, although they are not emphasized. The "word of the Lord" in 1 Thessalonians 4 is a rudimentary "apocalyptic timetable," complete with archangel's trumpet. The "architecture of heaven" can hardly have been unknown to someone who had been caught up to "the third heaven" (2 Cor. 12:2), who refrains from describing "visions and revelations" only because their content is unutterable (12:5).[36] Finally, Paul is evidently comfortable with judgment according to works (Rom. 2:6–11) and divine recompense for the wicked (Rom. 2:5; 12:19–20).[37] The net result of these observations is to situate Paul's thinking even more within the apocalyptic tradition. There is no good reason to marginalize the clearly apocalyptic viewpoint of 1 Corinthians 2 and 15 within Paul's thinking.[38]

Our unfamiliarity with "God's war of liberation" as a Pauline theme may also result from the way Colossians and Ephesians have shaped our perception of Paul's theology of the Powers. The pseudo-Pauline letters already began to modify Paul to serve the churches' agenda in the post-apostolic period, and to an extent to accommodate the word of the cross to the interests of empire. In the ears of the Roman dynasts of ancient Corinth, talk of Christ's having already defeated the powers would have seemed "a pleasantly harmless" myth; one can almost hear their collective sigh of relief at the Christian reassurance that "our struggle is not against human beings."[39]

---

34. Beker, *Paul the Apostle*, 168.

35. Beker declares that "the author of Colossians interprets Paul correctly on this point," citing Col. 2:15 and Eph. 1:20–22 (ibid., 190.)

36. On Paul's visionary experience see James D. Tabor, *Things Unutterable: Paul's Ascent to Paradise in Its Greco-Roman, Judaic, and Early Christian Contexts* (Lanham, Md.: University Press of America, 1986); Alan F. Segal, *Paul the Convert: The Apostolate and Apostasy of Saul the Pharisee* (New Haven: Yale University Press, 1990), chap. 2.

37. Klyne Snodgrass, "Justification by Grace — to the Doers: An Analysis of the Place of Romans 2 in the Theology of Paul," *NTS* 32 (1986): 72–93.

38. Kovacs, "Archons, the Spirit, and the Death of Christ," 224–25.

39. De Ste. Croix, *Class Struggle in the Ancient Greek World*, 432 (on the language of the Magnificat).

This is not Paul's theology of the Powers as it appears in 1 Corinthians. I want to stress the following differences between Paul's
theology of the Powers as it appears in 1 Corinthians and that of the
pseudo-Paulines:

1. Paul himself is not concerned to speculate on the origins of "the
powers." It is not important for him to affirm that they are "created"
(a point made in Col. 1:16). Paul was presumably familiar with the
myths of God apportioning the nations to the "sons of God," that
is, the "angels of the nations" (Deut. 32:8–9) and of the "fallen angels."[40] But he says no more than that "death entered by one man"
(1 Cor. 15:21; Rom. 5:12, 18), that "God subjected the creation to
futility [*mataiotēs*]," and that creation is consequently in "bondage to
corruption" or "decay [*phthora*]" (Rom. 8:20–21). He seems simply to
assume, with the apocalyptists, a worldview in which spiritual forces
stand behind political powers on earth.

2. Nor does Paul speak of the rehabilitation of the Powers; he speaks
rather of their "destruction" (RSV) or "neutralization," their *katargēsis*
(1 Cor. 2:6; 15:24). The language echoes the apocalypses, where God
will give dominion to the saints of the Most High (Dan. 7:22, 27) and
will "shatter these other kingdoms and make an end of them" (2:44).
Further, Paul locates this divine triumph "at the end," *not* in the cross
of Christ (vs. Col. 2:15).

3. Paul does not hesitate to describe the Powers as continuing in hostility against God. Death is "the last enemy to be destroyed" (1 Cor.
15:26). Similarly, the apparent intention of the "angels, principalities,
things present, things to come, powers" is to "separate us from the love
of God which is in Christ Jesus" (Rom. 8:38).

4. In Paul's own letters, the work of "heavenly" Powers opposed
to God ("angels, principalities") is clearly described as being carried
out through very human instruments: "oppression, distress, persecution, starvation, destitution, peril, sword" (Rom. 8:35–39). Paul here
lists "the sanctions of primarily human powers," things that "the evil
will of human beings can concoct."[41] These earthly sanctions cannot
separate us from the love of God, Paul says. It is hardly incidental
that this rhetorically powerful passage in Romans 8 gives way immediately to Paul's appeal for his audience's sympathy with the people
Israel (Romans 9–11),[42] an appeal motivated not only by recent im-

---

40. On the mythic background of "powers" language, see Wink, *Naming the Powers*,
13–35.

41. Romans 8:35 "refers not simply to hardships, such as 'famine' (RSV) but to things
done to us by 'someone' (*tis*) who wants to 'separate us from the love of Christ' " (ibid.,
48).

42. On the rhetorical connection between Romans 8 and 9, usually not recognized by
commentators, see Elliott, *Rhetoric of Romans*, 253–70.

perial legislation harshly restricting Jewish rights in the city of Rome, but perhaps also by the savagery in Roman Palestine during these same years.[43]

5. Corresponding to the view that the Powers continue to wreak violence and misery on earth, Paul understands "living in the Spirit" not as a turning away from earthly misery toward the contemplation of "things heavenly" (compare Col. 3:2), but rather as an agonized groaning in sympathy with an oppressed creation. The Spirit draws Christians into the trauma of a cosmic childbirth, as those who live in the Spirit await not only their own corporeal emancipation from the thrall of the Powers, but the liberation of the whole of creation itself (Rom. 8:22–23). This experience of the Spirit issues directly, for Paul and, he hopes, for his readers, in "great sorrow and unceasing anguish" for his own people, Israel, as they await the liberation of the messianic age which is their birthright (Rom. 9:1–5).

6. In contrast to the statement in Colossians that God "disarmed the principalities and powers and made a public example of them, triumphing over them" in Christ (Col. 2:15), Paul uses the metaphor of the triumphal procession more sparingly, and only to refer to his own physical abuse at the hands of very real earthly authorities. After his "affliction" (*thlipsis*) in Asia, when "we were so utterly, unbearably crushed that we despaired of life itself" and "felt that we had received the sentence of death" (2 Cor. 2:8–9), he describes himself as being "led about" by Christ in a triumphal procession, giving off the "stench of death" to those who see only the victim of Roman punishment (2 Cor. 2:14–16; compare 4:7–12).[44]

I conclude that, in contrast to Colossians and Ephesians, which have been allowed to play so dominant a role in scholarship on "the Powers," Paul's apocalyptic language about the Powers resists transposing the significance of Jesus' death from the earthly to the heavenly plane. It is precisely Paul's own insistence that the Powers remain unconquered until "the end," when they meet their decisive defeat at God's hands, that resists any narrowly spiritual interpretation of the Powers. Paul interprets Jesus' death as *the beginning of God's final "war of liberation"*

---

43. See Wolfgang Wiefel, "The Jewish Community in Ancient Rome and the Origins of Roman Christianity," in *The Romans Debate*, 2d ed. by Karl Donfried (Peabody, Mass.: Hendrickson Publishers, 1991); see my discussion in *Rhetoric of Romans*, 43–59. On Palestine under "The Roman Procurators A.D. 44–66," see *The History of the Jewish People in the Age of Jesus Christ*, vol. 1, ed. Geza Vermes, Fergus Millar, Matthew Black, and Pamela Vermes (Edinburgh: T. & T. Clark, 1973), 455–70.

44. On the metaphor of triumphal procession see Paul Brooks Duff, "Apostolic Suffering and the Language of Processions in 2 Corinthians 4:7–10," *BTB* 21:4 (1991): 158–65; idem, "Metaphor, Motif, and Meaning: The Rhetorical Strategy behind the Image 'Led in Triumph' in 2 Corinthians 2:14," *CBQ* 53:1 (1991): 79–92.

against all the Powers that hold creation in thrall through the instruments of earthly oppression. The death of Jesus unmasks the rulers of this age as intractably opposed to the wisdom of God, but *they are not yet overcome.*

Further, Paul speaks eloquently about his own freedom from the persistently lethal threats of the Powers: "We are afflicted in every way, but not crushed; perplexed, but not driven to despair; persecuted, but not forsaken; struck down, but not destroyed" (2 Cor. 4:8–9). This freedom marks his own identification with the crucifixion of Jesus: "We are always carrying about in the body the death of Jesus" (4:10). Paul is sustained in that freedom by a very traditionally apocalyptic hope in the resurrection of the dead, though to be sure this hope is confirmed for him by Jesus' resurrection.

Yes, the cross robs the Powers of Death of their "final sanction," exposing the Powers "as unable to make Jesus become what they wanted him to be, or to stop being who he was." "On the Cross these stupid powers displayed for all to see the one secret that they had to keep if they were to retain their power, the secret of founding violence."[45] But this is an insight possible for Paul only in light of the resurrection, for the crucifixion alone would only rehearse, not expose, the logic of founding violence. *It is the resurrection of Christ the crucified that reveals the imminent defeat of the Powers, pointing forward to the final triumph of God.* "The death and resurrection of Christ in their apocalyptic setting constitute the coherent core of Paul's thought."[46]

The mythological language with which Paul discusses the death of Jesus serves clear rhetorical purposes in 1 Corinthians, effectively extending the significance of Jesus' death at the hands of "the rulers" so as to determine how citizens of a flourishing Roman colony, hundreds of miles distant from dusty Judea, ought to conduct themselves toward the "scheme of this age, which is passing away" (7:31), on the one hand, and toward the "have-nots" in their own community (11:22) and in Judea itself (16:1–4), on the other. Given the profound distaste for the subject of crucifixion that Hengel documents for the Roman upper class, Paul's insistence on talking about the cross of Jesus, his insistence that this event has begun the dissolution of the Roman order, and his insistence that wealthy and prestigious Corinthians within the Christian congregation must now relate to the poor in a new way because of that crucifixion can scarcely be described as "minimizing the political aspects" of the cross!

---

45. Hamerton-Kelly, *Sacred Violence*, 85.
46. Beker, *Paul the Apostle*, 194–98; 205–8.

The Cross and the Justice of God

Paul's perspective on the death of Jesus is thoroughly and profoundly apocalyptic. Paul thus participates in a broad current in Second Temple Judaism through which Jews sought to "make sense of and to respond to concrete historical situations of oppression and even persecution." Apocalypticism empowered people to "remain steadfast in their traditions and to resist systematic attempts to suppress them."[47]

In the cross, God has annulled the wisdom of this age and of the rulers of this age. Further, since the one whom the rulers crucified has been raised from the dead, the rulers have clearly marked themselves out as doomed to destruction (1 Cor. 2:6–8; 15:51–58). The immediate consequence is that the Christian is no longer obligated to the scheme of this world, which is passing away (1 Cor. 7:31), but is called to obey the God who has chosen the weak, those "without rank or standing in the world, mere nothings, to overthrow the existing order" (1:28, Revised English Version).

This apocalyptic theology centers on the vindication of God's ancient purposes for the covenant people, and through them for the liberation of all creation. The questions at the heart of Paul's theology do not center on how the conscience-stricken individual may be saved, or on how a movement that includes Gentiles as well as Jews may be legitimized. His questions are the questions of his fellow apocalyptists: How shall God's justice be realized in a world dominated by evil powers?[48] For Paul, as for his pious contemporaries, the justice of God stood or fell with God's covenant faithfulness,[49] for the "plight" Paul conceived was dramatically focused in Israel's oppression, a "real, indubitable fact of first-century life. As long as Herod or Pilate ruled over her, Israel was still under the curse of 'exile.'" In this sense "nothing less than the framework of covenant theology will do justice" to Paul's thought.[50]

Paul's doctrine of the cross is thus a doctrine of God's justice and God's partiality toward the oppressed. In the crucifixion of the Messiah at the hands of the Roman oppressors, God has recapitulated the history of Israel's exile and brought it to a decisive climax; indeed, in a slave's

---

47. Horsley, *Jesus and the Spiral of Violence*, 139.

48. On the phrase "the righteousness of God," see Manfred Brauch's appendix in recent scholarship in E. P. Sanders, *Paul and Palestinian Judaism* (Philadelphia: Fortress, 1977), 523–42. Käsemann showed that the phrase has its background in Jewish apocalypticism and refers to God's "salvation-creating power" ("The Righteousness of God in Paul," *New Testament Questions of Today* [Philadelphia: Fortress, 1969], 168–82); Hays finds the same background already in the Bible ("Psalm 143 and the Logic of Romans 3," *JBL* 99 [1980]: 107–15). Against Käsemann, I doubt Paul's use of the phrase is directed against Jewish covenant theology (see Wright, *The Climax of the Covenant*, 234).

49. See J. Christiaan Beker, "The Faithfulness of God and the Priority of Israel in Paul's Letter to the Romans," *HTR* 79 (1986): 10–16.

50. Wright, *The Climax of the Covenant*, 261.

death on a cross (Phil. 2:8) the enslavement of the whole creation is embodied (Rom. 8:20–22).

Paul has not obscured the nature of the cross as historical and political oppression; rather he has focused it through the lens of Jewish apocalypticism. Only a gentile church unaccustomed to that perspective, and more familiar with the sacrificial logic of the blood cults, could have transformed Paul's message into a cult of atonement in Christ's blood (the letter to the Hebrews) and a charter of Israel's disfranchisement (the *Letter of Barnabas*). Paul's own letters show that he recognized these tendencies within the gentile church of his own day, and opposed them.

Romans 13:1–7
in the Context of
Imperial Propaganda

NEIL ELLIOTT

The exhortation to "be subject to the governing authorities" in Romans
13 (NRSV) is at once a notorious exegetical problem and a theological
scandal for us today. These verses have "caused more unhappiness and
misery in the Christian East and West than any other seven verses in
the New Testament by the license they have given to tyrants," as they
have been "used to justify a host of horrendous abuses of individual
human rights."[1] Here I address, first, the current state of historical scholarship on these verses; then, aspects of political rhetoric in the Roman
period, particularly under Nero's principate, that may offer us a new
angle of view.

The State of the Question...

"A persistent minority" of scholars have rejected Rom. 13:1–7 as a non-
Pauline interpolation into the letter.[2] Rom. 13:1–7 addresses a subject
that Paul discussed nowhere else; more significantly, the apparent sense
of these verses contradicts Paul's thought elsewhere in several particu-
lars. Absent here is any sense of "the estrangement of the world from
God" (cf. 2 Cor. 4:4, Gal. 1:4, 1 Cor. 7:31), or of the imminent expectation of the end of the age (cf. the following words in Rom. 13:11–13).
Neither do these verses betray any awareness that "the authorities" are
arrayed against God, as are the "rulers" of 1 Cor. 2:6–8. Here, in contrast, the world order is blithely approved as God-ordained. "Paul could
not have ascribed such an exalted status to Rome without being not

---

1. J. C. O'Neill, *Paul's Letter to the Romans* (London: Penguin, 1975), 209. See
also Neil Elliott, *Liberating Paul: The Justice of God and the Politics of the Apostle*
(Maryknoll, N.Y.: Orbis Books, 1994), 13–19.
2. Leander E. Keck, "What Makes Romans Tick?" in David M. Hay and E. Elizabeth
Johnson, eds., *Pauline Theology III: Romans* (Minneapolis: Fortress, 1995), 3–29.

only hypocritical and servile, but untrue to his whole theological position."[3] Even scholars who consider the passage authentic often regard it as "an alien body in Paul's exhortation,"[4] too questionable to support the weight of any reconstruction of Paul's political views.[5]

Other interpreters, however, declare that Rom. 13:1–7 makes a good deal of sense when read against the general climate of anti-Jewish sentiment in Rome. Rome had recently expelled Jews from the city because of riots "at the instigation of Chrestus" (Tacitus, *Annals* 15.44); mass discontent arose over exorbitant taxation during the reign of Nero (*Annals,* 13.50–51); and, more dubiously, Jews in Rome who were sympathetic with the revolutionary cause in Judea had supposedly expressed anti-Roman sentiments.[6] Moreover, gentile Christians were "putting themselves and their congregations at greater risk from the authorities" by accepting Jews back into their congregations.[7]

By highlighting important features of the historical context in which Romans was written, these studies have the effect of *relativizing* Paul's exhortation by tying it to a narrowly constrained political situation in Rome. This is an advance over universalizing Rom. 13:1–7 as a Christian "theology of the state."[8] On the other hand, these studies perpetuate several questionable assumptions about Paul's political stance. First, they imply that historical circumstances *adequately* explain the exhortation in 13:1–7 as a genuine and appropriate response, that the passage "makes good sense" once we understand its historical context. But the inconsistencies between 13:1–7 and Paul's thought elsewhere receive minimal attention. Second, these situational readings also imply that the posture of "political realism" Paul expresses here was

---

3. James Kallas, "Romans XIII. 7: An Interpolation," *NTS* 11 (1964–65): 365–74; Elliott, *Liberating Paul,* 217–18.

4. Ernst Käsemann, *Commentary on Romans,* trans. G. W. Bromiley (Grand Rapids: Eerdmans, 1973), 352; similarly Ernst Bammel, "Romans 13," in Ernst Bammel and C. F. D. Moule, eds., *Jesus and the Politics of His Day* (Cambridge: Cambridge University Press, 1984), 381.

5. Keck, "What Makes Romans Tick?" 16; similarly Bammel, "Romans 13," 381.

6. See the essays gathered with Keck's in Hay and Johnson, *Pauline Theology III;* N. T. Wright, "Romans and the Theology of Paul," 62; W. S. Campbell, "The Rule of Faith in Romans 12:1–15:13," 281; Mark Reasoner, "The Theology of Romans 12:1–15:13," 296. Also see J. Friedrich, W. Pöhlmann, and P. Stuhlmacher, "Zur historischen Situation und Intention von Röm 13,1–7," *ZTK* 73 (1976): 131–66; Marcus Borg, "A New Context for Romans XIII," *NTS* 19 (1972–73): 205–18; Bammel, "Romans 13," 367–71. Against Borg's "Zealotism" hypothesis see Friedrich et al., "Situation," 132–33; Ulrich Wilckens, "Römer 13,1–7," in *Rechtfertigung als Freiheit: Paulusstudien* (Neukirchen-Vluyn: Neukirchener Verlag, 1974), 230; Wolfgang Schrage, *The Ethics of the New Testament,* trans. David E. Green (Philadelphia: Fortress, 1988), 235.

7. James D. G. Dunn, *Romans 9–16* (Dallas: Word Publishing, 1988), 768–69; idem, "Romans 13:1–7 — A Charter for Political Quietism?" *Ex Auditu* 2 (1986): 55–68.

8. For example, Schrage, *Ethics,* 235.

inevitable,[9] rather than simply the most realistic *and responsible* approach to the situation.[10] Despite the confidence with which a number of scholars have identified "the Roman situation" that prompted 13:1–7, it is precisely in terms of the "inner logic of Paul's thought,"[11] both outside Romans and within the letter, that the benign, even benevolent characterization of "the governing authorities" (NRSV) here remains an enigma.[12]

... And the Question of the State

Paul's generous characterization of "the governing authorities" appears a "monumental contradiction" of Paul's thought, at several levels.[13]

Especially troubling, in the first instance, are *discrepancies within the immediate context of Romans 12–13*. These include the lapse of eschatological expectation in 13:1–7 (present again in 13:11–12!);[14] and the apparent assignment of God's prerogative to avenge wrongdoing (cf. 12:19–20) to the authority as the "minister" of divine wrath (13:4). Further, in 13:3 traditional social values of "good" and "bad" are accepted without qualification, while in the surrounding context Paul anticipates that Christians will suffer unjust persecution from their neighbors (12:17–21), and exhorts Christians to "cast off the works of darkness" that characterize the present evil age (13:11–13). Indeed, the iniquity of the pagan world is given searing attention at the very start of the letter (1:18–32). The resulting impression is of a stark moral double standard: The pagan world is characterized as hostile and shameful *except* for the governing authorities as they are presented in 13:1–7, who are benevolent and to be regarded with "honor" (*timē,* 13:7).

---

9. Dunn, *Romans 9–16,* 772; "Romans 13:1–7," 60.

10. Ernst Käsemann, "Principles of the Interpretation of Romans 13," in *New Testament Questions of Today,* trans. W. J. Montague (Philadelphia: Fortress, 1969), 212–13; Schrage, *Ethics,* 236, 238.

11. Keck, "What Makes Romans Tick?" 23.

12. Mark Nanos takes the entire passage to refer to *synagogue* authorities (*The Mystery of Romans: The Jewish Context of Paul's Letter* [Minneapolis: Fortress, 1996], chap. 6). Nanos recognizes, however, that a metaphorical or figurative reading of "the sword" as a reference to synagogue authority appears forced (310–14). In contrast, A. Strobel has shown that Paul's vocabulary here comes from the realm of Hellenistic political epideictic ("Zum Verständnis von Röm 13," *ZNW* 47 [1956]: 67–93; "Furcht wem Furcht gebührt. Zum profangriechischen Hintergrund von Röm 13,7," *ZNW* 55 [1964]: 58–62); see the refinements offered by Friedrich et al., "Situation," 135–40.

13. Victor Paul Furnish, *The Moral Teaching of Paul* (Nashville: Abingdon, 1979), 117.

14. Friedrich et al., "Situation," read 13:1–7 under the imminent "eschatological judgment of God" that is evident in the following verses ("Situation," 162). But any assurance of an eschatological end to the domination of the authorities is missing here: so also Bammel, "Romans 13," 367.

In one explanation of this double standard, "Paul accepted the system of honor operating on the public world of Graeco-Roman society, but rejected this society as shameful in the area of 'private life,' gender roles and sexuality."[15] But the immorality so floridly described in Romans 1, and referred to in Romans 6, is not particularly "private": The emphasis in Rom. 1:18–23 is on pagan idolatry, which was a thoroughly public affair in the Roman world.[16] Neither is the "vice list" in 1:28–32 restricted to the sphere of private life. As to the "degrading passions" referred to in Rom. 1:24–27, the notorious arrogance, brutality, and sensual over-indulgence of the ruling class in Rome and in the provinces alike — and their inevitable punishment by God — were a mainstay of Diaspora Jewish propaganda.[17] Josephus and Philo gave extraordinary attention to the assassination of the self-deified emperor Gaius (Caligula) in particular.[18] Although it cannot be proven that Paul had Gaius's grisly assassination particularly in mind as he wrote Rom. 1:18–27, his lurid description there of idolatry and depravity, punished in the very bodies of the depraved, would aptly have summarized the moral lesson that, according to his Diaspora contemporaries, divine providence had taught the whole world.[19]

Paul's talk of turning from "shameful" conduct to righteousness (Romans 6 and 12) clearly engages the Christian in the vicissitudes of public life: "Do not be conformed to this world" (12:2). Friction and opposition with urban neighbors are very serious possibilities for the Christians (12:14–21). Finally, given the clear eschatological declarations in the surrounding context (13:11–14), we can hardly suppose that Paul regarded the civil authorities with a resigned sense of inevitability.[20]

The puzzle remains why Paul should have allowed such glowing characterizations of the state to stand in this letter, *whatever* the situation that prompted it. Here I find Ernst Käsemann's perspective on Paul's rhetoric especially valuable. He observes that 13:1–7 "has a view toward universally valid realities," but this generality simply reflects the routine

---

15. See Halvor Moxnes, "Honor and Righteousness in Romans," *JSNT* 32 (1988): 66–68; "The Quest for Honor and the Unity of the Community in Romans 12 and in the Orations of Dio Chrysostom," in Troels Engberg-Pedersen, ed., *Paul in His Hellenistic Context* (Minneapolis: Fortress, 1995), 214.

16. Ramsay MacMullen, *Paganism in the Roman Empire* (New Haven: Yale University Press, 1981); S. R. F. Price, *Rituals and Power: The Roman Imperial Cult in Asia Minor* (Cambridge: Cambridge University Press, 1984).

17. On the death of Herod the Great, for example, see Josephus, *Ant.* 17:168–81, and Acts 12:20–23.

18. Josephus, *Ant.* 19:16. Philo may have followed his *Embassy to Gaius* with an account of the emperor's assassination as a proof of divine providence: see Philo, *The Embassy to Gaius,* trans. F. H. Colson, LCL (Cambridge: Harvard University Press, 1971), 186–87n.

19. Elliott, *Liberating Paul,* 190–95.

20. Vs. Moxnes, "Quest for Honor," 214; similarly Dunn, *Romans 9–16,* 772.

commonplaces of Diaspora Jewish propaganda and apologetic, "a long chain of tradition...dominated by the idea of divinely established authorities."[21] The notion expressed here, "that the authorities constantly seek to be God's servants, is obviously exaggerated if not wholly incredible"; the "proof" Paul offers for his exhortation is "forced" and lacking in persuasiveness.[22]

For interpretation, therefore, "the exhortation is decisive," not the premises on which Paul has somewhat incidentally based the exhortation. I conclude that Paul's statements regarding authorities as servants of God "are mere rhetorical commonplaces, meant only to focus the audience's attention on the discernment of 'the good,'" and thereby "to keep members of the *ekklēsia* from making trouble in the streets."[23] Attempts to inflate these premises into a "doctrine of the state" spring not from within Paul's text, but from extrinsic political interests on the part of the interpreters. In this way "the text has been misused for a millennium in the interests of political theory."[24]

Rom. 13:1–7 and the Question of the Letter's Purpose

Several of the "situational" readings of Rom. 13:1–7 discussed above imply that Paul's *first* concern here, and indeed throughout the letter, was the survival of predominantly *gentile-Christian* congregations, recently excluded from the "protective zone" of the synagogue. This implication is usually linked to the return to Rome of *Jews* exiled by Claudius, and to their precarious situation in the city. The result is a curious ambivalence, evident for example in James D. G. Dunn's reconstruction. On one hand, Dunn declares "the central factor" in interpreting Rom. 13:1–7 to be *"the ambiguous and vulnerable status of the Jews,"* a vulnerability made worse by official suspicion of foreign cults, and by popular resentment of Jewish privileges regarding the Temple tax.[25] Paul wished to protect the gentile church from mistakenly being "identified with Jews" by the Roman authorities. In the next moment, however, Dunn declares Paul's concern to be "the ambiguous and vulnerable status of the *Christian* congregations in Rome," caused in part by Paul's own efforts to "redefine the people of God" in "nonethnic terms." Now, it seems, the gentile Christians were in jeopardy precisely because they were *no longer* identified with the Jewish synagogue![26]

---

21. Käsemann, *Commentary,* 354–55; similarly Bammel, "Romans 13," 373.
22. Käsemann, *Commentary,* 357, 359; "Principles," 200.
23. Elliott, *Liberating Paul,* 223; similarly Friedrich et al., "Situation," 162.
24. Käsemann, *Commentary,* 354–55.
25. Dunn, "Romans 13:1–7," 58 (emphasis in original).
26. Ibid., 60–62.

This ambivalence regarding Paul's motive in 13:1–7 mirrors a larger debate over the "double character" of Romans. The letter is ostensibly directed to gentiles (1:6–13), and includes a climactic admonition against gentile-Christian "boasting" over Israel (11:13–35). It is nevertheless largely devoted to a critical discussion of "Jewish themes," including Torah's relevance, and Israel's standing before God.[27] On the currently prevailing reading of the letter, Romans is a theological defense of the gentile-Christian church, directed polemically against *Jewish* boasting or particularism. Correspondingly, Rom. 13:1–7 is intended to help protect the (predominantly gentile-Christian) Roman church from the dangerous political fallout of *Jewish* nationalist agitation.[28] Unfortunately, such suggestions must rely on extrapolating from what is assumed to be the overall purpose of the letter elsewhere; they fail to connect Rom. 13:1–7 with the argumentative flow that reaches its crest in Romans 11.

I find more compelling an alternative reading of the letter emerging from several recent studies. Romans is a paraenetic letter directed primarily against an emergent supersessionism among gentile Christians in Rome, an "incipient Marcionism."[29] Romans 9–11 constitutes the argumentative "climax" of the letter as Paul explicitly warns gentile Christians against boasting over an *apparently* vanquished Israel.[30] Even within chapters 1–8, long read as the dogmatic "core" of the letter, Paul's ultimate target is not Jewish boasting, but *gentile-Christian* arrogance. The rhetorical questions that shape the argument of Romans center around two main issues: gentile-Christian anti-Judaism, and a practical antinomianism which some gentile Christians may have confused with Paul's gospel.[31] "It is anachronistic and completely unwarranted to think that Paul has only the Jew in mind in 2:1–5 or that he characterizes the typical Jew"; Paul's target is rather the *gen-*

---

27. On the problem of the letter's "double character," see most recently my discussion in *Rhetoric of Romans: Argumentative Constraint and Strategy and Paul's Debate with Judaism* (Sheffield: Sheffield Academic Press, 1990), 9–43.

28. According to Borg, Paul wants Christians to subject themselves to the Roman government precisely because it restrains a troublesome nationalistic "particularity," namely, "Israel's cause" ("A New Context," 214–16, 218). Here Dunn detects Paul's fear "lest any other political or national entity made the same mistake as his fellow countrymen had — that of identifying God's purpose of salvation with one particular nation's well-being and political dominance" (*Romans 9–16*, 773–74).

29. William S. Campbell, *Paul's Gospel in an Intercultural Context: Jew and Gentile in the Letter to the Romans* (Frankfurt am Main: Peter Lang, 1992), 35. Nanos speaks of "misguided views that were gaining ground among the *gentile* believers in Rome toward Jews," an emerging "Christian-*gentile* exclusivism" (*Mystery of Romans*, 10 and passim).

30. See my essay, "Figure and Ground in the Interpretation of Romans 9–11," in Stephen E. Fowl, ed., *The Theological Interpretation of Scripture: Classic and Contemporary Readings* (Oxford: Blackwell, 1996), 371–89.

31. Campbell, *Paul's Gospel*, 31–33.

tile who judges others and presumes on God's mercy while doing the same things.[32] The same strategy recurs in chapters 9 and 10, where Paul "baits the trap" for the gentile Christian,[33] and in 14:1–15:13, where the indictment of "judging" others becomes specific in exhortation to the "strong," gentile Christians, not to judge the "weak," Torah-observant Jews.[34] The danger Paul addresses here is the threat that gentile-Christian contempt poses for Jewish acceptance of Jesus' messiahship.[35]

These analyses of the letter's argument correspond to a very different construal of the historical situation addressed. In fact the entire letter is directed to the same end as Paul's apocalyptic warning in 11:13–32. Given the extremely precarious situation of Jewish communities throughout the empire,[36] and not least of the Jews of Rome, who had already suffered expulsions under Tiberius (19 C.E.) and then Claudius (49 C.E.); given the insults which the Roman intelligentsia were only too glad to add to these injuries;[37] given, finally, the premises Paul apparently shared with his readers regarding Israel having "stumbled" (9:32, 10:11), the Christians of Rome were apparently ready to draw a theological conclusion as well: that Israel had stumbled, perhaps so as to fall (cf. Rom. 11:1, 11).[38] Paul wrote Romans to oppose this gentile-Christian "boasting" over Israel, and the corresponding indifference to the plight of real Jews in Rome in the wake of the Claudian expulsion.

---

32. Stanley K. Stowers, *The Diatribe and Paul's Letter to the Romans* (Chico, Calif.: Scholars Press, 1981), 112. See also Elliott, *Rhetoric of Romans,* 119–27; Stanley K. Stowers, *A Rereading of Romans: Justice, Jews, and Gentiles* (New Haven: Yale University Press, 1994), 100–109; Campbell, *Paul's Gospel,* 132–60.

33. Stowers, *A Rereading of Romans,* 299.

34. Wayne A. Meeks, "Judgement and the Brother: Romans 14:1–15:13," in G. F. Hawthorne and O. Betz, eds., *Tradition and Interpretation in the New Testament: Essays in Honor of E. Earle Ellis* (Grand Rapids: Eerdmans, 1987), 296.

35. Nanos's analysis of the "weak" and "strong" in Romans is critically important here: *Mystery of Romans,* 85–165.

36. See Paula Fredriksen, "Judaism, the Circumcision of Gentiles, and Apocalyptic Hope: Another Look at Galatians 1 and 2," *JTS* 42:2 (1991): esp. 556–58; idem, *From Jesus to Christ: The Origin of the New Testament Images of Jesus* (New Haven: Yale University Press, 1988), 154–55; E. Mary Smallwood, *The Jews under Roman Rule: From Pompey to Diocletian* (Leiden: E. J. Brill, 1976), 389–427.

37. John G. Gager, *The Origins of Anti-Semitism* (New York: Oxford University Press, 1981), 63–88; Peter Schäfer, *Judeophobia* (Cambridge, Mass.: Harvard University Press, 1997).

38. Daniel Fraikin argues that "somehow, at some point, the rejection of the gospel by individual Jews or synagogues has led to the theological conclusion [among Christians in Rome] that Israel has rejected the gospel" ("The Rhetorical Function of the Jews in Acts," in Peter Richardson and David Granskou, eds., *Anti-Judaism in Early Christianity,* vol. 1: *Paul and the Gospels* [Waterloo: Wilfrid Laurier University Press, 1986], 101; see also Nanos, *Mystery of Romans,* 119–28).

Historical Situation and
Sitz im Leben in Romans 13:1–7

These considerations suggest that *Paul's appeal to subjection to authorities in 13:1–7 would have functioned within the overall rhetorical purpose of Romans to advocate for the safety of the Jewish community in Rome.*[39] This suggestion proceeds from two lines of argument. First, *while reconstructions of the "historical situation" in Rome remain somewhat speculative, they may be reinforced by the evidence of similar situations* typically recurring in the Hellenistic and Roman *polis* (i.e., *Sitz im Leben*).[40] Jews were repeatedly endangered by "the hostility of local populations if Rome's attention were alienated or withdrawn."[41] Anti-Jewish violence was typically provoked not by religious differences but by social pressures, especially the pressure of Roman exploitation and colonization that Hellenistic aristocracies deflected onto more vulnerable Jewish populations. "Attacking the Romans directly...was out of the question. But attacking Roman clients [i.e., Jews] was not."[42]

Popular unrest occasioned by tax abuses might readily be deflected onto the Jews, who "by virtue not least of their special privileges regarding the temple tax, would be all the more open to charges of tax evasion."[43] The disastrous "war" in Alexandria in 38–41 C.E. (for so Claudius would later term it) had been fueled by native and Greek resentment of Jewish privileges, which Augustus had reaffirmed at the same moment he had imposed a capital tax on noncitizens. Although they had been harassed, rounded up out of their homes, herded together in the city and in the desert, tortured, even slaughtered by their Greek neighbors,[44] Claudius apparently held the Jews chiefly responsible for the violence. He forbade the Jewish survivors from receiving Jews from Syria, and threatened, "if they disobey, I shall proceed against them as fomenting a common plague for the whole world."[45]

---

39. See also my *Liberating Paul*, 221–26.

40. See Luise Schottroff, " 'Give to Caesar What Belongs to Caesar and to God What Belongs to God': A Theological Response of the Early Christian Church to Its Social and Political Environment," in Willard Swartley, ed., *The Love of Enemy and Nonretaliation in the New Testament* (Louisville: Westminster/John Knox Press, 1992), esp. 227–29.

41. Fredriksen, "Judaism," 556–58.

42. Christopher Stanley, " 'Neither Jew Nor Greek': Ethnic Conflict in Graeco-Roman Society," *JSNT* 64 (1996): 101–24.

43. Dunn, "Romans 13:1–7," 60.

44. See Philo, *Against Flaccus* 6.41–43; 8.53–57; 10.73–75; *Embassy to Gaius* 18.120–24; 19.127–20.134.

45. The papyrus letter of Claudius: *CPJ* 153 (V. Tcherikover and A. Fuks, eds., *Corpus Papyrorum Iudaicarum* [Cambridge: Harvard University Press, 1957], 2:25–43; see comments in 1:69–74). Compare Josephus, *Ant.* 19:281–91. Texts and bibliography in Louis H. Feldman and Meyer Reinhold, eds., *Jewish Life and Thought among Greeks and Romans: Primary Readings* (Minneapolis: Fortress, 1996), 89–92.

The brutality of the tax system was notorious and, in Philo's judgment, both deliberate and systematic (*Spec. Leg.* 2.92–95, 3.159–63). If Paul had any knowledge of the situation in Rome, he might reasonably have expected the empire to answer any agitation over taxes with the same force that had been used to crush dissent in nearby Puteoli, where a praetorian cohort had been brought in to "restore the town to concord" through an effective application of terror, including "a few executions" (Tacitus, *Annals* 13.48). The exhortation in Rom. 13:4–6 would have been particularly appropriate in this context: "Not for nothing do the authorities hold power to detain and to punish over any who violate their orders. Therefore pay your taxes and customs — if you don't want to expose yourselves to the brutal enforcement of the tax officials!"[46]

In short, Paul might well have expected the Jews of Rome to bear the brunt of violence in the event tax riots broke out within the city. A second line of argument reveals thematic connections between the exhortation in 13:1–7 and other parts of the letter where Paul is concerned to evoke gentile-Christian solicitude toward Jews. I note, first, *a series of correspondences between the characterization of being "in Christ" in Romans 8 and the exhortation in Romans 13,* represented in the accompanying table.[47] Further, I observe *a similar correspondence between the rhetorical movement across chapters 8–11 and that across 12–15.*

In chapter 8, Paul emphasizes perceiving rightly, having the mind "set on the things of the Spirit," having "the mind of the Spirit" (8:5, 6, 27). Perceiving rightly means reckoning the sufferings of the present world "not worth comparing with the glory to be revealed" (8:18). The righteous may suffer (8:17), the creation groans in its unredeemed futility (8:20–21), and those led by the Spirit groan as well as they await their own bodily liberation (8:23); none of this undermines hope which is set on what is unseen (8:24–25). Those whose minds are set on the things of the Spirit will know that God works in everything for good (8:28), that nothing will separate them from God's love, not all the sufferings of this age (8:35) — sufferings inflicted by "rulers" and "powers" (8:38–39).

These assurances of the object of hope, despite the suffering and futility of the present age, give way to Paul's solemn declarations that the sonship, the covenants, the promises are still Israel's (9:4); the word of God has not failed (9:6) — despite the apparent evidence of Israel's

---

46. Friedrich et al., "Situation," 144.

47. These correspondences do not overshadow marked differences between these passages, of course. Although the eschatological hope so central in chap. 8 (vv. 18–25) is absent from 13:1–7, it is expressed in the surrounding context (13:11–14), where hope and the patient endurance of tribulation are again in view (12:12; cf. 8:25). There is no thought in 13:1–7 about the coming redemption of the authorities, or of their awareness of their own subjection to God, to correspond to the creation's subjection to futility in chap. 8.

Thematic Correspondences between Romans 8 and Romans 13

Romans 8	*Romans 13*
Paul speaks of "subordination" as appropriate to the Christian, specifically subordination to the Law of God (8:7).	Paul speaks of "subordination" to God's "disposition" or ordering (*diatagē*, 13:2).
This subordination is contrasted with the "mind of the flesh," which cannot subject itself to the Law of God (8:7).	This subordination is contrasted with those who oppose the ordering of God by setting themselves against the governing authorities (13:2).
Correspondingly, Christians are under an obligation as "debtors" (*opheiletai*) to the Spirit rather than to the flesh (8:12).	Subordination to the authorities is expressed as giving what is owed to each (*tas opheilas*, 13:7).
Those who "walk according to the Spirit" are able to fulfill the Law's just requirement (8:4).	(Paul goes on to say that Christians should "owe" nothing to anyone but love, for love fulfills the Law, 13:8.)
Christian obligation must be lived out in an antagonistic world that has been subordinated to God: "creation was subjected [*hypetagē*] to futility" by God, and now experiences a "bondage to decay" (8:20–21).	Christians must subordinate themselves to the authorities currently in power (*hyperechousai*), who have in turn been set in rank by God (*hypo theou tetagmenai*, 13:1).
While this environment is hostile, a sphere of suffering (8:18), of inflicted harm, including the threat of "the sword" (*machaira*, 8:35), Christians are assured they need not live in fear (8:15).	While the authorities wield the threat of punishment ("the sword," *machaira*) and "wrath" (13:3–4), Christians are assured they need not live in fear (13:3).
Despite the sufferings inflicted in the present age, Christians know that "all things work together for good [*eis to agathon*] for those who love God, who are called according to his purpose" (8:28, NRSV).	Christians may pay taxes, knowing that the authority is "God's servant for the good" (*eis to agathon*, 13:4, 6).

---

stumbling (9:31–33, 11:11). "God has not rejected his people" (11:1); all Israel will be saved (11:26); for "the gifts and the call of God are irrevocable" (11:29). From a powerfully intimate declaration of anguished sympathy for Israel (9:1–4), Paul moves to an apocalyptically clothed warning to the gentile Christians in his audience to avoid boasting over

Israel (11:13–24), for God has caused the present "hardening" of Israel, only until the full number of the gentiles has come in (11:25–26).[48] That this "hardening" is part of God's sovereign plan is the message of Scripture, interpreted rightly; it is also a supernatural insight, provided through the medium of revelation (*to mystērion*, 11:25).

Thus the initial emphasis on right perception and the distinction between "what is seen" and "what is not seen" (chap. 8) prepare the audience to accept a new perspective on the "stumbling" of Israel (chaps. 9–11). Paul's citation of Psalm 44:23 in Rom. 8:36, "For your sake . . . we are led as sheep to the slaughter," evokes the ancient question of Israel's exilic suffering to address the sufferings of the present age. "The answering echo is found in Rom. 11:1," where Paul insists that God has not cast off his people.[49] The use of the psalm is no mere metaphorical trope. The juxtaposition of the psalm and the "sufferings of the present age" point to the present sufferings *of Israel*: "Israel undergoes rejection for the sake of the world, bearing suffering vicariously."[50] The afflictions listed in 8:35, "tribulation, distress, persecution, famine, nakedness, peril, sword," are not merely pieces of eschatological tradition, they are a pointed summary of Israel's experience under Roman rule. No doubt these words would have evoked sharp echoes of very recent events in Rome itself.[51]

Similarly, the paraenesis in chapters 12–15 begins with general comments about the renewal of the mind, in opposition to conformity to this world (12:2), and about right perceptions of oneself in relation to others (*mē hyperphronein par ho dei phronein, alla phronein eis to sophronein*, 12:3). Beneath this heading, general paraenesis about mutual regard and living peaceably with others (12:9–21) and the "obligation" (*opheilete*) of love for others as fulfilling the Law (13:8) give way to the more specific exhortation in 14:1–15:13, which reframes the conduct of "the strong" toward "the weak" in terms of obligation: "We who are powerful are obligated [*opheilomen*] to bear with the weaknesses of the weak and not to please ourselves" (15:1). The attitudes and practices attributed to the "strong" are such as "might be expected to arise among gentiles who have come to the Christian faith without an appreciation of

---

48. On the rhetorical coherence of Rom. 8:14–11:36, see Elliott, *Rhetoric of Romans*, 253–70s; "Figure and Ground," 379–80.

49. Richard B. Hays, *Echoes of Scripture in the Letters of Paul* (New Haven: Yale University Press, 1989), 59.

50. Ibid., 61.

51. Käsemann takes these terms with concrete seriousness: *Commentary*, 249–50. While Hays initially reads 8:18–38 as concerning "the suffering that Christians experience in the present age" (*Echoes of Scripture*, 57), then later uses "his [i.e., God's] people" to refer to Israel (59, 61), I consider the physical afflictions of Israel to be in view from 8:18 on. The possibility that God had "rejected Israel" arose not only from numerous Jews declining to accept Jesus as messiah, but from the perception that the Jews' physical distress was God's punishment.

how their new faith is linked . . . with the faith of the historical people of God. . . . Indeed, they are not unlike the kind of gentile prejudices toward Jews and the practice of their faith that were prevalent in the gentile city of Rome in the first century C.E."[52] The "weak" of 14:1–15:6, like the "stumbling" of 9:30–33, are (non-Christian) Jews offended by the failure of gentile Christians to observe the halakot expected of converts to Judaism.[53]

The later chapters develop the paraenesis of 12:1–2. The responsibility, the obligation, of the strong is "to have their minds 'renewed' rather than 'conformed to this world' so that they 'prove what the will of God is, that which is good and acceptable and perfect' (12:2), instead of asserting their rights regardless of the impact on the 'weak.' "[54] The Roman Christians' positive response to Paul's exhortation will mean nothing less than a foretaste of the eschatological worship in which Israel and the nations are joined (15:7–12); further, it will fulfill his sacred service by guaranteeing the sanctity of his "offering of the nations" (15:14–16). To buttress this argument, at last, he hails other Greek congregations who have recognized that they are "obligated" (opheilousin), both spiritually and physically, to "the poor of Jerusalem," i.e., the Jewish community there (15:27).

These correspondences of vocabulary, theme, and rhetorical movement across chapters 8–11 and chapters 12–15 suggest a similar structure of thought undergirding Paul's talk of "subjection" in Romans 8–11 and in Romans 13. Paul wants the Christians of Rome to understand that Israel's being "subjected" to God's hardening was not through their own fault (11:25–32),[55] just as God's subjecting the whole creation to futility was against its will (8:20). The result is that Israel has "stumbled," and in its exile must suffer the distresses of the present age. But Israel's present circumstances ("what is seen") say nothing about Israel's ultimate destiny ("what is not seen," but what is revealed as "a mystery"), which is secure in God's unfailing promises. Similarly Paul declares that God has set political authorities in rank so that others must be subordinated to them (13:1–2), with the result that in the present age the authorities mete out "wrath" against those who violate the established order. This subjection (like the others) is never described as "good" in itself, or permanent; it is simply "the way things are," for

---

52. The label "strong" has negative connotations within Romans: " 'presumption,' 'arrogance,' " which echo the state of mind confronted in chap. 11 (par heautois phronimoi, 11:25) and 12 (hyperphronein par' ho dei phronein, 12:3; ta hypsēla phronountes, par' heautois phronimoi, 12:16), and indeed "throughout this letter" (Nanos, Mystery of Romans, 99–101).

53. Ibid., 123–35.

54. Ibid., 134; on implications for the reading of the letter as a whole, 159–65.

55. Stowers, A Rereading of Romans, 305.

now. Within the constraints of this situation, Paul requires subordination rather than defiant opposition of the authorities, "doing good" rather than evil to avoid wrath (13:3–4; compare 12:17–21).

The broad rhetorical movement across chapters 12–15, like that across chapters 8–11, is meant to quell gentile-Christian arrogance and to evoke sympathy and solidarity with Israel. That context suggests that Rom. 13:1–7 was intended to head off the sort of public unrest that could have further jeopardized the already vulnerable situation of the beleaguered Jewish population of Rome. Paul meant simply to deflect the Roman Christians from the trajectory of anti-Jewish attitudes and ideology along which they were already traveling, a trajectory that would implicate them ever more in the scapegoating of the Jews already visible in Roman culture — a scapegoating that would become a mainstay of Christian orthodoxy within a generation.[56]

"Conscience," "Fear," and the "Idle Sword"

One significant obstacle to reading Rom. 13:1–7 as a consistent and coherent response to a particular Roman situation is that *this passage itself does not express a univocally positive attitude toward "the governing authorities."* On the one hand, we read absurdly positive comments about the purpose and function of the authorities. They are "instituted by God" (13:1, NRSV); they approve or reward those who do good (13:3); they are "God's ministers for good" (13:4), "God's servants" (13:6). While such affirmations are traditional in Hellenistic Jewish propaganda, "what is missing in Romans 13:1–7 is the characteristic criticism of those foreign powers in the present evil age. For the call to subordination in Judaism carried an implicit, if not always explicit, judgment of such foreign governments, even if God was somehow using their evil intentions to accomplish his ultimate goals."[57] Further, Paul assures his readers that "rulers are not a terror to good conduct," so the one who does good will have nothing to fear (13:3). Surely, to such benign authorities any reasonable person would eagerly give both honor (*timē*, 13:7) and the consent of conscience (*syneidēsis*, 13:5).

Yet Paul also warns against opposing the governing authorities, though he maintains a stolid silence about how or why such opposition

---

56. Elliott, *Liberating Paul*, 221–25. This reading is diametrically opposed to the suppositions, which I consider gratuitous, that the jeopardy in which the Christians find themselves involves "the hostile synagogue" (Friedrich et al., "Situation," 159), or "Jewish attempts to divert the activities of anti-Jewish officials against the Christians" (Bammel, "Romans 13," 370).

57. Nanos, *Mystery of Romans,* 299. There are no criteria here for distinguishing "just" from "unjust" authorities, nor do I think such criteria are "implicit" in the passage (against Stanley E. Porter, "Romans 13:1–7 as Pauline Rhetoric," *Filologia neotestamentaria* 3 (1990): 115; Dunn, "Romans 13:1–7," 64).

might arise (13:2). He warns that the wrongdoer should fear the authority as the instrument of God's wrath, who "does not bear the sword in vain!" (13:4). To "conscience," then, is added the motive of the fear of wrath (13:5), so that Paul can at last conclude that *both* honor and "fear" (*phobos*) are due the authorities.

The weight of these warnings threatens to sink more buoyant readings of the passage. Why should any decent citizen need to be exhorted to "be subject" to authorities who always "reward the good"? Why should "fear" of the authorities be urged (13:7) from those who have just been told they need have no fear if they do good (13:3)?[58] This last question is even more urgent when we observe that nowhere else in the New Testament (or Jewish scripture) is "fear" urged toward human authorities, being usually reserved for God alone. Two alternatives have presented themselves to interpreters: either translate the two uses of *phobos* differently, e.g., "terror" of the authorities in 13:3 and "respect" for the authorities in 13:7 (so the NRSV), or assign the phrases in 13:7 to different objects. In the latter case, "fear to whom fear is due" would refer to God alone; "honor to whom honor is due," to the civil authority. But while this second alternative gains plausibility from other early Christian writings, it can hardly be described as the clear meaning of Rom. 13:7.[59]

And why should the proper subjects of any such benign authorities need to be reminded of the threat of the sword (13:4)?[60] The answer that would seem to arise naturally from Rom. 12:14 and 17 is that Christians may unjustly suffer persecution from their pagan neighbors (cf. 1 Peter 4:12–19). *This possibility is quietly elided in Rom. 13:1–7, however.* The logic of reward for good and punishment for evil (13:3–4) could be expected to result in a single, straightforward admonition: "Therefore do good." No urging to "be subject" would be necessary for those who consent to do "the good" envisioned by the authorities. "It fits in such a context to remind people to fulfil duties and pay taxes

---

58. So Strobel notes that the urge to "fear" in 13:7 seems to contradict the theological thought of 13:2–3 ("Furcht wem Furcht gebührt," 59).

59. C. E. B. Cranfield suggests that the phrase in 13:7 be aligned with the language of 1 Peter 2:17 ("Fear God; honor the king") and the second-century *Acts of the Scilitan Martyrs* ("Give honor to Caesar as unto Caesar, but fear to God"), arguing that the pattern reflected an early (pre-Pauline) Christian catechetical pattern (*The Epistle to the Romans,* ICC [Edinburgh: T. & T. Clark, 1979], 2:670–73). Friedrich et al. point out, however, that neither Paul (13:3) nor the Jewish tradition (Prov. 7:1; 24:21; Sirach 3:11) observes this distinction consistently ("Situation," 165; cf. Käsemann, *Commentary,* 359).

60. "The sword" refers to the lethal power enforcing Roman hegemony, "the presence of power which unavoidably as such causes terror and anxiety" (Käsemann, *Commentary,* 358; cf. Friedrich et al., "Situation," 144). Earlier in this same letter (8:35), "the sword" clearly refers to lethal force, and is arrayed among very real calamities that threaten the existence of the people of God in the last days.

and customs *without constraint.*"[61] But contrary to that very reasonable expectation, forceful "constraint" is quite explicitly threatened here!

It is not sufficient to identify a specific convergence of circumstances that might have prompted Paul to write a passage like ours. In order to explicate "the inner logic of his thought," we must ask not only why Paul might have made such amenable comments about civil authority as we find here, but why those comments are entwined with clear references to causes of "terror and anxiety" in the body politic as well.

An answer is to be found in contemporary discussions of the maintenance of public order in the period of the Roman republic and empire. Again and again we find that "fear" is yoked with "consent" as a motive for conformity to social standards, though fear is expected to be more effective among those, especially from the lower classes, who do not have the sense willingly to embrace the society's values as their own.

Addressing this subject, Cicero, whose political speeches are of prime value for the study of Roman propaganda, described how a society encouraged the values of "praise and glory and disgrace and dishonor," the values at the heart of ceremonial rhetoric (epideictic). The "best men" are deterred from crime, Cicero declared, not so much by "the fear of the penalties ordained by law as by the sense of shame which Nature has given to man in the form of a certain fear of justified censure." Thus the wise statesman has recourse both to rhetoric, which provides training in shame, and to the evocation of fear, in maintaining order (*De republica* 5.6). We may suppose that in Cicero's view, lesser men were more naturally motivated by the fear of punishment, and that for them force would have been more effective than rhetoric. Contrasting rule by consent (among the upper classes) with rule by force (for slaves), Cicero worried that an increase of "lawlessness" might cause a reversion to force alone, "so that those who up to now obeyed us willingly would be held faithful by fear alone" (3,41).

We find the same candor about the coincidence of persuasion and coercion in the propaganda of the principate. Extolling the accession of Tiberius, the historian Velleius Paterculus declared that "justice, equity, and industry, long buried in oblivion, have been restored to the state....Rioting in the theater has been suppressed; *all citizens have either been impressed with the wish to do right, or have been forced to do so by necessity*" (*History of Rome* 2.126). Still later, Plutarch would contrast the Romans' obsession with Fortune, the god who had delivered countless military triumphs into their hands, with the devotion to "Wisdom or Prudence" found among peoples, like the Greeks, who placed value on persuasion (*The Fortune of the Romans* 318).

While persuasion and coercion were yoked in imperial rhetoric, Jews

---

61. Käsemann, *Commentary*, 352 (emphasis added).

of the Roman Diaspora *contrasted* the order imposed through coercion with the concord won by persuasion among equals, and identified the latter with the Jewish *politeia*. According to Philo, in the giving of the Torah Moses had avoided "issuing orders without words of exhortation, as though to slaves instead of free men," for this "savored of tyranny and despotism." Rather, "in his commands and prohibitions he suggests and admonishes rather than commands," with laws written "in order to exhort rather than to enforce" (*De Vita Mosis* 2.49–51). Similarly Josephus declared that Moses had created, not a monarchy or an oligarchy, but a theocracy based upon persuasion, setting in supreme position the priests, men "preeminently gifted with persuasive eloquence and discretion" (*Against Apion* 2.164–67, 186–87, 218–19). And 4 Maccabees has the pious Eleazar defy the Greek tyrant who threatens him with torture: "We who are firmly persuaded that we must lead our lives in accordance with the divine Law recognize no compulsion violent enough to overcome our own willing obedience to the Law" (5:16).

These last are brave words, spoken in extremity. The three texts just cited show that a single *topos,* the contrast between persuasion and forceful coercion, could be used in more accommodating texts — as when Josephus or Philo seek to show Moses as a model of persuasive rhetoric — as well as in texts representing open defiance of imperial power. For his part, Philo recognizes both possibilities, of accommodation and of defiance, as appropriate responses for the empire's subjects, *depending on the circumstances.* It is critically important for Philo — as for his Jewish reader! — to distinguish "speaking most freely" (*eleutherotomeitō phaskein*), "boldness of speech" (*parrēsia*), from "untimely frankness" (*akairon parrēsia*), the reckless defiance by which some Jews have put their entire community into mortal jeopardy (*De Somniis* 2.83–84).

Although those who display "untimely frankness" risk dreadful destruction at the hands of the overlords — "they are branded and beaten and mutilated and suffer before they die every savage and pitiless torture, and then are led away to execution and killed"[62] — open defiance of tyranny is the birthright of the Jew, *made when circumstances allow.* Thus, "when the times are right, it is good to set ourselves against the violence of our enemies and subdue it; *but when the circumstances do not present themselves, the safe course is to stay quiet*" (2.92).

Philo's theme is caution (*eulabeia*). The wise person "knows how mightily blow the winds of necessity, fortune, opportunity, force, violence, and princedom," and will therefore take caution "as an inseparable safeguard to prevent any grave disaster." Again, the wise person is

---

62. Philo, loc. cit.; trans. E. R. Goodenough, *An Introduction to Philo Judaeus*, 2d ed. (Oxford: Basil Blackwell, 1962), 55.

like Abraham, who did obeisance to the sons of Cheth "when the fitness of the circumstances prompted him to do so" (2.89). This is the caution of a ship's pilot, who prefers the safety of the harbor when a hurricane appears on the horizon; like those who charm poisonous snakes rather than provoke them (2.85–89). Significantly, Josephus knows the same *topos*, put for example into the mouth of Agrippa as he appeals to the rebels of Jerusalem to surrender to the Romans: "It would be good while your ship is still in port to foresee the coming storm, and not to put out into the midst of the hurricane and meet your doom!" (*War* 2.396). Since far mightier peoples have submitted to Rome, Agrippa argues, how much more should the Jews, "to whom thralldom is hereditary," submit? (2.358–89). Indeed, "the powers that be should be conciliated by flattery, not irritated"; "there is nothing to check blows like submission" (2.350–51).

For Josephus, however, recognition that divine assistance "is ranged on the side of the Romans," and submission to those "to whom Fortune has transferred her favors," is always the proper response of the devout. Philo's "political realism," in contrast, is merely pragmatic. All who recognize the "vainglory" of the powers will rightly hate it, loathe it, abhor it (*De Somniis* 2.98). One submits to ferocious, brutal rulers, and seeks to "tame and soothe" them, simply because opposing them avails nothing (2.89). Thus "it was not out of any feeling of respect [*timē*] for those who by nature and race and custom were the enemies of reason . . . that [Abraham] brought himself to do obeisance. Rather it was just because he feared their power at the time and their formidable strength and took care to give no provocation" (2.90).

The same prudential caution is appropriate when Philo's Jewish contemporaries go into the Alexandrian marketplace (2.91–92). They quickly make way "for the rulers, and for beasts beneath the yoke." Of course, Philo protests, the motive is different: "With the rulers, we act out of respect [*timē*]; to beasts beneath the yoke, we act on account of fear [*phobon*], so we suffer no serious injury from them." E. R. Goodenough quite perceptively noted Philo's political doubletalk in this, "one of the most vital passages from ancient literature," which functions as a tract of political counsel.[63] Abraham did obeisance to pagan rulers out of "fear of their power," not out of respect — and yet the Jews of Alexandria naturally give way to their overlords out of respect, not fear!

"The sarcasm at the end is obvious," Goodenough writes:

> Philo has compared harsh rulers to savage and deadly animals throughout. When he mentions how in the marketplace the Jews have to make place for their rulers and the pack animals alike, it

---

63. *An Introduction to Philo Judaeus*, 55–57.

is part of the very caution he is counselling that he should distinguish between the two, once the rulers in Alexandria have been
distinctly referred to, and say that one gives way out of honor to
the rulers, but out of fear to the beasts.... But his Jewish readers
would quite well have understood that the reason Philo gave way
to each was the same, because he knew that if he did not he would
be crushed.[64]

"Philo is truly the Jewish champion, ready to die for the people and
the law which are dearer to him than life; but, bold as he can be under
favorable conditions, he still never loses his astute sense of where to
stop." As his characterizations of official brutality show, "Philo detests
the Roman political power and longs for the day of its overthrow, but
with realistic caution will praise Roman rulers to their face in the hope
that they will help and support the Jews." He is thus representative of
the Jews under Roman rule generally, for whom "political activity consisted, in dealing with the Romans, largely in flattery, obsequiousness,
and insinuation. All people of the Empire had to do the same."[65]

In light of Philo's guarded language, the ambivalent remarks in Rom.
13:1–7 become clearer. "Honor" may be due the authorities — at least
some of them — but so, given the reality of the Roman sword, is fear.
The comparison with Philo allows us to see that the "political realism"
expressed by Paul has nothing to do with an "inevitable" social order,
to which Christians simply must accustom themselves. "Fear" (of the
sword) and "conscience," i.e., consent to the good to which the authorities are supposed to be dedicated, are equally powerful motives for
civic behavior. Given the realities of Roman rule, one may "do good"
and hope for the best (13:3); but under the circumstances, open resistance cannot be contemplated, so long as the authorities wield the sword
(13:4).

*Just this ambivalence regarding the authorities was quite out of
pace with the contemporary propaganda of the empire.* It had been a
rhetorical mainstay of the principate that Augustus's wars had achieved
spectacular peace throughout the world: Augustus congratulated himself
on "peace, secured by victory, throughout the whole domain of the Roman people on land and sea" (*Res Gestae* 2.13). The historian Velleius
Paterculus proclaimed that on Octavius's return to Rome after his victory at Actium, "The civil wars were ended after twenty years, foreign
wars suppressed, peace restored, the frenzy of arms everywhere lulled
to rest; validity was restored to the laws, authority to the courts, and
dignity to the senate; the power of the magistrates was reduced to its
former limits.... The old traditional form of the republic was restored.

---

64. Ibid., 57.
65. Ibid., 60, 62; 54.

Agriculture returned to the fields, respect to religion, to mankind freedom from anxiety, and to each citizen his property rights were now
assured" (*History* 2.89).

Closer to Paul's time, the propaganda of imperial peace reached its
fulsome zenith upon Nero's accession. Explicitly contrasted with the *Pax
Augusta*, peace under Nero had not been established through war. His
propagandists set themselves to the unprecedented challenge of hymning
the lapse even of the memory of war. Thus Calpurnius Siculus:

> The unholy War-Goddess [*Bellona*] shall yield and have her van-
> quished hands bound behind her back, and, stripped of weapons,
> turn her furious teeth into her own entrails; upon herself shall she
> wage the civil wars which of late she spread o'er all the world....
> Fair peace shall come, fair not in visage alone.... Clemency has
> commanded every vice that wears the disguise of peace to betake
> itself afar: she has broken every maddened sword-blade.... Peace
> in her fullness shall come; knowing not the drawn sword, she shall
> renew once more the reign of Saturn in Latium, once more the
> reign of Numa who first taught the tasks of peace to armies that
> rejoiced in slaughter. (Eclogue 1.45–65)

The so-called Einsiedeln Eclogues take the theme of the "undrawn
sword" to a new poetic height, as herdsmen in a bucolic paradise glorify
the peace brought by Nero:

> We reap with no sword, nor do towns in fast-closed walls prepare
> unutterable war: there is not any woman who, dangerous in her
> motherhood, gives birth to an enemy. Unarmed our youth can dig
> the fields, and the boy, trained to the slow-moving plow, marvels at
> the sword hanging in the abode of his fathers. (Eclogue 25–31)[66]

Nero's accession was carefully orchestrated. His advisor Seneca prepared a series of speeches with which Nero announced how his newly
inaugurated rule would diverge from that of his predecessor, Claudius:
he would abandon the proscriptions of political enemies and personal
interventions in capital cases. Whether or not Seneca's *De Clementia*
("On Mercy") was one of these speeches, it expresses the propaganda
theme admirably. Seneca proposes the emperor reflect on his absolute
power over "this vast throng — discordant, factious, and unruly, ready
to run riot alike for the destruction of itself and others if it should break
its yoke" (1.1):

> I am the arbiter of life and death for the nations.... All those many
> thousands of swords which my peace restrains will be drawn at

---

66. Texts in J. Wight Duff and Arnold M. Duff, eds., *Minor Latin Poets*, LCC
(Cambridge: Harvard University Press, 1954).

my nod; what nations shall be utterly destroyed, which banished,
... this it is mine to decree. With all things thus at my disposal, I
have been moved neither by anger nor youthful impulse to unjust
punishment.... With me the sword is hidden, nay, is sheathed; I
am sparing to the utmost of even the meanest blood; no man fails
to find favor at my hands though he lack all else but the name of
man. (*De Clem.* 1.2–4)

In contrast to the military triumphs of Augustus, Nero's gift is "a
state unstained by blood, and your prideful boast that in the whole
world you have shed not a drop of human blood is the more significant
and wonderful because no one ever had the sword put into his hands at
an earlier age" (11.3). Nero would be that good prince who, "protected
by his own good deeds, needs no bodyguard; the arms he wears are for
adornment only" (13.5).

History would give the proof of these vaunted claims. The sword
would be deployed to murderous effect during Nero's reign, within
Rome as well as in distant Judaea, where legions would be dispatched
to suppress the Jewish revolt. But our present interest is not with Nero's
murderousness, or with the question, much belabored in scholarship,
of the extent to which the personal proclivities of a *princeps* would
influence the structural violence of the institution.[67] I stress the contrast between the propaganda theme of the idle sword — undrawn,
unbloodied, unremembered, a quaint relic of bygone days — and Paul's
testy declaration that the authority "does not bear the sword in vain."

To any within the Roman churches tempted to take the imperial self-
advertisements at face value, and correspondingly to divide the world's
people into those who enjoyed a new age of perfect peace and harmony,
on the one hand, and those barbarians who stood at the periphery of
empire, on the other (cf. Rom. 1:14–15), even the naively optimistic
remarks in 13:1–7 betray a sobering caution. The imperial sword is *not*
idle: it continues to threaten destruction and bloodshed.

Against the keen eschatological tenor of his letters elsewhere, Paul's
positive characterization of "the governing authorities" here appears a
foreign body. Within the rhetorical structure of Romans, however, these
remarks have an important function: to encourage submission, for now,
to the authorities, rather than desperate resistance; and thus to safeguard
the most vulnerable around and among the Roman Christians, those
Jews struggling to rebuild their shattered community in the wake of imperial violence. There is hope here: in the diligence of the authorities for
the common good (*proskarterountes*, 13:6), as in the diligence of the
Christians (*proskarterountes*, 12:12) who pray, endure, share their food

---

67. See Miriam Griffin, *Nero: The End of a Dynasty* (New Haven: Yale University
Press, 1984).

and their homes, stand with those who rejoice or mourn, "make their way with those who have been humbled" (12:16).

There is also warning here, against arrogance, presumption, the scapegoating of the weak and the vanquished; and warning against any disruptive action that could bring crashing down on the poor community of Israel the ominous storm clouds of imperial power overhead. Only the most pernicious twists of fate would later enlist these verses in the service of the empire itself.[68]

---

68. Elliott, *Liberating Paul,* 7–9, 13–20, 221–26.

Part IV

Building an alternative society

Introduction

> When any of you has a grievance against another, do you dare to take it to court before the unrighteous, instead of taking it before the saints? Do you not know that the saints will judge the world?
>
> (1 Cor. 6:1–2)

To believe that Paul founded a religion is anachronistic, as explained in the general introduction above, although his letters did indeed become a central part of the scriptures of the Christianity that developed partly as a result of his mission. Nor can Paul be understood to have "converted" from one religion to another, although the stories of Paul on the road to Damascus in the book of Acts became paradigmatic for later conversions to Christianity. It is historically unjustified to imagine that a religion called Judaism or another called Christianity already existed at the time of Paul. If we are going to use modern concepts and analogies for ancient historical realities and relationships, then we need to reexamine the sources such as Paul's letters in the wider context of the Roman empire and from a wider perspective of a more comprehensive and inclusive picture of social relations. The movement that Paul joined and then spearheaded in the area of Greece and Asia Minor clearly began in Galilee and Judea and was a development of Israelite traditions. And it clearly had a religious dimension. Reexamination of Paul's letters in wider historical context, however, suggests that Paul understood his mission as far more than setting up a new religious cult or a sect of Judaism.

When Paul refers to his origins he writes not that he was a believer or practicer of "Judaism," but that he was of the "people" or "race" of Israel, which had tribal subdivisions and varying understandings of the Law and varying degrees of enthusiasm or "patriotism" within "Israel" for the traditional way of life (Phil. 3:4–6). The *ioudaismos* in which he was "advanced beyond many among my people of the same age" (Gal. 1:14) cannot justifiably be translated simply as "Judaism." It probably meant a group or movement among contemporary Jews to enforce within Jewish communities a communal discipline of maintaining the traditional way of life, over against the pressure from the Roman empire and its Hellenistic predecessors to adopt the Greek way of life (*hellenismos*).[1] Paul's description of his own fanaticism in Gal. 1:13–

---

1. The first appearance of these terms is in 2 Maccabees, an epitome of Jason of

206

14 and Phil. 3:6 fits just such an understanding of *ioudaismos.* In his *zēlos* for the traditions of his ancestors, the traditional Israelite way of life, he was attempting to destroy the *ekklēsia,* the fledging "Jesus movement" that was breaking with Jewish communal discipline as Paul then understood it. The religious and political dimensions were inseparable in the *ioudaismos* movement within the contemporary people of Israel that Paul was involved in prior to his joining the very Jesus movement he had been attempting to suppress. Its agenda was evidently to maintain the independence of Israel insofar as possible in the context of the Roman empire and over against both the pressures of assimilation and overt anti-Roman activity that might evoke Roman military action against Israel.

Studies of Paul have generally placed credibility in Paul's comment that he was "a Pharisee as to the Law." It is unwarranted, however, to categorize a Pharisaic background or training as narrowly religious. Recent studies of the Pharisees are broadening the picture of them as having narrowed their concerns from temple-state politics to religion under Herod the Great, supposedly becoming merely an eating club devoted to priestly purity in everyday life.[2] As can be seen in Josephus's reports of their intrigue against Herod and their prominent role in the high priestly junta after the outbreak of the great revolt against Roman rule in 66 C.E., they continued their activities as a political interest group among the scribal retainers of the temple state.[3] In the imperial situation of the Judean temple state, the Pharisees and other scribal retainers were perpetually "caught in the middle." In their role as the professional cultivators and guardians of the traditional Judean-Israelite way of life, they attempted to hold Judean society together according to "the laws of the Judeans" (Josephus's term), while also serving, in effect, as the mediators of the Roman imperial order under their high priestly patrons who served as client rulers for Rome.[4] It is understandable that

---

Cyrene's history of the Maccabean struggle against the Hellenizing reform in Jerusalem, surely meant to inspire such resistance elsewhere among Jewish communities subject to Hellenistic imperial rule. On the hypothesis that *ioudaismos* was developed over against and on the model of such *hellenismos,* see Jonathan Goldstein, *II Maccabees,* Anchor Bible 41A (Garden City, N.Y.: Doubleday, 1983).

2. This is the highly influential construction documented from rabbinic sources by Jacob Neusner in *The Rabbinic Traditions about the Pharisees before 70,* 3 vols. (Leiden: Brill, 1971), and popularized in *From Politics to Piety: The Emergence of Pharisaic Judaism* (Englewood Cliffs, N.J.: Prentice-Hall, 1973).

3. For construction of the social (religious-economic-political) role of the Pharisees as scribal "retainers" according to standard sociology of traditional agrarian societies, see Anthony J. Saldarini, *Pharisees, Scribes, and Sadducees in Palestinian Society: A Sociological Approach* (Wilmington, Del.: Glazier, 1988); for a critical reexamination of Josephus's accounts of the Pharisees and their history in second temple society, see Steve Mason, *Flavius Josephus on the Pharisees* (Leiden: Brill, 1991), summarized in *Josephus and the New Testament* (Peabody, Mass.: Hendrickson, 1992), 132–48.

4. See the provisional sketch in Richard A. Horsley, *Jesus and the Spiral of Violence:*

a Pharisee in the Judean temple state, emphasizing the maintenance of the traditional way of life while attempting to suppress any provocative outbreak of popular resistance against Rome rule, would have become involved in the *ioudaismos* movement. Both the Pharisees and the fanatical advocates of *ioudaismos* were engaged in the difficult maneuver of maintaining the traditional way of life in resistance to empire while serving as mediators of the *pax Romana*.

If the language Paul used with reference to the movement and communities he was building is any indication, he clearly did not think of them in explicitly religious terms. "Cultic borrowing from Hellenistic-Roman socioreligous clubs (cf. *thiasos* and *eranos*) and the usual Hellenistic-Roman language for worship are absent."[5] When Paul does use cultic-sacrificial language, he applies it metaphorically to social-ethical behavior of believers or to his own potential martyrdom (Rom. 12:1; Phil. 2:17). Paul was not establishing a religious cult in worship of (a) God. That believers underwent baptism as a rite of entrance into the movement did not make it into a mystery religion such as the initiation into Isis, the Queen of heaven. Nor — despite some similar features — were Paul's communities modeled on the associations or guilds (*collegia*) devoted to some god that multiplied under the early empire and with which later Roman opponents of Christian groups identified them. Besides "the almost complete absence of common terminology for the groups themselves or for their leaders," Paul's communities were both far more comprehensive (even totalistic) in their common purpose, exclusive over against the dominant society, and parts of an intercity, international movement.[6]

The principal term Paul uses with reference both to the movement as a whole and to the particular local communities is *ekklēsia*. By general consensus, while *ekklēsia* comes to Paul from the Septuagint (the Jewish Bible in Greek) with strong connotations of the "assembly" of (all) Israel, its primary meaning in the Greek-speaking eastern Roman empire was the citizen "assembly" of the Greek *polis*. *Ekklēsia* is thus a political term with certain religious overtones. It is misleading to continue to translate *ekklēsia* as "church," particularly insofar as that implies wor-

---

Popular Jewish Resistance in Roman Palestine (San Francisco: Harper & Row, 1987), chaps. 1, 3, 5.

5. J. Christiaan Beker, *Paul the Apostle: The Triumph of God in Life and Thought* (Philadelphia: Fortress, 1984), 319–20. E. A. Judge, "Cultural Conformity and Innovation in Paul: Some Clues from Contemporary Documents," *Tyndale Bulletin* 35 (1984): 6–7.

6. See the fuller comparison and contrast by Wayne A. Meeks, *First Urban Christians: The Social World of the Apostle Paul* (New Haven: Yale University Press, 1983), 77–80. He also points out (81–84) that the "religious fellowships" of the Pythagorean and Epicurean philosophical schools (about which we know little until late antiquity) are not a credible model for Paul's communities. Despite their lack of explicitly religious language Meeks still thinks of the Pauline communities as new "cultic" communities (e.g., 190).

ship or ritual activity.[7] On the other hand, the "assembly" of the Greek *polis* certainly involved praise, acclamation, and discussion of issues of concern to the citizenry, which were also some of the principal activities that Paul's communities carried on at gatherings of the "assemblies." Paul evidently understood the *ekklēsia* of a Thessalonica or Corinth not as a "cultic community," but as the political assembly of the people "in Christ" in pointed juxtaposition and "competition" with the official city assembly (e.g., 1 Thess. 1:1; 1 Cor. 11:18; cf. all the "assemblies" of a given Roman province, 1 Cor. 16:1; 16:19; 2 Cor. 8:1; Gal. 1:2; 1 Thess. 2:14).[8] Paul, moreover, understood that in catalyzing local assemblies among the peoples and cities, he was building an international political-religious movement also known by the political term *ekklēsia,* in either singular or plural.

Paul's *ekklēsiai* are thus local communities of an alternative society to the Roman imperial order.[9] The alternative society, moreover, is rooted in the history of Israel, in opposition to the *pax Romana.* Those familiar with the Hebrew Bible immediately recognize that when Paul speaks of "the *ekklēsia* of God," the underlying foundation is the *qehal yhwh,* the "assembly of the LORD," the assembly of historical Israel (either as a whole or in a given region; cf. 1 Cor. 1:2; 10:32). In God's guidance of human affairs, history, which had been running through Israel and not through Rome, has finally come to fulfillment. The promises to Abraham that all peoples would receive blessings through his seed have now been fulfilled in the crucifixion of Jesus Christ and his exaltation in heaven as the eschatological Lord (over and displacing Caesar, the imperial lord and savior). This is consistently present in Paul's letters, explicitly and centrally in Galatians, 1 Corinthians, and Romans, and implicitly in 1 Thessalonians, Philippians, and sections of 2 Corinthians. This fulfillment of history that runs through Israel stands over against the Roman imperial order. The fulfillment of the promises to Abraham has now come to the other (non-Israelite) nations. The movement, especially in Paul's mission area, was thus "international," with "assemblies" in the various provinces. But those from among the "peoples/

---

7. Beker, *Paul the Apostle,* 317. Although he still translates *ekklēsia* as "church," Beker understands it as far more than a religious community throughout chap. 14.

8. Similarly Dieter Georgi, *Theocracy in Paul's Praxis and Theology* (Minneapolis: Fortress, 1991), 57; and Meeks, *First Urban Christians,* 108.

9. Georgi uses a less politically "realistic" but similar term, "a concrete alternative social utopia" (*Theocracy,* 51, in connection with Galatians 3–6). Whereas he sees several central ideals of "Hellenistic society" as the basis of Paul's communities, I suggest we look to Paul's background in the traditions of Israel, including the Mosaic covenant, which he seems to deemphasize into a historically limited role in Galatians 3. Vincent L. Wimbush similarly concludes that Paul's "early Christianity," in effect, "took the 'heart' out of the Empire not only in its radial allegiance to another power, but also in its creation of whole new basic units of social existence" (*Paul, the Worldly Ascetic* [Macon, Ga.: Mercer University Press, 1987], 93.)

nations" who joined the movement were no longer *of* those nations, no longer belonged to them (see 1 Cor. 12:2;[10] cf. the disparagement of "Gentiles who do not know God," 1 Thess. 4:5; Gal. 2:15). Those "baptized into Christ" or "belong[ing] to Christ" were changed into "Abraham's offspring according to the promise," no longer slaves or minors but heirs of the blessings promised to Abraham (Gal. 3:26–4:7; Rom. 15:7–13).[11] Believers from among the nations were branches cut off from "wild olive" trees and grafted into a "cultivated olive tree" (Rom. 11:17–24).[12]

It has often been observed that Paul's communities were exclusive, separated from "the world." More than that, however, Paul's alternative society stood sharply against the Roman imperial order. The most vivid expression of this comes in 1 Thess. 5:1–11 (discussed in the selection by Helmut Koester in Part III above), where the Thessalonians are engaged defensively in a virtual war with the empire, shielding themselves against its attacks with the metaphorical "breastplate of faith and love and the helmet of the hope of salvation."[13] In the first selection below, Karl Donfried juxtaposes Paul's portrayal of the hostility and opposition that his mission and community in Thessalonica experienced with the imperial cult and other manifestations of the imperial order there. "Acceptance and integration into society at large" would have been the last thing Paul wanted for his assemblies.[14] To the Corinthians, for example, he insisted rather that they not have recourse to or cooperate with the official courts; indeed "the saints" themselves would "judge the world" (1 Cor. 6:1–6). Similarly, he forbade them to participate in temple banquets of food sacrificed to gods — sacrificial meals which, in effect, constituted a given kinship, urban, or imperial community (1 Cor. 10:14–22). His general principle was that, while remaining open to the society at large in order to recruit more people into the movement, the Corinthians (and presumably other assemblies) were to live "as if they had no dealings with the world" (1 Cor. 7:29–31). Certain

---

10. Note that both (N)RSV and (N)JB transform the ethnic/political "nations/gentiles" into the religious term "pagans."

11. But Paul does not think of the *ekklēsia* as the new or true Israel ("the Israel of God" in Gal. 6:16 is surely Israel). It is not the displacement or replacement, but part of the fulfillment (of the history) of Israel.

12. John M. G. Barclay (*Jews in the Mediterranean Diaspora from Alexander to Trajan (232 B.C.E.–117 C.E.)* [Edinburgh: T. & T. Clark, 1996], 393), suggests that "In his conceptuality Paul is most at home among the particularistic and least accommodated segments of the Diaspora; . . . yet he employs the language of a culturally antagonistic Judaism to establish a new social entity which transgresses the boundaries of the Diaspora synagogues." As suggested in that last phrase, however, Barclay's treatment is problematic insofar as it ignores the imperial context, as if the only issue were Jews vs. Gentiles.

13. Georgi, *Theocracy,* 27–28.

14. Versus the functionalism that informs Halvor Moxnes, "Honor and Righteousness in Romans," *JSNT* 32 (1988): 67–68.

diaspora Jewish *synagogai* ("assemblies") had their own semi-separate *politeuma* (constitution or form of self-government), but one officially or tacitly approved by the Roman authorities. By contrast, Paul insists that "our *politeuma* is in heaven, and it is from there that we are expecting a *Sōtēr*" (Phil. 3:20) — both an alternative constitution or form of government and an alternative emperor for an alternative society.[15]

Strangely enough, a key aspect of Paul's mission strategy by which he was building an alternative society was the way in which he used the basic forms and key terms of Greco-Roman political rhetoric in order to persuade his assemblies to maintain their solidarity over against the dominant imperial society. In the rediscovery of ancient rhetorical forms and their appearance in Paul's letters, special attention has been paid to Paul's adaptation of deliberative arguments to persuade his communities to take a particular course of action. In 1 Corinthians, in particular, many of the key terms are those standardly used in political rhetoric to urge cities to pursue concord and the common advantage, and not be divided into factions.[16] But Paul is precisely not urging the Corinthians to "be united in the same mind and the same purpose" and to seek mutual advantage with the rest of Corinthian society. He is rather attempting to unite his Corinthian assembly, through their mutual "building up" of the community, so that they can stand in solidarity against the official courts and overlapping communities constituted by sacrificial meals in temples (1 Cor. 6:1–9 and 10:14–22).

Recognition that this is the way Paul uses the rhetoric he has borrowed/learned from the dominant culture leads to a more precise reconstruction about Paul's relation to Hellenistic culture in general. Debate continues about Paul's degree of acculturation and assimilation into Hellenistic culture and how that meshes with the way his orientation and perspective was formed during his time in Judea (in Pharisaic and/or apocalyptic circles?). It is impossible to engage that debate in

---

15. On *politeuma* see Gert Lüderitz, "What Is Politeuma?" in Jan W. Van Henten and Pieter W. Van der Horst, eds., *Studies in Early Jewish Epigraphy* (Leiden: Brill, 1994), 181–225; Stanley K. Stowers, "Friends and Enemies in the Politics of Heaven," in Jouette M. Bassler, ed., *Pauline Theology* (Minneapolis: Fortress, 1991), 1:112–13. The standard view that Paul was socially "(extremely) conservative," "not willing or able to challenge the social structures of his society," precisely because in his apocalyptic enthusiasm he was expecting its termination (e.g., Beker, *Paul the Apostle,* 322–26; cf. the sketch of this view by Neil Elliott, *Liberating Paul: The Justice of God and the Politics of the Apostle* [Maryknoll, N.Y.: Orbis Books, 1994], 37–40) thus seems to be an inappropriate characterization. If modern analogies of questionable applicability are to be used, then Paul is a "radical" in his rejection of the established order, although not a "revolutionary" who attempted to overthrow it.

16. See, e.g., Margaret M. Mitchell, *Paul and the Rhetoric of Reconciliation* (Louisville: Westminster/John Knox, 1992); Stephen M. Pogoloff, *Logos and Sophia: The Rhetorical Situation of 1 Corinthians,* SBLDS 134 (Atlanta: Scholars Press, 1992); Lawrence L. Welborn, "On the Discord in Corinth: 1 Corinthians 1–4 and Ancient Politics," *JBL* 106 (1987): 85–111.

this context.[17] Yet it is worth noting briefly that most of the passages in which Paul is seen to be utilizing particular motifs and forms from Hellenistic culture are in the Corinthian correspondence. More precise investigations of the particular terms, phrases, and ideas in 1 Corinthians (and 2 Cor. 2:14–6:2) are suggesting that Paul is responding not to some form of Gnosticism, but to a form of Hellenistic Jewish wisdom theology, similar to that in Wisdom of Solomon and Philo of Alexandria, that had probably been introduced into the Corinthian assembly by Apollos.[18] Thus the principal passages in which Paul seems to speak and think in standard Hellenistic terms and forms are not "typical" of Paul. And those standard Hellenistic terms and forms come to him not necessarily from his own education, but mediated through a Hellenistic Jewish theology that had itself assimilated Hellenistic cultural forms in developing a spirituality that provided transcendence of the dominant social order. The framing perspective within which Paul discusses issues arising from the introduction of wisdom theology into Corinth is Paul's adaptation of Judean apocalyptic language and orientation toward the fulfillment of history (as in passages such as 1 Cor. 2:6–8, discussed by Elliott in chapter 10 above, 3:12–15; 10:5–11; and 15). Throughout the letter the burden of his arguments is to insist on the solidarity and "building up" of the community (separate from the wider society) and against individual spiritual transcendence of the mundane expressed in terms of wisdom, enlightenment theology, and immortality of soul.[19]

While he articulates only vague images of the concrete shape of the future life he anticipated in the "kingdom of God" following the *parousia,* Paul does indicate at several points how social relations in his assemblies should be conducted. And although in his practice Paul may not have lived up to his ideal principles, the latter represent an opposition to and breakthrough of the dominant patterns of social relations in imperial Roman society. The selection by Elisabeth Schüssler Fiorenza below explains how the "baptismal formula" that "there is no

---

17. E.g., E. P. Sanders, *Paul and Palestinian Judaism* (Minneapolis: Fortress, 1977); Abraham Malherbe, *Paul and the Popular Philosophers* (Minneapolis: Fortress, 1989); and Troels Engberg-Pedersen, ed., *Paul in His Hellenistic Context* (Minneapolis: Fortress, 1995). Barclay (*Jews in the Mediterranean Diaspora,* 390–91) comments that "to turn to Paul after reading most other Diaspora literature is to be struck by his minimal use of Hellenistic theology, anthropology or ethics," and that "the main thrust of Pauline theology was inherently antipathetic to any such attempt to find common cause with Hellenistic culture."

18. See esp. Birger Pearson, *The Pneumatos-Psychikos Terminology in 1 Corinthians,* SBLDS 12 (Missoula, Mont.: Scholars Press, 1973); and Richard A. Horsley, "Wisdom of Word and Word of Wisdom," *CBQ* 39 (1977): 223–39; "How Can Some of You Say, 'There Is No Resurrection of the Dead?' Spiritual Elitism in Corinth," *NovT* 20 (1978): 203–31; "Gnosis in Corinth: 1 Corinthians 8:1–6," *NTS* 27 (1980): 32–51.

19. Mitchell, *The Rhetoric of Reconciliation;* Richard A. Horsley, *1 Corinthians,* Abingdon Bible Commentaries (Nashville: Abingdon, forthcoming).

longer Jew or Greek, . . . slave or free, . . . male and female" (Gal. 3:28) symbolized a transcendence of the principal divisions within the dominant society, particularly as embodied in the patriarchal slave-holding household, and how Paul adapted and applied that formula.

Egalitarian, in contrast to hierarchical, social relations even extended into the economic dimension in Paul's pursuit of his alternative society, although again his practice may not have embodied his intentions. When Paul became an "apostle" in the Jesus movement following his commissioning with his own distinctive "gospel" by Christ, he identified with the horizontal reciprocity of social-economic relations of a movement rooted in the peasant villages of Galilee, with their Israelite covenantal traditions (Gal. 1:13–24). These relatively egalitarian social relations stood in sharp opposition to the hierarchical relations of the Roman patronage system in general and the similar "patron-client" arrangement in which he had (apparently) been involved as a zealous Pharisee. Paul's own otherwise baffling refusal to accept economic support from Corinthians, contrary to the "right" of an apostle and the general practice within the movement (1 Cor. 9:1–18; cf. 2 Cor. 11:7–11), can best be explained as his attempt to avoid being pulled into a typical patron-client relationship with one or more of the heads of households in which the Corinthian assembly members met.[20] Ironically, while attempting to embody an alternative to the patronage system economically in Corinth, he may have, in effect, established his own little patronage network with the household heads Gaius, Crispus, and particularly Stephanas (1 Cor. 1:14–16; 16:15–17). Over against the hierarchical social-economic patronage system by which the whole imperial society became structured and the hierarchical political economy of subject peoples rendering tribute to the empire, moreover, Paul aggressively organized and administered a "collection" for "the poor among the saints in Jerusalem" (Rom. 15:25–28; 1 Cor. 16:1–4; 2 Corinthians 8; 9). In concrete terms, the collection amounted to an international horizontal reciprocal economic relationship, as opposed to the vertical system of tributary relations. My own essay below explores these and other facets of the alternative society that Paul was attempting to build in his assemblies.

Paul understood his commission to include more than simply preaching a gospel of Christ's crucifixion and resurrection, a gospel about the fulfillment of history in decisive events of the recent past. His gospel also included the *parousia* of Christ in the imminent future. And he understood his commission with the gospel to include establishing assemblies of believers among the nations of Asia Minor and Greece (and

---

20. See Victor P. Furnish, *II Corinthians,* Anchor Bible (Garden City, N.Y.: Doubleday, 1984), 507–8.

eventually of Spain). Indeed, his own commissioned role was second in importance to that of Christ himself in the fulfillment of history. He somehow felt responsible for seeing those assemblies of a society alternative to the Roman imperial order remain intact until the *parousia* of their true *Sōtēr* and the establishment of the kingdom of God. And that is why he wrote his ad hoc letters to his communities, insisting that they maintain their solidarity in the struggle over against the dominant imperial order until Christ had made "all things subject to himself" (Phil. 3:20–21), that is, "destroyed every rule and every authority and power" (1 Cor. 15:24). But "none of the rulers of this age understood this; for if they had, they would not have crucified the Lord of glory" (1 Cor. 2:8).

The Imperial Cults of Thessalonica and Political Conflict in 1 Thessalonians

KARL P. DONFRIED

The starting point for the interpretation of the Thessalonian correspondence must be the reconstruction, as best we can, of the religious and political history of Thessalonica, at least to the time of the earliest Christian community.

In Acts 17 the Jews together with some persons from the *agora* in Thessalonica attacked the home of Paul's sponsor, Jason. When they could not find them, they dragged Jason and some of the brethren before the city authorities, crying, "These men who have turned the world upside down have come here also, and Jason has received them; and they are all acting against the decrees of Caesar (*tōn dogmatōn Kaisaros*), saying that there is another king, Jesus." What are these *dogmata Kaisaros* which Paul and his associates violated? Is Luke here spinning an entertaining story or is he faithfully describing the reality of the Thessalonian situation?

E. A. Judge cites a number of imperial decrees which might have been referred to as "decrees of Caesar" in Thessalonica.[1] Among them is the following intensified ban on prediction from Tiberius in 16 C.E.:

> But as for all the other astrologers and magicians and such as practiced divination in anyway whatsoever, he put to death those who were foreigners and banished all the citizens that were accused of still employing the art at this time after the previous decree (*dogma*) by which it had been forbidden to engage in any such business in the city....[2]

While this reference is helpful the question still remains why the Thessalonian politarchs rather than the proconsul of Macedonia would have

---

1. E. A. Judge, "The Decrees of Caesar at Thessalonica," *Reformed Theological Review* 30 (1971): 2.
2. Dio Chrysostom 57 15.8; Judge, "Decrees of Caesar," 4.

been asked to enforce a ban of this type. "We must assume that in some respect the politarchs were obliged to take cognisance of offences against the 'decrees of Caesar.' "[3] But why — on what basis? Judge cites three pieces of evidence in the order of increasing specificity. First, there is an extant oath of personal loyalty by the *inhabitants* of Paphlagonia to the Caesarian house. This oath includes Roman and non-Romans alike and reads as follows:

> I swear...that I will support Caesar Augustus, his children and descendants, throughout my life, in word, deed and thought...that in whatsoever concerns them I will spare neither body nor soul nor life nor children...that whenever I see or hear of anything being said, planned or done against them I will report it...and whomsoever they regard as enemies I will attack and pursue with arms and the sword by land and by sea....[4]

Secondly he cites a Cypriot oath of allegiance to Tiberius on his assumption of power. What is new here are the specific pledges to reverence (*sebasesthai*) and obedience (*hypakousesthai* and *peitharchesein*). A "formula of this kind might be sufficient to lead to the Thessalonians treating the oath as a 'decree' of Caesar."[5] Thirdly, an inscription from Samos strongly suggests that local magistrates were responsible for administering the oath of loyalty as well as to receive complaints concerning violations of such an oath.[6]

In all likelihood the politarchs in Thessalonica were responsible for administering the oath of loyalty and for dealing with violations of the oath. In view of this situation we need to ask whether there were elements in the proclamation of Paul and his co-workers in Thessalonica which might have been perceived as politically inflammatory and whether the unusually strong civic cult in the city would have created an environment particularly hostile to early Christian proclamation and language.

It is difficult, if not impossible, to reconstruct the original Pauline message proclaimed in the city, and all we can hope for are glimmers of it in the written correspondence. If 1 Thessalonians is at all representative of his original preaching then we certainly do find elements which could be understood or misunderstood in a distinctly political sense. In 2:12 God, according to the Apostle, calls the Thessalonian Christians "into his own kingdom"; in 5:3 there is a frontal attack on the *Pax et*

---

3. Judge, "Decrees of Caesar," 5.
4. Ibid., 6.
5. Ibid., 7.
6. Ibid.

Securitas program of the early Principate;[7] and in the verses just preceding this attack one finds three heavily loaded political terms: *parousia, apantēsis* and *kyrios. Parousia* is related to "the 'visit' of the king, or some other official."[8] When used as court language *parousia* refers to the arrival of Caesar, a king or an official.[9] *Apantēsis* refers to the citizens meeting a dignitary who is about to visit the city.[10] These two terms are used in this way by Josephus (*Ant.* XI.327ff.) and also similarly referred to by such Greek writers as Chrysostom. The term *kyrios,* especially when used in the same context as the two preceding terms, also has a definite political sense. People in the eastern Mediterranean applied the term *kyrios* to the Roman emperors from Augustus on, although the first verifiable inscription of the *Kyrios*-title in Greece dates to the time of Nero.[11] All of this, coupled with the use of *euaggelion* and its possible association with the eastern ruler cult,[12] suggests that Paul and his associates could easily be understood as violating the "decrees of Caesar" in the most blatant manner.

Thessalonica was founded in 316 B.C.E. by Cassander, a general in Alexander's army. The new city included the ancient Therme and some thirty-five other towns. When Macedonia became a Roman province in 146 B.C.E., Thessalonica was made the capital and thus the center of Roman administration.

Holland Hendrix shows not only that the Thessalonians' fortunes were determined heavily by Roman interests from the middle of the second century to the middle of the first century B.C.E., but also that in view of this situation it was necessary for the Thessalonians to develop ways to honor their Roman benefactors so that they would be able "to attract and sustain influential Romans' commitments and favors."[13]

As Roman benefaction gains in importance for the citizens of Thessalonica, increasingly the Roman benefactors are included as objects of honor alongside the gods. Holland Hendrix in his thesis adds that while " 'the gods' of the city were due honors as the source of Thessalonica's continued well-being, important foreign agents of its immediate interests were acknowledged in concert with its divine sustainers.... Honors *for*

---

7. W. H. C. Frend, *Martyrdom and Persecution in the Early Church* (Oxford: Blackwell, 1965), 96; see also 124, n. 69.

8. George Milligan, *St. Paul's Epistles to the Thessalonians* (New York: Macmillan, n.d.), 145–48.

9. Martin Dibelius, HNT 11, no. 3 (Tübingen, 1937), 14–15.

10. Ernest Best, The *First and Second Epistles to the Thessalonians* (London: Adams & Charles Black, 1972). See p. 199 for bibliography.

11. Adolf Deissmann, *Light from the Ancient East* (New York: Doran, 1922), 351–58.

12. Peter Stuhlmacher, *Das paulinische Evangelium,* I (Göttingen: Vandenhoeck & Ruprecht, 1968), 196–206.

13. Holland L. Hendrix, "Thessalonicans Honor Romans," Th.D. thesis, Harvard Divinity School, 1984, 253.

the gods and Roman benefactors expressed a hierarchy of benefaction extending from the divine sphere into human affairs" (336).

During the first century B.C.E. the goddess Roma is joined to the Roman benefactors and "it is clear that in establishing a priesthood for Roma and the Roman benefactors, Thessalonians acknowledged her divine status" (287). While conventions concerning Roma may have been borrowed from elsewhere, her status and function in Thessalonica is quite different; she is not granted honors as an independent figure nor was she specifically related to an individual such as Augustus, but rather "she was grafted onto a previously existing object of honor, the Roman benefactors....As an object of devotion she was linked inextricably to those Romans who tangibly benefited the city" (287). Once Roma is joined to the benefactors it now becomes easy for the priesthood of the gods to become associated with these Roman benefactors. Honors to the gods, Roma and the Roman benefactors become increasingly interrelated in the practice of the city.

But there is yet another important step in this trajectory: a temple of Caesar is built. This took place in the reign of Augustus and associated with this temple is a "priest and agonothete of the Imperator" (62). Most helpful as an aid in understanding this development is the numismatic evidence. From this it is clear that "Thessalonica acclaimed Julius as god" (108). These coins were minted in Thessalonica about 27 B.C.E. and are the first coins which portray the heads of Romans (173). In the case of Julius "a Roman is designated explicitly as 'god.'" Although "the title 'son of god' (*theou huios*) does not appear with Octavian/Augustus on any of the coins, the juxtaposition of the Divine Julius with his son may reflect Thessalonican awareness of the Imperator's status as *divi filius* and is indicative perhaps of local importance to it" (170). Also significant in this overall process is that at this time the head of Augustus displaces the head of Zeus on the coins of the city.

This unequivocal numismatic designation of a Roman ruler as divine was "an extension of Thessalonica's earlier policies of monumental recognition for distinguished Romans whose benefactions were important to the city...because of his status as sole ruler and his supreme responsibility in assuring Thessalonica's well-being" (299, 308). Thus, "Thessalonica added Augustus, his divine father and his successors to the honors granted 'the gods and Roman benefactors' and 'Roma and Roman benefactors'" (308). As a result of acknowledging "the divine sanction of the new order" (310) a temple of Caesar is built and a priest and agonothete of the Imperator Augustus "son of god" is appointed and now is given priority over the other priesthoods. In "every extant instance in which the 'priest and agonothete of the Imperator' is mentioned, he is listed first in what appears to be a strict observance of protocol. The Imperator's priest and agonothete assumes priority, the priest of 'the gods' is cited next followed by the priest of Roma and Roman benefactors" (312). The process of cult interaction and inter-relationship proceeds, but it is clear at this point in the history of Thessalonica which office "demanded superior attention" (312). Supe-rior attention is called for precisely because that "particular strand of royal theology which is most apparent in Thessalonica's honorific ac-tivity is the attention paid to the legitimation of Augustus's rule and his successors" (311). "Augustus' dynastic prospects were publicly ac-claimed on coin types honoring Gaius and Tiberius. Numismatic honors previously granted only selectively became a conventional feature of the city's coinage. The impact of developments in royal theologies and re-ligious activities directed to rulers which had been cultivated in certain quarters of the Hellenistic Greek world and late Republican Rome are manifested clearly in the city's honors" (310).

Given this emphasis on royal theology in Thessalonica at the time of Paul's visit and the accusation recorded in Acts that he and his associates are "all acting against the decrees of Caesar, saying that there is another king, Jesus..." (17:7), let us proceed by lifting out certain elements in 1 Thessalonians which are not unrelated to this overall political climate.

What situation/s is Paul referring to with his several references to affliction and suffering in 1 Thessalonians? In 1:6 he reminds the Thes-salonians that they "received the word in much affliction (*thlipsei pollē*); in 2:14 he refers to their suffering (*epathete*); in 3:3 he sends Timo-thy to them so "that no one be moved by these afflictions (*thlipsesin*)." This theme is well summarized in 3:4: "For when we were with you, we told you beforehand that we were to suffer affliction (*thlibesthai*); just as it has come to pass, and as you know." What did Paul have in mind when he made this warning to the congregation during his visit and what exactly had come to pass?

Also related to this are the Satan/tempter references. In 1 Thess. 2:18 Paul indicates that Satan repeatedly hindered him from visiting the Thes-salonian congregation. Is this an indication that the political opposition to him remained so strong that it was impossible for Paul to reenter the city? "Paul might well discern Satanic opposition behind the politarchs' decision...."[14] This also relates to the "tempter" reference in 3:5: "For this reason, when I could bear it no longer, I sent that I might know your faith, for fear that somehow the tempter (*ho peirazōn*) had tempted you and that our labor would be in vain."[15] It is fully possible that the Apos-tle is concerned that the political opposition and pressure on the young Christians might be so strong that they would be tempted to abandon their faith in Christ. That the climate of such a concern is a realistic

---

14. F. F. Bruce, *The Acts of the Apostles* (Grand Rapids: Eerdmans, 1951), 327.
15. Note also 1 Cor. 7:5 — "Satan tempts...."

possibility should be evident in light of our review of the civic cult in Thessalonica.

In the midst of this situation of affliction and suffering, produced in all likelihood by political opposition, 1 Thessalonians assures the congregation that God has chosen them (1:4)[16] and emphatically stresses the twin themes of hope and parousia. How does this emphasis fit into the overall perspective of the situation and what specifically caused Paul to place such emphasis on these twin themes of hope and parousia?

It is noteworthy that 1 Thessalonians opens in 1:3 and closes in 5:8 with the triadic formulation "faith, love and hope." However, when Timothy reports back to Paul about the condition of the Thessalonian church he only brings the good news of their "faith and love" (3:6). The element of hope is absent. This section of the letter ends with Paul praying that he might see them soon face to face so that he might "supply what is lacking" (ta hysterēmata) in their faith (3:10). Given the strong emphasis on hope (elpis) in such strategic locations as 1:10, 2:19 and 3:13, locations which mark the closing of the first three chapters, and the fact that a similar situation exists with regard to the term parousia in 2:19, 3:13, 4:15 and 5:23, it is likely that what is lacking in the faith of the Thessalonians is the dimension of hope. This observation is underscored by the many "you know" type references (1:5; 2:1, 2, 5, 9, 10, 11, etc.). These "superfluous rehearsals and reminders"[17] come to an abrupt halt in 4:13, the beginning of the section dealing with those persons who have died prior to the parousia. The verb agnoeō, a word not found elsewhere in the Thessalonian correspondence, is used by Paul as a literary device to signal that new information is to follow. To indicate that the new information has come to an end, the Apostle uses another rehearsal formula in 5:1: "But as to the times and the seasons, brethren, you have no need to have anything written to you." Thus, 4:13–18 is a section of critical importance for 1 Thessalonians; within the eschatological framework of Paul's initial proclamation, a new issue has arisen: what is the status of those who have died in Christ prior to the parousia? Negatively, Paul argues that the Thessalonian Christians should not be like the remainder of the Gentile population who have no hope. Underscoring the accuracy of Paul's description of pagan hopelessness in the face of death,

> In all the "Oriental" cults in general, whether of Atargatis, Mithra, Isis or Cybele, the element of resurrection has received emphatic attention in studies old and new — attention emphatic but not al-

---

16. The choice of this language may well be related to the persecution/affliction theme of the letter.

17. Nils Dahl in reflections made to the Society of Biblical Literature's Paul Seminar in 1972, p. 2.

ways firmly controlled. It should really not be taken for granted, as it often is assumed, that people who believe a god might rise from death also believed in such a blessing for themselves as well. The conjecture needs support — and finds none.[18]

Paul's positive response to this issue is to refer to the faith they hold in common: "We believe that Jesus died and rose again." By the use of an apocalyptic "word of the Lord" (4:15), the Apostle can draw the consequence that when the Lord comes "the dead in Christ will rise first; then we who are alive..." (4:16–17).

It is important to ask why this issue concerning the "dead in Christ" (*hoi nekroi en Christǭ*; 4:16) is so central to the letter, and, further, we must ask whether it is possible to identify those who have fallen asleep (*tous koimēthentas*; 4:14). "Perhaps those who 'fell asleep' so soon (1 Thess. 4:13) were victims of this persecution [the one referred to in Acts 17]."[19] Few scholars[20] discuss the matter of death by persecution this early in Christian history. Yet there are a number of items which could give positive support to Bruce's suggestion: (1) The use of *koimaō* in Acts 7:60 is remarkable: "And as they were stoning Stephen, he prayed, 'Lord Jesus, receive my spirit.' And he knelt down and cried with a loud voice, 'Lord, do not hold this sin against them.' And when he had said this, he fell asleep (*ekoimēthē*)." In this text the verb *koimaō* refers explicitly to one who has suffered death through persecution. (2) In 1 Thess. 2:14–16, which we have argued elsewhere as authentic,[21] Paul makes a very clear parallel between the situation of the Thessalonian church and that of the churches in Judea; they "became imitators of the churches of God in Christ Jesus which are in Judea" and they "suffered the *same things*" (*ta auta epathete*) from their countrymen and that clearly involves the dimension of death (2:14–15). (3) The Thessalonian congregation became an example to all the believers in Macedonia and in Achaia precisely because they "received the word in much affliction..." (1 Thess. 1:6–8). Further they became "imitators" of Paul, Silvanus and Timothy (1 Thess. 1:6) in suffering, a theme which Paul articulates in 2:2: "But though we had already suffered and had been shamefully treated in Philippi, as you know, we had courage in our God to declare to you the gospel of God in the face of great opposition (*en pollǭ agōni*)." Paul uses this same term, *agōn*, only once again, in a very similar context, in Phil. 1:30. It is precisely in this first chapter

---

18. Ramsay MacMullen, *Paganism in the Roman Empire* (New Haven: Yale University, 1981), 55.

19. Bruce, *Acts*, 327–28; unfortunately, Bruce does not mention this suggestion in his new commentary, *1 and 2 Thessalonians*, Word 45 (Waco, Tex.: Word, 1982).

20. Perhaps Frend, *Martyrdom and Persecution*, 83.

21. K. P. Donfried, "Paul and Judaism: 1 Thessalonians 2:13–16 as a Test Case," *Interpretation* 38 (1984): 242–53.

of Philippians that the apostle expresses "full courage" so that "Christ will be honored in my body, whether by life or by death" (Phil. 1:20), and it is in this same letter that Paul once again expresses the possible nearness of death: "Even if I am to be poured as a libation upon the sacrificial offering of your faith, I am glad and rejoice with you all" (Phil. 2:17). Most commentators are agreed that Paul is alluding to the possibility of his own death as a martyr;[22] Paul and the congregation are bound together in this threat of martyrdom. Referring to Paul's anticipated trip to Philippi, Lohmeyer remarks: "It is a journey to martyrdom, more precisely, to lasting personal union of apostle and community in martyrdom."[23]

Is it probable that the afflictions and persecutions in Thessalonica could lead to occasional deaths?[24] When Paul in Romans 8:35–36 speaks of tribulation, distress, persecution, famine, nakedness, peril and sword and then cites Ps. 44:23, "For thy sake we are being killed all the day long; we are regarded as sheep to be slaughtered," is he merely speaking rhetorically? "The list of afflictions is strengthened by the citation of Ps. 44:23. The rabbis applied Ps. 44:23 to martyr-death (2 Maccabees 7)."[25] We are hard pressed to see that Paul had any other intention in mind.

If our inclination is to take seriously the possibility of persecutions in Thessalonica and elsewhere as leading to occasional death, do we have any extra-biblical evidence which would lend further credibility to this suggestion? The Paphlagonian oath of loyalty to the Caesarian house in 3 B.C.E., which we cited earlier, compels Romans and non-Romans alike to report cases of disloyalty and to physically hunt down the offenders. The seriousness by which this is meant to be taken — even to the point of death for those who are disloyal — is self-evident. If this possible parallel has any relevance for the political situation in Thessalonica at the time of Paul, then certainly the Apostle's "political preaching" and his direct attack on the *Pax et Securitas* emphasis of the early principate was not likely to lead the citizens to give Paul a warm or extended welcome.

Paul's review of his work in Thessalonica in 1 Thess. 2:1–12 is sandwiched between the themes of suffering and death. We suggest the following as background to Paul's response: Paul had to leave Thessalonica hurriedly after a brief stay[26] due to opposition. As a result

---

22. Joachim Gnilka, *Der Philipperbrief*, HTKNT X, 3 (Freiburg: Herder, 1968), 154–55; J. B. Lightfoot, *Saint Paul's Epistle to the Philippians* (London: Macmillan, 1891), 118–19; Ernst Lohmeyer, *Die Brief an die Philipper, an die Kolosser und an Philemon*, MeyerK (Göttingen: Vandenhoeck & Ruprecht, 1964), 111–14.

23. Lohmeyer, *Brief an die Philipper*, 111.

24. We certainly do not wish to imply any systematic persecutions.

25. Otto Michel, *Der Brief an die Römer*, MeyerK (Göttingen: Vandenhoeck & Ruprecht, 1963), 217.

26. The reference to three weeks in Acts 17 deals with Paul's activity in the synagogue

Paul travels to Athens but the Thessalonian Christians must remain and continue to experience the consequences of this attack. They experience persecution and, perhaps, in the case of a few, even to the point of death. Dio Chrysostom speaks negatively about certain philosophers who "merely utter a phrase or two, and then, after railing at you rather than teaching you, they make a hurried exit, anxious lest before they have finished you may raise an outcry and send them packing."[27] Not to be confused with those wandering philosophers who did not become involved in the *agōn* of life, Paul reminds them that he and his co-workers preached the gospel of God to them "in the face of great opposition (*en pollō agōni*)" (1 Thess. 2:2), a reference placed very deliberately at the beginning of the apostle's "apology." Certainly 1 Thess. 3:7, "in all our distress and affliction," refers to Paul's situation at the time he is writing 1 Thessalonians. To demonstrate that his preaching was not a "cloak for greed" (1 Thess. 2:5) the apostle recounts how hard Silvanus, Timothy and he worked and how "righteous and blameless" (1 Thess. 2:9–12) was their behavior toward the Christian community in Thessalonica.

In terms of the substantive issue raised in 1 Thess. 4:13–18, Paul attempts to assure the community that those who have died will not be forgotten and that those who are alive at the parousia will not have precedence. The apocalyptic language serves to support this conclusion. The relationship between the problem of being dead or alive at the parousia and the centrality of the parousia to his thought is summarized in 1 Thess. 5:9–10: "For God has not destined us for wrath, but to obtain salvation through our Lord Jesus Christ, who died for us so that whether we wake or sleep we might live with him."

---

and not necessarily his total stay. Note Bruce, *Acts,* 324: "We are not told what space of time elapsed between his leaving the synagogue and leaving the city." See also Gerd Lüdemann, *Paulus, der Heidenapostel,* I (Göttingen: Vandenhoeck & Ruprecht, 1980), 203–4, for a brief discussion of his and other positions. We are inclined to stress the brevity of Paul's visit to Thessalonica.

27. Dio Chrysostom, *Oration* 32, 11; see Abraham Malherbe, "Gentle as a Nurse: The Cynic Background to I Thess ii," *NovT* 12 (1970): 208.

thirteen

The Praxis of Coequal Discipleship

ELISABETH SCHÜSSLER FIORENZA

The contemporary discussion linking Gal. 3:28 and the household-code tradition seems to point to a historical-political dynamic that does not come to the fore when it is forced into the oppositions of "order of creation" and "order of redemption" on the one hand, and of "enthusiastic excess, or gnostic heresy" and "Pauline theology and New Testament orthodoxy" on the other. Commentaries on Galatians "have consistently denied that Paul's statements have political implications."[1] Such commentaries are prepared to state the opposite of what Paul actually says in order to preserve a "purely religious" interpretation. In doing so, they can strongly emphasize the reality of equality before God sacramentally and at the same time "deny that any conclusions can be drawn from this in regard to the ecclesiastical offices (!) and the political order" — all of which, I would add, rest on the assumed natural differences between the sexes institutionalized in patriarchal marriage.

Analysis and Interpretation of Galatians 3:28

Form critical analyses converge in the delineation of Gal. 3:26–28 and its classification as a baptismal confession quoted by Paul.[2]

    i. 3:26a For you are all children of God

    ii. 3:27a For as many as were baptized into Christ
            b have put on Christ

---

1. H. D. Betz, *Galatians,* Hermeneia (Philadelphia: Fortress, 1979), 189, n. 68.

2. W. A. Meeks, "The Image of the Androgyne: Some Uses of a Symbol in Earliest Christianity," *History of Religions* 13 (1974): 165–208; see also H. D. Betz, "Spirit, Freedom, Law: Paul's Message to the Galatian Churches," *Svensk Exegetisk Årsbok* 39 (1974): 145–60, and his *Galatians,* 181–201; J. Becker, *Auferstehung der Toten im Urchristentum,* SBS 82 (Stuttgart: Katholisches Bibelwerk, 1976), 56f.; H. Paulsen, "Einheit und Freiheit der Söhne Gottes — Gal. 3:26–29," *ZNW* 71 (1980): 74–95, for literature.

iii. 3:28a There is neither Jew nor Greek
        b There is neither slave nor free
        c There is no male and female

iv. 3:28d For you are all one

Reinforced by dramatic gestures (disrobing, immersion, robing), such a declaration would carry — within the community for which its language was meaningful — the power to assist in shaping the symbolic universe by which that group distinguished itself from the ordinary "world" of the larger society. As a "performative utterance" it makes a factual claim about an "objective" change in reality that fundamentally modifies social roles. New attitudes and altered behavior would follow — but only if the group succeeds in clothing the novel declaration with an "aura of factuality."[3]

Such new behavior was engendered by this baptismal declaration, at least with respect to women who exercised leadership roles in the house churches and mission of the early Christian movement. A letter of Pliny to the Emperor Trajan confirms that at the beginning of the second century women "servants" (slaves?) were ministers in the church of Bithynia.[4] Around the same time, Ignatius writes to the bishop Polycarp of Smyrna, telling him not to set free either male or female slaves at the expense of the church (4:3). This exhortation presupposes that slaves who joined the Christian community expected their freedom to be bought by the church.

Such expectations were supported by the Christians' belief that they were truly set free by Christ. Such formulas occur again and again in the Pauline letters: "You were bought with a price, do not become human slaves" (1 Cor. 6:20; 7:23). Or "For freedom Christ has set us free...do not submit again to a yoke of slavery" (Gal. 5:1). The goal of Christian calling is freedom: "You were called to freedom" (Gal. 5:13), because "where the Spirit of the Lord is there is freedom" (2 Cor. 3:17). To argue that Christian slaves who understood their call to freedom had only "a superficial understanding of the gospel"[5] is to minimize the impact of this language in a world where slavery was a commonly accepted institution. Liberation from the slavery of sin, law, and death,

---

3. Meeks, "Image of the Androgyne," 182.
4. Pliny *Epistles* 10.96. According to A. N. Sherwin-White, "Pliny treats the *diakonoi* as these 'servants' evidently were, as slaves, whose evidence was commonly taken under torture. The torture of freeborn witnesses in ordinary criminal procedures was an innovation of the Late Empire.... Pliny stresses that many of 'every age, every class, and of both sexes are being accused...'" (*The Letters of Pliny: A Historical and Social Commentary* [Oxford: Clarendon Press, 1966], 708).
5. Cf. J. E. Crouch, *The Origin and Intention of the Colossian Haustafel*, FRLANT 109 (Göttingen: Vandenhoeck & Ruprecht, 1972), 127.

from the conditions of the "present evil age" (Gal. 1:4), has "freedom" as its purpose and destiny. "As a result, *eleutheria* (freedom) is the central theological concept which sums up the Christian's situation before God as well as in this world."[6] Therefore, a slave woman who became a Christian in the first century heard this baptismal pronunciation as a ritual, "performative utterance," which not only had the power to shape the "symbolic universe" of the Christian community but also determined the social interrelationships and structures of the church.

That such an expectation of free status on the grounds of baptism was not merely excessive enthusiasm is apparent if we look at the first opposites of the baptismal formula — Jew/Greek. One could show that Paul's whole work centered around the abolition of the religious distinctions between Jew and Greek. "For there is no distinction between Jew and Greek. The same Lord is Lord of all and bestows his riches upon all who call upon him" (Rom. 10:12). Equality among all those who call upon the Lord is based on the fact that they have all one and the same master who shares his wealth with all of them (cf. also Rom. 3:22). That such "religious equality" had social-ecclesial consequences for the interrelationship between Jewish and gentile Christians is apparent from the Antioch incident, which seems to have been well known in the early church.[7] Peter and Barnabas had entered into table sharing with the gentile Christians in Antioch but, after pressure from Jerusalem, discontinued it. They again adhered to the Pharisaic Christian purity rules against eating together with the "unclean." Paul publicly confronts Cephas and the Jewish Christian group around him because "they did not act in consistency with the truth of the gospel" (Gal. 2:14). The whole letter to the Galatians is written to make the same point. It is not circumcision or uncircumcision that counts, but the new creation.

This struggle of Paul for equality between gentile and Jewish Christians had important ramifications for Jewish and gentile Christian women alike. If it was no longer circumcision but baptism which was the primary rite of initiation, then women became full members of the people of God with the same rights and duties. This generated a fundamental change, not only in their standing before God but also in their ecclesial-social status and function, because in Judaism religious differences according to the law were also expressed in communal behavior and social practice. While one was *born* into Judaism — even the full proselyte could not achieve the status of the male Israelite — the Christian movement was based not on racial and national inheritance and

---

6. Betz, *Galatians*, 255.
7. For literature and discussion, cf. ibid., 103f.

kinship lines, but on a new kinship in Jesus Christ.[8] In baptism Christians entered into a kinship relationship with people coming from very different racial, cultural, and national backgrounds. These differences were not to determine the social structures of the community, nor were those of family and clan. Therefore both Jewish and gentile women's status and role were drastically changed, since family and kinship did not determine the social structures of the Christian movement.

This seems to be stated explicitly in the final pair of the baptismal pronunciation: "There is no male and female." This last pair differs in formulation from the preceding two, insofar as it does not speak of opposites but of man *and* woman. Exegetes have speculated a good deal over the fact that "male and female" are used here, but not "man and woman."[9] It is often argued that not only "the *social* differences (roles) between men and women are involved but the *biological* distinctions" as well.[10] Therefore, as we have seen, it is conjectured that the formulation is gnostic and advocates androgyny. Paul does not repeat the formulation in 1 Cor. 12:13 — according to this argument — because he had special problems in Corinth due to the gnostic or enthusiastic consequences women drew from Gal. 3:28. However, such a conjecture is based on the unproven assumption that the behavior of Corinthian women was determined by gnostic beliefs and not by early Christian prophetic experiences.

The argument, moreover, overlooks the fact that designations of the sexes in the neuter can simply be used in place of "woman and man." Such designations do not imply a denial of biological sex differences.[11] The reference here probably alludes to Gen. 1:27, where humanity created in the image of God is qualified as "male and female" in order to introduce the theme of procreation and fertility. Jewish exegesis understood "male and female," therefore, primarily in terms of marriage and family. In early Christian theology the expression also evokes the image of the first couple, and not that of an androgynous being, as can be seen from Mark 10:6. "No longer male and female" is best understood, therefore, in terms of marriage and gender relationships. As such, Gal. 3:28c does not assert that there are no longer men and women in Christ, but that patriarchal marriage — and sexual relationships between male and female — is no longer constitutive of the new community in

---

8. This is stressed by R. Loewe: "The sociological basis on which Christianity rests is not the tie of kinship as in the case of Judaism, but that of fellowship — fellowship in Christ" (*The Position of Women in Judaism* [London: SPCK, 1966], 52).

9. See especially H. Thyen, " '...nicht mehr männlich und weiblich...' Eine Studie zu Galater 3.28," in F. Crüsemann and H. Thyen, eds., *Als Mann und Frau geschaffen* (Gelnhausen: Burkardthaus-Verlag, 1978), 109f.

10. Betz, *Galatians*, 195.

11. For documentation, see M. de Merode, "Une théologie primitive de la femme?" *Revue Théologique de Louvain* 9 (1978): 176–89, esp. 184ff.

Christ.[12] Irrespective of their procreative capacities and of the social roles connected with them, persons will be full members of the Christian movement in and through baptism.

In antiquity not only were sexual or gender roles considered to be grounded in biological nature but also cultural, racial, and social differences. Religious, social, racial, and sexual properties were not differentiated in antiquity as much as they are today. Although most would concede today that racial or class differences are not natural or biological, but cultural and social, sexual differences and gender roles are still proclaimed as given by nature. However, feminist studies have amply documented that most perceived sex differences or gender roles are cultural-social properties. We are socialized into sex and gender roles as soon as we are born. Every culture gives different symbolic significance and derives different social roles from the human biological capacities of sexual intercourse, childbearing, and lactation.[13] Sexual dimorphism and strictly defined gender roles are products of a patriarchal culture, which maintain and legitimize structures of control and domination — the exploitation of women by men.[14] Gal. 3:28 not only advocates the abolition of religious-cultural divisions and of the domination and exploitation wrought by institutional slavery but also of domination based on sexual divisions. It repeats with different categories and words that within the Christian community no structures of dominance can be tolerated. Gal. 3:28 is therefore best understood as a communal Christian self-definition rather than a statement about the baptized individual. It proclaims that in the Christian community all distinctions of religion, race, class, nationality, and gender are insignificant. All the baptized are equal, they are one in Christ. Thus, taken at face value, the baptismal declaration of Gal. 3:28 does not express "excessive enthusiasm" or a "gnosticizing" devaluation of procreative capacities.

We do not know the social effects initiation into Judaism had upon women, but we have some indication that it could spell "freedom" for

---

12. For a similar exegetical argument but a different systematic conclusion, see also B. Witherington, "Rite and Rights for Women — Galatians 3.28," *NTS* 27 (1981): 593–604. According to Witherington, the "Judaizers may have been insisting on the necessity of marriage and propagation, perhaps as a way of including women into the community and giving them an important role.... " But he insists that the mere fact that Paul speaks here of such sexual, racial, religious, and class distinctions means Paul recognizes quite well that they exist. "He wishes not to obliterate them but to orient them properly.... Thus he rejects their *abuse* and not their proper *use*" (601f.). However, such a conclusion cannot be derived from the text.

13. See especially M. Zimbalist Rosaldo, "The Use and Abuse of Anthropology: Reflections on Feminism and Cross-Cultural Understandings," *Signs* 5 (1980): 389–417; and chap. 1 of Elisabeth Schüssler Fiorenza, *In Memory of Her: A Feminist Theological Reconstruction of Christian Origins* (New York: Crossroad, 1983).

14. For the delineation of sex and gender, see A. Oackley, *Sex, Gender and Society* (New York: Harper & Row, 1972), 158ff.

slaves. The manumission or setting free of the slave was an act of the slave owner performed with the assent of the synagogue. The slave gained complete freedom except for the requirement to attend the synagogue. Connected with the act of manumission was a second washing that corresponded so closely to proselyte baptism that both could be seen as one and the same. Against the background of oriental cultic and Jewish religious manumission practices it is obvious that slaves would expect freedom from their initiation into the Christian community.[15] Paul seems to assume this when he sends the baptized Onesimus back to Philemon "no longer as a slave" but as a beloved brother "both in the flesh and in the Lord," that is, socially as well as ecclesially, as a human being as well as a Christian (Philem. 16). Paul has neither the legal ability to set Onesimus free himself nor the authority to *command* Philemon to do so. But by sending Onesimus back as a new member of the church in Philemon's house, he expects Philemon to acknowledge the new *status* of the former slave as a "brother."

Insofar as the Christian community did not withdraw from society, as the Epicurean Garden or the Jewish Therapeutae did, it provided an experience of an alternative community in the midst of the Greco-Roman city for those who came in contact with it. As an alternative association which accorded women- and slave-initiates equal status and roles, the Christian missionary movement was a conflict movement which stood in tension with the institutions of slavery and the patriarchal family. Such conflict could arise not only *within* the community but even more within the larger society, since Christians admitted to their membership women as well as slaves who continued to live in pagan marriages and households. This tension between the alternative Christian community and the larger society had to cause conflicts that demanded resolution, often in different ways. The Pauline exhortations and the household-code tradition within the New Testament testify to these tensions.

Yet unconsciously these injunctions of men, which demand the subordination of slaves, women, and children, may also express the interests of the "owner and patron class"[16] — as well as reflect the interests of husbands and masters, the heads of families, who felt that their prerogatives were being undermined. Of course, it is difficult for us to decide whether or not such motivations played a role in the modifications of the Christian baptismal self-understanding, that is, which admonitions to subordination were due to a genuine concern for the Christian group's embattled situation and which arose from a defense of patriarchal dom-

---

15. See Crouch, *Colossian Haustafel,* 126–29.
16. E. A. Judge, *The Social Pattern of the Christian Groups in the First Century* (London: Tyndale Press, 1960), 60.

inance couched in theological terms. The theological counterarguments by slaves or women have not survived in history.

Conversion and baptism into Christ for men, therefore, implied a much more radical break with their former social and religious self-understandings — especially for those who were also wealthy slave owners — than it did for women and slaves. While the baptismal declaration in Gal. 3:28 offered a new religious vision to women and slaves, it denied all male religious prerogatives in the Christian community based on gender roles. Just as born Jews had to abandon the privileged notion that they alone were the chosen people of God, so masters had to relinquish their power over slaves, and husbands that over wives and children. Since these social-political privileges were, at the same time, religious privileges, conversion to the Christian movement for men also meant relinquishing their religious prerogatives. It is often argued that it was impossible for the tiny Christian group to abolish the institution of slavery and other social hierarchies. That might have been the case or it might not. However, what is often overlooked is that relinquishment of religious male prerogatives within the Christian community was possible and that such a relinquishment included the abolition of social privileges as well. The legal-societal and cultural-religious male privileges were no longer valid for Christians. Insofar as this egalitarian Christian self-understanding did away with all male privileges of religion, class, and caste, it allowed not only gentiles and slaves but also women to exercise leadership functions within the missionary movement.

Paul's Modifications of Galatians 3:28

The introduction to 1 Corinthians 7 clearly states that Paul is responding here to matters about which the Christians had written him. Although all the problems raised seem to refer in one way or another to marriage and the relationship between the sexes, Paul also mentions in 7:17–24 the question of circumcision/uncircumcision and slave/free. Since he also speaks in this section about the Christian calling by God, he clearly had the baptismal formula in mind when elaborating the general theological foundation for his advice in chapter 7. His reference to circumcision/uncircumcision in particular indicates that he has the three pairs Jew/gentile, slave/free, male/female in mind, since this reference to circumcision does not quite fit the tenor of the whole chapter, that is, it is not the social situation in which one finds oneself as a Christian that determines one's Christian standing, but rather living according to the will of God.[17] Exegetes misread Paul's advice to Jewish or gentile Chris-

---

17. For a different interpretative emphasis, see H. Conzelmann, *1 Corinthians*, Hermeneia (Philadelphia: Fortress, 1975), 126: "And grace embraces the world and holds

tians, when they argue that Paul here means to say that they should remain in the social state and religious role they had when they heard the call to conversion. Paul clearly does not advise the former Jew or the former gentile to remain in their Jewish or pagan state. Rather he insists that the religious/biological sign of initiation to Jewish religion is no longer of any relevance to Christians.

Similarly, the advice to slaves cannot mean that slaves should remain in the state in which they were called. The advice in 7:21 is difficult to understand, since it is not clear whether they should "use" freedom or slavery to their advantage, if they have the possibility of being set free.[18] Although most exegetes and translators assume that slaves were to remain in the state of slavery when they became Christians, in my opinion the context speaks against such an interpretation. The injunction of v. 23 — "You were bought with a price, do not become slaves of people" — prohibits such an interpretation. The advice Paul gives to Christian slaves, then, seems best understood as: "If you still must live in the bondage of slavery, with no possibility of being freed, even though you were called to freedom, do not worry about it. However, if you have the opportunity to be set free, by all means use this opportunity and live in accordance with your calling to freedom. Those of you who were slaves when called to become a Christian are now freedwomen and freedmen of the Lord, just as those of you who were freeborn have now a master in Jesus Christ." Paul argues here, then, that both slaves and freeborn are equal in the Christian community, because they have one Lord. Therefore, it is possible to be a Christian even as a slave, if no possibility of becoming free exists. Of course it is more in line with one's calling to freedom to live as a free person. Much would be gained by a change in social status, if such a change is possible. Regardless of one's social status, however, the decisive thing is to continue in the calling to freedom which one has heard and entered into in baptism.[19] Thus it seems clear that Paul had the baptismal declaration of Gal. 3:28 in mind when addressing the problem of the relationship between the sexes in chapter 7, even though the reference to the first two pairs of the formula is made only in passing.[20]

me fast in my worldliness. No change of status brought about by myself can further my salvation."

18. See S. Scott Bartchy, *First-Century Slavery and 1 Corinthians 7:21,* SBLDS 11 (Missoula, Mont.: Scholars Press, 1973), 6–7, for a synopsis of the interpretations of 1 Cor. 7:21.

19. For a similar interpretation, see also P. Trummer, "Die Chance der Freiheit: Zur Interpretation des *mallon chrēsai* in 1 Kor 7,21," *Biblica* 56 (1975): 344–68.

20. See, e.g., D. Cartlidge, "1 Cor. 7 as a Foundation for a Christian Sex-Ethic," *Journal of Religion* 55 (1975): 220–34; W. Schrage, "Zur Frontstellung der paulinischen Ehebewertung in 1 Kor 7.1–7," *ZNW* 67 (1976): 214–34; and the commentaries for bibliographical reviews.

Paul's theological advice with respect to the relationship between the sexes is basically similar to the advice given to slaves. It is quite possible to live a Christian life as a married person, if that was the state in which one lived when becoming a Christian. However, Paul explicitly bases his argument not on the social order, but on a word of the Lord that prohibits divorce. The eschatological ideal of Jesus' declaration on marriage is here turned into an injunction of Jesus against divorce. However, despite this explicit instruction of the Lord, wives — who are mentioned first and with more elaboration in 7:10f. — still have the possibility of fleeing themselves from the bondage of patriarchal marriage, in order to live a marriage-free life. If they have done so, however, they must remain in this marriage-free state. They are allowed to return to their husbands, but they may not marry someone else.

It is not only remarkable that Paul insists on equality and mutuality in sexual relationships between husbands and wives, but even more that he advises Christians, especially women, to remain free from the marriage bond. This is often overlooked because Paul's option for celibacy has become "the higher calling" in Christian tradition. However, in the first century, permanent abstinence from sexual relations and remaining unmarried were quite exceptional. The discoveries of Qumran and Philo's description of the community of the Therapeutae give evidence of such an ascetic lifestyle within Judaism, but it was lived in isolation from the mainstream urban culture. Temporary chastity was known in most oriental cults; castration was practiced in the worship of the Great Mother, and in Rome the Vestal Virgins remained chaste for the thirty years of their service; but virginity was a privilege and not a right according to Roman law.

> The lives of the Vestals were severely regulated but in some respects they were the most emancipated women in Rome. As noted in our discussions of unmarried goddesses, the most liberated females are those who are not bound to males in a permanent relationship. . . . Further evidence of the freedom from the restrictions of ordinary women is to be found in the privileges enjoyed by the Vestals. . . . These privileges had such implications of status that the "rights of Vestals" were often conferred upon female members of the imperial family, who were frequently portrayed as Vestals on coins.[21]

The privileges of virginity were not open to "ordinary women" in the Roman empire. In order to strengthen the traditional Roman family,

---

21. S. B. Pomeroy, *Goddesses, Whores, Wives, and Slaves* (New York: Schocken Books, 1975), 213f.

Augustus had introduced severe marriage legislation and openly used religion to promote his marriage ideals.[22] In order to increase the birthrate, he granted freeborn women with three children and freedwomen who had given birth to four children emancipation from patriarchal tutelage. However, since he gave this privilege to his wife, the Vestal Virgins, and soldiers who could not marry during their time of service, other women who had not fulfilled the prescribed number of births also acquired this privilege. The rate of birth and the number of children were of great political concern, however, to the patriarchal establishment of the empire. The emperor levied sanctions and taxes upon those who were still bachelors. Moreover, widowers and divorcees of both sexes were expected to remarry after a period of one month. Widows at first were expected to remarry after a one year period, but, following protests, this period was extended to three years. Only those who were over fifty years of age were allowed to remain unmarried. Although these laws were probably not strictly kept throughout the empire, they evidence the general cultural ethos and the legal situation with respect to a marriage-free state. At the end of the first century, the emperor Domitian reinforced the Augustan marriage legislation particularly in order to strengthen the leading families of the empire.

It is therefore important to note that Paul's advice to remain free from the marriage bond was a frontal assault on the intentions of existing law and the general cultural ethos, especially since it was given to people who lived in the urban centers of the Roman empire. It stood over and against the dominant cultural values of Greco-Roman society. Moreover, his advice to women to remain nonmarried was a severe infringement of the right of the *paterfamilias* since, according to Roman law, a woman remained under the tutorship of her father and family, even after she married. Paul's advice to widows who were not necessarily "old" — since girls usually married between twelve and fifteen years of age — thus offered a possibility for "ordinary" women to become independent. At the same time, it produced conflicts for the Christian community in its interaction with society.

Paul's theological argument, however, that those who marry are "divided" and not equally dedicated to the affairs of the Lord as the nonmarried, implicitly limited married women to the confines of the patriarchal family. It disqualified married people theologically as less engaged missionaries and less dedicated Christians. It posited a rift between the married woman, concerned about her husband and family, and the unmarried virgin who was pure and sacred and therefore would

---

22. See N. Lewis, *Roman Civilization* (New York: Columbia University Press, 1955), 52ff.; P. E. Corbett, *The Roman Law of Marriage* (Oxford: Oxford University Press, 1930), 106–46:120f.

receive the pneumatic privileges of virginity. One can only wonder how Paul could have made such a theological point when he had Prisca as his friend and knew other missionary couples who were living examples that his theology was wrong.

Thus Paul's impact on women's leadership in the Christian missionary movement is double-edged.[23] On the one hand he affirms Christian equality and freedom. He opens up a new independent lifestyle for women by encouraging them to remain free of the bondage of marriage. On the other hand, he subordinates women's behavior in marriage and in the worship assembly to the interests of Christian mission, and restricts their rights not only as "pneumatics" but also as "women," for we do not find such explicit restrictions on the behavior of men qua men in the worship assembly. The post-Pauline and pseudo-Pauline tradition will draw out these restrictions in order to change the equality in Christ between women and men, slaves and free, into a relationship of subordination in the household which, on the one hand, eliminates women from the leadership of worship and community and, on the other, restricts their ministry to women.

Christian Mission and the Patriarchal Household

As we have seen, the early Christian vision of the discipleship of equals practiced in the house church attracted especially slaves and women to Christianity but also caused tensions and conflicts with the dominant cultural ethos of the patriarchal household. True, women as well as men, slaves as well as free, Asians as well as Greeks and Romans, participated fully in the cult of the Great Goddess; and in such a religious context the baptismal confession of Gal. 3:28 was not utopian. However, in contrast to the public cult of the goddess, in the Christian context, the public religious sphere of the church and the private sphere of the patriarchal house were not clearly separated. Insofar as Christians understood themselves as the new family[24] and expressed this self-understanding institutionally in the house church, the public-religious and private patriarchal spheres were no longer distinguished. In fact, it was the religious ethos — of equality — that was transferred to and came in conflict with the patriarchal ethos of the household. The Christian missionary movement thus provided an alternative vision and praxis to that of the dominant society and religion.

---

23. If this practical tension in Paul's writings is overlooked, then Paul is alternately condemned as a "chauvinist" or hailed as a "liberationist."

24. For a survey of NT writings, see R. Hamerton-Kelly, *God the Father: Theology and Patriarchy in the Teaching of Jesus* (Philadelphia: Fortress, 1979), 82–99.

Colossians, written by a disciple of Paul,[25] quotes Gal. 3:28 but changes it considerably. Moreover, he balances it out with a household code of patriarchal submission. The relationship of Jews and gentiles was no longer a great problem and concern for the author. The separation between the Jewish and Christian communities probably had already taken place at the time of his writing. In quoting the baptismal formula[26] Colossians mentions Greeks first and elaborates the second member of the pair circumcision and uncircumcision with "barbarian and Scythian," in order to stress that national and cultural differences and inequalities are overcome in the new humanity of Christ. Since Scythians were the proverbial boors of antiquity, it is obvious that the author of Colossians is especially interested in the opposite pair Greek and barbarian. While the third pair of Gal. 3:28 — male and female — is not mentioned at all, Col. 3:11 also dissolves the slave-free polarization that defines the social-political stratifications of institutional slavery. Col. 3:11 no longer juxtaposes slave-free as opposite alternatives but adds them to the enumeration and elaboration of those who are uncircumcised: barbarian, Scythian, slave, freeborn.

Although the letter to the Colossians still refers to the baptismal liturgy and theology of the Asian churches,[27] it celebrates not so much the restoration of human equality in the new community but rather "a cosmic event, in which the opposing elements of the universe were reconciled to each other." The so-called enthusiastic theology ascribed to Paul's opponents in Corinth is fully expressed here. Baptism means resurrection and enthronement with Christ in heaven, "stripping away the body of flesh" (2:11), and life in heaven rather than on earth (2:1–4; cf. 2:12, 20). The baptized are delivered from "the dominion of darkness" and transferred into "the kingdom of his beloved son" (1:13). They are "dead to the cosmos," have received a secret mystery (1:26f.; 2:2–3), and have the assurance of an inheritance among the "holy ones" in the realm of light. The writer of Colossians agrees with his audience on this theology of exaltation but disagrees with some of the Colossians on how this baptismal "symbolic universe" and drama should be remembered and made effective. While some in the community of Colossae believed that the "removal of the fleshly body" and the "new human-

---

25. See E. Lohse, *Colossians and Philemon,* Hermeneia (Philadelphia: Fortress, 1971), 177–83, for a comparison of Colossians and Pauline theology; see also J. Lähnemann, *Der Kolosserbrief* (Gütersloh: Mohn, 1971), 11–28, 153–82.

26. Lohse (*Colossians and Philemon,* 142–47) argues that the series has been adopted from tradition. But whereas the tradition insists that the "new humanity" or "new creation" realized in the Christian community has "cut through distinctions of social position," Colossians understands the "putting on of the new human" in moral terms.

27. See especially W. A. Meeks, "In One Body: The Unity of Humankind in Colossians and Ephesians," in J. Jervell and W. A. Meeks, eds., *God's Christ and His People: Studies in Honor of Nils Alstrup Dahl* (Oslo: Universitatsvorlaget, 1977), 209–21.

ity" in baptism must be realized in ascetic practices and elaborate ritual observances, the author insists on the finality of Christ's reconciliation and unification. The new "angelic religion" and the life in heaven are not to be realized by ascetic and ritual practice but in ethical behavior and communal life.[28] Since they have been raised with Christ, they are to "seek the things that are above," and to set their "minds on the things that are above." They do so "by putting away" anger, wrath, malice, slander, and foul talk and by "putting on" compassion, kindness, lowliness, meekness, and patience, forbearing one another and forgiving each other. Above all, they should "put on love, which binds everything together in perfect harmony" (3:5–17). They should behave wisely to outsiders and be able to answer everyone (4:5f.).

This is the context of the household code (3:18–4:1), the first and most precise form of the domestic code in the New Testament. The basic form of this code consists of three pairs of reciprocal exhortations addressing the relationship between wife and husband, children and father, and slaves and masters. In each case, the socially subordinate first member of the pair is exhorted to obedience to the superordinate second. The formal structure of such a household code, then, consists of address (wives), exhortation (submit to your husbands), and motivation (as is fitting in the Lord). The only Christian element in the Colossian code is the addition "in the Lord."[29] However, the author of Colossians quotes the code here, not because he is concerned about the behavior of wives, but that of slaves.

The expansion of the code's third pair, slave-master, indicates that the obedience and acceptance of servitude by Christian slaves are of utmost concern.[30] Colossians asks slaves to fulfill their task with single-mindedness of heart and dedication "as serving the Lord and not men" (3:23). It not only promises eschatological reward for such behavior but also threatens eschatological judgment and punishment for misbehavior (3:24f). The injunction to masters, in turn, is very short and has no Christian component except the reminder that they, too, have a master in heaven. Slave behavior is likened here to the Christian service of the Lord, while the "masters" are likened to the "Master" in heaven. It is obvious that the good behavior of slaves, according to the author, is the concrete realization of Gal. 3:28, insofar as both slaves and free-born have one Lord in heaven, Christ, and belong to the new humanity,

---

28. For the many attempts to identify the "opponents" of Colossians, see F. O. Francis and W. A. Meeks, eds., *Conflict at Colossai*, SBLSBS 4 (Missoula, Mont.: Scholars Press, 1973).

29. However, Lohse (*Colossians and Philemon*, 156f.) argues that this addition is not a "mere formal element. Rather the entire life, thought and conduct of believers is subordinated to the lordship of the Kyrios."

30. See Crouch, *Colossian Haustafel*, 150f.

now "hid with Christ in God" (3:3). What we hear in these injunctions is "the voice of the propertied class."[31] We have no way of determining whether "those who are your earthly masters" are only pagan or also Christian masters. The injunction to the masters presupposes that they still have slaves who might or might not have been Christian.

In taking over the Greco-Roman ethic of the patriarchal household code, Colossians not only "spiritualizes" and moralizes the baptismal community understanding expressed in Gal. 3:28 but also makes this Greco-Roman household ethic a part of "Christian" social ethic. However, it is important to keep in mind that such a reinterpretation of the Christian baptismal vision is late — it did not happen before the last third of the first century. Moreover, it is found only in one segment of early Christianity, the post-Pauline tradition, and had no impact on the Jesus traditions. The insistence on equality and mutuality within the Christian community that seems to have been expressed by slaves as well as by women is not due to later "enthusiastic excesses"[32] or to illegitimate agitation for emancipation. The opposite is true. Colossians shows how a so-called "enthusiastic" realized eschatological perspective can produce an insistence on patriarchal behavior as well as an acceptance of the established political-social status quo of inequality and exploitation in the name of Jesus Christ.

In discussing the *Sitz im Leben* of the household code form, exegetes have arrived at different interpretations. While a few scholars think that the demands for the obedience and submission of wives, children, and slaves are genuinely Christian, the majority sees the domestic code as a later Christian adaptation of a Greco-Roman or Jewish-Hellenistic philosophical-theological code.

Most recently scholars have pointed to the treatises on economics and politics that reflect a form already codified by Aristotle and at home in the philosophical schools and morals of the first century C.E. The moralists of the early empire sought to formulate an ethics that would find a balance between the absolute traditional demands of subordination and obedience to the *paterfamilias* and the ideals of equality formulated in the Hellenistic age. What comes to the fore in the household code form of the New Testament is the option for "an ethically softened or humanized notion of domination and rule."[33] The right order of the house and economics are intertwined because in antiquity the household was economically independent, self-sufficient, hierarchically ordered, and as such the basis of the state. Therefore, the three

---

31. Judge, *The Social Pattern of Christian Groups*, 60, 71.
32. See Crouch, *Colossian Haustafel*, 141.
33. K. Thraede, "Zum historischen Hintergrund der 'Haustafeln' des NT," JAC Ergänzungsband 8 (1981): 359–68:365.

topoi, "concerning the state," "concerning household management," and "concerning marriage," were closely interrelated.[34]

Aristotle, who has decisively influenced Western political philosophy as well as American legal concepts,[35] argues against Plato that one must begin the discussion of politics with thoughts about marriage, defined by him as a union of "natural ruler and natural subject."[36] When slaves are added to the family, it can be called a "house." Several households constitute a village and several villages a city-state, or *politeia:*

> The investigation of everything should begin with its smallest parts, and the smallest and primary parts of the household are master and slave, husband and wife, father and children. We ought therefore to examine the proper constitution and character of each of the three relationships, I mean that of mastership, that of marriage and thirdly the progenitive relationship. [*Politics* I.1253b]

It is part of the household science to rule over wife and children as freeborn. However, this is not done with the same form of government. Whereas the father rules over his children as a monarch rules, the husband exercises republican government over the wife:

> for the male is by nature better fitted to command than the female... and the older and fully developed person than the younger and immature. It is true that in most cases of republican government the ruler and ruled interchange in turn... but the male stands in this relationship to the female continuously. The rule of the father over the children on the other hand is that of a king. [*Politics* I.1259b]

Against those who argue that slavery is contrary to nature, Aristotle points to the rule of the soul over the body.

> It is manifest that it is natural and expedient for the body to be governed by the soul and for the emotional part to be governed by the intellect, the part possessing reason, whereas for the two parties to be on equal [*ison*] footing or in the contrary positions is harmful in all cases.... Also as between the sexes, the male is by nature superior and the female inferior, the male ruler and

---

34. F. Wilhelm, "Die Oeconomica der Neupythagoreer Bryson, Kallikdratidas, Periktione, Phintys," *Rheinisches Museum* 70 (1915): 161–223:222.

35. Cf. especially S. Moller Okin, *Women in Western Political Thought* (Princeton: Princeton University Press, 1979), 234–304.

36. For this whole section, see ibid., 15–96, on Plato and Aristotle; and David L. Balch, *Let Wives Be Submissive: The Domestic Code in 1 Peter,* SBLMS 26 (Chico, Calif.: Scholars Press, 1981), 33–38. For the translation on Aristotle's *Politics,* see H. Rackham, LCL (Cambridge, Mass.: Harvard University Press, 1926).

the female subject. And the same must also necessarily apply in the case of humankind generally; therefore all human beings that differ as widely as the soul does from the body . . . these are by nature slaves for whom to be governed by this kind of authority is advantageous. [*Politics* I.1254b]

These "natural" differences justify the relationships of domination in household and state.

Hence there are by nature various classes of rulers and ruled. For the free rules the slave, the male the female, the man the child in a different way. And all possess the various parts of the soul but possess them in different ways; for the slave has not got the deliberative part at all, and the female has it but without full authority, while the child has it but in an undeveloped form. [*Politics* I.1260a]

Interestingly enough, Aristotle acknowledges one exception when women can rule with "authority." Usually the relationship between husband and wife is that of "aristocracy" but when the husband controls everything it becomes an "oligarchy," "for he governs in violation of fitness and not in virtue of superiority." "And sometimes when the wife is an heiress, it is she who rules. In these cases, then, authority goes not by virtue but by wealth and power, as in an oligarchy" (*Nicomachean Ethics* VIII.1160b).

Since, however, every household is part of the state, the state is jeopardized if the different forms of household rule are not exercised faithfully.

The freedom in regard to women is detrimental both in regard to the purpose of the *politeia* and in regard to the happiness of the state. For just as man and wife are part of a household, it is clear that the state also is divided nearly in half into its male and female population, so that in all *politeia* in which the position of women is badly regulated one half of the state must be deemed neglected in framing the law. [*Politics* II.1269b]

Such was the case in Sparta, where women controlled their own wealth. Although the Spartans did attempt to bring their women under the law, they gave up when the women resisted. Therefore, they loved and respected wealth and were under the sway of their women. The women controlled not only many things but also ruled their own rulers! These remarks make it clear that Aristotle knows of a historical state that was differently constituted.

Although the negative influence of Aristotle on Christian anthropology is widely acknowledged today,[37] it is not sufficiently recognized that such an anthropology was rooted in Aristotle's understanding of political rule and domination. Just as he defined the "nature" of slaves with respect to their status as property and to their economic function, so Aristotle defined the "nature" of woman as that of someone who does not have "full authority" to rule, although he is well aware that such rule was an actual historical possibility and reality. The definition of "woman's nature" and "woman's proper sphere" is thus rooted in a certain relation of domination and subordination between man and woman having a concrete political background and purpose. Western misogynism has its root in the rules for the household as the model of the state. A feminist theology therefore must not only analyze the anthropological dualism generated by Western culture and theology, but also uncover its political roots in the patriarchal household of antiquity.

Aristotle's political philosophy was revitalized in neo-Pythagorean and Stoic philosophy.[38] It was also accepted in Hellenistic Judaism, as the writings of Philo and Josephus demonstrate. Philo insists that Jews are not impious, they respect father and mother, and wives must be in servitude to their husbands (*Hypothetica* VIII.7.14). In discussing the *politeia* of Moses and comparing it to that of Romulus, Josephus stresses that Jewish laws do not teach impiety but piety, not the hatred of others but the communal life. They oppose injustice and teach justice, they deter from war and encourage people to work. Therefore, there can be nowhere a greater justice, piety, and harmony than among the Jews. In their marriage laws and the birth and upbringing of children Jews fulfilled the laws of Romulus's *politeia,* which the Romans had imposed on the whole empire. Jewish women were good Roman citizens:

> The woman, says the Law, is in all things inferior to the man. Let her accordingly be submissive, not for her humiliation, but that she may be directed, for the authority has been given by God to the man. [*Against Apion* II.201]

Alongside this Aristotelian ethics of submission and rule, a marriage ethos developed which stressed the harmony between the couples.[39] Plutarch describes the ideal marriage as a copartnership:

> It is a lovely thing for a wife to sympathize with her husband's concerns and the husband with the wife's so that, as ropes, by

---

37. See, e.g., K. E. Børresen, *Subordination and Equivalence: The Nature and Role of Women in Augustine and Thomas Aquinas* (Washington, D.C.: University Press of America, 1981).

38. D. L. Balch, "Household Ethical Codes in Peripatetic, Neopythagorean and Early Christian Moralists," *SBL Seminar Papers* 11 (1977): 397–404.

39. Thraede, "Zum historischen Hintergrund," 364; see also his article "Gleichheit," in *RAC* 10 (1978), 122–64.

being intertwined, get strength from each other, thus...the co-partnership may be preserved through the joint action of both. [*Conjugal Precepts* 140e]

Plutarch also emphasizes that the wife should not only share her husband's friends but also his gods. She must therefore "shut the front door tight upon all queer rituals and outlandish superstitions. For with no god do stealthy and secret rites performed by a woman find any favor" (140d). Thus it is apparent that in antiquity rules of the household are part of economics and politics, as are religious rites and ancestral customs. The well-being of the state and the religious observance of the laws and customs of the patriarchal family are intertwined. Slaves and wives who do not worship the gods of the *paterfamilias* violate not only their household duties but also the laws of the state.

The praxis of coequal discipleship between slaves and masters, women and men, Jews and Greeks, Romans and barbarians, rich and poor, young and old, brought the Christian community into tension with its social-political environment. This tension, engendered by the alternative Christian vision of Gal. 3:28, and not by "enthusiastic excesses," became the occasion for introducing the Greco-Roman patriarchal order into the house church. Colossians and Ephesians testify that realized eschatology, rooted in the dualism between this world and the world above, is responsible for developing a theological justification of the patriarchal order.

fourteen

1 Corinthians: A Case Study of Paul's Assembly as an Alternative Society

RICHARD A. HORSLEY

First Corinthians has traditionally been a generous source of proof texts that Christians have used as scriptural bases for theological doctrines such as the pre-existence of Christ and social institutions, such as slavery. More recently it has been the focus of debates on the degree to which Paul subordinated women and urged slaves to remain in their servile status.[1] In the excitement of these debates, however, little attention has been given to the wider horizon within which Paul understands the assembly's struggles, that is, to the fulfillment of history between the crucifixion and exaltation of Christ, in the immediate past and the *parousia* and general resurrection in the imminent future, and to Paul's adamant opposition to Roman imperial society. Since, among Paul's letters, it covers the greatest number of different facets of assembly life in relation to the dominant society, 1 Corinthians may provide a good case study of the ways in which Paul appears to be fostering an alternative society.[2]

The relations between Rome and Corinth exemplify the most extreme forms of Roman imperial practice and of the imperial society it produced. Having maneuvered Corinth and the Achaian league into war,

---

1. Major recent treatments, with references to previous discussion, are Elisabeth Schüssler Fiorenza, *In Memory of Her: A Feminist Theological Reconstruction of Christian Origins* (New York: Crossroad, 1983), excerpted above; Antoinette C. Wire, *Corinthian Women Prophets: A Reconstruction through Paul's Rhetoric* (Minneapolis: Fortress, 1991); Amos Jones, Jr., *Paul's Message of Freedom: What Does It Mean to the Black Church?* (Valley Forge, Pa.: Judson, 1984); Neil Elliott, *Liberating Paul: The Justice of God and the Politics of the Apostle* (Maryknoll, N.Y.: Orbis Books, 1994). See also my forthcoming *1 Corinthians,* Abingdon New Testament Commentaries (Nashville: Abingdon, 1998); and the forthcoming issue of *Semeia* (1998) devoted to "Slavery in Text and History."

2. It is also the letter with which I am most familiar, from a series of programmatic articles in the late 1970s and a commentary (*1 Corinthians,* on the research for which much of the analysis and construction below is based).

in 146 B.C.E. the Romans ruthlessly sacked the city, killed its men, and enslaved its women and children. A century later Julius Caesar established a colony at Corinth to which were sent, along with some army veterans, large numbers of urban poor from Rome, over half of them freed slaves (Strabo, *Geogr.* 8.6.23). Ambitious freedmen and others of low social status thus set the tone in a hypercompetitive urban ethos (e.g., Apuleius, *Met.* 10.19, 25). The elite, hungry for honor and office, cultivated the patronage of governors and emperors and sponsored construction of new civic and imperial temples in the city center and festivals such as the newly instituted Caesarean Games (see further the Chow selection in Part II above). Populated by the descendants of Roman riffraff and deracinated former slaves, Corinth was the epitome of urban society created by empire: a conglomeration of atomized individuals cut off from the supportive communities and particular cultural traditions that had formerly constituted their corporate identities and solidarities as Syrians, Judeans, Italians, or Greeks. As freedpeople and urban poor isolated from any horizontal supportive social network, they were either already part of or readily vulnerable for recruitment into the lower layers of patronage pyramids extending downwards into the social hierarchy as the power bases of those clambering for high honor and office expanded. Amidst all the luxuries provided by the increasingly munificent and honored elite, Corinthians had a reputation as uncultured and lacking in social graces, partly because the wealthy so grossly exploited the poor (Alciphron, *Letters* 15 and 24).

The letter as a whole is framed by discussion of the crucifixion of Christ in the opening of the first major argument (1:17–2:8) and the resurrection in the last major argument (chap. 15). In those arguments, moreover, Paul articulates his basic (Judean) apocalyptic orientation and perspective. The crucifixion and resurrection of Christ has become the turn of the ages, from "this age" (1:20; 2:6, 8) to the next. Paul reminds the Corinthians about just this historical crisis throughout the letter, with references to the imminent judgment (3:12–15; 4:5; 5:5; 6:2–3), to the appointed time of fulfillment having been foreshortened so that the scheme of the present order is passing away (7:29, 31), to "the ends of the ages" having come upon them (10:11), and to the Lord's coming anticipated in the very celebration of the Lord's death (11:26). Paul also mentions explicitly that the events of the crucifixion and resurrection are happening according to God's (now revealed) *mystery* or plan for the fulfillment of history (2:7; 15:51; cf. "the wisdom of God" in 1:21, used parallel with the more technical Judean apocalyptic "mystery," e.g., Dan. 2:18–19, 27–28; 1QS 3:13–4:25; 1QpHab 7:1–5).

What we may not notice immediately, because of the assumption that we are reading about the formation of a religion, is just how politically Paul conceives of these events by which "this age" is being terminated and the next inaugurated. To be sure, God has also turned the tables on pretentious aristocratic Hellenistic culture. The gospel of Christ crucified is indeed utter foolishness to the elite who benefit from Roman terrorization of subject peoples through crucifixion of rebellious provincials and intransigent slaves. But it is through the despicably crucified Christ and now his lowborn, weak, and despised followers, the Corinthian believers themselves, that God has shamed the pretentious elite questing after power, wealth, wisdom, noble birth, and honorific public office (1:21–23, 26–29; 4:8, 10). Those terms, of course, in their literal meaning, describe not simply a cultural elite but the provincial (Corinthian) political elite. The most important casualties of God's implementation of his plan (mystery), however, are the imperial "rulers of this age" (2:6–8). Here as elsewhere in Paul (cf. Rom. 13:3) and the New Testament, "rulers" (*archontes*) refers to earthly political rulers.[3] While Paul probably does not have Pontius Pilate explicitly in mind, he is thinking of the Romans and their imperial system who, precisely in crucifying Christ in their unthinking practice of violence, have now been "doomed to destruction." In 15:24–28 Paul comes around to the completion of the eschatological events in which the imperial rulers will be destroyed, along with all other "enemies": At "the end" Christ will hand the kingdom to God the Father, "after he has destroyed every rule and every (governing) authority and power." *Dynamis* in this case may well point to "powers" such as Death. But *archē* and *exousia,* parallel to "the rulers of this age," appear to be the rulers of the Roman imperial system (cf. "governing authority" in Rom. 13:1–3).[4] As argued variously in Part III above for Paul in general, so in 1 Corinthians his gospel, mission, and the struggles of his assembly are part of God's fulfillment of history in the doom and destruction of Roman imperial rule.

In that context, then, we can perceive how at several points in 1 Corinthians Paul articulates ways in which the assembly of saints is to constitute a community of a new society alternative to the dominant imperial society.

First, 1 Corinthians and related references in other letters provide just enough information for us to discern the structure of the mission and the nascent assembly(ies) in Corinth and the surrounding area.[5] Paul was

---

3. With no real linguistic evidence indicating demonic powers; see Gordon D. Fee, *The First Epistle to the Corinthians,* NIC (Grand Rapids: Eerdmans, 1987), esp. 103–4; and Wesley Carr, "The Rulers of this Age — 1 Corinthians II.6–8," *NTS* 23 (1976–77): 20–35.

4. The Christian scholarly mystification of "rule and governing authority" here and "rulers of this age" in 2:6–8 into "cosmic forces" is heavily influenced by their original spiritualization by Paul's "disciples" in Colossians and Ephesians (see the introduction to Part III and the first essay by Neil Elliott above).

5. Wayne S. Meeks, *The First Urban Christians: The Social World of the Apostle Paul* (New Haven: Yale University Press, 1983), chap. 3, topically organizes much useful

teamed with a number of coworkers, not simply Timothy and Silvanus, who had worked with him earlier (1 Thess. 1:1; 2 Cor. 1:19). He formed a special collaborative bond with Prisca and her husband, Aquila, perhaps because of their common "trade" (cf. Acts 18:2–3). Contrary to the popular image of Paul preaching the gospel in public places, he and his coworkers almost certainly avoided the marketplace of religious competition (cf. 2 Cor. 2:17) for the more intensive interaction of small groups in people's houses. From references to "the assembly in the house of Prisca and Aquila" (1 Cor. 16:19; Rom. 16:5; cf. Philemon 2) it seems clear that the movement in Corinth (and again in Ephesus) took the form of a number of small "assemblies" based in households. Paul's references to "the whole assembly" coming together for certain purposes such as the Lord's Supper and discussion (1 Cor. 14:23; cf. 10:20; Rom. 16:23) indicate that at other times only a portion of the whole assembly functioned semi-separately in some way. This is the basis for surmising that households of figures such as Stephanas, Gaius, and possibly Crispus hosted house-based (sub-)assemblies (1 Cor. 16:16–17; 1:14–16). The hosts of the latter then constituted leaders and, in effect, additional coworkers in the movement on whom Paul could rely for communication, coordination, and group discipline.[6] The assembly at Cenchreae in which Phoebe was the principal leader (Rom. 16:1) illustrates how the network of smaller household-based communities spread out from Corinth into the satellite towns and villages. The picture that emerges from such observations is not one of a religious cult, but of a nascent social movement comprised of a network of cells based in Corinth but spreading more widely into the province of Achaia. That is surely indicated when Paul, writing later in coordination of the collection "for the poor among the saints in Jerusalem," refers not to Corinth alone but to Achaia more generally, just as he refers not simply to the Thessalonians or Philippians but to "the assemblies of Macedonia" in general (2 Cor. 8:2; 9:2, 4).

Second, besides urging group solidarity, Paul insisted that the Corinthian assembly conduct its own affairs autonomously, in complete independence of "the world," as he writes in no uncertain terms in 1 Corinthians 5–6. That did not mean completely shutting themselves off from the society in which they lived. The purpose of the mission, of course, was to bring people into the community. The believers should thus not cut off all contact with "the immoral of this world, or the greedy and robbers" (5:10). The assembly, however, should not only

---

information, but sacrifices a sense of the dynamics of a developing movement for analysis in terms of social "Models from the Environment."

6. Although structurally the "house assemblies" also posed an obvious problem for integration and potential conflict, illustrated by the divisiveness to which Paul responds in 1 Corinthians (e.g., 1 Cor. 1:11–13; 11:17–34).

(a) maintain ethical purity and group discipline in stark opposition to the injustice of the dominant society, but also (b) it should handle its own disputes in absolute independence of the established courts.

The assembly stands diametrically opposed to "the world" as a community of "saints." As often observed, in Paul holiness refers to social-ethical behavior and relations, the maintenance of justice. In these paragraphs Paul states rather bluntly that those who run the civil courts, as well as those "in the world" outside the assembly generally, are "unjust" (6:1). His list of unjust outsiders in 5:10 pointedly features the economic injustices of coveting and theft. That surely sets up his suggestion in 6:7–8 that the issue over which one member had taken another to civil court was economic (most likely the plaintiff defrauding the defendant precisely by that action).[7] Thus economic matters as well as matters of sexual morality were included in Paul's concern that the assembly embody just social relations within its autonomous community. By implication in both paragraphs, 5:1–13 and 6:1–11, the assembly of "saints" should be exercising strict group discipline (cf. the stringent standards and discipline of the Qumran community in 1QS and of the [idealized!] early Jerusalem community of Jesus followers in Acts 2:44– 45 and 5:1–6). For Paul, the assemblies at Corinth and elsewhere, as the eschatological people of God, were set over against "the world" which stood under God's judgment. Indeed, as paralleled in Judean apocalyptic writings (e.g., 1QpHab 5:4; 1 Enoch 1:9; 95:3; cf. Rev. 20:4), at the judgment the "saints will judge the world" (6:2).

The assembly's independence and autonomy, moreover, meant that members should work out any and all disputes within the community and have no relations with the dominant society, such as resorting to the established courts. The law and the courts in the Roman empire were instruments of social control, a vested interest of the wealthy and powerful elite which operated for their advantage over that of those of lesser status. Paul does indeed have just such a concern about economic relations in mind, hence his concern cannot be reduced to the later separation of "church" and "state" that tends to block recognition of the political-economic dimension of his statement here.[8] His concern, however, is not simply a parallel to that of diaspora Jewish communities to conduct their own internal community affairs semiautonomously insofar as possible by permission of the Roman authorities. Paul's insistence that the assembly run its own affairs was more of a complete declaration of

---

7. See further the suggestive discussion of the issues in 1 Corinthians 5–6 in the context of the patronage system by John K. Chow, *Patronage and Power* (Sheffield: JSOT Press, 1992), 123–41.

8. Many commentators (e.g., Fee, *First Corinthians*, 232; H. Conzelmann, *1 Corinthians*, Hermeneia [Philadelphia: Fortress, 1975], 105), still projecting the "church-state" separation back into the situation of Paul, claim that Paul was not rejecting the civil courts.

independence and autonomy, as in apocalyptic literature, where Judean scribes advocate independence of Judea or their own circles from imperial governments or their local clients. Statements of self-government from Qumran and branches of the Jesus movement appear to parallel Paul's statement to the Corinthians (cf. 1QS 5:25–6:1; CD 9:2–8; Matt. 18:15–17 ‖ Luke 17:2–3; 12:57–59 ‖ Matt. 5:25–26).

Third, Paul's prohibition of the Corinthians' eating of "food sacrificed to idols," despite their *gnosis* that "no idol in the world really exists" and that "there is no God but one," cut the Corinthians off from participation in the fundamental forms of social relations in the dominant society. Christian theological interpretation of 1 Corinthians has tended to forget that religion in the ancient Roman world did not consist primarily of personal belief and was often inseparable from political, economic, and other fundamental social forms. We have been reminded recently from outside the field that temples and shrines to the emperor, located in the very center of public space, and citywide festivals played an important role in constituting the cohesion of the Roman empire as well as the local society under the domination of the sponsoring local elite.[9] From within the field, moreover, we are reminded that sacrifice was integral to, indeed constitutive of, community life in Greco-Roman antiquity at every social level from extended families to guilds and associations to citywide celebrations, including imperial festivals.[10] With that in mind, it should be possible to realize that Paul's discussion in 1 Corinthians 8–10 is about far more than individual ethics.

Contrary to a prominent tradition of Pauline interpretation, Paul did not share the enlightened theology that informed the "liberty" (*exousia*) of the Corinthians he was addressing in chapters 8–10. In fact, he not only rejects its effects rather bluntly in 8:1–3, but he also contradicts their *gnosis* that "no idol in the world really exists" and "there is no God but one" in the awkward aside of 8:5b: "in fact there are many gods and many lords" alive and functioning in the world. The issue addressed in 1 Corinthians 8–10, moreover, is not the dispute imagined by modern scholars between the "weak" and the "strong," that is, between Jews or Jewish Christians still obsessed with traditional Jewish food codes and enlightened Christians, including Paul. The term "food offered to idols," which does not occur in Jewish texts prior to Paul, always refers to food eaten in a temple.[11] And that is clearly what Paul

9. See esp. S. R. F. Price, *Rituals and Power: The Roman Imperial Cult in Asia Minor* (Cambridge: Cambridge University Press: 1984), excerpted in chap. 3 above.

10. Stanley K. Stowers, "Greeks Who Sacrifice and Those Who Do Not: Toward an Anthropology of Greek Religion," in L. M. White and L. Yarbrough, eds., *The Social World of the First Christians: Essays in Honor of Wayne Meeks* (Minneapolis: Fortress, 1995), 293–333.

11. Ben Witherington III, "Not So Idle Thoughts about *Eidolothuton*," *Tyndale Bulletin* 44 (1993): 237–54.

has in mind, as indicated both in 8:10 and 10:14–20. Thus the strongly Lutheran reading of 1 Corinthians 8–10 that found the main point in 10:23–11:1, with 10:1–13 and 14–22 as digressions, should be abandoned. Paul is addressing enlightened Corinthians who presume that they have the liberty to banquet in temples (since the gods supposedly honored there do not exist). His argument climaxes in 10:14–22 with the absolute prohibition of such banqueting, with 10:23–11:1 being a conciliatory afterthought and summary of his argument.[12]

If we come to the text with the assumptions of ancient Greco-Roman society instead of modern theological ones, then we can see precisely in the climax of Paul's argument, 10:14–22, not a "sacramental" realism, but the societal or "political" realism that Paul shared with both the nonenlightened majority of ancient Greeks and Romans and the biblical traditions of nonenlightened Israelites/Judeans. In the preceding paragraph, 10:1–13, Paul insisted that biblical traditions not be taken as symbols of spiritual realities ("spiritual food/drink/rock"), but as histories of events that had happened to the Israelites who were en route in the wilderness from their liberation from Egyptian oppression to the land in which they would become a firmly implanted independent people. That many Israelites were struck down by God because of their idolatry served as warnings to the Corinthians to maintain their group discipline until, analogously, they reached their goal now "at the ends of the ages." In 10:14–22 Paul makes even more explicit the exclusivity of the assembly of believers. He starts with their own celebration of the Lord's Supper. The cup of blessing is "a *sharing* or fellowship (*koinonia*) in the blood of Christ" and the bread a "sharing in the body of Christ." As becomes clearer in chapter 12, "body" was also a well-established political metaphor for the "body politic," the citizen body of a city-state (*polis*). With Israel also, those who ate the sacrifices were sharers in the altar. Similarly, those who eat food sacrificed to idols are sharers or partners with the demons (idols/gods) to whom they sacrifice, establishing social bonds of sharing. In contrast to the dominant society in which many overlapping social bonds were established in sacrifices to multiple gods, however, the assembly of sharers in the body of Christ was exclusive. It was simply impossible and forbidden therefore for members of the body politic established and perpetuated in the cup and table of the Lord to partake also in the cup and table of demons.

For Paul the sharing of "food offered to idols" was not an issue of ethics, but of the integrity and survival of the Corinthians' assembly as an exclusive alternative community to the dominant society and its

---

12. More fully explained in Fee, *First Corinthians*; and Horsley, *1 Corinthians*, both of which contain documentation and explanation that supports the interpretation of 1 Corinthians 8–10 which follows below.

social networks. In his concern to "build up" the assembly of saints over against the networks of power relations by which the imperial society was constituted, he could not allow those who had joined the assembly to participate in the sacrificial banquets by which those so-cial relations were ritually established. In 10:14–22 Paul insists on political-religious solidarity over against the dominant society which was constituted precisely in such banquets or "fellowship/sharing" with gods. For the members of the new alternative community that meant cutting themselves off from the very means by which their previously essential social-economic relations were maintained.

Fourth, at several points Paul indicates that his assembly(ies) should embody economic relations dramatically different from those in Roman imperial society. As noted above, in 1 Cor. 5:10 and 6:7–8 he insinu-ated disapprovingly that the assembly member who was taking another to civil court was defrauding him economically. Economics play a more obvious and important role in 1 Corinthians 8–10. In the structure of his argument, Paul offers an autobiographically framed principle to guide behavior with regard to the Corinthians' "liberty" (*exousia*) to eat "food offered to idols" in 8:13, which he then proceeds to illustrate autobiographically, telling how he refrains from using his own apostolic "right" (*exousia*) in chapter 9. His illustration, far more elaborate and "defensive" than necessary to illustrate the principle, becomes an ex-plicit defense (9:3) of his practice of not accepting economic support for his ministry, contrary to the standard practice among apostles of the movement. That had been his practice in Thessalonica (1 Thess. 2:7, 8–9), and he apparently continued the practice in Corinth, judging from his repeated references to how he had not wanted to "burden them" or "sponge off of them" in his later Corinthian correspondence (2 Cor. 11:9; 12:13, 16). His mention of Barnabas in this connection indicates that his peculiar practice of not accepting economic support dated from at least the time he was working with Barnabas in a mission based in Antioch. But why does he refuse support, contrary to the norm within the movement, and what point is he driving at here in his "defense" in 1 Corinthians 9?

Prior to his "calling" Paul presumably would have received support in the tributary system of the Jerusalem temple state whereby the high priestly rulers "redistributed" revenues they took from Judean and other villagers (that is, if Paul had indeed been a Pharisee, Phil. 3:5). By contrast with the tributary flow of goods upwards from peasant pro-ducers to their rulers, the early Jesus movement adapted the horizontal economic reciprocity of village communities following the traditional Mosaic covenantal ideal of maintaining the subsistence level of all community members (see, e.g., Leviticus 25). Households and villages provided for the economic subsistence of apostles and prophets moving from place to place building the movement (Mark 6:8–10; Luke 10:2–9). Paul's distinctive refusal of such support may have been rooted in his distinctive background prior to becoming an apostle in the movement. The original apostles, themselves from the peasantry, were used to sharing in the poverty of village life. But Paul as a former scribal "retainer" may have been sensitive about continuing to live off of poverty-stricken people once he identified with them in joining the movement. "Paying his own way" by working with his own hands, despised as it was in aristocratic Hellenistic culture, may also have been another way he could identify with the humiliation of the crucified Christ (cf. 1 Cor. 4:12).

The Corinthians who were "examining" him on this matter must have been still attuned to the values of the patronage system that had permeated the provincial cities of Greece during the early empire. Perhaps one or more of the Corinthian householders who were able to contribute to Paul's and other apostles' support were eager to enhance their own prestige and honor by serving as patron(s). It seems that Apollos, Paul's rival in Corinth, had accepted such patronage (3:5–15; 4:3–5; 9:12). According to the protocol of the patronage system, Paul's refusal of such support would have been an offensive repudiation of the prospective patron's "friendship." His shameful working with his own hands would have constituted a further humiliation for their proud posture as potential patrons.[13] Paul's personal concern was surely to avoid becoming a "house apostle" to some Corinthian patron. But his larger concern may have been to prevent the assembly he was attempting to "build up" from replicating the controlling and exploitative power relations of the dominant society.

It is conceivable, of course, that in warding off the unwanted patronage of some, he in effect began to build his own network of "friends" in the assemblies of Achaia as he began to rely on Stephanas and his household as his own mediators with the Corinthians and Phoebe in relation with the assembly in Cenchreae (1 Cor. 16:15–18; Rom. 16:1–2). Paul did not come up with any vision of an alternative political economy for his alternative society — which would have been extraordinary for antiquity. In his explanation of why he did not accept support, he simply resorted to the imagery of household administration ("commission," 9:17), with the implied image of God as the divine estate owner and himself as the steward. Such imagery fits with similar controlling metaphors, such as God as a monarch, Christ as the alternative emperor, and himself as the Lord's "servant" or "slave." He used his overall con-

---

13. On such "friendship" and "enmity" in the patronage system, see Peter Marshall, *Enmity in Corinth: Social Convention in Paul's Relations with the Corinthians* (Tübingen: Mohr [Siebeck], 1987).

trolling vision of the "kingdom" of God as a basis for rejecting the patronage system, but remained within that traditional biblical vision.

Fifth, at the close of 1 Corinthians Paul mentions briefly another economic aspect of the movement that is unprecedented and probably unique in antiquity: the collection for the poor among the saints in Jerusalem (16:1–4).[14] This project which Paul pushes so adamantly in the Corinthian correspondence (see further the two short letters contained in 2 Corinthians 8 and 9) was an outgrowth of an agreement with James, Peter, and John that Paul and Barnabas, then based in the Antioch assembly, could expand the movement among the nations, but that they should "remember the poor" (Gal. 2:9–10). In reciprocal relations with the assembly in Jerusalem, other nascent assemblies were to send economic assistance to the poor there. According to Paul's later rationalization, the nations should "be of service" to Israel in material goods since they had come to share in Israel's "spiritual blessings" (Rom. 15:27; cf. Isa. 56:7, about the nations bringing tribute in gratitude to Jerusalem at the final time of fulfillment).

Paul's instructions about the collection in 1 Cor. 16:1–4 (and 2 Corinthians 8; 9) indicate that the network of assemblies had an "international" political-economic dimension diametrically opposed to the tributary political economy of the empire. Even before Paul set out on his own independent mission into Asia Minor and Greece, the movement had developed its distinctive way of practicing international economic solidarity and (horizontal) reciprocity, the (relative) "haves" sharing with the "have-nots." Besides belonging to a larger international movement, the local assemblies shared economic resources across the "nations" and across considerable distances. Both the international character of the movement and its international economic reciprocity were unusual, perhaps unique, in the Roman empire or in any ancient empire.[15] By contrast with the vertical and centripetal movement of resources in the tributary political economy of the empire, Paul organized a horizontal movement of resources from one subject people to another for the support of "the poor among the saints at Jerusalem" (Rom. 15:26).

The purpose and rhetoric of 1 Corinthians itself, finally, indicates how Paul is attempting to "build up" his assemblies as independent communities over against the dominant society. As recent studies of

---

14. For fuller treatment, see the suggestive study by Dieter Georgi, *Remembering the Poor: The History of Paul's Collection for Jerusalem* (Nashville: Abingdon, 1992).

15. The collection embodied the politics as well as the economics of the movement, with delegates chosen by the assemblies themselves designated to bring the resources to the assembly in Jerusalem. Surely one of Paul's motives in pressing the project was to demonstrate to the Jerusalem leaders he had alienated that his labors among the nations had indeed borne fruit.

Paul's rhetoric have shown, he uses the basic forms of Greco-Roman political rhetoric.[16] The arguments in 1 Corinthians are "deliberative" rhetoric, attempting to persuade the group addressed about a particular course of action they should take. The key terms in the arguments, moreover, are those of political discourse, particularly terms focused on the unity, concord, best advantage, and mutual cooperation within the *polis*. Far from urging the Corinthian "saints" to conform with Corinthian society, however, he insisted that they maintain their solidarity as an exclusive community that stands against the larger society.[17] First Corinthians and his other letters were Paul's instruments to shore up the assemblies' group discipline and solidarity over against the imperial society, "the present evil age" (Gal. 1:4), "the present form of this world [that is] passing away" (1 Cor. 7:31).

---

16. Margaret M. Mitchell, *Paul and the Rhetoric of Reconciliation: An Exegetical Investigation of the Language and Composition of 1 Corinthians* (Louisville: Westminster/John Knox, 1992); Stephen M. Pogoloff, *Logos and Sophia: The Rhetorical Situation of 1 Corinthians,* SBLDS 134 (Atlanta: Scholars Press, 1992); Lawrence L. Welborn, "On the Discord in Corinth: 1 Corinthians 1–4 and Ancient Politics," *JBL* 106 (1987): 83–113.

17. We need be under no illusions, however, that in dealing with the divisiveness in the Corinthian assembly, Paul consistently implemented the ideal enunciated in the baptismal formula of Gal. 3:28. On the "slippage" and inconsistency, see Schüssler Fiorenza, *In Memory of Her,* esp. chaps. 6 and 7, excerpted above; and Wire, *Corinthian Women Prophets.*

Index